Philosophers of Process

PHILOSOPHERS
of
PROCESS

edited by
DOUGLAS BROWNING *and*
WILLIAM T. MYERS

 FORDHAM UNIVERSITY PRESS
New York • 1998

Copyright © 1998 by Fordham University Press
All rights reserved
LC 98–25568
ISBN 0–8232–1878–3 (hardcover)
ISBN 0–8232–1879–1 (paperback)

Library of Congress Cataloging-in-Publication Data

Philosophers of process / edited by Douglas Browning and William T.
Myers. — 2nd ed.
   p.   cm.
   Includes bibliographical references.
   ISBN 0-8232-1878-3 (hc.). — ISBN 0-8232-1879-1 (pbk.)
   1. Process philosophy.   2. Philosophers, Modern—United
States.   3. Philosphers, Modern—Europe.   I. Browning,
Douglas, 1929–   .   II. Myers, William T.
BD372.P54   1998
146'.7—dc21   98-25568
                                                        CIP

Printed in the United States of America

CONTENTS

COPYRIGHT ACKNOWLEDGMENTS

PREFACE TO THE SECOND EDITION

The first edition of *Philosophers of Process* has been out of print for just over twenty years. During that time, process metaphysics has continued to grow in importance and in popularity. A second edition of this book seems especially timely right now, given the continued revival of interest in American Pragmatism and the process metaphysics which serves as its grounding. Indeed, the strength of this movement is shown by several factors: 1) There is the growth of interest in the works of both Peirce and Dewey. That this growth is significant is shown by the fact that their respective complete works have either been published (in the case of Dewey) or are in the process of being published (in the case of Peirce). In addition to this, two of the most successful Internet discussion groups focus on their works. 2) The Society for the Advancement of American Philosophy has a vigorously growing membership and influence. Each year, the group sees substantial growth. 3) The rise of neo-pragmatism, under the influence of Richard Rorty and Hilary Putnam, has contributed to this growth. The authors included in this book are either right in the middle of that tradition or are at least important influences on it.

But this is only one side of the story. In addition to the rise of pragmatism, there is another group whose interest is more straightforwardly metaphysical, as opposed to the more varied interests of the pragmatists. The philosophical interests of this group tend to be the works of Whitehead, Hartshorne, and sometimes Bergson and James. The growing importance of this school is shown both by the activities of the Center for Process Studies, especially its publication of the journal *Process Studies*, and by another vigorous Internet discussion list focusing on process philosophy.

Between these two groups, there are quite a number of philosophers who are interested in teaching process metaphysics on both the undergraduate and graduate level. Up until now, there has been no good single text to use in such a course. In order to teach a course on process metaphysics from primary sources, one either has to buy numerous primary sources or take the time and expense of making a very cumbersome course packet. Currently, the only general, basic book on process metaphysics available is Nicholas Rescher's *Process Metaphysics*. While Professor Rescher's book is fine in and of itself, it contains no primary texts. This book is intended to fill this need.

For this second edition, we have made a number of changes that we believe make this a more complete volume. From the first edition, one philosopher was deleted and two were added. C. Lloyd Morgan was deleted. The reason for his inclusion originally was for his work on the concept of emergence. We decided that John Dewey's discussion was better suited to the task, so Morgan was deleted and portions of Chapter Seven of Dewey's *Experience and Nature* were added. The two additions are Friedrich Nietzsche and Charles Hartshorne. The Nietzsche section was added to reflect his critique of substance metaphysics and to reflect a growing acknowledgment in the field that Nietzsche was indeed an early process philosopher. The reasons for adding Hartshorne should be evident. He is an important process metaphysician in his own right. Indeed, his introduction to the first edition has been retained as the first chapter of his own section. That piece still stands as the best introduction to this book.

The selections included from Peirce, James, Alexander, Bergson, and Mead remain the same. We believe that these selections still reflect the best offerings from each philosopher. For Dewey, in addition to the added selections from *Experience and Nature,* his fine 1930 essay "Qualitative Thought" has been added. The only other changes concern the Whitehead selections. Conspicuously absent from the first edition was any significant selection from Whitehead's main work *Process and Reality*. The addition of "Fact and Form" corrects that. As well, we have added some additional pages from *Science and the Modern World* in order to fill out Whitehead's critique of scientific materialism to a greater degree than the original. Finally, the short section called "A Metaphysical Description," which was from *Religion in the Making,* was deleted.

The first edition included biographical sketches and bibliographies for each philosopher at the beginning of their respective chapters. For this edition, these bibliographies have been updated to reflect current scholarship. For brevity's sake, the bibliographies are narrowly selective; they are slanted in favor of works that focus on the process metaphysical views of the authors in question, and we have tried not to duplicate points of view among commentators.

One final note on changes to the text. The order of placement has been changed to reflect a chronological order from date of birth. The order and the dates, then, go as follows: Peirce, 1839; James, 1842; Nietzsche, 1844; Alexander, 1859; Bergson, 1859; Dewey, 1859; Whitehead, 1861; Mead, 1863; and Hartshorne, 1898. One way of dividing these thinkers is into three groups of three. The first three are the pioneers. The second three, all born in 1859, the same year as the publication of Darwin's *Origin of Species*, were the great consolidators. The final three, then, could be viewed as representing the culmination of the metaphysics.

A number of folks have made very helpful suggestions for making this edition more complete. For their suggestions for either readings or bibliographical references, we want to thank Randall Auxier of Oklahoma City University; Larry Hickman, Director of the Dewey Center; Kathleen Higgins of the University of Texas at Austin; Gregory Pappas of Texas A&M University; and Charlene Haddock Seigfried of Purdue University.

W. M.

PREFACE TO THE FIRST EDITION

Process philosophy is fundamentally a metaphysical position. Its basic doctrine is that the universe is essentially to be understood as creative, organic, and temporal. In this metaphysical soil a pragmatic epistemology and a teleological ethics seem to grow naturally, while a distinctive theology and philosophy of language may be easily nurtured. The spatial limitations of this volume of readings from the major figures of recent process philosophy dictate a very selective approach. Since process philosophy is at bottom metaphysics, it seemed wise to emphasize these doctrines. Hence, though many of the readings lead us into epistemology, ethics, theology, aesthetics, philosophy of language, etc., one criterion for their inclusion has been their relevance to the elaboration of the metaphysics of process.

In his introductory essay, Professor Hartshorne makes clear that process philosophy constitutes a neoclassical tradition which has existed alongside the classical approach since the dawn of both Oriental and Occidental philosophy. In the Western world, a neoclassical theology remained, until recent times, in the shadow of such classical systems as those of Aristotle and Aquinas. Descartes presided at the opening of the modern era of philosophy by carrying the classical tradition forward. It will be worth a brief space to set out the essentials of Cartesian classicism and to show how it ordained the subsequent development of Western thought.

As any undergraduate student of philosophy knows, Descartes held that there existed in the universe three sorts of substance: mind, matter, and God. Presupposed in this doctrine are the two classical principles of substance and causality, i.e., the principle that all appearances are attributes inhering in a substance and the principle that there can be no more in the effect than in the cause. Descartes ran into difficulty when he tried to account for the obvious interaction between mind and the external world of matter. The dualism of natural substances begets puzzles both on the metaphysical level (How can the body and the mind possibly affect each other?) and on the epistemological level (How can we have knowledge of the external world?). The metaphysicians who inherited these problems and set about to solve them fall into two broad classes: those who, retaining Descartes' two natural substances and one supernatural substance, attempted to work out some explanation of the appearance of interaction, and those who, retaining only one of the substances, attempted to solve the problems of interaction by dispensing with the other parties involved. It was this last monistic group which came nearest success. Hobbes and the French *philosophes* championed matter, Berkeley and Leibniz championed mind, and Spinoza decided for God. The rise and fall of these monistic systems take up the greater part of the metaphysical enterprise for three centuries. Hume, of course, and empiricists after him, criticized the knowledge claims of all of these metaphysicians, but he offered no alternative theory of reality. Kant tried to defend the traditional view against Hume's arguments by reinstating its concepts of substance and causality at the level of constructive mind while at the same time denying the possibility of a constructive metaphysics of the foundational reality.

It was in the last half of the nineteenth century that increasing dissatisfaction with the adequacy and consistency of this entire tradition served to bring about a radical shift of thought. Philosophers of profound metaphysical temperament such as Henri Bergson, Charles Sanders Peirce, and William James began to question not only the knowledge claims (as had Hume) but the explanatory value of the basic presuppositions of the Cartesian tradition, principles which were assumed by Descartes himself as self-evident and which indeed were assumed by philosophers throughout the classical tradition as a whole, namely, the principles of substance and causality. In the place of these principles the new philosophers suggested principles of process and creativity. Eventually, the attack upon Cartesianism was supplanted by construction; by the close of the 1920s the details of a new and comprehensive process philosophy had been worked out.

This neoclassical renaissance may be easily dated from the 1880s to the present. The greatest figures of the movement are represented by selections in this volume. The ideational and historical unity of this movement, together with the fact that it represents the most thoroughly elaborated Western philosophy of process, justifies the exclusion from this volume of the several Western neoclassicists who lived and wrote in previous times, and of the Buddhists, who have developed their own distinctive and important tradition.

I would like to interject a personal note. My editing of this book is a mark of my profound respect for the type of philosophy it represents and for the particular philosophers included herein. Process philosophy, particularly as it is found in Whitehead, is the culmination in coherence, scope, and relevance of man's attempts at a systematic understanding of the universe. For all that, I cannot count myself a process philosopher. This fact is a partial explanation of why I invited Professor Hartshorne, as the major living philosopher of process, to contribute the introduction to this volume. It is obvious that if he had not graciously consented to the writing of an essay especially for this project, it would have been necessary to include among the selections something from his previously published material.

I have no one to thank for the idea of this volume but myself. Nonetheless, it is clear to me that I would not have conceived the idea at all had I not been infected with an enthusiasm for Whitehead's philosophy some years ago by my friend and colleague Mahlon Barnes. Many helpful suggestions for the choice of selections and the biographical notes came from Professor Hartshorne and Professor David L. Miller, both of the University of Texas. I am greatly indebted to them for their help.

D. B.

CHARLES SANDERS PEIRCE

Charles Sanders Peirce was born in Cambridge, Massachusetts, on September 10, 1839, the son of the renowned astronomer and distinguished Harvard Professor of Mathematics Benjamin Peirce. After receiving an M.A. and Sc.B. at Harvard in 1862 and 1863, respectively, he appeared destined for an academic career, but except for two brief one-year lectureships at Harvard in philosophy (1864–1865 and 1869–1870) and a longer tenure as Lecturer in Logic at the first American graduate school at Johns Hopkins (1879–1884, during which time John Dewey and Thorstein Veblen took courses from him), he spent the bulk of his career in association with the United States Coast and Geodesic Survey (off and on from 1859 to 1891). It appears that Peirce was unsuited for the sort of harnessing of his energies required for a sustained academic career. It is said that after his abrupt dismissal from Johns Hopkins for reasons never made public, he lived in virtual seclusion in Milford, Pennsylvania, financially supported to a large extent by the charity of his friend William James. He died in 1914. His first wife had deserted him in 1876. His second wife, a Frenchwoman, outlived him. He left no children.

Peirce was not only a philosopher of first rank, he was a logician and scientist of international repute. It is worth remarking that his Photometric Researches (1878), which was well received abroad, was the only full-length book he ever published. Peirce's career offers a sharp contrast to that of Bergson. While the latter gained sudden fame which evaporated during his lifetime, the former, whose reputation has increased steadily since his death, lived and died philosophically unknown. Bergson fitted well into academic life; Peirce could not. But the contrast is even more striking in terms of writing and publication. Bergson was a systematic philosopher; he felt most comfortable expanding his insights into books. Peirce dreamed of the day when he would work the various pieces of his philosophy into a grand system, but his many attempts to begin such a project ended in frustration. However, he wrote many short pieces, a large number of which were published in journals, and he left among his effects when he died most of his abandoned attempts at synopsis and system. Fortunately, almost all of these pieces, published and unpublished, which are of philosophical interest have been brought together in an eight-volume edition of his *Collected Papers*.

It has just been pointed out that Peirce's published writings are numerous but short. However, on three separate occasions he published a series of articles in a single journal in an attempt to develop a set of common themes. In the following selective bibliography only the articles in each of these series are listed.

MAJOR PHILOSOPHICAL WORKS BY PEIRCE

1868   *Journal of Speculative Philosophy*, Vol. 2.
  1. "Questions Concerning Certain Faculties Claimed for Man," pp. 103–114.
  2. "Some Consequences of Four Incapacities," pp. 140–157.
  3. "Ground of Validity of the Laws of Logic: Further Consequences of Four Incapacities," pp. 193–208.
1877–1878   *Popular Science Monthly*, Vols. 12, 13. Series entitled "Illustrations of the Logic of Science."
  1. "The Fixation of Belief," Vol. 12, pp. 1–15.
  2. "How to Make Our Ideas Clear," Vol. 12, pp. 286–302.
  3. "The Doctrine of Chances," Vol. 12, pp. 604–615.
  4. "The Probability of Induction," Vol. 12, pp. 705–718.
  5. "The Order of Nature," Vol. 13, pp. 203–217.
  6. "Deduction, Induction and Hypothesis," Vol. 13, pp. 470–482.
1891–1893   *The Monist*, Vols. 1–3.
  1. "The Architecture of Theories," January, 1891.
  2. "The Doctrine of Necessity Examined," April, 1892.
  3. "The Law of Mind," July, 1892.
  4. "Man's Glassy Essence," October, 1892.
  5. "Evolutionary Love," January, 1893.
1898   *Reason and the Logic of Things: The Cambridge Conference Lectures of 1898*. Edited by K. L Ketner, with "Comments on the Lectures" by Hilary Putnam. Cambridge, Mass.: Harvard University Press, 1992.

1903 *Pragmatism as a Principle and Method of Right Thinking: The 1903 Harvard "Lectures on Pragmatism."* Edited with commentary by P. A. Turrisi. Albany: SUNY Press, 1997.

IMPORTANT COLLECTIONS OF WORKS BY PEIRCE

Collected Papers of Charles Sanders Peirce. Vols. 1–6, edited by C. Hartshorne and P. Weiss. Cambridge, Mass.: Harvard University Press, 1931–1935. Vols. 7–8, edited by A. W. Burks. Cambridge, Mass.: Harvard University Press, 1958.

Writings of Charles S. Peirce: A Chronological Edition. Vols. 1–5 (1857–1886). Edited by C. J. W. Kloesel, N. Hauser, et al. Bloomington, Ind.: Indiana University Press, 1980–1993. (This project is ongoing.)

RECOMMENDED WORKS ON PEIRCE

Esposito, Joseph L. *Evolutionary Metaphysics: The Development of Peirce's Theory of Categories.* Athens, Ohio: Ohio University Press, 1980.

Ketner, Kenneth Laine (ed.). *Peirce and Contempory Thought: Philosophical Inquiries.* New York: Fordham University Press, 1995.

Moore, Edward C., and Robin, Richard S. (eds.). *Studies in the Philosophy of Charles Sanders Peirce*, Second Series. Amherst: University of Massachusetts Press, 1964.

Murphey, Murray G. *The Development of Peirce's Philosophy.* Cambridge: Harvard University Press, 1961.

Thompson, Manley. *The Pragmatic Philosophy of C. S. Peirce.* Chicago: University of Chicago Press, 1953.

Wiener, Philip P., and Young, Frederic H. (eds.). *Studies in the Philosophy of Charles Sanders Peirce.* Cambridge: Harvard University Press, 1952.

The Architecture of Theories

Of the fifty or hundred systems of philosophy that have been advanced at different times of the world's history, perhaps the larger number have been, not so much results of historical evolution, as happy thoughts which have accidentally occurred to their authors. An idea which has been found interesting and fruitful has been adopted, developed, and forced to yield explanations of all sorts of phenomena. The English have been particularly given to this way of philosophizing; witness, Hobbes, Hartley, Berkeley, James Mill. Nor has it been by any means useless labor; it shows us what the true nature and value of the ideas developed are, and in that way affords serviceable materials for philosophy. Just as if a man, being seized with the conviction that paper was a good material to make things of, were to go to work to build a *papier mâché* house, with roof of roofing-paper, foundations of pasteboard, windows of paraffined paper, chimneys, bath tubs, locks, etc., all of different forms of paper, his experiment would probably afford valuable lessons to builders, while it would certainly make a detestable house, so those one-idea'd philosophies are exceedingly interesting and instructive, and yet are quite unsound.

The remaining systems of philosophy have been of the nature of reforms, sometimes amounting to radical revolutions, suggested by certain difficulties which have been found to beset systems previously in vogue; and such ought certainly to be in large part the motive of any new theory. This is like partially rebuilding a house. The faults that have been committed are, first, that the repairs of the dilapidations have generally not been sufficiently thoroughgoing, and second, that not sufficient pains had been taken to bring the additions into deep harmony with the really sound parts of the old structure.

When a man is about to build a house, what a power of thinking he has to do before he can safely break ground! With what pains he has to excogitate the precise wants that are to be supplied! What a study to ascertain the most available and suitable materials, to determine the mode of construction to which those materials are best adapted, and to answer a hundred such questions! Now, without riding the metaphor too far, I think we may safely say that the studies preliminary to the construction of a great theory should be at least as deliberate and thorough as those that are preliminary to the building of a dwelling-house.

That systems ought to be constructed architectonically has been preached since Kant, but I do not think the full import of the maxim has by any means been apprehended. What I would recommend is that every person who wishes to form an opinion concerning fundamental problems, should first of all make a complete survey of human knowledge, should take note of all the valuable ideas in each branch of science, should observe in just what respect each has been successful and where it has failed, in order that, in the light of the thorough acquaintance so attained of the available materials for a philosophical theory and of the nature and strength of each, he may proceed to the study of what the problem of philosophy consists in, and of the proper way of solving it. I must not be understood as endeavoring to state fully all that these preparatory studies should embrace; on the contrary, I purposely slur over many points in order to give emphasis to one special recommendation, namely, to make a systematic study of the conceptions out of which a philosophical theory may be built, in order to ascertain what place each conception may fitly occupy in such a theory, and to what uses it is adapted.

The adequate treatment of this single point would fill a volume, but I shall endeavor to illustrate my meaning by glancing at several sciences and indicating conceptions in them serviceable for philosophy. As to the results to which long studies thus commenced have led me, I shall just give a hint at their nature.

We may begin with dynamics—field in our day of perhaps the grandest conquest human science has ever made—I mean the law of the conservation of energy. But let us revert to the first step taken by modern scientific thought—and a great stride it was—the inauguration of dynamics by Galileo. A modern physicist on examining Galileo's works is surprised to find how little experiment had to do with the establishment of the foundations of mechanics. His principal appeal is to common sense and *il lume naturale*. He always assumes that the true theory will be found to be a simple and natural one. And we can see why it should indeed be so in dynamics. For instance, a body left to its own inertia, moves in a straight line, and a straight line appears to us the simplest of curves. In *itself,* no curve is simpler than another. A system of straight lines has intersections precisely corresponding to those of a system of like parabolas similarly placed, or to those of any one of an infinity of systems of curves. But the straight line appears to us simple, because, as Euclid says, it lies evenly between its extremities; that is, because viewed endwise it appears as a point. That is, again, because light moves in straight lines. Now, light moves in straight lines because of the part which the straight line plays in the laws of dynamics. Thus it is that our minds having been formed under the influence of phenomena governed by the laws of mechanics, certain conceptions entering into those laws become implanted in our minds, so that we readily guess at what the laws are. Without such a natural prompting, having to search blindfold for a law which would suit the phenomena, our chance of finding it would be as one to infinity. The further physical studies depart from phenomena which have directly influenced the growth of the mind, the less we can expect to find the laws which govern them "simple," that is, composed of a few conceptions natural to our minds.

The researches of Galileo, followed up by Huyghens and others, led to those modern conceptions of *Force* and *Law*, which have revolutionized the intellectual world. The great attention given to mechanics in the seventeenth century soon so emphasized these conceptions as to give rise to the Mechanical Philosophy, or doctrine that all the phenomena of the physical universe are to be explained upon mechanical principles. Newton's great discovery imparted a new impetus to this tendency. The old notion that heat consists in an agitation of corpuscles was now applied to the explanation of the chief properties of gases. The first suggestion in this direction was that the pressure of gases is explained by the battering of the particles against the walls of the containing vessel, which explained Boyle's law of the compressibility of air. Later, the expansion of gases, Avogadro's chemical law, the diffusion and viscosity of gases, and the action of Crooke's radiometer were shown to be consequences of the same kinetical theory; but other phenomena, such as the ratio of the specific heat at constant volume to that at constant pressure, require additional hypotheses, which we have little reason to suppose are simple, so that we find ourselves quite afloat. In like manner with regard to light. That it consists of vibrations was almost proved by the phenomena of diffraction, while those of polarization showed the excursions of the particles to be perpendicular to the line of propagation; but the phenomena of dispersion, etc., require additional hypotheses which may be very complicated. Thus, the further progress of molecular speculation appears quite uncertain. If hypotheses are to be tried haphazard, or simply because they will suit certain phenomena, it will occupy the mathematical physicists of the world say half a century on the average to bring each theory to the test, and since the number of possible theories may go up into the trillions, only one of which can be true, we have little prospect of making further solid additions to the subject in our time. When we come to atoms, the presumption in favor of a simple law seems very slender. There is room for serious doubt whether the fundamental laws of mechanics hold good for single atoms, and it seems quite likely that they are capable of motion in more than three dimensions.

To find out much more about molecules and atoms, we must search out a natural history of laws of nature, which may fulfill that function which the presumption in favor of simple laws fulfilled in the early days of dynamics, by showing us what kind of laws we have to expect and by answering such questions as this: Can we with reasonable prospect of not wasting time, try the supposition that atoms attract one another inversely as the seventh power of their distances, or can we not? To suppose universal laws of nature capable of being apprehended by the mind and yet having no reason for their special forms, but standing inexplicable and irrational, is hardly a justifiable position. Uniformities are precisely the sort of facts that need to be accounted for. That a pitched coin should sometimes turn up heads and sometimes tails calls for no particular explanation; but if it shows heads every time, we wish to know how this result has been brought about. Law is *par excellence* the thing that wants a reason.

Now the only possible way of accounting for the laws of nature and for uniformity in general is to suppose them results of evolution. This supposes them not to be absolute, not to be obeyed precisely. It makes an element of indeterminacy, spontaneity, or absolute chance in nature. Just as, when we attempt to verify any physical law, we find our observations cannot be precisely satisfied by it, and rightly attribute the discrepancy to errors of observation, so we must suppose far more minute discrepancies to exist owing to the imperfect cogency of the law itself, to a certain swerving of the facts from any definite formula.

Mr. Herbert Spencer wishes to explain evolution upon mechanical principles. This is illogical, for four reasons. First, because the principle of evolution requires no extraneous cause, since the tendency to growth can be supposed itself to have grown from an infinitesimal germ accidentally started. Second, because law ought more than anything else to be supposed a result of evolution. Third, because exact law obviously never can produce heterogeneity out of homogeneity; and arbitrary heterogeneity is the feature of the universe the most manifest and characteristic. Fourth, because the law of the conservation of energy is equivalent to the proposition that all operations governed by mechanical laws are reversible; so that an immediate corollary from it is that growth is not explicable by those laws, even if they be not violated in the process of growth. In short, Spencer is not a philosophical evolutionist, but only a half-evolutionist—or, if you will, only a semi-Spencerian. Now philosophy requires thorough-going evolutionism or none.

The theory of Darwin was that evolution had been brought about by the action of two factors: first, heredity, as a principle making offspring nearly resemble their parents, while yet giving room for "sporting," or accidental variations—for very slight variations often, for wider ones rarely; and, second, the destruction of breeds or races that are unable to keep the birth rate up to the death rate. This Darwinian principle is plainly capable of great generalization. Wherever there are large numbers of objects having a tendency to retain certain characters unaltered, this tendency, however, not being absolute but giving room for chance variations, then, if the amount of variation is absolutely limited in certain directions by the destruction of everything which reaches those limits, there will be a gradual tendency to change in direction of departure from them. Thus, if a million players sit down to bet at an even game, since one after another will get ruined, the average wealth of those who remain will perpetually increase. Here is indubitably a genuine formula of possible evolution, whether its operation accounts for much or little in the development of animal and vegetable species.

The Lamarckian theory also supposes that the development of species has taken place by a long series of insensible changes, but it supposes that those changes have taken place during the lives of the individuals, in consequence of effort and exercise, and that reproduction plays no part in the process except in preserving these modifications. Thus, the Lamarckian theory only explains the development of characters for which individuals strive, while the Darwinian theory only explains the production of characters really beneficial to the race, though these may be fatal to individuals.[1] But more broadly and philo-sophically conceived, Darwinian evolution is evolution by the opera-tion of chance, and the destruction of bad results, while Lamarckian evolution is evolution by the effect of habit and effort.

A third theory of evolution is that of Mr. Clarence King. The testi-mony of monuments and of rocks is that species are unmodified or scarcely modified, under ordinary circumstances, but are rapidly al-tered after cataclysms or rapid geological changes. Under novel cir-cumstances, we often see animals and plants sporting excessively in reproduction, and sometimes even undergoing transformations during individual life, phenomena no doubt due partly to the enfeeblement of vitality from the breaking up of habitual modes of life, partly to changed food, partly to direct specific influence of the element in which the organism is immersed. If evolution has been brought about in this way, not only have its single steps not been insensible, as both Darwinians and Lamarckians suppose, but they are furthermore neither haphazard on the one hand, nor yet determined by an inward striving on the other, but on the contrary are effects of the changed environ-ment, and have a positive general tendency to adapt the organism to that environment, since variation will particularly affect organs at once enfeebled and stimulated. This mode of evolution, by external forces and the breaking up of habits, seems to be called for by some of the broadest and most important facts of biology and paleontology; while it certainly has been the chief factor in the historical evolution of insti-tutions as in that of ideas; and cannot possibly be refused a very promi-nent place in the process of evolution of the universe in general.

Passing to psychology, we find the elementary phenomena of mind fall into three categories. First, we have Feelings, comprising all that is immediately present, such as pain, blue, cheerfulness, the feeling that arises when we contemplate a consistent theory, etc. A feeling is a state of mind having its own living quality, independent of any other state of mind. Or, a feeling is an element of consciousness which might conceivably override every other state until it monopolized the mind, although such a rudimentary state cannot actually be realized, and would not properly be consciousness. Still, it is conceivable, or suppos-able, that the quality of blue should usurp the whole mind, to the exclu-

---

[1] The new-Darwinian, Weisman, has shown that mortality would almost necessarily result from the action of the Darwinian principle.

sion of the ideas of shape, extension, contrast, commencement and cessation, and all other ideas whatsoever. A feeling is necessarily perfectly simple, *in itself,* for if it had parts these would also be in the mind, whenever the whole was present, and thus the whole could not monopolize the mind.[2]

Besides Feelings, we have Sensations of reaction; as when a person blindfold suddenly runs against a post, when we make a muscular effort, or when any feeling gives way to a new feeling. Suppose I had nothing in my mind but a feeling of blue, which were suddenly to give place to a feeling of red; then, at the instant of transition there would be a shock, a sense of reaction, my blue life being transmuted into red life. If I were further endowed with a memory, that sense would continue for some time, and there would also be a peculiar feeling or sentiment connected with it. This last feeling might endure (conceivably I mean) after the memory of the occurrence and the feelings of blue and red had passed away. But the *sensation* of reaction cannot exist except in the actual presence of the two feelings blue and red to which it relates. Wherever we have two feelings and pay attention to a relation between them of whatever kind, there is the sensation of which I am speaking. But the sense of action and reaction has two types: it may either be a perception of relation between two ideas, or it may be a sense of action and reaction between feeling and something out of feeling. And this sense of external reaction again has two forms; for it is either a sense of something happening to us, by no act of ours, we being passive in the matter, or it is a sense of resistance, that is, of our expending feeling upon something without. The sense of reaction is thus a sense of connection or comparison between feelings, either, *A,* between one feeling and another, or *B,* between feeling and its absence or lower degree; and under *B* we have, First, the sense of the access of feeling, and Second, the sense of remission of feeling.

Very different both from feelings and from reaction-sensations or disturbances of feeling are general conceptions. When we think, we are conscious that a connection between feelings is determined by a general rule, we are aware of being governed by a habit. Intellectual power is nothing but facility in taking habits and in following them in cases essentially analogous to, but in nonessentials widely remote from, the

---

[2] A feeling may certainly be compound, but only in virtue of a perception which is not the feeling nor any feeling at all.

normal cases of connections of feelings under which those habits were formed.

The one primary and fundamental law of mental action consists in a tendency to generalization. Feeling tends to spread; connections between feelings awaken feelings; neighboring feelings become assimilated; ideas are apt to reproduce themselves. These are so many formulations of the one law of the growth of mind. When a disturbance of feeling takes place, we have a consciousness of gain, the gain of experience; and a new disturbance will be apt to assimilate itself to the one that preceded it. Feelings, by being excited, become more easily excited, especially in the ways in which they have previously been excited. The consciousness of such a habit constitutes a general conception.

The cloudiness of psychological notions may be corrected by connecting them with physiological conceptions. Feeling may be supposed to exist, wherever a nerve-cell is in an excited condition. The disturbance of feeling, or sense of reaction, accompanies the transmission of disturbance between nerve-cells or from a nerve-cell to a muscle-cell or the external stimulation of a nerve-cell. General conceptions arise upon the formation of habits in the nerve-matter, which are molecular changes consequent upon its activity and probably connected with its nutrition.

The law of habit exhibits a striking contrast to all physical laws in the character of its commands. A physical law is absolute. What it requires is an exact relation. Thus, a physical force introduces into a motion a component motion to be combined with the rest by the parallelogram of forces; but the component motion must actually take place exactly as required by the law of force. On the other hand, no exact conformity is required by the mental law. Nay, exact conformity would be in downright conflict with the law, since it would instantly crystallize thought and prevent all further formation of habit. The law of mind only makes a given feeling *more likely* to arise. It thus resembles the "non-conservative" forces of physics, such as viscosity and the like, which are due to statistical uniformities in the chance encounters of trillions of molecules.

The old dualistic notion of mind and matter, so prominent in Cartesianism as two radically different kinds of substance, will hardly find defenders to-day. Rejecting this, we are driven to some form of hylopathy, otherwise called monism. Then the question arises whether physical laws on the one hand, and the Psychical law on the other are to be taken—

(A) as independent, a doctrine often called *monism,* but which I would name *neutralism*; or,

(B) the Psychical law as derived and special, the physical law alone as primordial, which is *materialism*; or,

(C) the physical law as derived and special, the Psychical law alone as primordial, which is *idealism.*

The materialistic doctrine seems to me quite as repugnant to scientific logic as to common sense; since it requires us to suppose that a certain kind of mechanism will feel, which would be a hypothesis absolutely irreducible to reason—an ultimate, inexplicable regularity; while the only possible justification of any theory is that it should make things clear and reasonable.

Neutralism is sufficiently condemned by the logical maxim known as Ockham's razor, i.e., that not more independent elements are to be supposed than necessary. By placing the inward and outward aspects of substance on a par, it seems to render both primordial.

The one intelligible theory of the universe is that of objective idealism, that matter is effete mind, inveterate habits becoming physical laws. But before this can be accepted it must show itself capable of explaining the tridimensionality of space, the laws of motion, and the general characteristics of the universe, with mathematical clearness and precision; for no less should be demanded of every philosophy.

*   *   *

Now, metaphysics has always been the ape of mathematics. Geometry suggested the idea of a demonstrative system of absolutely certain philosophical principles; and the ideas of the metaphysicians have at all times been in large part drawn from mathematics. The metaphysical axioms are imitations of the geometrical axioms; and now that the latter have been thrown overboard, without doubt the former will be sent after them. It is evident, for instance, that we can have no reason to think that every phenomenon in all its minutest details is precisely determined by law. That there is an arbitrary element in the universe we see—namely, its variety. This variety must be attributed to spontaneity in some form.

Had I more space, I now ought to show how important for philosophy is the mathematical conception of continuity. Most of what is true in Hegel is a darkling glimmer of a conception which the mathematicians had long before made pretty clear, and which recent researches have still further illustrated.

Among the many principles of Logic which find their application in Philosophy, I can here only mention one. Three conceptions are perpetually turning up at every point in every theory of logic, and in the most rounded systems they occur in connection with one another. They are conceptions so very broad and consequently indefinite that they are hard to seize and may be easily overlooked. I call them the conceptions of First, Second, Third. First is the conception of being or existing independent of anything else. Second is the conception of being relative to, the conception of reaction with, something else. Third is the conception of mediation, whereby a first and second are brought into relation. To illustrate these ideas, I will show how they enter into those we have been considering. The origin of things, considered not as leading to anything, but in itself, contains the idea of First, the end of things that of Second, the process mediating between them that of Third. A philosophy which emphasizes the idea of the One, is generally a dualistic philosophy in which the conception of Second receives exaggerated attention; for this One (though of course involving the idea of First) is always the other of a manifold which is not one. The idea of the Many, because variety is arbitrariness and arbitrariness is repudiation of any Secondness, has for its principal component the conception of First. In psychology Feeling is First, Sense of reaction Second, General conception Third, or mediation. In biology, the idea of arbitrary sporting is First, heredity is Second, the process whereby the accidental characters become fixed is Third. Chance is First, Law is Second, the tendency to take habits is Third. Mind is First, Matter is Second, Evolution is Third.

Such are the materials out of which chiefly a philosophical theory ought to be built, in order to represent the state of knowledge to which the nineteenth century has brought us. Without going into other important questions of philosophical architectonic, we can readily foresee what sort of a metaphysics would appropriately be constructed from those conceptions. Like some of the most ancient and some of the most recent speculations it would be a Cosmogonic Philosophy. It would suppose that in the beginning—infinitely remote—there was a chaos of unpersonalized feeling, which being without connection or regularity would properly be without existence. This feeling, sporting here and

there in pure arbitrariness, would have started the germ of a generalizing tendency. Its other sportings would be evanescent, but this would
have a growing virtue. Thus, the tendency to habit would be started;
and from this with the other principles of evolution all the regularities
of the universe would be evolved. At any time, however, an element
of pure chance survives and will remain until the world becomes an
absolutely perfect, rational, and symmetrical system, in which mind is
at last crystallized in the infinitely distant future.

That idea has been worked out by me with elaboration. It accounts
for the main features of the universe as we know it—the characters of
time, space, matter, force, gravitation, electricity, etc. It predicts many
more things which new observations can alone bring to the test. May
some future student go over this ground again, and have the leisure to
give his results to the world.

The Doctrine of Necessity Examined

In *The Monist* for January, 1891, I endeavored to show what elementary ideas ought to enter into our view of the universe. I may mention that on those considerations I had already grounded a cosmical theory, and from it had deduced a considerable number of consequences capable of being compared with experience. This comparison is now in progress, but under existing circumstances must occupy many years.

I propose here to examine the common belief that every single fact in the universe is precisely determined by law. It must not be supposed that this is a doctrine accepted everywhere and at all times by all rational men. Its first advocate appears to have been Democritus, the atomist, who was led to it, as we are informed, by reflecting upon the "impenetrability, translation, and impact of matter." . . . That is to say, having restricted his attention to a field where no influence other than mechanical constraint could possibly come before his notice, he straightway jumped to the conclusion that throughout the universe that was the sole principle of action—a style of reasoning so usual in our day with men not unreflecting as to be more than excusable in the infancy of thought. But Epicurus, in revising the atomic doctrine and repairing its defenses, found himself obliged to suppose that atoms swerve from their courses by spontaneous chance; and thereby he conferred upon the theory life and entelechy. For we now see clearly that the peculiar function of the molecular hypothesis in physics is to open an entry for the calculus of probabilities. Already, the prince of philosophers had repeatedly and emphatically condemned the dictum of Democritus (especially in the "Physics," Book II, chapters iv, v, vi), holding that events come to pass in three ways, namely, (1) by external compulsion, or the action of efficient causes, (2) by virtue of an inward nature, or the influence of final causes, and (3) irregularly without definite cause, but just by absolute chance; and this doctrine is of the inmost essence of Aristotelianism. It affords, at any rate, a valuable

enumeration of the possible ways in which anything can be supposed
to have come about. The freedom of the will, too, was admitted both
by Aristotle and by Epicurus. But the Stoa, which in every department
seized upon the most tangible, hard, and lifeless element, and blindly
denied the existence of every other, which, for example, impugned the
validity of the inductive method and wished to fill its place with the
reductio ad absurdum, very naturally became the one school of ancient
philosophy to stand by a strict necessitarianism, thus returning to a
single principle of Democritus that Epicurus had been unable to swal-
low. Necessitarianism and materialism with the Stoics went hand in
hand, as by affinity they should. At the revival of learning, Stoicism
met with considerable favor, partly because it departed just enough
from Aristotle to give it the spice of novelty, and partly because its
superficialities well adapted it for acceptance by students of literature
and art who wanted their philosophy drawn mild. Afterwards, the great
discoveries in mechanics inspired the hope that mechanical principles
might suffice to explain the universe; and though without logical justification, this hope has since been continually stimulated by subsequent
advances in physics. Nevertheless, the doctrine was in too evident conflict with the freedom of the will and with miracles to be generally
acceptable, at first. But meantime there arose that most widely spread
of philosophical blunders, the notion that associationalism belongs
intrinsically to the materialistic family of doctrines; and thus was
evolved the theory of motives; and libertarianism became weakened.
At present, historical criticism has almost exploded the miracles, great
and small, so that the doctrine of necessity has never been in so great
vogue as now.

The proposition in question is that the state of things existing at any
time, together with certain immutable laws, completely determine the
state of things at every other time (for a limitation to *future* time is
indefensible). Thus, given the state of the universe in the original neb-
ula, and given the laws of mechanics, a sufficiently powerful mind
could deduce from these data the precise form of every curlicue of
every letter I am now writing.

Whoever holds that every act of the will as well as every idea of the
mind is under the rigid governance of a necessity coordinated with that
of the physical world, will logically be carried to the proposition that
minds are part of the physical world in such a sense that the laws of
mechanics determine everything that happens according to immutable

attractions and repulsions. In that case, the instantaneous state of things from which every other state of things is calculable consists in the positions and velocities of all the particles at any instant. This, the usual and most logical form of necessitarianism, is called the mechanical philosophy.

When I have asked thinking men what reason they had to believe that every fact in the universe is precisely determined by law, the first answer has usually been that the proposition is a "presupposition" or postulate of scientific reasoning. Well, if that is the best that can be said for it, the belief is doomed. Suppose it be "postulated": that does not make it true, nor so much as afford the slightest rational motive for yielding it any credence. It is as if a man should come to borrow money, and when asked for his security, should reply he "postulated" the loan. To "postulate" a proposition is no more than to hope it is true. There are, indeed, practical emergencies in which we act upon assumptions of certain propositions as true, because if they are not so, it can make no difference how we act. But all such propositions I take to be hypotheses of individual facts. For it is manifest that no universal principle can in its universality be comprised in a special case or can be requisite for the validity of any ordinary inference. To say, for instance, that the demonstration by Archimedes of the property of the lever would fall to the ground if men were endowed with free-will, is extravagant; yet this is implied by those who make a proposition incompatible with the freedom of the will the postulate of all inference. Considering, too, that the conclusions of science make no pretense to being more than probable, and considering that a probable inference can at most only suppose something to be most frequently, or otherwise approximately, true, but never that anything is precisely true without exception throughout the universe, we see how far this proposition in truth is from being so postulated.

But the whole notion of a postulate being involved in reasoning appertains to a by-gone and false conception of logic. Non-deductive, or ampliative inference, is of three kinds: induction, hypothesis, and analogy. If there be any other modes, they must be extremely unusual and highly complicated, and may be assumed with little doubt to be of the same nature as those enumerated. For induction, hypothesis, and analogy, as far as their ampliative character goes, that is, so far as they conclude something not implied in the premises, depend upon one principle and involve the same procedure. All are essentially inferences from sampling. Suppose a ship arrives at Liverpool laden with wheat in bulk. Suppose that by some machinery the whole cargo be stirred up with great thoroughness. Suppose that twenty-seven thimblefuls be taken equally from the forward, midships, and aft parts, from the starboard, center, and larboard parts, and from the top, half depth, and lower parts of her hold, and that these being mixed and the grains counted, four-fifths of the latter are found to be of quality A. Then we infer, experientially and provisionally, that approximately four-fifths of all the grain in the cargo is of the same quality. I say we infer this *experientially* and *provisionally*. By saying that we infer it *experientially,* I mean that our conclusion makes no pretension to knowledge of wheat-in-itself; our ἀλήθεια, as the derivation of that word implies, has nothing to do with *latent* wheat. We are dealing only with the matter of possible experience—experience in the full acceptation of the term as something not merely affecting the senses but also as the subject of thought. If there be any wheat hidden on the ship, so that it can neither turn up in the sample nor be heard of subsequently from purchasers—or if it be half-hidden, so that it may, indeed, turn up, but is less likely to do so than the rest—or if it can affect our senses and our pockets, but from some strange cause or causelessness cannot be reasoned about—all such wheat is to be excluded (or have only its proportional weight) in calculating that true proportion of quality A, to which our inference seeks to approximate. By saying that we draw the inference *provisionally,* I mean that we do not hold that we have reached any assigned degree of approximation as yet, but only hold that if our experience be indefinitely extended, and if every fact of whatever nature, as fast as it presents itself, be duly applied, according to the inductive method, in correcting the inferred ratio, then our approximation will become indefinitely close in the long run; that is to say, close to the experience *to come* (not merely close by the exhaustion of a finite collection) so that if experience in general is to fluctuate irregularly to and fro, in a manner to deprive the ratio sought of all definite value, we shall be able to find out approximately within what limits it fluctuates, and if, after having one definite value, it changes and assumes another, we shall be able to find that out, and in short, whatever may be the variations of this ratio in experience, experience indefinitely extended will enable us to detect them, so as to predict rightly, at last, what its ultimate value may be, if it have any ultimate value, or what the ultimate law of succession of values may be, if there be any such ultimate law, or that it ultimately fluctuates irregularly within certain limits, if it does so ultimately fluctuate. Now our inference, claiming to be no more than thus experiential and provisional, manifestly involves no postulate whatever.

For what is a postulate? It is the formulation of a material fact which we are not entitled to assume as a premise, but the truth of which is requisite to the validity of an inference. Any fact, then, which might be supposed postulated, must either be such that it would ultimately present itself in experience, or not. If it will present itself, we need not postulate it now in our provisional inference, since we shall ultimately be entitled to use it as a premise. But if it never would present itself in experience, our conclusion is valid but for the possibility of this fact being otherwise than assumed, that is, it is valid as far as possible experience goes, and that is all that we claim. Thus, every postulate is cut off, either by the provisionality or by the experientiality of our inference. For instance, it has been said that induction postulates that, if an indefinite succession of samples be drawn, examined, and thrown back each before the next is drawn, then in the long run every grain will be drawn as often as any other, that is to say, postulates that the ratio of the numbers of times in which any two are drawn will indefinitely approximate to unity. But no such postulate is made; for if, on the one hand, we are to have no other experience of the wheat than from such drawings, it is the ratio that presents itself in those drawings and not the ratio which belongs to the wheat in its latent existence that we are endeavoring to determine; while if, on the other hand, there is some other mode by which the wheat is to come under our knowledge, equivalent to another kind of sampling, so that after all our care in stirring up the wheat, some experiential grains will present themselves in the first sampling operation more often than others in the long run, this very singular fact will be sure to get discovered by the inductive method, which must avail itself of every sort of experience; and our inference, which was only provisional, corrects itself at last. Again, it has been said, that induction postulates that under like circumstances like events will happen, and that this postulate is at bottom the same as the principle of universal causation. But this is a blunder, or *bévue*, due to thinking exclusively of inductions where the concluded ratio is either 1 or 0. If any such proposition were postulated, it would be that under like circumstances (the circumstances of drawing the different samples) different events occur in the same proportions in all the different sets—a proposition which is false and even absurd. But in truth no such thing is postulated, the experiential character of the inference reducing the condition of validity to this, that if a certain result does not occur, the opposite result will be manifested, a condition assured by the provisionality of the inference. But it may be asked whether it is not conceivable that every instance of a certain class destined to be ever employed as a datum of induction should have one character, while every instance destined not to be so employed should have the opposite character. The answer is that in that case, the instances excluded from being subjects of reasoning would not be experienced in the full sense of the word, but would be among these *latent* individuals of which our conclusion does not pretend to speak.

To this account of the rationale of induction I know of but one objection worth mention: it is that I thus fail to deduce the full degree of force which this mode of inference in fact possesses; that according to my view, no matter how thorough and elaborate the stirring and mixing process had been, the examination of a single handful of grain would not give me any assurance, sufficient to risk money upon, that the next handful would not greatly modify the concluded value of the ratio under inquiry, while, in fact, the assurance would be very high that this ratio was not greatly in error. If the true ratio of grains of quality A were 0.80 and the handful contained a thousand grains, nine such handfuls out of every ten would contain from 780 to 820 grains of quality A. The answer to this is that the calculation given is correct when we know that the units of this handful and the quality inquired into have the normal independence of one another, if for instance the stirring has been complete and the character sampled for has been settled upon in advance of the examination of the sample. But in so far as these conditions are not known to be complied with, the above figures cease to be applicable. Random sampling and predesignation of the character sampled for should always be striven after in inductive reasoning, but when they cannot be attained, so long as it is conducted honestly, the inference retains some value. When we cannot ascertain how the sampling has been done or the sample-character selected, induction still has the essential validity which my present account of it shows it to have.

I do not think a man who combines a willingness to be convinced with a power of appreciating an argument upon a difficult subject can resist the reasons which have been given to show that the principle of universal necessity cannot be defended as being a postulate of reasoning. But then the question immediately arises whether it is not proved to be true, or at least rendered highly probable, by observation of nature.

Still, this question ought not long to arrest a person accustomed to reflect upon the force of scientific reasoning. For the essence of the necessitarian position is that certain continuous quantities have certain exact values. Now, how can observation determine the value of such a quantity with a probable error absolutely *nil*? To one who is behind the scenes, and knows that the most refined comparisons of masses, lengths, and angles, far surpassing in precision all other measurements, yet fall behind the accuracy of bank-accounts, and that the ordinary determinations of physical constants, such as appear from month to month in the journals, are about on a par with an upholsterer's measurements of carpets and curtains, the idea of mathematical exactitude being demonstrated in the laboratory will appear simply ridiculous. There is a recognized method of estimating the probable magnitudes of errors in physics—the method of least squares. It is universally admitted that this method makes the errors smaller than they really are; yet even according to that theory an error indefinitely small is indefinitely improbable; so that any statement to the effect that a certain continuous quantity has a certain exact value, if well-founded at all, must be founded on something other than observation.

Still, I am obliged to admit that this rule is subject to a certain qualification. Namely, it only applies to continuous[1] quantity. Now, certain kinds of continuous quantity are discontinuous at one or at two limits, and for such limits the rule must be modified. Thus, the length of a line cannot be less than zero. Suppose, then, the question arises how long a line a certain person had drawn from a marked point on a piece of paper. If no line at all can be seen, the observed length is zero; and the only conclusion this observation warrants is that the length of the line is less than the smallest length visible with the optical power employed. But indirect observations—for example, that the person supposed to have drawn the line was never within fifty feet of the paper—may make it probable that no line at all was made, so that the concluded length will be strictly zero. In like manner, experience no doubt would warrant

---

[1] *Continuous* is not exactly the right word, but I let it go to avoid a long an irrelevant discussion.

the conclusion that there is absolutely *no* indigo in a given ear of wheat, and absolutely *no* attar in a given lichen. But such inferences can only be rendered valid by positive experiential evidence, direct or remote, and cannot rest upon a mere inability to detect the quantity in question. We have reason to think there is no indigo in the wheat, because we have remarked that wherever indigo is produced it is produced in considerable quantities, to mention only one argument. We have reason to think there is no attar in the lichen, because essential oils seem to be in general peculiar to single species. If the question had been whether there was iron in the wheat or the lichen, though chemical analysis should fail to detect its presence, we should think some of it probably was there, since iron is almost everywhere. Without any such information, one way or the other, we could only abstain from any opinion as to the presence of the substance in question. It cannot, I conceive, be maintained that we are in any *better* position than this in regard to the presence of the element of chance or spontaneous departures from law in nature.

Those observations which are generally adduced in favor of mechanical causation simply prove that there is an element of regularity in nature, and have no bearing whatever upon the question of whether such regularity is exact and universal, or not. Nay, in regard to this *exactitude,* all observation is directly *opposed* to it; and the most that can be said is that a good deal of this observation can be explained away. Try to verify any law of nature, and you will find that the more precise your observations, the more certain they will be to show irregular departures from the law. We are accustomed to ascribe these, and I do not say wrongly, to errors of observation; yet we cannot usually account for such errors in any antecedently probable way. Trace their causes back far enough, and you will be forced to admit they are always due to arbitrary determination, or chance.

But it may be asked whether if there were an element of real chance in the universe it must not occasionally be productive of signal effects such as could not pass unobserved. In answer to this question, without stopping to point out that there is an abundance of great events which one might be tempted to suppose were of that nature, it will be simplest to remark that physicists hold that the particles of gases are moving about irregularly, substantially as if by real chance, and that by the principles of probabilities there must occasionally happen to be concentrations of heat in the gases contrary to the second law of thermodynamics, and these concentrations, occurring in explosive mixtures, must sometimes have tremendous effects. Here, then, is in substance the very situation supposed; yet no phenomena ever have resulted which we are forced to attribute to such chance concentration of heat, or which anybody, wise or foolish, has ever dreamed of accounting for in that manner.

In view of all these considerations, I do not believe that anybody, not in a state of case-hardened ignorance respecting the logic of science, can maintain that the precise and universal conformity of facts to law is clearly proved, or even rendered particularly probable, by any observations hitherto made. In this way, the determined advocate of exact regularity will soon find himself driven to *a priori* reasons to support his thesis. These received such a sockdolager from Stuart Mill in his examination of Hamilton, that holding to them now seems to me to denote a high degree of imperviousness to reason; so that I shall pass them by with little notice.

To say that we cannot help believing a given proposition is no argument, but it is a conclusive fact if it be true; and with the substitution of "I" for "we," it is true in the mouths of several classes of minds, the blindly passionate, the unreflecting and ignorant, and the person who has overwhelming evidence before his eyes. But that which has been inconceivable today has often turned out indisputable on the morrow. Inability to conceive is only a stage through which every man must pass in regard to a number of beliefs—unless endowed with extraordinary obstinacy and obtuseness. His understanding is enslaved to some blind compulsion which a vigorous mind is pretty sure soon to cast off.

Some seek to back up the *a priori* position with empirical arguments. They say that the exact regularity of the world is a natural belief, and that natural beliefs have generally been confirmed by experience. There is some reason in this. Natural beliefs, however, if they generally have a foundation of truth, also require correction and purification from natural illusions. The principles of mechanics are undoubtedly natural beliefs; but, for all that, the early formulations of them were exceedingly erroneous. The general approximation to truth in natural beliefs is, in fact, a case of the general adaptation of genetic products to recognizable utilities or ends. Now, the adaptations of nature, beautiful and often marvelous as they verily are, are never found to be quite perfect;

so that the argument is quite *against* the absolute exactitude of any natural belief, including that of the principle of causation.

Another argument, or convenient commonplace, is that absolute chance is *inconceivable.* (This word has eight current significations. The *Century Dictionary* enumerates six.) Those who talk like this will hardly be persuaded to say in what sense they mean that chance is inconceivable. Should they do so, it would easily be shown either that they have no sufficient reason for the statement or that the inconceivability is of a kind which does not prove that chance is non-existent.

Another *a priori* argument is that chance is unintelligible; that is to say, while it may perhaps be conceivable, it does not disclose to the eye of reason the how or why of things; and since a hypothesis can only be justified so far as it renders some phenomenon intelligible, we never can have any right to suppose absolute chance to enter into the production of anything in nature. This argument may be considered in connection with two others. Namely, instead of going so far as to say that the supposition of chance can *never* properly be used to explain any observed fact, it may be alleged merely that no facts are known which such a supposition could in any way help in explaining. Or again, the allegation being still further weakened, it may be said that since departures from law are not unmistakably observed, chance is not a *vera causa,* and ought not unnecessarily to be introduced into a hypothesis.

These are no mean arguments, and require us to examine the matter a little more closely. Come, my superior opponent, let me learn from your wisdom. it seems to me that every throw of sixes with a pair of dice is a manifest instance of chance.

"While you would hold a throw of deuce-ace to be brought about by necessity?" (The opponent's supposed remarks are placed in quotation marks.)

Clearly one throw is as much chance as another.

"Do you think throws of dice are of a different nature from other events?"

I see that I must say that all the diversity and specificalness of events is attributable to chance.

"Would you, then, deny that there is any regularity in the world?"

That is clearly undeniable. I must acknowledge there is an approximate regularity, and that every event is influenced by it. But the diversification, specificalness, and irregularity of things I suppose is chance.

A throw of sixes appears to me a case in which this element is particularly obtrusive.

"If you reflect more deeply, you will come to see that *chance* is only a name for a cause that is unknown to us."

Do you mean that we have no idea whatever what kind of causes could bring about a throw of sixes?

"On the contrary, each die moves under the influence of precise mechanical laws."

But it appears to me that it is not these *laws* which made the die turn up sixes; for these laws act just the same when other throws come up. The chance lies in the diversity of throws; and this diversity cannot be due to laws which are immutable.

"The diversity is due to the diverse circumstances under which the laws act. The dice lie differently in the box, and the motion given to the box is different. These are the unknown causes which produce the throws, and to which we give the name of chance; not the mechanical law which regulates the operation of these causes. You see you are already beginning to think more clearly about this subject."

Does the operation of mechanical law not increase the diversity?

"Properly not. You must know that the instantaneous state of a system of particles is defined by six times as many numbers as there are particles, three for the coordinates of each particle's position, and three more for the components of its velocity. This number of numbers, which expresses the amount of diversity in the system, remains the same at all times. There may be, to be sure, some kind of relation between the coordinates and component velocities of the different particles, by means of which the state of the system might be expressed by a smaller number of numbers. But, if this is the case, a precisely corresponding relationship must exist between the coordinates and component velocities at any other time, though it may doubtless be a relation less obvious to us. Thus, the intrinsic complexity of the system is the same at all times."

Very well, my obliging opponent, we have now reached an issue. You think all the arbitrary specifications of the universe were introduced in one dose, in the beginning, if there was a beginning, and that the variety and complication of nature has always been just as much as it is now. But I, for my part, think that the diversification, the specification, has been continually taking place. Should you condescend to ask me why I so think, I should give my reasons as follows:

(1) Question any science which deals with the course of time. Consider the life of an individual animal or plant, or of a mind. Glance at the history of states, of institutions, of language, of ideas. Examine the successions of forms shown by paleontology, the history of the globe as set forth in geology, of what the astronomer is able to make out concerning the changes of stellar systems. Everywhere the main fact is growth and increasing complexity. Death and corruption are mere accidents or secondary phenomena. Among some of the lower organisms, it is a moot point with biologists whether there be anything which ought to be called death. Races, at any rate, do not die out except under unfavorable circumstances. From these broad and ubiquitous facts we may fairly infer, by the most unexceptionable logic, that there is probably in nature some agency by which the complexity and diversity of things can be increased; and that consequently the rule of mechanical necessity meets in some way with interference.

(2) By thus admitting pure spontaneity or life as a character of the universe, acting always and everywhere though restrained within narrow bounds by law, producing infinitesimal departures from law continually, and great ones with infinite infrequency, I account for all the variety and diversity of the universe, in the only sense in which the really *sui generis* and new can be said to be accounted for. The ordinary view has to admit the inexhaustible multitudinous variety of the world, has to admit that its mechanical law cannot account for this in the least, that variety can spring only from spontaneity, and yet denies without any evidence or reason the existence of this spontaneity, or else shoves it back to the beginning of time and supposes it dead ever since. The superior logic of my view appears to me not easily controverted.

(3) When I ask the necessitarian how he would explain the diversity and irregularity of the universe, he replies to me out of the treasury of his wisdom that irregularity is something which from the nature of things we must not seek to explain. Abashed at this, I seek to cover my confusion by asking how he would explain the uniformity and regularity of the universe, whereupon he tells me that the laws of nature are immutable and ultimate facts, and no account is to be given of them. But my hypothesis of spontaneity does explain irregularity, in a certain sense; that is, it explains the general fact of irregularity, though not, of course, what each lawless event is to be. At the same time, by thus loosening the bond of necessity, it gives room for the influence of

another kind of causation, such as seems to be operative in the mind in the formation of associations, and enables us to understand how the uniformity of nature could have been brought about. That single events should be hard and unintelligible, logic will permit without difficulty: we do not expect to make the shock of a personally experienced earthquake appear natural and reasonable by any amount of cogitation. But logic does expect things *general* to be understandable. To say that there is a universal law, and that it is a hard, ultimate, unintelligible fact, the why and wherefore of which can never be inquired into, at this a sound logic will revolt; and will pass over at once to a method of philosophizing which does not thus barricade the road of discovery.

(4) Necessitarianism cannot logically stop short of making the whole action of the mind a part of the physical universe. Our notion that we decide what we are going to do, if as the necessitarian says, it has been calculable since the earliest times, is reduced to illusion. Indeed, consciousness in general thus becomes a mere illusory aspect of a material system. What we call red, green, and violet are in reality only different rates of vibration. The sole reality is the distribution of qualities of matter in space and time. Brain-matter is protoplasm in a certain degree and kind of complication—a certain arrangement of mechanical particles. Its feeling is but an inward aspect, a phantom. For, from the positions and velocities of the particles at any one instant, and the knowledge of the immutable forces, the positions at all other times are calculable; so that the universe of space, time, and matter is a rounded system uninterfered with from elsewhere. But, from the state of feeling at any instant, there is no reason to suppose the states of feeling at all other instants are thus exactly calculable; so that feeling is, as I said, a mere fragmentary and illusive aspect of the universe. This is the way, then, that necessitarianism has to make up its accounts. It enters consciousness under the head of sundries, as a forgotten trifle; its scheme of the universe would be more satisfactory if this little fact could be dropped out of sight. On the other hand, by supposing the rigid exactitude of causation to yield, I care not how little—be it but by a strictly infinitesimal amount—we gain room to insert mind into our scheme, and to put it into the place where it is needed, into the position which, as the sole self-intelligible thing, it is entitled to occupy, that of the fountain of existence; and in so doing we resolve the problem of the connection of soul and body.

(5) But I must leave undeveloped the chief of my reasons, and can

only adumbrate it. The hypothesis of chance-spontaneity is one whose inevitable consequences are capable of being traced out with mathematical precision into considerable detail. Much of this I have done and find the consequences to agree with observed facts to an extent which seems to me remarkable. But the matter and methods of reasoning are novel, and I have no right to promise that other mathematicians shall find my deductions as satisfactory as I myself do, so that the strongest reason for my belief must for the present remain a private reason of my own, and cannot influence others. I mention it to explain my own position; and partly to indicate to future mathematical speculators a veritable gold mine, should time and circumstances and the abridger of all joys prevent my opening it to the world.

If now I, in my turn, inquire of the necessitarian why he prefers to suppose that all specification goes back to the beginning of things, he will answer me with one of those last three arguments which I left unanswered.

First, he may say that chance is a thing absolutely unintelligible, and, therefore, that we never can be entitled to make such a supposition. But does not this objection smack of naive impudence? It is not mine, it is his own conception of the universe which leads abruptly up to hard, ultimate, inexplicable, immutable law, on the one hand, and to inexplicable specification and diversification of circumstances on the other. My view, on the contrary, hypothesizes nothing at all, unless it be hypothesis to say that all specification came about in some sense, and is not to be accepted as unaccountable. To undertake to account for anything by saying boldly that it is due to chance would, indeed, be futile. But this I do not do. I make use of chance chiefly to make room for a principle of generalization, or tendency to form habits, which I hold has produced all regularities. The mechanical philosopher leaves the whole specification of the world utterly unaccounted for, which is pretty nearly as bad as to boldly attribute it to chance. I attribute it altogether to chance, it is true, but to chance in the form of a spontaneity which is to some degree regular. It seems to me clear at any rate that one of these two positions must be taken, or else specification must be supposed due to a spontaneity which develops itself in a certain and not in a chance way, by an objective logic like that of Hegel. This last way I leave as an open possibility, for the present; for it is as much opposed to the necessitarian scheme of existence as my own theory is.

Secondly, the necessitarian may say there are, at any rate, no observed phenomena which the hypothesis of chance could aid in explaining. In reply, I point first to the phenomenon of growth and developing complexity, which appears to be universal, and which though it may possibly be an affair of mechanism perhaps, certainly presents all the appearance of increasing diversification. Then, there is variety itself, beyond comparison the most obtrusive character of the universe: no mechanism can account for this. Then, there is the very fact the necessitarian most insists upon, the regularity of the universe which for him serves only to block the road of inquiry. Then, there are the regular relationships between the laws of nature—similarities and comparative characters, which appeal to our intelligence as its cousins, and call upon us for a reason. Finally, there is consciousness, feeling, a patent fact enough, but a very inconvenient one to the mechanical philosopher.

Thirdly, the necessitarian may say that chance is not a *vera causa,* that we cannot know positively there is any such element in the universe. But the doctrine of the *vera causa* has nothing to do with elementary conceptions. Pushed to that extreme, it at once cuts off belief in the existence of a material universe; and without that necessitarianism could hardly maintain its ground. Besides, variety is a fact which must be admitted; and the theory of chance merely consists in supposing this diversification does not antedate all time. Moreover, the avoidance of hypotheses involving causes nowhere positively known to act is only a recommendation of logic, not a positive command. It cannot be formulated in any precise terms without at once betraying its untenable character—I mean as rigid rule, for as a recommendation it is wholesome enough.

I believe I have thus subjected to fair examination all the important reasons for adhering to the theory of universal necessity, and have shown their nullity. I earnestly beg that whoever may detect any flaw in my reasoning will point it out to me, either privately or publicly; for if I am wrong, it much concerns me to be set right speedily. If my argument remains unrefuted, it will be time, I think, to doubt the absolute truth of the principle of universal law; and when once such a doubt has obtained a living root in any man's mind, my cause with him, I am persuaded, is gained.

The Law of Mind

In an article published in *The Monist* for January, 1891, I endeavored to show what ideas ought to form the warp of a system of philosophy, and particularly emphasized that of absolute chance. In the number of April, 1892, I argued further in favor of that way of thinking, which it will be convenient to christen *tychism*. . . . A serious student of philosophy will be in no haste to accept or reject this doctrine; but he will see in it one of the chief attitudes which speculative thought may take, feeling that it is not for an individual, nor for an age, to pronounce upon a fundamental question of philosophy. That is a task for a whole era to work out. I have begun by showing that *tychism* must give birth to an evolutionary cosmology, in which all the regularities of nature and of mind are regarded as products of growth, and to a Schelling-fashioned idealism which holds matter to be mere specialized and partially deadened mind. I may mention, for the benefit of those who are curious in studying mental biographies, that I was born and reared in the neighborhood of Concord—I mean in Cambridge—at the time when Emerson, Hedge, and their friends were disseminating the ideas that they had caught from Schelling, and Schelling from Plotinus, from Boehm, or from God knows what minds stricken with the monstrous mysticism of the East. But the atmosphere of Cambridge held many an antiseptic against Concord transcendentalism; and I am not conscious of having contracted any of that virus. Nevertheless, it is probable that some cultural bacilli, some benignant form of the disease was implanted in my soul, unawares, and that now, after long incubation, it comes to the surface, modified by mathematical conceptions and by training in physical investigations.

The next step in the study of cosmology must be to examine the general law of mental action. In doing this, I shall for the time drop my tychism out of view, in order to allow a free and independent expansion to another conception signalized in my first *Monist* paper as one of the most indispensable to philosophy, though it was not there dwelt upon; I mean the idea of continuity. The tendency to regard continuity, in the sense in which I shall define it, as an idea of prime importance in philosophy may conveniently be termed *synechism*. The present paper is intended chiefly to show what synechism is, and what it leads to. I attempted, a good many years ago, to develop this doctrine in the *Journal of Speculative Philosophy* (Vol. 11); but I am able now to improve upon that exposition, in which I was a little blinded by nominalistic prepossessions. I refer to it, because students may possibly find that some points not sufficiently explained in the present paper are cleared up in those earlier ones.

WHAT THE LAW IS

Logical analysis applied to mental phenomena shows that there is but one law of mind, namely, that ideas tend to spread continuously and to affect certain others which stand to them in a peculiar relation of affectibility. In this spreading they lose intensity, and especially the power of affecting others, but gain generality and become welded with other ideas.

I set down this formula at the beginning, for convenience; and now proceed to comment upon it.

INDIVIDUALITY OF IDEAS

We are accustomed to speak of ideas as reproduced, as passed from mind to mind, as similar or dissimilar to one another, and, in short, as if they were substantial things; nor can any reasonable objection be raised to such expressions. But taking the word "idea" in the sense of an event in an individual consciousness, it is clear that an idea once past is gone forever, and any supposed recurrence of it is another idea. These two ideas are not present in the same state of consciousness, and therefore cannot possibly be compared. To say, therefore, that they are similar can only mean that an occult power from the depths of the soul forces us to connect them in our thoughts after they are both no more. We may note, here, in passing, that of the two generally recognized principles of association, contiguity and similarity, the former is a connection due to a power without, the latter a connection due to a power within.

But what can it mean to say that ideas wholly past are thought of at all, any longer? They are utterly unknowable. What distinct meaning can attach to saying that an idea in the past in any way affects an idea in the future, from which it is completely detached? A phrase between the assertion and the denial of which there can in no case be any sensible difference is mere gibberish.

I will not dwell further upon this point, because it is a commonplace of philosophy.

CONTINUITY OF IDEAS

We have here before us a question of difficulty, analogous to the question of nominalism and realism. But when once it has been clearly formulated, logic leaves room for one answer only. How can a past idea be present? Can it be present vicariously? To a certain extent, perhaps; but not merely so; for then the question would arise how the past idea can be related to its vicarious representation. The relation, being between ideas, can only exist in some consciousness: now that past idea was in no consciousness but that past consciousness that alone contained it; and that did not embrace the vicarious idea.

Some minds will here jump to the conclusion that a past idea cannot in any sense be present. But that is hasty and illogical. How extravagant, too, to pronounce our whole knowledge of the past to be mere delusion! Yet it would seem that the past is as completely beyond the bounds of possible experience as a Kantian thing-in-itself.

How can a past idea be present? Not vicariously. Then, only by direct perception. In other words, to be present, it must be *ipso facto* present. That is, it cannot be wholly past; it can only be going, infinitesimally past, less past than any assignable past date. We are thus brought to the conclusion that the present is connected with the past by a series of real infinitesimal steps.

It has already been suggested by psychologists that consciousness necessarily embraces an interval of time. But if a finite time be meant, the opinion is not tenable. If the sensation that precedes the present by half a second were still immediately before me, then, on the same principle the sensation preceding that would be immediately present, and so on *ad infinitum*. Now, since there is a time, say a year, at the end of which an idea is no longer *ipso facto* present, it follows that this is true of any finite interval, however short.

But yet consciousness must essentially cover an interval of time; for if it did not, we could gain no knowledge of time, and not merely no veracious cognition of it, but no conception whatever. We are, therefore, forced to say that we are immediately conscious through an infinitesimal interval of time.

This is all that is requisite. For, in this infinitesimal interval, not only is consciousness continuous in a subjective sense, that is, considered as a subject or substance having the attribute of duration; but also, because it is immediate consciousness, its object is *ipso facto* continuous. In fact, this infinitesimally spread-out consciousness is a direct feeling of its contents as spread out. This will be further elucidated below. In an infinitesimal interval we directly perceive the temporal sequence of its beginning, middle, and end—not, of course, in the way of recognition, for recognition is only of the past, but in the way of immediate feeling. Now upon this interval follows another, whose beginning is the middle of the former, and whose middle is the end of the former. Here, we have an immediate perception of the temporal sequence of its beginning, middle, and end, or say of the second, third, and fourth instants. From these two immediate perceptions, we gain a mediate, or inferential, perception of the relation of all four instants. This mediate perception is objectively, or as to the object represented, spread over the four instants; but subjectively, or as itself the subject of duration, it is completely embraced in the second moment. (The reader will observe that I use the word *instant to* mean a point of time, and *moment* to mean an infinitesimal duration.) If it is objected that, upon the theory proposed, we must have more than a mediate perception of the succession of the four instants, I grant it; for the sum of the two infinitesimal intervals is itself infinitesimal, so that it is immediately perceived. It is immediately perceived in the whole interval, but only mediately perceived in the last two-thirds of the interval. Now, let there be an indefinite succession of these inferential acts of comparative perception; and it is plain that the last moment will contain objectively the whole series. Let there be, not merely an indefinite succession, but a continuous flow of inference through a finite time; and the result will be a mediate objective consciousness of the whole time in the last moment. In this last moment, the whole series will be recognized, or known as known before, except only the last moment, which of course will be absolutely unrecognizable to itself. Indeed, even this last moment will be recognized like the rest, or, at least, be just beginning to be so. There is a little *elenchus,* or appearance of contradiction, here, which the ordinary logic of reflection quite suffices to resolve.

*   *   *

. . . Suppose a surface to be part red and part blue; so that every point on it is either red or blue, and, of course, no part can be both red and blue. What, then, is the color of the boundary line between the red and blue? The answer is that red or blue, to exist at all, must be spread over a surface; and the color of the surface is the color of the surface in the immediate neighborhood of the point. I purposely use a vague form of expression. Now, as the parts of the surface in the immediate neighborhood of any ordinary point upon a curved boundary are half of them red and half blue, it follows that the boundary is half red and half blue. In like manner, we find it necessary to hold that consciousness essentially occupies time; and what is present to the mind at any ordinary instant, is what is present during a moment in which that instant occurs. Thus, the present is half past and half to come. Again, the color of the parts of a surface at any finite distance from a point, has nothing to do with its color just at that point; and, in the parallel, the feeling at any finite interval from the present has nothing to do with the present feeling, except vicariously. Take another case: the velocity of a particle at any instant of time is its mean velocity during an infinitesimal instant in which that time is contained. Just so my immediate feeling is my feeling through an infinitesimal duration containing the present instant.

ANALYSIS OF TIME

One of the most marked features about the law of mind is that it makes time to have a definite direction of flow from past to future. The relation of past to future is, in reference to the law of mind, different from the relation of future to past. This makes one of the great contrasts between the law of mind and the law of physical force, where there is no more distinction between the two opposite directions in time than between moving northward and moving southward.

In order, therefore, to analyze the law of mind, we must begin by asking what the flow of time consists in. Now, we find that in reference to any individual state of feeling, all others are of two classes, those which affect this one (or have a tendency to affect it, and what this means we shall inquire shortly), and those which do not. The present is affectible by the past but not by the future.

Moreover, if state A is affected by state B, and state B by state C, then A is affected by state C, though not so much so. It follows, that if A is affectible by B, B is not affectible by A.

If, of two states, each is absolutely unaffectible by the other, they are to be regarded as parts of the same state. They are contemporaneous.

To say that a state is *between* two states means that it affects one and is affected by the other. Between any two states in this sense lies an innumerable series of states affecting one another; and if a state lies between a given state and any other state which can be reached by inserting states between this state and any third state, these inserted states not immediately affecting or being affected by either, then the second state mentioned immediately affects or is affected by the first, in the sense that in the one the other is *ipso facto* present in a reduced degree.

These propositions involve a definition of time and of its flow. Over and above this definition they involve a doctrine, namely, that every state of feeling is affectible by every earlier state.

THAT FEELINGS HAVE INTENSIVE CONTINUITY

Time with its continuity logically involves some other kind of continuity than its own. Time, as the universal form of change, cannot exist unless there is something to undergo change, and to undergo a change continuous in time, there must be a continuity of changeable qualities. Of the continuity of intrinsic qualities of feeling we can now form but a feeble conception. The development of the human mind has practically extinguished all feelings, except a few sporadic kinds, sound, colors, smells, warmth, etc., which now appear to be disconnected and disparate. In the case of colors, there is a tridimensional spread of feelings. Originally, all feelings may have been connected in the same way, and the presumption is that the number of dimensions was endless. For development essentially involves a limitation of possibilities. But given a number of dimensions of feeling, all possible varieties are obtainable by varying the intensities of the different elements. Accordingly, time logically supposes a continuous range of intensity in feeling. It follows, then, from the definition of continuity, that when any particular kind of feeling is present, an infinitesimal continuum of all feelings differing infinitesimally from that is present.

THAT FEELINGS HAVE SPATIAL EXTENSION

Consider a gob of protoplasm, say an amoeba or a slime-mold. It does not differ in any radical way from the contents of a nerve-cell, though its functions may be less specialized. There is no doubt that this slime-mold, or this amoeba, or at any rate some similar mass of protoplasm feels. That is to say, it feels when it is in its excited condition. But note how it behaves. When the whole is quiescent and rigid, a place upon it is irritated. Just at this point, an active motion is set up, and this gradually spreads to other parts. In this action, no unity nor relation to a nucleus, or other unitary organ can be discerned. It is a mere amorphous continuum of protoplasm, with feeling passing from one part to another. Nor is there anything like a wave-motion. The activity does not advance to new parts, just as fast as it leaves old parts. Rather, in the beginning, it dies out at a slower rate than that at which it spreads. And while the process is going on, by exciting the mass at another point, a second quite independent state of excitation will be set up. In some places, neither excitation will exist, in others each separately, in still other places, both effects will be added together. Whatever there is in the whole phenomenon to make us think there is feeling in such a mass of protoplasm—*feeling*, but plainly no *person*ality—goes logically to show that that feeling has a subjective, or substantial spatial extension, as the excited state has. This is, no doubt, a difficult idea to seize, for the reason that it is a subjective, not an objective, extension. It is not that we have a feeling of bigness; though Professor James, perhaps rightly, teaches that we have. It is that the feeling, as a subject of inhesion, is big. Moreover, our own feelings are focused in attention to such a degree that we are not aware that ideas are not brought to an absolute unity; just as nobody not instructed by special experiment has any idea how very, very little of the field of vision is distinct. Still, we all know how the attention wanders about among our feelings; and this fact shows that those feelings that are not coordinated in attention have a reciprocal externality, although they are present at the same time. But we must not tax introspection to make a phenomenon manifest which essentially involves externality.

Since space is continuous, it follows that there must be an immediate community of feeling between parts of mind infinitesimally near together. Without this, I believe it would have been impossible for minds external to one another, ever to become coordinated, and equally impossible for any coordination to be established in the action of the nerve-matter of one brain.

AFFECTIONS OF IDEAS

But we are met by the question, what is meant by saying that one idea affects another. The unravelment of this problem requires us to trace out phenomena a little further.

Three elements go to make up an idea. The first is its intrinsic quality as a feeling. The second is the energy with which it affects other ideas, an energy which is infinite in the here-and-nowness of immediate sensation, finite and relative in the recency of the past. The third element is the tendency of an idea to bring along other ideas with it.

As an idea spreads, its power of affecting other ideas gets rapidly reduced; but its intrinsic quality remains nearly unchanged. It is long years now since I last saw a cardinal in his robes; and my memory of their color has become much dimmed. The color itself, however, is not remembered as dim. I have no inclination to call it a dull red. Thus, the intrinsic quality remains little changed; yet more accurate observation will show a slight reduction of it. The third element, on the other hand, has increased. As well as I can recollect, it seems to me the cardinals I used to see wore robes more scarlet than vermilion is, and highly luminous. Still, I know the color commonly called cardinal is on the crimson side of vermilion and of quite moderate luminosity, and the original idea calls up so many other hues with it, and asserts itself so feebly, that I am unable any longer to isolate it.

A finite interval of time generally contains an innumerable series of feelings; and when these become welded together in association, the result is a general idea. For we have just seen how by continuous spreading an idea becomes generalized.

The first character of a general idea so resulting is that it is living feeling. A continuum of this feeling, infinitesimal in duration, but still embracing innumerable parts, and also, though infinitesimal, entirely unlimited, is immediately present. And in its absence of boundedness a vague possibility of more than is present is directly felt.

Second, in the presence of this continuity of feeling, nominalistic maxims appear futile. There is no doubt about one idea affecting another, when we can directly perceive the one gradually modified and shaping itself into the other. Nor can there any longer be any difficulty about one idea resembling another, when we can pass along the continuous field of quality from one to the other and back again to the point which we had marked.

Third, consider the insistency of an idea. The insistency of a past idea with reference to the present is a quantity which is less the further back that past idea is, and rises to infinity as the past idea is brought up into coincidence with the present. Here we must make one of those inductive applications of the law of continuity which have produced such great results in all the positive sciences. We must extend the law of insistency into the future. Plainly, the insistency of a future idea with reference to the present is a quantity affected by the minus sign; for it is the present that affects the future, if there be any effect, not the future that affects the present. Accordingly, the curve of insistency is a sort of equilateral hyperbola. (See the figure.) Such a conception is none the less mathematical, that its quantification cannot now be exactly specified.

Now consider the induction which we have here been led into. This curve says that feeling which has not yet emerged into immediate consciousness is already affectible and already affected. In fact, this is habit, by virtue of which an idea is brought up into present consciousness by a bond that had already been established between it and another idea while it was still *in futuro*.

We can now see what the affection of one idea by another consists in. It is that the affected idea is attached as a logical predicate to the affecting idea as subject. So when a feeling emerges into immediate consciousness, it always appears as a modification of a more or less general object already in the mind. The word suggestion is well adapted to expressing this relation. The future is suggested by, or rather is influenced by the suggestions of, the past.

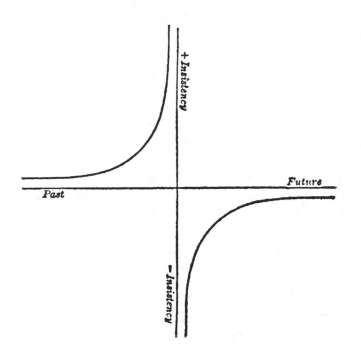

IDEAS CANNOT BE CONNECTED EXCEPT BY CONTINUITY

That ideas can nowise be connected without continuity is sufficiently evident to one who reflects upon the matter. But still the opinion may be entertained that after continuity has once made the connection of ideas possible, then they may get to be connected in other modes than through continuity. Certainly, I cannot see how anyone can deny that the infinite diversity of the universe, which we call chance, may bring ideas into proximity which are not associated in one general idea. It may do this many times. But then the law of continuous spreading will produce a mental association; and this I suppose is an abridged statement of the way the universe has been evolved. But if I am asked whether a blind ἀνάγκη cannot bring ideas together, first I point out that it would not remain blind. There being a continuous connection between the ideas, they would infallibly become associated in a living, feeling, and perceiving general idea. Next, I cannot see what the must-ness or necessity of this ἀνάγκη would consist in. In the absolute uniformity of the phenomenon, says the nominalist. Absolute is well put in; for if it merely happened so three times in succession, or three million times in succession, in the absence of any reason, the coincidence could only be attributed to chance. But absolute uniformity must extend over the whole infinite future; and it is idle to talk of that except as an idea. No; I think we can only hold that wherever ideas come together they tend to weld into general ideas; and wherever they are generally connected, general ideas govern the connection; and these general ideas are living feelings spread out.

MENTAL LAW FOLLOWS THE FORMS OF LOGIC

The three main classes of logical inference are Deduction, Induction, and Hypothesis. These correspond to three chief modes of action of the human soul. In deduction the mind is under the dominion of a habit or association by virtue of which a general idea suggests in each case a corresponding reaction. But a certain sensation is seen to involve that idea. Consequently, that sensation is followed by that reaction. That is the way the hind legs of a frog, separated from the rest of the body, reason, when you pinch them. It is the lowest form of Psychical manifestation.

By induction, a habit becomes established. Certain sensations, all involving one general idea, are followed each by the same reaction; and an association becomes established, whereby that general idea gets to be followed uniformly by that reaction.

Habit is that specialization of the law of mind whereby a general idea gains the power of exciting reactions. But in order that the general idea should attain all its functionality, it is necessary, also, that it should become suggestible by sensations. That is accomplished by a Psychical process having the form of hypothetic inference. By hypothetic inference, I mean, as I have explained in other writings, an induction from qualities. For example, I know that the kind of man known and classed as a "mugwump" has certain characteristics. He has a high self-respect and places great value upon social distinction. He laments the great part that rowdyism and unrefined good-fellowship play in the dealings of American politicians with their constituency. He thinks that the reform which would follow from the abandonment of the system by which the distribution of offices is made to strengthen party organizations and a return to the original and essential conception of office-filling would be found an unmixed good. He holds that monetary considerations should usually be the decisive ones in questions of public policy. He respects the principle of individualism and of *laissez-faire* as the greatest agency of civilization. These views, among others, I know to be obstrusive marks of a "mugwump." Now, suppose I casually meet a man in a railway-train, and falling into conversation find that he holds opinions of this sort; I am naturally led to suppose that he is a "mugwump." That is hypothetic inference. That is to say, a number of readily verifiable marks of a mugwump being selected, I find this man has these, and infer that he has all the other characters which go to make a thinker of that stripe. Or let us suppose that I meet a man of a semi-clerical appearance and a sub-pharisaical sniff, who appears to look at things from the point of view of a rather wooden dualism. He cites several texts of Scripture and always with particular attention to their logical implications; and he exhibits a sternness, almost amounting to vindictiveness, toward evil-doers, in general. I readily conclude that he is a minister of a certain denomination. Now the mind acts in a way similar to this, every time we acquire a power of coordinating reactions in a peculiar way, as in performing any act requiring skill. Thus, most persons have a difficulty in moving the two hands simultaneously and in opposite directions through two parallel circles nearly in the medial plane of the body. To learn to do this, it is necessary to attend, first, to the different actions in different parts of the motion, when suddenly a general conception of the action springs up and it becomes perfectly easy. We think the motion we are trying to do involves this action, and this, and this. Then, the general idea comes which unites all those actions, and thereupon the desire to perform the motion calls up the general idea. The same mental process is many times employed whenever we are learning to speak a language or are acquiring any sort of skill.

Thus, by induction, a number of sensations followed by one reaction become united under one general idea followed by the same reaction; while by the hypothetic process, a number of reactions called for by one occasion get united in a general idea which is called out by the same occasion. By deduction, the habit fulfills its function of calling out certain reactions on certain occasions.

UNCERTAINTY OF MENTAL ACTION

The inductive and hypothetic forms of inference are essentially probable inferences, not necessary; while deduction may be either necessary or probable.

But no mental action seems to be necessary or invariable in its character. In whatever manner the mind has reacted under a given sensation, in that manner it is the more likely to react again; were this, however, an absolute necessity, habits would become wooden and ineradicable, and no room being left for the formation of new habits, intellectual life would come to a speedy close. Thus, the uncertainty of the mental law is no mere defect of it, but is on the contrary of its essence. The truth is, the mind is not subject to "law," in the same rigid sense that matter is. It only experiences gentle forces which merely render it more likely to act in a given way than it otherwise would be. There always remains a certain amount of arbitrary spontaneity in its action, without which it would be dead.

Some psychologists think to reconcile the uncertainty of reactions with the principle of necessary causation by means of the law of fatigue. Truly for a *law,* this law of fatigue is a little lawless. I think it is merely a case of the general principle that an idea in spreading loses its insistency. Put me tarragon into my salad, when I have not tasted it for years, and I exclaim, "What nectar is this!" But add it to every dish I taste for week after week, and a habit of expectation has been created; and in thus spreading into habit, the sensation makes hardly any more impression upon me; or, if it be noticed, it is on a new side from which it appears as rather a bore. The doctrine that fatigue is one of the primordial phenomena of mind I am much disposed to doubt. It seems a somewhat little thing to be allowed as an exception to the great principle of mental uniformization. For this reason, I prefer to explain it in the manner here indicated, as a special case of that great principle. To consider it as something distinct in its nature, certainly somewhat strengthens the necessitarian position; but even if it be distinct, the hypothesis that all the variety and apparent arbitrariness of mental action ought to be explained away in favor of absolute determinism does not seem to me to recommend itself to a sober and sound judgment, which seeks the guidance of observed facts and not that of prepossessions.

RESTATEMENT OF THE LAW

Let me now try to gather up all these odds and ends of commentary and restate the law of mind, in a unitary way.

First, then, we find that when we regard ideas from a nominalistic, individualistic, sensualistic way, the simplest facts of mind become utterly meaningless. That one idea should resemble another or influence another, or that one state of mind should so much as be thought of in another is, from that standpoint, sheer nonsense.

Second, by this and other means we are driven to perceive, what is quite evident of itself, that instantaneous feelings flow together into a continuum of feeling, which has in a modified degree the peculiar vivacity of feeling and has gained generality. And in reference to such general ideas, or continua of feeling, the difficulties about resemblance and suggestion and reference to the external, cease to have any force.

Third, these general ideas are not mere words, nor do they consist in this, that certain concrete facts will every time happen under certain descriptions of conditions; but they are just as much, or rather far more, living realities than the feelings themselves out of which they are concreted. And to say that mental phenomena are governed by law does not mean merely that they are describable by a general formula; but that there is a living idea, a conscious continuum of feeling, which pervades them, and to which they are docile.

Fourth, this supreme law, which is the celestial and living harmony, does not so much as demand that the special ideas shall surrender their peculiar arbitrariness and caprice entirely; for that would be self-destructive. It only requires that they shall influence and be influenced by one another.

Fifth, in what measure this unification acts, seems to be regulated only by special rules; or, at least, we cannot in our present knowledge say how far it goes. But it may be said that, judging by appearances, the amount of arbitrariness in the phenomena of human minds is neither altogether trifling nor very prominent.

Personality

Having thus endeavored to state the law of mind, in general, I descend to the consideration of a particular phenomenon which is remarkably prominent in our own consciousness, that of personality. A strong light is thrown upon this subject by recent observations of double and multiple personality. The theory which at one time seemed plausible that two persons in one body corresponded to the two halves of the brain will, I take it, now be universally acknowledged to be insufficient. But that which these cases make quite manifest is that personality is some kind of coordination or connection of ideas. Not much to say, this, perhaps. Yet when we consider that, according to the principle which we are tracing out, a connection between ideas is itself a general idea, and that a general idea is a living feeling, it is plain that we have at least taken an appreciable step toward the understanding of personality. This personality, like any general idea, is not a thing to be apprehended in an instant. It has to be lived in time; nor can any finite time embrace it in all its fullness. Yet in each infinitesimal interval it is present and living, though specially colored by the immediate feelings of that moment. Personality, so far as it is apprehended in a moment, is immediate self-consciousness.

But the word coordination implies somewhat more than this; it implies a teleological harmony in ideas, and in the case of personality this teleology is more than a mere purposive pursuit of a predeterminate end; it is a developmental teleology. This is personal character. A general idea, living and conscious now, it is already determinative of acts in the future to an extent to which it is not now conscious.

This reference to the future is an essential element of personality. Were the ends of a person already explicit, there would be no room for development, for growth, for life; and consequently there would be no personality. The mere carrying out of predetermined purposes is mechanical. This remark has an application to the philosophy of religion. It is that a genuine evolutionary philosophy, that is, one that makes the principle of growth a primordial element of the universe, is so far from being antagonistic to the idea of a personal creator, that it is really inseparable from that idea; while a necessitarian religion is in an altogether false position and is destined to become disintegrated. But a pseudo-evolutionism which enthrones mechanical law above the principle of growth, is at once scientifically unsatisfactory, as giving no possible hint of how the universe has come about, and hostile to all hopes of personal relations to God.

COMMUNICATION

Consistently with the doctrine laid down in the beginning of this paper, I am bound to maintain that an idea can only be affected by an idea in continuous connection with it. By anything but an idea, it cannot be affected at all. This obliges me to say, as I do say, on other grounds, that what we call matter is not completely dead, but is merely mind hidebound with habits. It still retains the element of diversification; and in that diversification there is life. When an idea is conveyed from one mind to another, it is by forms of combination of the diverse elements of nature, say by some curious symmetry, or by some union of a tender color with a refined odor. To such forms the law of mechanical energy has no application. If they are eternal, it is in the spirit they embody; and their origin cannot be accounted for by any mechanical necessity. They are embodied ideas; and so only can they convey ideas. Precisely how primary sensations, as colors and tones, are excited, we cannot tell, in the present state of psychology. But in our ignorance, I think that we are at liberty to suppose that they arise in essentially the same manner as the other feelings, called secondary. As far as sight and hearing are in question, we know that they are only excited by vibrations of inconceivable complexity; and the chemical senses are probably not more simple. Even the least Psychical of peripheral sensations, that of pressure, has in its excitation conditions which, though apparently simple, are seen to be complicated enough when we consider the molecules and their attractions. The principle with which I set out requires me to maintain that these feelings are communicated to the nerves by continuity, so that there must be something like them in the excitants themselves. If this seems extravagant, it is to be remembered that it is the sole possible way of reaching any explanation of sensation, which otherwise must be pronounced a general fact, absolutely inexplicable and ultimate. Now absolute inexplicability is a hypothesis which sound logic refuses under any circumstances to justify.

I may be asked whether my theory would be favorable or otherwise to telepathy. I have no decided answer to give to this. At first sight, it seems unfavorable. Yet there may be other modes of continuous connection between minds other than those of time and space.

The recognition by one person of another's personality takes place by means to some extent identical with the means by which he is conscious of his own personality. The idea of the second personality, which is as much as to say that second personality itself, enters within the field of direct consciousness of the first person, and is as immediately perceived as his ego, though less strongly. At the same time, the opposition between the two persons is perceived, so that the externality of the second is recognized.

The psychological phenomena of intercommunication between two minds have been unfortunately little studied. So that it is impossible to say, for certain, whether they are favorable to this theory or not. But the very extraordinary insight which some persons are able to gain of others from indications so slight that it is difficult to ascertain what they are, is certainly rendered more comprehensible by the view here taken.

A difficulty which confronts the synechistic philosophy is this. In considering personality, that philosophy is forced to accept the doctrine of a personal God; but in considering communication, it cannot but admit that if there is a personal God, we must have a direct perception of that person and indeed be in personal communication with him. Now, if that be the case, the question arises how it is possible that the existence of this being should ever have been doubted by anybody. The only answer that I can at present make is that facts that stand before our face and eyes and stare us in the face are far from being, in all cases, the ones most easily discerned. That has been remarked from time immemorial.

CONCLUSION

I have thus developed as well as I could in a little space the *synechistic* philosophy, as applied to mind. I think that I have succeeded in making it clear that this doctrine gives room for explanations of many facts which without it are absolutely and hopelessly inexplicable; and further that it carries along with it the following doctrines: first, a logical realism of the most pronounced type; second, objective idealism; third, tychism, with its consequent thoroughgoing evolutionism. We also notice that the doctrine presents no hindrances to spiritual influences, such as some philosophies are felt to do.

Man's Glassy Essence

In *The Monist* for January, 1891, I tried to show what conceptions ought to form the brick and mortar of a philosophical system. Chief among these was that of absolute chance for which I argued again in last April's number.[1] In July, I applied another fundamental idea, that of continuity, to the law of mind. Next in order, I have to elucidate, from the point of view chosen, the relation between the Psychical and physical aspects of a substance.

*   *   *

But what is to be said of the property of feeling? If consciousness belongs to all protoplasm, by what mechanical constitution is this to be accounted for? The slime is nothing but a chemical compound. There is no inherent impossibility in its being formed synthetically in the laboratory, out of its chemical elements; and if it were so made, it would present all the characters of natural protoplasm. No doubt, then, it would feel. To hesitate to admit this would be puerile and ultra-puerile. By what element of the molecular arrangement, then, would that feeling be caused? This question cannot be evaded or pooh-poohed. Protoplasm certainly does feel; and unless we are to accept a weak dualism, the property must be shown to arise from some peculiarity of the mechanical system. Yet the attempt to deduce it from the three laws of mechanics, applied to never so ingenious a mechanical contrivance, would obviously be futile. It can never be explained, unless we admit that physical events are but degraded or undeveloped forms of Psychical events. But once grant that the phenomena of matter are but the result of the sensibly complete sway of habits upon mind, and it only remains to explain why in the protoplasm these habits are to some slight extent broken up, so that according to the law of mind,

---

[1] I am rejoiced to find, since my last paper was printed, that a philosopher as subtle and profound as Dr. Edmund Montgomery has long been arguing for the same element in the universe. Other world-renowned thinkers, as M. Renouvier and M. Delboeuf, appear to share this opinion.

in that special clause of it sometimes called the principle of accommo-dation,[2] feeling becomes intensified. Now the manner in which habits generally get broken up is this. Reactions usually terminate in the re-moval of a stimulus; for the excitation continues as long as the stimulus is present. Accordingly, habits are general ways of behavior which are associated with the removal of stimuli. But when the expected removal of the stimulus fails to occur, the excitation continues and increases, and nonhabitual reactions take place; and these tend to weaken the habit. If, then, we suppose that matter never does obey its ideal laws with absolute precision, but that there are almost insensible fortuitous departures from regularity, these will produce, in general, equally min-ute effects. But protoplasm is in an excessively unstable condition; and it is the characteristic of unstable equilibrium, that near that point excessively minute causes may produce startlingly large effects. Here, then, the usual departures from regularity will be followed by others that are very great; and the large fortuitous departures from law so produced, will tend still further to break up the laws, supposing that these are of the nature of habits. Now, this breaking up of habit and renewed fortuitous spontaneity will, according to the law of mind, be accompanied by an intensification of feeling. The nerve-protoplasm is, without doubt, in the most unstable condition of any kind of matter; and consequently, there the resulting feeling is the most manifest.

Thus we see that the idealist has no need to dread a mechanical theory of life. On the contrary, such a theory, fully developed, is bound to call in a tychistic idealism as its indispensable adjunct. Wherever chance-spontaneity is found, there, in the same proportion, feeling ex-ists. In fact, chance is but the outward aspect of that which within itself is feeling. I long ago showed that real existence, or thing-ness, consists in regularities. So, that primeval chaos in which there was no regularity was mere nothing, from a physical aspect. Yet it was not a blank zero; for there was an intensity of consciousness there in comparison with which all that we ever feel is but as the struggling of a molecule or two to throw off a little of the force of law to an endless and innumerable diversity of chance utterly unlimited.

But after some atoms of the protoplasm have thus become partially emancipated from law, what happens next to them? To understand this,

---

[2] "Physiologically . . . accommodation means the breaking up of a habit. . . . Psycho-logically, it means reviving consciousness," Baldwin, *Psychology*, Part III, ch. 1, S. 5.

we have to remember that no mental tendency is so easily strengthened by the action of habit as is the tendency to take habits. Now, in the higher kinds of protoplasm, especially, the atoms in question have not only long belonged to one molecule or another of the particular mass of slime of which they are parts; but before that, they were constituents of food of a protoplasmic constitution. During all this time, they have been liable to lose habits and to recover them again; so that now, when the stimulus is removed, and the foregone habits tend to reassert themselves, they do so in the case of such atoms with great promptness. Indeed, the return is so prompt that there is nothing but the feeling to show conclusively that the bonds of law have ever been relaxed.

In short, diversification is the vestige of chance-spontaneity; and wherever diversity is increasing, there chance must be operative. On the other hand, wherever uniformity is increasing, habit must be operative. But wherever actions take place under an established uniformity, there so much feeling as there may be takes the mode of a sense of reaction. That is the manner in which I am led to define the relation between the fundamental elements of consciousness and their physical equivalents.

It remains to consider the physical relations of general ideas. It may be well here to reflect that if matter has no existence except as a specialization of mind, it follows that whatever affects matter according to regular laws is itself matter. But all mind is directly or indirectly connected with all matter, and acts in a more or less regular way; so that all mind more or less partakes of the nature of matter. Hence, it would be a mistake to conceive of the Psychical and the physical aspects of matter as two aspects absolutely distinct. Viewing a thing from the outside, considering its relations of action and reaction with other things, it appears as matter. Viewing it from the inside, looking at its immediate character as feeling, it appears as consciousness. These two views are combined when we remember that mechanical laws are nothing but acquired habits, like all the regularities of mind, including the tendency to take habits, itself; and that this action of habit is nothing but generalization, and generalization is nothing but the spreading of feelings. But the question is, how do general ideas appear in the molecular theory of protoplasm?

The consciousness of a habit involves a general idea. In each action of that habit certain atoms get thrown out of their orbit, and replaced by others. Upon all the different occasions it is different atoms that are thrown off, but they are analogous from a physical point of view, and there is an inward sense of their being analogous. Every time one of the associated feelings recurs, there is a more or less vague sense that there are others, that it has a general character, and of about what this general character is. We ought not, I think, to hold that in protoplasm habit never acts in any other than the particular way suggested above. On the contrary, if habit be a primary property of mind, it must be equally so of matter, as a kind of mind. We can hardly refuse to admit that wherever chance motions have general characters, there is a tendency for this generality to spread and to perfect itself. In that case, a general idea is a certain modification of consciousness which accompanies any regularity or general relation between chance actions.

The consciousness of a general idea has a certain "unity of the ego" in it, which is identical when it passes from one mind to another. It is, therefore, quite analogous to a person, and, indeed, a person is only a particular kind of general idea. . . .

WILLIAM JAMES

William James was born in New York City in 1842, the son of a theologian and the elder brother of the novelist Henry James. His education was varied and somewhat diffuse. He began his schooling in New York, but in 1855 he set out with his family for Europe and continued his learning for the following three years through schools, tutors, and French governesses in England and France. It was during this period that young William, full of enthusiasm for Delacroix, set his heart upon a career of art. There followed a year's residence and schooling at Newport, Rhode Island, and then another year of schools and tutors in Switzerland and Germany. Returning to Newport, James studied painting for a time with W. M. Hunt. But his enthusiasm for art gradually waned and in 1861 he turned to Harvard and the vocation of science. Prevented by physical frailty and poor health from participating in the raging Civil War, James quietly pursued his studies. It was during this time that he made two lifelong friendships, with Charles Sanders Peirce and Oliver Wendell Holmes. In 1864 he entered the Medical School at Harvard but he did not receive his M.D. until 1869. During these five years his travels continued, first to Brazil on a scientific expedition with Louis Agassiz, then to Germany again to study experimental physiology and to explore his new-found interest in philosophy. He had begun to experience at this time declining health and spells of profound melancholia. In 1870 his depression was deepened by a spiritual crisis not unlike the famous tribulations of John Stuart Mill. Life seemed to James to lose its zest and meaning and his own development seemed hopeless. At this point, no doubt, the somewhat boyish infatuation with the charms of philosophy became the need of a man. His complete recovery was signaled in 1873 by his acceptance of an instructorship in comparative anatomy at Harvard. In 1879 be began teaching philosophy and published one of his most famous essays, "The Sentiment of Rationality." In 1880 he was made an assistant professor of philosophy and in 1885 a full professor. In 1890, after twelve years of research and writing, the two-volume *Principles of Psy-*

chology was published, establishing his leadership in American thought. From that time until his death in 1910 he worked diligently at the development of a pluralistic and empiricistic philosophy of change. He acknowledged graciously the early influence of Peirce upon his thinking, but toward the end of his life it was Bergson to whom he looked as his master. It must be admitted that James was not as original as either Peirce or Bergson, but he supplemented the foundations they laid for the development of a new metaphysics and he performed the important service of saying persuasively and clearly what his two contemporaries too often said only sketchily or obscurely.

MAJOR PHILOSOPHICAL WORKS BY JAMES

In 1988, Harvard University Press completed their republication of corrected editions of James's works in *The Works of William James*, under the editorships of Frederick H. Burkhardt, Fredson Bowers, and Ignas K. Skrupskelis. All of the following works of James are included in that collection.

1890   *Principles of Psychology.*
1892   *Psychology: Briefer Course.*
1897   *The Will to Believe, and Other Essays in Popular Philosophy.*
1898   *Human Immortality: Two Supposed Objections to the Doctrine.*
1902   *The Varieties of Religious Experience: A Study in Human Nature.* (Gifford Lectures.)
1907   *Pragmatism: A New Name for Some Old Ways of Thinking.*
1909   *The Meaning of Truth, A Sequel to "Pragmatism."*
1909   *A Pluralistic Universe.* (Hibbert Lectures.)
1911   *Some Problems of Philosophy: A Beginning of an Introduction to Philosophy.* (Posthumous.)
1911   *Memories and Studies.* (Posthumous.)
1912   *Essays in Radical Empiricism.* (Posthumous.)
1920   *Collected Essays and Reviews.* Edited by R. B. Perry.

RECOMMENDED WORKS ON JAMES

Cotkin, George. *William James: Public Philosopher.* Baltimore: Johns Hopkins University Press, 1990.
Donnelly, Margaret E. (ed.). *Reinterpreting the Legacy of William*

James. Washington D.C.: American Psychological Association Press, 1992.

Ford, Marcus Peter. *William James's Philosophy: A New Perspective.* Amherst: The University of Massachusetts Press, 1982.

Gavin, William J. *William James and the Reinstatement of the Vague.* Philadelphia: Temple University Press, 1992.

Moore, Edward C. *William James.* New York: Washington Square Press, 1965.

Myers, Gerald E. *William James: His Life and Thought.* New Haven: Yale University Press, 1988.

Perry, R. B. *The Thought and Character of William James.* Two volumes. Boston: Little, Brown & Co., 1935. (Briefer one-volume edition published in 1948.)

Seigfried, Charlene Haddock. *Chaos and Context: A Study in William James.* Athens, Ohio: Ohio University Press, 1978.

————. *William James's Radical Reconstruction of Philosophy.* New York: SUNY Press, 1990.

The Dilemma of Determinism

A common opinion prevails that the juice has ages ago been pressed out of the free-will controversy, and that no new champion can do more than warm up stale arguments which everyone has heard. This is a radical mistake. I know of no subject less worn out, or in which inventive genius has a better chance of breaking open new ground— not, perhaps, of forcing a conclusion or of coercing assent, but of deepening our sense of what the issue between the two parties really is, of what the ideas of fate and of free will imply. At our very side almost, in the past few years, we have seen falling in rapid succession from the press works that present the alternative in entirely novel lights. Not to speak of the English disciples of Hegel, such as Green and Bradley; not to speak of Hinton and Hodgson, nor of Hazard here—we see in the writings of Renouvier, Fouillée, and Delbœuf how completely changed and refreshed is the form of all the old disputes. I cannot pretend to vie in originality with any of the masters I have named, and my ambition limits itself to just one little point. If I can make two of the necessarily implied corollaries of determinism clearer to you than they have been made before, I shall have made it possible for you to decide for or against that doctrine with a better understanding of what you are about. And if you prefer not to decide at all, but to remain doubters, you will at least see more plainly what the subject of your hesitation is. I thus disclaim openly on the threshold all pretension to prove to you that the freedom of the will is true. The most I hope is to induce some of you to follow my own example in assuming it true, and acting as if it were true. If it be true, it seems to me that this is involved in the strict logic of the case. Its truth ought not to be forced willy-nilly down our indifferent throats. It ought to be freely espoused by men who can equally well turn their backs upon it. In other words, our first act of freedom, if we are free, ought in all inward propriety to be to affirm that we are free. This should exclude, it seems to me, from the freewill side of the question all hope of a coercive demonstration—a demonstration which I, for one, am perfectly contented to go without.

With thus much understood at the outset, we can advance. But not without one more point understood as well. The arguments I am about to urge all proceed on two suppositions: first, when we make theories about the world and discuss them with one another, we do so in order to attain a conception of things which shall give us subjective satisfaction; and, second, if there be two conceptions, and the one seems to us, on the whole, more rational than the other, we are entitled to suppose that the more rational one is the truer of the two. I hope that you are all willing to make these suppositions with me; for I am afraid that if there be any of you here who are not, they will find little edification in the rest of what I have to say. I cannot stop to argue the point; but I myself believe that all the magnificent achievements of mathematical and physical science—our doctrines of evolution, of uniformity of law, and the rest—proceed from our indomitable desire to cast the world into a more rational shape in our minds than the shape into which it is thrown there by the crude order of our experience. The world has shown itself, to a great extent, plastic to this demand of ours for rationality. How much farther it will show itself plastic no one can say. Our only means of finding out is to try; and I, for one, feel as free to try conceptions of moral as of mechanical or of logical rationality. If a certain formula for expressing the nature of the world violates my moral demand, I shall feel as free to throw it overboard, or at least to doubt it, as if it disappointed my demand for uniformity of sequence, for example; the one demand being, so far as I can see, quite as subjective and emotional as the other is. The principle of causality, for example—what is it but a postulate, an empty name covering simply a demand that the sequence of events shall some day manifest a deeper kind of belonging of one thing with another than the mere arbitrary juxtaposition which now phenomenally appears? It is as much an altar to an unknown god as the one that Saint Paul found at Athens. All our scientific and philosophic ideals are altars to unknown gods. Uniformity is as much so as is free will. If this be admitted, we can debate on even terms. But if anyone pretends that while freedom and variety are, in the first instance, subjective demands, necessity and uniformity are something altogether different, I do not see how we can debate at all.

To begin, then, I must suppose you acquainted with all the usual arguments on the subject. I cannot stop to take up the old proofs from causation, from statistics, from the certainty with which we can foretell one another's conduct, from the fixity of character, and all the rest. But there are two *words* which usually encumber these classical arguments, and which we must immediately dispose of if we are to make any progress. One is the eulogistic word *freedom,* and the other is the opprobrious word *chance.* The word "chance" I wish to keep, but I wish to get rid of the word "freedom." Its eulogistic associations have so far overshadowed all the rest of its meaning that both parties claim the sole right to use it, and determinists today insist that they alone are freedom's champions. Old-fashioned determinism was what we may call *hard* determinism. It did not shrink from such words as fatality, bondage of the will, necessitation, and the like. Nowadays, we have a *soft* determinism which abhors harsh words, and, repudiating fatality, necessity, and even predetermination, says that its real name is freedom; for freedom is only necessity understood, and bondage to the highest is identical with true freedom. Even a writer as little used to making capital out of soft words as Mr. Hodgson hesitates not to call himself a "free-will determinist."

Now, all this is a quagmire of evasion under which the real issue of fact has been entirely smothered. Freedom in all these senses presents simply no problem at all. No matter what the soft determinist means by it—whether he means the acting without external constraint; whether he means the acting rightly, or whether he means the acquiescing in the law of the whole—who cannot answer him that sometimes we are free and sometimes we are not? But there *is* a problem, an issue of fact and not of words, an issue of the most momentous importance, which is often decided without discussion in one sentence—nay, in one clause of a sentence—by those very writers who spin out whole chapters in their efforts to show what "true" freedom is; and that is the question of determinism, about which we are to talk tonight.

Fortunately, no ambiguities hang about this word or about its opposite, indeterminism. Both designate an outward way in which things may happen, and their cold and mathematical sound has no sentimental associations that can bribe our partiality either way in advance. Now, evidence of an external kind to decide between determinism and indeterminism is, as I intimated a while back, strictly impossible to find. Let us look at the difference between them and see for ourselves. What does determinism profess?

It professes that those parts of the universe already laid down absolutely appoint and decree what the other parts shall be. The future has no ambiguous possibilities bidden in its womb; the part we call the

present is compatible with only one totality. Any other future complement than the one fixed from eternity is impossible. The whole is in
each and every part, and welds it with the rest into an absolute unity,
an iron block, in which there can be no equivocation or shadow of
turning.

> With earth's first clay they did the last man knead,
> And there of the last harvest sowed the seed.
> And the first morning of creation wrote
> What the last dawn of reckoning shall read.

Indeterminism, on the contrary, says that the parts have a certain
amount of loose play on one another, so that the laying down of one of
them does not necessarily determine what the others shall be. It admits
that possibilities may be in excess of actualities, and that things not yet
revealed to our knowledge may really in themselves be ambiguous. Of
two alternative futures which we conceive, both may now be really
possible; and the one becomes impossible only at the very moment
when the other excludes it by becoming real itself. Indeterminism thus
denies the world to be one unbending unit of fact. It says there is a
certain ultimate pluralism in it; and, so saying, it corroborates our ordinary unsophisticated view of things. To that view, actualities seem to
float in a wider sea of possibilities from out of which they are chosen;
and, *somewhere,* indeterminism says, such possibilities exist, and form
a part of truth.

Determinism, on the contrary, says they exist *nowhere,* and that necessity on the one hand and impossibility on the other are the sole
categories of the real. Possibilities that fail to get realized are, for determinism, pure illusions: they never were possibilities at all. There is
nothing inchoate, it says, about this universe of ours, all that was or is
or shall be actual in it having been from eternity virtually there. The
cloud of alternatives our minds escort this mass of actuality withal is a
cloud of sheer deceptions, to which "impossibilities" is the only name
that rightfully belongs.

The issue, it will be seen, is a perfectly sharp one, which no eulogistic terminology can smear over or wipe out. The truth *must* lie with one
side or the other, and its lying with one side makes the other false.

The question relates solely to the existence of possibilities, in the
strict sense of the term, as things that may, but need not, be. Both sides
admit that a volition, for instance, has occurred. The indeterminists say

another volition might have occurred in its place: the determinists swear that nothing could possibly have occurred in its place. Now, can science be called in to tell us which of these two point-blank contradicters of each other is right? Science professes to draw no conclusions but such as are based on matters of fact, things that have actually happened; but how can any amount of assurance that something actually happened give us the least grain of information as to whether another thing might or might not have happened in its place? Only facts can be proved by other facts. With things that are possibilities and not facts, facts have no concern. If we have no other evidence than the evidence of existing facts, the possibility-question must remain a mystery never to be cleared up.

And the truth is that facts practically have hardly anything to do with making us either determinists or indeterminists. Sure enough, we make a flourish of quoting facts this way or that; and if we are determinists, we talk about the infallibility with which we can predict one another's conduct; while if we are indeterminists, we lay great stress on the fact that it is just because we cannot foretell one another's conduct, either in war or statecraft or in any of the great and small intrigues and businesses of men, that life is so intensely anxious and hazardous a game. But who does not see the wretched insufficiency of this so-called objective testimony on both sides? What fills up the gaps in our minds is something not objective, not external. What divides us into *possibility* men and *anti-possibility* men is different faiths or postulates— postulates of rationality. To this man the world seems more rational with possibilities in it—to that man more rational with possibilities excluded; and talk as we will about having to yield to evidence, what makes us monists or pluralists, determinists or indeterminists, is at bottom always some sentiment like this.

The stronghold of the deterministic sentiment is the antipathy to the idea of chance. As soon as we begin to talk indeterminism to our friends, we find a number of them shaking their heads. This notion of alternative possibilities, they say, this admission that any one of several things may come to pass, is, after all, only a roundabout name for chance; and chance is something the notion of which no sane mind can for an instant tolerate in the world. What is it, they ask, but barefaced crazy unreason, the negation of intelligibility and law? And if the slightest particle of it exists anywhere, what is to prevent the whole fabric from falling together, the stars from going out, and chaos from recommencing her topsy-turvy reign?

Remarks of this sort about chance will put an end to discussion as quickly as anything one can find. I have already told you that "chance" was a word I wished to keep and use. Let us then examine exactly what it means, and see whether it ought to be such a terrible bugbear to us. I fancy that squeezing the thistle boldly will rob it of its sting.

The sting of the word "chance" seems to lie in the assumption that it means something positive, and that if anything happens by chance, it must needs be something of an intrinsically irrational and preposterous sort. Now, chance means nothing of the kind. It is a purely negative and relative[1] term, giving us no information about that of which it is predicated, except that it happens to be disconnected with something else—not controlled, secured, or necessitated by other things in advance of its own actual presence. As this point is the most subtile one of the whole lecture, and at the same time the point on which all the rest hinges, I beg you to pay particular attention to it. What I say is that it tells us nothing about what a thing may be in itself to call it "chance." It may be a bad thing, it may be a good thing. It may be lucidity, transparency, fitness incarnate, matching the whole system of other things, when it has once befallen, in an unimaginably perfect way. All you mean by calling it "chance" is that this is not guaranteed, that it may also fall out otherwise. For the system of other things has no positive hold on the chance-thing. Its origin is in a certain fashion negative: it escapes, and says, Hands off! coming, when it comes, as a free gift, or not at all.

This negativeness, however, and this opacity of the chance-thing when thus considered *ab extra,* or from the point of view of previous things or distant things, do not preclude its having any amount of positiveness and luminosity from within, and at its own place and moment. All that its chance-character asserts about it is that there is something in it really of its own, something that is not the unconditional property of the whole. If the whole wants this property, the whole must wait till it can get it, if it be a matter of chance. That the universe may actually be a sort of joint-stock society of this sort, in which the sharers have

---

[1] Speaking technically, it is a word with a positive denotation, but a connotation that is negative. Other things must be silent about *what* it is: it alone can decide that point at the moment in which it reveals itself.

both limited liabilities and limited powers, is of course a simple and conceivable notion.

Nevertheless, many persons talk as if the minutest dose of disconnectedness of one part with another, the smallest modicum of independence, the faintest tremor of ambiguity about the future, for example, would ruin everything, and turn this goodly universe into a sort of insane sand-heap or nulliverse—no universe at all. Since future human volitions are as a matter of fact the only ambiguous things we are tempted to believe in, let us stop for a moment to make ourselves sure whether their independent and accidental character need be fraught with such direful consequences to the universe as these.

What is meant by saying that my choice of which way to walk home after the lecture is ambiguous and matter of chance as far as the present moment is concerned? It means that both Divinity Avenue and Oxford Street are called; but that only one, and that one *either* one, shall be chosen. Now, I ask you seriously to suppose that this ambiguity of my choice is real; and then to make the impossible hypothesis that the choice is made twice over, and each time falls on a different street. In other words, imagine that I first walk through Divinity Avenue, and then imagine that the powers governing the universe annihilate ten minutes of time with all that it contained, and set me back at the door of this hall just as I was before the choice was made. Imagine then that, everything else being the same, I now make a different choice and traverse Oxford Street. You, as passive spectators, look on and see the two alternative universes—one of them with me walking through Divinity Avenue in it, the other with the same me walking through Oxford Street. Now, if you are determinists you believe one of these universes to have been from eternity impossible: you believe it to have been impossible because of the intrinsic irrationality or accidentality somewhere involved in it. But looking outwardly at these universes, can you say which is the impossible and accidental one, and which the rational and necessary one? I doubt if the most ironclad determinist among you could have the slightest glimmer of light on this point. In other words, either universe *after the fact* and once there would, to our means of observation and understanding, appear just as rational as the other. There would be absolutely no criterion by which we might judge one necessary and the other matter of chance. Suppose now we relieve the gods of their hypothetical task and assume my choice, once made, to be made forever. I go through Divinity Avenue for good and all. If, as good determinists, you now begin to affirm, what all good determinists punctually do affirm, that in the nature of things I *couldn't* have gone through Oxford Street—had I done so it would have been chance, irrationality, insanity, a horrid gap in nature—I simply call your attention to this, that your affirmation is what the Germans call a *Machtspruch,* a mere conception fulminated as a dogma and based on no insight into details. Before my choice, either street seemed as natural to you as to me. Had I happened to take Oxford Street, Divinity Avenue would have figured in your philosophy as the gap in nature; and you would have so proclaimed it with the best deterministic conscience in the world.

But what a hollow outcry, then, is this against a chance which, if it were presented to us, we could by no character whatever distinguish from a rational necessity! I have taken the most trivial of examples, but no possible example could lead to any different result. For what are the alternatives which, in point of fact, offer themselves to human volition? What are those futures that no seem matters of chance? Are they not one and all like the Divinity Avenue and Oxford Street of our example? Are they not all o them *kinds* of things already here and based in the existing frame of nature? Is anyone ever tempted to produce an *absolute* accident, something utterly irrelevant to the rest of the world? Do not an the motives that assail us, all the futures that offer themselves to our choice, spring equally from the soil of the past; and would not either one of them, whether realized through chance or through necessity, the moment it was realized, seem to us to fit that past, and in the completest and most continuous manner to interdigitate with the phenomena already there?[2]

The more one thinks of the matter, the more one wonders that so empty and gratuitous a hubbub as this outcry against chance should have found so great an echo in the hearts of men. It is a word which tells us absolutely nothing about what chances, or about the *modus*

---

[2] A favorite argument against free will is that if it be true, a man's murderer may as probably be his best friend as his worst enemy, a mother be as likely to strangle as to suckle her first-born, and all of us be as ready to jump from fourth-story windows as to go out of front doors, etc. Users of this argument should properly be excluded from debate till they learn what the real question is. "Free will" does not say that everything that is physically conceivable is also morally possible. It merely says that of alternatives that really *tempt* our will more than one is really possible. Of course, the alternatives that do thus tempt our will are vastly fewer than the physical possibilities we can coldly fancy. Persons really tempted often do murder their best friends, mothers do strangle their first-born, people do jump out of fourth-story windows, etc.

operandi of the chancing; and the use of it as a war cry shows only a temper of intellectual absolutism, a demand that the world shall be a solid block, subject to one control—which temper, which demand, the world may not be found to gratify at all. In every outwardly verifiable and practical respect, a world in which the alternatives that now actually distract *your* choice were decided by pure chance would be by *me* absolutely undistinguished from the world in which I now live. I am, therefore, entirely willing to call it, so far as your choices go, a world of chance for me. To *yourselves,* it is true, those very acts of choice, which to me are so blind, opaque, and external, are the opposites of this, for you are within them and effect them. To you they appear as decisions; and decisions, for him who makes them, are altogether peculiar psychic facts. Self-luminous and self-justifying at the living moment at which they occur, they appeal to no outside moment to put its stamp upon them or make them continuous with the rest of nature. Themselves it is rather who seem to make nature continuous; and in their strange and intense function of granting consent to one possibility and withholding it from another, to transform an equivocal and double future into an unalterable and simple past.

But with the psychology of the matter we have no concern this evening. The quarrel which determinism has with chance fortunately has nothing to do with this or that psychological detail. It is a quarrel altogether metaphysical. Determinism denies the ambiguity of future volitions, because it affirms that nothing future can be ambiguous. But we have said enough to meet the issue. Indeterminate future volitions *do* mean chance. Let us not fear to shout it from the house-tops if need be; for we now know that the idea of chance is, at bottom, exactly the same thing as the idea of gift—the one simply being a disparaging, and the other a eulogistic, name for anything on which we have no effective *claim.* And whether the world be the better or the worse for having either chances or gifts in it will depend altogether on *what* these uncertain and unclaimable things turn out to be.

And this at last brings us within sight of our subject. We have seen what determinism means: we have seen that indeterminism is rightly described as meaning chance; and we have seen that chance, the very name of which we are urged to shrink from as from a metaphysical pestilence, means only the negative fact that no part of the world, however big, can claim to control absolutely the destinies of the whole. But although, in discussing the word "chance" I may at moments have seemed to be arguing for its real existence, I have not meant to do so yet. We have not yet ascertained whether this be a world of chance or no; at most, we have agreed that it seems so. And I now repeat what I said at the outset, that, from any strict theoretical point of view, the question is insoluble. To deepen our theoretic sense of the *difference* between a world with chances in it and a deterministic world is the most I can hope to do; and this I may now at last begin upon, after all our tedious clearing of the way.

I wish first of all to show you just what the notion that this is a deterministic world implies. The implications I call your attention to are all bound up with the fact that it is a world in which we constantly have to make what I shall, with your permission, call judgments of regret. Hardly an hour passes in which we do not wish that something might be otherwise; and happy indeed are those of us whose hearts have never echoed the wish of Omar Khayam—

> That we might clasp, ere closed, the book of fate,
> And make the writer on a fairer leaf
> Inscribe our names, or quite obliterate.

> Ah! Love, could you and I with fate conspire
> To mend this sorry scheme of things entire,
> Would we not shatter it to bits, and then
> Remold it nearer to the heart's desire?

Now, it is undeniable that most of these regrets are foolish, and quite on a par in point of philosophic value with the criticisms on the universe of that friend of our infancy, the hero of the fable "The Atheist and the Acorn"—

> Fool! had that bough a pumpkin bore,
> Thy whimsies would have worked no more, etc.

Even from the point of view of our own ends, we should probably make a botch of remodeling the universe. How much more then from the point of view of ends we cannot see! Wise men therefore regret as little as they can. But still some regrets are pretty obstinate and hard to stifle—regrets for acts of wanton cruelty or treachery, for example, whether performed by others or by ourselves. Hardly any one can remain *entirely* optimistic after reading the confession of the murderer at Brockton the other day: how, to get rid of the wife whose continued existence bored him, he inveigled her into a desert spot, shot her four times, and then, as she lay on the ground and said to him, "You didn't do it on purpose, did you, dear?" replied, "No, I didn't do it on purpose," as he raised a rock and smashed her skull. Such an occurrence, with the mild sentence and self-satisfaction of the prisoner, is a field for a crop of regrets, which one need not take up in detail. We feel that, although a perfect mechanical fit to the rest of the universe, it is a bad moral fit, and that something else would really have been better in its place.

But for the deterministic philosophy the murder, the sentence, and the prisoner's optimism were all necessary from eternity; and nothing else for a moment had a ghost of a chance of being put in their place. To admit such a chance, the determinists tell us, would be to make a suicide of reason; so we must steel our hearts against the thought. And here our plot thickens, for we see the first of those difficult implications of determinism and monism, which it is my purpose to make you feel. If this Brockton murder was called for by the rest of the universe, if it had to come at its preappointed hour, and if nothing else would have been consistent with the sense of the whole, what are we to think of the universe? Are we stubbornly to stick to our judgment of regret, and say, though it *couldn't* be, yet it *would* have been a better universe with something different from this Brockton murder in it? That, of course, seems the natural and spontaneous thing for us to do; and yet it is nothing short of deliberately espousing a kind of pessimism. The judgment of regret calls the murder bad. Calling a thing bad means, if it means anything at all, that the thing ought not to be, that something else ought to be in its stead. Determinism, in denying that anything else can be in its stead, virtually defines the universe as a place in which what ought to be is impossible—in other words, as an organism whose constitution is afflicted with an incurable taint, an irremediable flaw. The pessimism of a Schopenhauer says no more than this—that the murder is a symptom; and that it is a vicious symptom because it belongs to a vicious whole, which can express its nature no otherwise than by bringing forth just such a symptom as that at this particular spot. Regret for the murder must transform itself, if we are determinists and wise, into a larger regret. It is absurd to regret the murder alone. Other things being what they are, *it* could not be different. What we should regret is that whole frame of things of which the murder is one member. I see no escape whatever from this pessimistic conclusion if, being determinists, our judgment of regret is to be allowed to stand at all.

The only deterministic escape from pessimism is everywhere to abandon the judgment of regret. That this can be done, history shows to be not impossible. The devil, *quoad existentiam,* may be good. That is, although he be a *principle* of evil, yet the universe, with such a principle in it, may practically be a better universe than it could have been without. On every hand, in a small way, we find that a certain amount of evil is a condition by which a higher form of good is brought. There is nothing to prevent anybody from generalizing this view, and trusting that if we could but see things in the largest of all ways, even such matters as this Brockton murder would appear to be paid for by the uses that follow in their train. An optimism *quand même,* a systematic and infatuated optimism like that ridiculed by Voltaire in his *Candide,* is one of the possible ideal ways in which a man may train himself to look on life. Bereft of dogmatic hardness and lit up with the expression of a tender and pathetic hope, such an optimism has been the grace of some of the most religious characters that ever lived.

> Throb thine with Nature's throbbing breast,
> And all is clear from east to west.

Even cruelty and treachery may be among the absolutely blessed fruits of time, and to quarrel with any of their details may be blasphemy. The only real blasphemy, in short, may be that pessimistic temper of the soul which lets it give way to such things as regrets, remorse, and grief.

Thus, our deterministic pessimism may become a deterministic optimism at the price of extinguishing our judgments of regret.

But does not this immediately bring us into a curious logical predicament? Our determinism leads us to call our judgments of regret wrong, because they are pessimistic in implying that what is impossible yet ought to be. But how then about the judgments of regret themselves? If they are wrong, other judgments, judgments of approval presumably, ought to be in their place. But as they are necessitated, nothing else *can* be in their place; and the universe is just what it was before—namely, a place in which what ought to be appears impossible. We have got one foot out of the pessimistic bog, but the other one sinks all the deeper. We have rescued our actions from the bonds of evil, but our judgments are now held fast. When murders and treacheries cease to be sins, regrets are theoretic absurdities and errors. The theoretic and the active life thus play a kind of see-saw with each other on the ground of evil. The rise of either sends the other down. Murder and treachery cannot be good without regret being bad: regret cannot be good without treachery and murder being bad. Both, however, are supposed to have been foredoomed; so something must be fatally unreasonable, absurd, and wrong in the world. It must be a place of which either sin or error forms a necessary part. From this dilemma there seems at first sight no escape. Are we then so soon to fall back into the pessimism from which we thought we had emerged? And is there no possible way by which we may, with good intellectual consciences, call the cruelties and treacheries, the reluctances and the regrets, *all* good together?

Certainly there is such a way, and you are probably most of you ready to formulate it yourselves. But, before doing so, remark how inevitably the question of determinism and indeterminism slides us into the question of optimism and pessimism, or, as our fathers called it, "the question of evil." The theological form of all these disputes is the simplest and the deepest, the form from which there is the least escape—not because, as some have sarcastically said, remorse and regret are clung to us with a morbid fondness by the theologians as spiritual luxuries, but because they are existing facts of the world, and as such must be taken into account in the deterministic interpretation of all that is fated to be. If they are fated to be error, does not the bat's wing of irrationality still cast its shadow over the world?

The refuge from the quandary lies, as I said, not far off. The necessary acts we erroneously regret may be good, and yet our error in so regretting them may be also good, on one simple condition; and that condition is this: The world must not be regarded as a machine whose final purpose is the making real of any outward good, but rather as a contrivance for deepening the theoretic consciousness of what goodness and evil in their intrinsic natures are. Not the doing either of good or evil is what nature cares for, but the knowing of them. Life is one long eating of the fruit of the tree of *knowledge*. I am in the habit, in thinking to myself, of calling this point of view the *gnostical* point of view. According to it, the world is neither an optimism nor a pessimism, but a *gnosticism*. But as this term may perhaps lead to some misunderstandings, I will use it as little as possible here, and speak rather of *subjectivism*, and the *subjectivistic* point of view.

Subjectivism has three great branches—we may call them scientificism, sentimentalism, and sensualism, respectively. They all agree essentially about the universe, in deeming that what happens there is subsidiary to what we think or feel about it. Crime justifies its criminality by awakening our intelligence of that criminality and eventually our remorses and regrets; and the error included in remorses and regrets, the error of supposing that the past could have been different, justifies itself by its use. Its use is to quicken our sense of *what* the irretrievably lost is. When we think of it as that which might have been ("the saddest words of tongue or pen"), the quality of its worth speaks to us with a wilder sweetness; and, conversely, the dissatisfaction wherewith we think of what seems to have driven it from its natural place gives us the severer pang. Admirable artifice of nature! we might be tempted to exclaim—deceiving us in order the better to enlighten us, and leaving nothing undone to accentuate to our consciousness the yawning distance of those opposite poles of good and evil between which creation swings.

We have thus clearly revealed to our view what may be called the dilemma of determinism, so far as determinism pretends to think things out at all. A merely mechanical determinism, it is true, rather rejoices in not thinking them out. It is very sure that the universe must satisfy its postulate of a physical continuity and coherence, but it smiles at anyone who comes forward with a postulate of moral coherence as well. I may suppose, however, that the number of purely mechanical or hard determinists among you this evening is small. The determinism to whose seductions you are most exposed is what I have called soft determinism—the determinism which allows considerations of good and bad to mingle with those of cause and effect in deciding what sort of a universe this may rationally be held to be. The dilemma of this determinism is one whose left horn is pessimism and whose right horn is subjectivism. In other words, if determinism is to escape pessimism, it must leave off looking at the goods and ills of life in a simple objective way, and regard them as materials, indifferent in themselves, for the production of consciousness, scientific and ethical, in us.

To escape pessimism is, as we all know, no easy task. Your own studies have sufficiently shown you the almost desperate difficulty of making the notion that there is a single principle of things, and that principle absolute perfection, rhyme together with our daily vision of the facts of life. If perfection be the principle, how comes there any imperfection here? If God be good, how came he to create—or, if he did not create, how comes he to permit—the devil? The evil facts must be explained as seeming: the devil must be whitewashed, the universe must be disinfected, if neither God's goodness nor His unity and power are to remain impugned. And of all the various ways of operating the disinfection, and making bad seem less bad, the way of subjectivism appears by far the best.[3]

For, after all, is there not something rather absurd in our ordinary notion of external things being good or bad in themselves? Can murders and treacheries, considered as mere outward happenings, or motions of matter, be bad without anyone to feel their badness? And could paradise properly be good in the absence of a sentient principle by which the goodness was perceived? Outward goods and evils seem practically indistinguishable except in so far as they result in getting moral judgments made about them. But then the moral judgments seem the main thing, and the outward facts mere perishing instruments for their production. This is subjectivism. Everyone must at some time have wondered at that strange paradox of our moral nature, that, though the pursuit of outward good is the breath of its nostrils, the attainment of outward good would seem to be its suffocation and death. Why does the painting of any paradise or utopia, in heaven or on earth, awaken such yawnings for nirvana and escape? The white-robed harp-playing heaven of our sabbath-schools, and the ladylike tea-table elysium represented in Mr. Spencer's *Data of Ethics,* as the final consummation of progress, are exactly on a par in this respect—lubberlands, pure and simple, one and all. We look upon them from this delicious mess of insanities and realities, strivings and deadnesses, hopes and fears, agonies and exultations, which forms our present state, and *tedium vitae* is the only sentiment they awaken in our breasts. To our crepuscular natures, born for the conflict, the Rembrandtesque moral *chiaroscuro,* the shifting struggle of the sunbeam in the gloom, such pictures of light upon light are vacuous and expressionless, and neither to be enjoyed

---

[3] To a reader who says he is satisfied with a pessimism, and has no objection to thinking the whole bad, I have no more to say: he makes fewer demands on the world than I, who, making them, wish to look a little further before I give up all hope of having them satisfied. If, however, all he means is that the badness of some parts does not prevent his acceptance of a universe whose *other* parts give him satisfaction, I welcome him as an ally. He has abandoned the notion of the *Whole,* which is the essence of deterministic monism, and views things as a pluralism, just as I do in this paper.

nor understood. If *this* be the whole fruit of the victory, we say; if the generations of mankind suffered and laid down their lives; if prophets confessed and martyrs sang in the fire, and all the sacred tears were shed for no other end than that a race of creatures of such unexampled insipidity should succeed, and protract *in saecula saeculorum* their contented and inoffensive lives—why, at such a rate, better lose than win the battle, or at all events better ring down the curtain before the last act of the play, so that a business that began so importantly may be saved from so singularly flat a winding-up.

All this is what I should instantly say, were I called on to plead for gnosticism; and its real friends, of whom you will presently perceive I am not one, would say without difficulty a great deal more. Regarded as a stable finality, every outward good becomes a mere weariness to the flesh. It must be menaced, be occasionally lost, for its goodness to be fully felt as such. Nay, more than occasionally lost. No one knows the worth of innocence till he knows it is gone forever, and that money cannot buy it back. Not the saint, but the sinner that repenteth, is he to whom the full length and breadth, and height and depth, of life's meaning is revealed. Not the absence of vice, but vice there, and virtue holding her by the throat, seems the ideal human state. And there seems no reason to suppose it not a permanent human state. There is a deep truth in what the school of Schopenhauer insists on—the illusoriness of the notion of moral progress. The more brutal forms of evil that go are replaced by others more subtle and more poisonous. Our moral horizon moves with us as we move, and never do we draw nearer to the far-off line where the black waves and the azure meet. The final purpose of our creation seems most plausibly to be the greatest possible enrichment of our ethical consciousness, through the intensest play of contrasts and the widest diversity of characters. This of course obliges some of us to be vessels of wrath, while it calls others to be vessels of honor. But the subjectivist point of view reduces all these outward distinctions to a common denominator. The wretch languishing in the felon's cell may be drinking draughts of the wine of truth that will never pass the lips of the so-called favorite of fortune. And the peculiar consciousness of each of them is an indispensable note in the great ethical concert which the centuries as they roll are grinding out of the living heart of man.

So much for subjectivism! If the dilemma of determinism be to choose between it and pessimism, I see little room for hesitation from the strictly theoretical point of view. Subjectivism seems the more rational scheme. And the world may possibly, for aught I know, be nothing else. When the healthy love of life is on one, and all its forms and its appetites seem so unutterably real; when the most brutal and the most spiritual things are lit by the same sun, and each is an integral part of the total richness—why, then it seems a grudging and sickly way of meeting so robust a universe to shrink from any of its facts and wish them not to be. Rather take the strictly dramatic point of view, and treat the whole thing as a great unending romance which the spirit of the universe, striving to realize its own content, is eternally thinking out and representing to itself.

No one, I hope, will accuse me, after I have said all this, of underrating the reasons in favor of subjectivism. And now that I proceed to say why those reasons, strong as they are, fail to convince my own mind, I trust the presumption may be that my objections are stronger still.

I frankly confess that they are of a practical order. If we practically take up subjectivism in a sincere and radical manner and follow its consequences, we meet with some that make us pause. Let a subjectivism begin in never so severe and intellectual a way, it is forced by the law of its nature to develop another side of itself and end with the corruptest curiosity. Once dismiss the notion that certain duties are good in themselves, and that we are here to do them, no matter how we feel about them; once consecrate the opposite notion that our performances and our violations of duty are for a common purpose, the attainment of subjective knowledge and feeling, and that the deepening of these is the chief end of our lives—and at what point on the downward slope are we to stop? In theology, subjectivism develops as its "left wing" antinomianism. In literature, its left wing is romanticism. And in practical life it is either a nerveless sentimentality or a sensualism without bounds.

Everywhere it fosters the fatalistic mood of mind. It makes those who are already too inert more passive still; it renders wholly reckless those whose energy is already in excess. All through history we find how subjectivism, as soon as it has a free career, exhausts itself in every sort of spiritual, moral, and practical license. Its optimism turns to an ethical indifference, which infallibly brings dissolution in its train. It is perfectly safe to say now that if the Hegelian gnosticism, which has begun to show itself here and in Great Britain, were to become a popular philosophy, as it once was in Germany, it would certainly develop its left wing here as there, and produce a reaction of disgust. Already I have heard a graduate of this very school express in the pulpit his willingness to sin like David, if only he might repent like David. You may tell me he was only sowing his wild, or rather his tame, oats; and perhaps he was. But the point is that in the subjectivistic or gnostical philosophy oat-sowing, wild or tame, becomes a systematic necessity and the chief function of life. After the pure and classic truths, the exciting and rancid ones must be experienced; and if the stupid virtues of the philistine herd do not then come in and save society from the influence of the children of light, a sort of inward putrefaction becomes its inevitable doom.

Look at the last runnings of the romantic school, as we see them in that strange contemporary Parisian literature, with which we of the less clever countries are so often driven to rinse out our minds after they have become clogged with the dullness and heaviness of our native pursuits. The romantic school began with the worship of subjective sensibility and the revolt against legality of which Rousseau was the first great prophet: and through various fluxes and refluxes, right wings and left wings, it stands today with two men of genius, M. Renan and M. Zola, as its principal exponents—one speaking with its masculine, and the other with what might be called its feminine, voice. I prefer not to think now of less noble members of the school, and the Renan I have in mind is of course the Renan of latest dates. As I have used the term gnostic, both he and Zola are gnostics of the most pronounced sort. Both are athirst for the facts of life, and both think the facts of human sensibility to be of all facts the most worthy of attention. Both agree, moreover, that sensibility seems to be there for no higher purpose—certainly not, as the Philistines say, for the sake of bringing mere outward rights to pass and frustrating outward wrongs. One dwells on the sensibilities for their energy, the other for their sweetness; one speaks with a voice of bronze, the other with that of an Aeolian harp; one ruggedly ignores the distinction of good and evil, the other plays the coquette between the craven unmanliness of his *Philosophic Dialogues* and the butterfly optimism of his *Souvenirs de Jeunesse*. But under the pages of both there sounds incessantly the hoarse bass of *vanitas vanitatum, omnia vanitas,* which the reader may hear, whenever he will, between the lines. No writer of this French romantic school has a word of rescue from the hour of satiety with the things of life—the hour in which we say, "I take no pleasure in them"—or from the hour of terror at the world's vast meaningless grinding, if perchance such hours should come. For terror and satiety are facts of sensibility like any others, and at their own hour they reign in their own right. The heart of the romantic utterances, whether poetical, critical, or historical, is this inward remedilessness, what Carlyle calls this far-off whimpering of wail and woe. And from this romantic state of mind there is absolutely no possible *theoretic* escape. Whether, like Renan, we look upon life in a more refined way, as a romance of the spirit; or whether, like the friends of M. Zola, we pique ourselves on our "scientific" and "analytic" character, and prefer to be cynical, and call the world a *roman expérimental* on an infinite scale—in either case the world appears to us potentially as what the same Carlyle once called it, a vast, gloomy, solitary Golgotha and mill of death.

The only escape is by the practical way. And since I have mentioned the nowadays much-reviled name of Carlyle, let me mention it once more, and say it is the way of his teaching. No matter for Carlyle's life, no matter for a great deal of his writing. What was the most important thing he said to us? He said: "Hang your sensibilities! Stop your snivelling complaints, and your equally snivelling raptures! Leave off your general emotional tomfoolery, and get to WORK like men!" But this means a complete rupture with the subjectivist philosophy of things. It says conduct, and not sensibility, is the ultimate fact for our recognition. With the vision of certain works to be done, of certain outward changes to be wrought or resisted, it says our intellectual horizon terminates. No matter how we succeed in doing these outward duties, whether gladly and spontaneously, or heavily and unwillingly, do them we somehow must; for the leaving of them undone is perdition. No matter how we feel; if we are only faithful in the outward act and refuse to do wrong, the world will in so far be safe, and we quit of our debt toward it. Take, then, the yoke upon our shoulders; bend our neck beneath the heavy legality of its weight; regard something else than our feeling as our limit, our master, and our law; be willing to live and die in its service—and, at a stroke, we have passed from the subjective into the objective philosophy of things, much as one awakens from some feverish dream, full of bad lights and noises, to find one's self bathed in the sacred coolness and quiet of the air of the night.

But what is the essence of this philosophy of objective conduct so old-fashioned and finite, but so chaste and sane and strong, when compared with its romantic rival? It is the recognition of limits, foreign and opaque to our understanding. It is the willingness, after bringing about some external good, to feel at peace; for our responsibility ends with the performance of that duty, and the burden of the rest we may lay on higher powers.[4]

> Look to thyself, O Universe,
> Thou are better and not worse—

we may say in that philosophy, the moment we have done our stroke of conduct, however small. For in the view of that philosophy the universe belongs to a plurality of semi-independent forces, each one of which may help or hinder, and be helped or hindered by, the operations of the rest.

But this brings us right back, after such a long detour, to the question of indeterminism and to the conclusion of all I came here to say to-night. For the only consistent way of representing a pluralism and a world whose parts may affect one another through their conduct being either good or bad is the indeterministic way. What interest, zest, or excitement can there be in achieving the right way, unless we are enabled to feel that the wrong way is also a possible and a natural way—nay, more, a menacing and an imminent way? And what sense can there be in condemning ourselves for taking the wrong way, unless we need have done nothing of the sort, unless the right way was open to us as well? I cannot understand the willingness to act, no matter how we feel, without the belief that acts are really good and bad. I cannot understand the belief that an act is bad, without regret at its happening. I cannot understand regret without the admission of real, genuine possibilities in the world. Only *then* is it other than a mockery to feel, after we have failed to do our best, that an irreparable opportunity is gone from the universe, the loss of which it must forever after mourn.

If you insist that this is all superstition, that possibility is in the eye of science and reason impossibility, and that if I act badly 'tis that the universe was foredoomed to suffer this defect, you fall right back into the dilemma, the labyrinth, of pessimism and subjectivism, from out of whose toils we have just found our way.

Now, we are of course free to fall back, if we please. For my own part, though, whatever difficulties may beset the philosophy of objec-

---

[4] The burden, for example, of seeing to it that the *end* of all our righteousness be some positive universal gain.

tive right and wrong, and the indeterminism it seems to imply, determinism, with its alternative of pessimism or romanticism, contains
difficulties that are greater still. But you will remember that I expressly
repudiated a while ago the pretension to offer any arguments which
could be coercive in a so-called scientific fashion in this matter. And I
consequently find myself, at the end of this long talk, obliged to state
my conclusions in an altogether personal way. This personal method
of appeal seems to be among the very conditions of the problem; and
the most anyone can do is to confess as candidly as he can the grounds
for the faith that is in him, and leave his example to work on others as
it may.

Let me, then, without circumlocution say just this. The world is enig-
matical enough in all conscience, whatever theory we may take up
toward it. The indeterminism I defend, the free-will theory of popular
sense based on the judgment of regret, represents that world as vulnera-
ble, and liable to be injured by certain of its parts if they act wrong.
And it represents their acting wrong as a matter of possibility or accident, neither inevitable nor yet to be infallibly warded off. In all this, it
is a theory devoid either of transparency or of stability. It gives us a
pluralistic, restless universe, in which no single point of view can ever
take in the whole scene; and to a mind possessed of the love of unity
at any cost, it will, no doubt, remain forever unacceptable. A friend
with such a mind once told me that the thought of my universe made
him sick, like the sight of the horrible motion of a mass of maggots in
their carrion bed.

But while I freely admit that the pluralism and the restlessness are
repugnant and irrational in a certain way, I find that every alternative
to them is irrational in a deeper way. The indeterminism with its maggots, if you please to speak so about it, offends only the native absolutism of my intellect—an absolutism which, after all, perhaps, deserves
to be snubbed and kept in check. But the determinism with its necessary carrion, to continue the figure of speech, and with no possible
maggots to eat the latter up, violates my sense of moral reality through
and through. When, for example, I imagine such carrion as the Brockton murder, I cannot conceive it as an act by which the universe, as a
whole, logically and necessarily expresses its nature without shrinking
from complicity with such a whole. And I deliberately refuse to keep
on terms of loyalty with the universe by saying blankly that the murder,
since it does flow from the nature of the whole, is not carrion. There

are *some* instinctive reactions which I, for one, will not tamper with. The only remaining alternative, the attitude of gnostical romanticism, wrenches my personal instincts in quite as violent a way. It falsifies the simple objectivity of their deliverance. It makes the goose flesh the murder excites in me a sufficient reason for the perpetration of the crime. It transforms life from a tragic reality into an insincere melodramatic exhibition, as foul or as tawdry as anyone's diseased curiosity pleases to carry it out. And with its consecration of the *roman naturalists* state of mind, and its enthronement of the baser crew of Parisian *littérateurs* among the eternally indispensable organs by which the infinite spirit of things attains to that subjective illumination which is the task of its life, it leaves me in presence of a sort of subjective carrion considerably more noisome than the objective carrion I called it in to take away.

No! better a thousand times, than such systematic corruption of our moral sanity, the plainest pessimism, so that it be straightforward; but better far than that the world of chance. Make as great an uproar about chance as you please, I know that chance means pluralism and nothing more. If some of the members of the pluralism are bad, the philosophy of pluralism, whatever broad views it may deny me, permits me, at least, to turn to the other members with a clean breast of affection and an unsophisticated moral sense. And if I still wish to think of the world as a totality, it lets me feel that a world with a *chance* in it of being altogether good, even if the chance never come to pass, is better than a world with no such chance at all. That "chance" whose very notion I am exhorted and conjured to banish from my view of the future as the suicide of reason concerning it, that "chance" is—what? Just this—the chance that in moral respects the future may be other and better than the past has been. This is the only chance we have any motive for supposing to exist. Shame, rather, on its repudiation and its denial! For its presence is the vital air which lets the world live, the salt which keeps it sweet.

And here I might legitimately stop, having expressed all I care to see admitted by others tonight. But I know that if I do stop here, misapprehensions will remain in the minds of some of you, and keep all I have said from having its effect; so I judge it best to add a few more words.

In the first place, in spite of all my explanations, the word "chance" will still be giving trouble. Though you may yourselves be adverse to the deterministic doctrine, you wish a pleasanter word than "chance" to name the opposite doctrine by; and you very likely consider my preference for such a word a perverse sort of a partiality on my part. It certainly *is* a bad word to make converts with; and you wish I had not thrust it so butt-foremost at you—you wish to use a milder term.

Well, I admit there may be just a dash of perversity in its choice. The spectacle of the mere word-grabbing game played by the soft determinists has perhaps driven me too violently the other way; and, rather than be found wrangling with them for the good words, I am willing to take the first bad one which comes along, provided it be unequivocal. The question is of things, not of eulogistic names for them; and the best word is the one that enables men to know the quickest whether they disagree or not about the things. But the word "chance," with its singular negativity, is just the word for this purpose. Whoever uses it instead of "freedom," squarely and resolutely gives up all pretense to control the things he says are free. For *him,* he confesses that they are no better than mere chance would be. It is a word of *impotence,* and is therefore the only sincere word we can use, if, in granting freedom to certain things, we grant it honestly, and really risk the game. "Who chooses me must give and forfeit all he hath." Any other word permits of quibbling, and lets us, after the fashion of the soft determinists, make a pretense of restoring the caged bird to liberty with one hand, while with the other we anxiously tie a string to it leg to make sure it does not get beyond our sight.

But now you will bring up your final doubt. Does not the admission of such an unguaranteed chance or freedom preclude utterly the notion of a Providence governing the world? Does it not leave the fate of the universe at the mercy of the chance-possibilities, and so far insecure? Does it not, in short, deny the craving of our nature for an ultimate peace behind all tempests, for a blue zenith above all clouds?

To this my answer must be very brief. The belief in free will is not in the least incompatible with the belief in Providence, provided you do not restrict the Providence to fulminating nothing but *fatal* decrees. If you allow him to provide possibilities as well as actualities to the universe, and to carry on his own thinking in those two categories just as we do ours, chances may be there, uncontrolled even by him, and the course of the universe be really ambiguous; and yet the end of all things may be just what he intended it to be from all eternity.

An analogy will make the meaning of this clear. Suppose two men before a chessboard—the one a novice, the other an expert player of the game. The expert intends to beat. But he cannot foresee exactly what any one actual move of his adversary may be. He knows, however, all the *possible* moves of the latter; and he knows in advance how to meet each of them by a move of his own which leads in the direction of victory. And the victory infallibly arrives, after no matter how devious a course, in the one predestined form of check-mate to the novice's king.

Let now the novice stand for us finite free agents, and the expert for the infinite mind in which the universe lies. Suppose the latter to be thinking out his universe before he actually creates it. Suppose him to say, I will lead things to a certain end, but I will not *now*[5] decide on all the steps thereto. At various points, ambiguous possibilities shall be left open, *either* of which, at a given instant, may become actual. But whichever branch of these bifurcations becomes real, I know what I shall do at the *next* bifurcation to keep things from drifting away from the final result I intend.[6]

The creator's plan of the universe would thus be left blank as to many of its actual details, but all possibilities would be marked down. The realization of some of these would be left absolutely to chance;

---

[5]This of course leaves the creative mind subject to the law of time. And to anyone who insists on the timelessness of that mind I have no reply to make. A mind to whom all time is simultaneously present must see all things under the form of actuality, or under some form to us unknown. If he thinks certain moments as ambiguous in their content while future, he must simultaneously know how the ambiguity will have been decided when they are past. So that none of his mental judgments can possibly be called hypothetical, and his world is one from which chance is excluded. Is not, however, the timeless mind rather a gratuitous fiction? And is not the notion of eternity being given at a stroke to omniscience only just another way of whacking upon us the block-universe, and of denying that possibilities exist?—just the point to be proved. To say that time is an illusory appearance is only a roundabout manner of saying there is no real plurality, and that the frame of things is an absolute unit. Admit plurality, and time may be its form.

[6] And this of course means "miraculous" interposition, but not necessarily of the gross sort our fathers took such delight in representing, and which has so lost its magic for us. Emerson quotes some Eastern sage as saying that if evil were really done under the sun, the sky would incontinently shrivel to a snakeskin and cast it out in spasms. But, says Emerson, the spasms of Nature are years and centuries; and it will tax man's patience to wait so long. We may think of the reserved possibilities God keeps in his own hand, under as invisible and molecular and slowly self-summating a form as we please. We may think of them as counteracting human agencies which he inspires *ad hoc*. In short, signs and wonders and convulsions of the earth and sky are not the only neutralizers of obstruction to a god's plans of which it is possible to think.

that is, would only be determined when the moments of realization came. Other possibilities would be *contingently* determined; that is, their decision would have to wait till it was seen how the matters of absolute chance fell out. But the rest of the plan, including its final upshot, would be rigorously determined once for all. So the creator himself would not need to know all the details of actuality until they came; and at any time his own view of the world would be a view partly of facts and partly of possibilities, exactly as ours is now. Of one thing, however, he might be certain; and that is that his world was safe, and that no matter how much of it might zigzag he could surely bring it home at last.

Now, it is entirely immaterial, in this scheme, whether the creator leave the absolute chance-possibilities to be decided by himself, each when its proper moment arrives, or whether, on the contrary, he alienate this power from himself, and leave the decision out and out to finite creatures such as we men are. The great point is that the possibilities are really *here*. Whether it be we who solve them, or he working through us, at those soul-trying moments when fate's scales seem to quiver, and good snatches the victory from evil or shrinks nerveless from the fight, is of small account, so long as we admit that the issue is decided nowhere else than *here* and *now*. *That* is what gives the palpitating reality to our moral life and makes it tingle, as Mr. Mallock says, with so strange and elaborate an excitement. This reality, this excitement, are what the determinisms, hard and soft alike, suppress by their denial that *anything* is decided here and now, and their dogma that all things were foredoomed and settled long ago. If it be so, may you and I then have been foredoomed to the error of continuing to believe in liberty.[7] It is fortunate for the winding up of controversy that in every discussion with determinism this *argumentum ad hominem* can be its adversary's last word.

---

7 As long as languages contain a future perfect tense, determinists, following the bent of laziness or passion, the lines of least resistance, can reply in that tense, saying, "It will have been fated," to the still small voice which urges an opposite course; and thus excuse themselves from effort in a quite unanswerable way.

The Stream of Consciousness

The order of our study must be analytic.—We are now prepared to begin the introspective study of the adult consciousness itself. Most books adopt the so-called synthetic method. Starting with "simple ideas of sensation," and regarding these as so many atoms, they proceed to build up the higher states of mind out of their "association," "integration," or "fusion,"as houses are built by the agglutination of bricks. This has the didactic advantages which the synthetic method usually has. But it commits one beforehand to the very questionable theory that our higher states of consciousness are compounds of units; and instead of starting with what the reader directly knows, namely his total concrete states of mind, it starts with a set of supposed "simple ideas" with which he has no immediate acquaintance at all, and concerning whose alleged interactions he is much at the mercy of any plausible phrase. On every ground, then, the method of advancing from the simple to the compound exposes us to illusion. All pedants and abstractionists will naturally hate to abandon it. But a student who loves the fullness of human nature will prefer to follow the "analytic" method, and to begin with the most concrete facts, those with which he has a daily acquaintance in his own inner life. The analytic method will discover in due time the elementary parts, if such exist, without danger of precipitate assumption. The reader will bear in mind that our own chapters on sensation have dealt mainly with the physiological conditions thereof. They were put first as a mere matter of convenience, because incoming currents come first. *Psychologically* they might better have come last. Pure sensations were described . . . as processes which in adult life are well-nigh unknown, and nothing was said which could for a moment lead the reader to suppose that they were the *elements of composition* of the higher states of mind.

The Fundamental Fact.—The first and foremost concrete fact which every one will affirm to belong to his inner experience is the fact that *consciousness of some sort goes on. "States of mind" succeed each other in him.* If we could say in English "it thinks," as we say "it rains" or "it blows," we should be stating the fact most simply and with the minimum of assumption. As we cannot, we must simply say that *thought goes on.*

Four Characters in Consciousness.—How does it go on? We notice immediately four important characters in the process, of which it shall be the duty of the present chapter to treat in a general way:

1. Every "state" tends to be part of a personal consciousness.
2. Within each personal consciousness states are always changing.
3. Each personal consciousness is sensibly continuous.
4. It is interested in some parts of its object to the exclusion of others, and welcomes or *rejects—chooses* from among them, in a word—all the while.

In considering these four points successively, we shall have to plunge *in medias res* as regards our nomenclature and use psychological terms which can only be adequately defined in later chapters of the book. But everyone knows what the terms mean in a rough way; and it is only in a rough way that we are now to take them. This chapter is like a painter's first charcoal sketch upon his canvas, in which no niceties appear.

When I say *every "state"* or *"thought" is part of a personal consciousness,* "personal consciousness" is one of the terms in question. Its meaning we know so long as no one asks us to define it, but to give an accurate account of it is the most difficult of philosophic tasks. This task we must confront in the next chapter; here a preliminary word will suffice.

In this room—this lecture-room, say—there are a multitude of thoughts, yours and mine, some of which cohere mutually, and some not. They are as little each-for-itself and reciprocally independent as they are all-belonging-together. They are neither; no one of them is separate, but each belongs with certain others and with none beside. My thought belongs with *my* other thoughts, and your thoughts with *your* other thoughts. Whether anywhere in the room there be a *mere* thought, which is nobody's thought, we have no means of ascertaining, for we have no experience of its like. The only states of consciousness that we naturally deal with are found in personal consciousness, minds, selves, concrete particular I's and you's.

Each of these minds keeps its own thoughts to itself. There is no giving or bartering between them. No thought even comes into direct *sight* of a thought in another personal consciousness than its own. Absolute insulation, irreducible pluralism, is the law. It seems as if the elementary psychic fact were not *thought* or *this thought* or *that thought,* but *my thought,* every thought being *owned.* Neither contemporaneity, nor proximity in space, nor similarity of quality and content are able to fuse thoughts together which are sundered by this barrier of belonging to different personal minds. The breaches between such thoughts are the most absolute breaches in nature. Everyone will recognize this to be true, so long as the existence of *something* corresponding to the term 'personal mind' is all that is insisted on, without any particular view of its nature being implied. On these terms the personal self rather than the thought might be treated as the immediate datum in psychology. The universal conscious fact is not "feelings and thoughts exist," but "I think" and "I feel." No psychology, at any rate, can question the *existence* of personal selves. Thoughts connected as we feel them to be connected are *what we mean* by personal selves. The worst a psychology can do is so to interpret the nature of these selves as to rob them of their *worth.*

Consciousness is in constant change.—I do not mean by this to say that no one state of mind has any duration—even if true, that would be hard to establish. What I wish to lay stress on is this, that *no state once gone can recur and be identical with what it was before.* Now we are seeing, now hearing; now reasoning, now willing; now recollecting, now expecting; now loving, now hating; and in a hundred other ways we know our minds to be alternately engaged. But all these are complex states, it may be said, produced by combination of simpler ones;—do not the simpler ones follow a different law? Are not the *sensations* which we get from the same object, for example, always the same? Does not the same piano key, struck with the same force, make us hear in the same way? Does not the same grass give us the same feeling of green, the same sky the same feeling of blue, and do we not get the same olfactory sensation no matter how many times we put our nose to the same flask of cologne? It seems a piece of metaphysical sophistry to suggest that we do not; and yet a close attention to the matter shows that *there is no proof that an incoming current ever gives us just the same bodily sensation twice.*

What is got twice is the same OBJECT. We hear the same *note* over and over again; we see the same *quality* of green, or smell the same objective perfume, or experience the same *species* of pain. The reali-

ties, concrete and abstract, physical and ideal, whose permanent existence we believe in, seem to be constantly coming up again before our
thought, and lead us, in our carelessness, to suppose that our "ideas"
of them are the same ideas. When we come, some time later, to the
chapter on Perception, we shall see how inveterate is our habit of simply using our sensible impressions as stepping-stones to pass over to
the recognition of the realities whose presence they reveal. The grass
out of the window now looks to me of the same green in the sun as in
the shade, and yet a painter would have to paint one part of it dark
brown, another part bright yellow, to give its real sensational effect.
We take no heed, as a rule, of the different way in which the same
things look and sound and smell at different distances and under different circumstances. The sameness of the *things* is what we are concerned to ascertain; and any sensations that assure us of that will
probably be considered in a rough way to be the same with each other.
This is what makes offhand testimony about the subjective identity of
different sensations well-nigh worthless as a proof of the fact. The
entire history of what is called Sensation is a commentary on our inability to tell whether two sensible qualities received apart are exactly
alike. What appeals to our attention far more than the absolute quality
of an impression is its *ratio to* whatever other impressions we may
have at the same time. When everything is dark, a somewhat less dark
sensation makes us see an object white. Helmholtz calculates that the
white marble painted in a picture representing an architectural view by
moonlight is, when seen by daylight, from ten to twenty thousand times
brighter than the real moonlit marble would be.

Such a difference as this could never have been *sensibly* learned; it
had to be inferred from a series of indirect considerations. These make
us believe that our sensibility is altering all the time, so that the same
object cannot easily give us the same sensation over again. We feel
things differently accordingly as we are sleepy or awake, hungry or
full, fresh or tired; differently at night and in the morning, differently
in summer and in winter; and above all, differently in childhood, man-
hood, and old age. And yet we never doubt that our feelings reveal the
same world, with the same sensible qualities and the same sensible
things occupying it. The difference of the sensibility is shown best by
the difference of our emotion about the things from one age to another,
or when we are in different organic moods. What was bright and excit-

ing becomes weary, flat, and unprofitable. The bird's song is tedious, the breeze is mournful, the sky is sad.

To these indirect presumptions that our sensations, following the mutations of our capacity for feeling, are always undergoing an essential change, must be added another presumption, based on what must happen in the brain. Every sensation corresponds to some cerebral action. For an identical sensation to recur it would have to occur the second time *in an unmodified brain.* But as this, strictly speaking, is a physiological impossibility, so is an unmodified feeling an impossibility; for to every brain-modification, however small, we suppose that there must correspond a change of equal amount in the consciousness which the brain subserves.

But if the assumption of "simple sensations" recurring in immutable shape is so easily shown to be baseless, how much more baseless is the assumption of immutability in the larger masses of our thought!

For there it is obvious and palpable that our state of mind is never precisely the same. Every thought we have of a given fact is, strictly speaking, unique, and only bears a resemblance of kind with our other thoughts of the same fact. When the identical fact recurs, we *must* think of it in a fresh manner, see it under a somewhat different angle, apprehend it in different relations from those in which it last appeared. And the thought by which we cognize it is the thought of it-in-those-relations, a thought suffused with the consciousness of all that dim context. Often we are ourselves struck at the strange differences in our successive views of the same thing. We wonder how we ever could have opined as we did last month about a certain matter. We have outgrown the possibility of that state of mind, we know not how. From one year to another we see things in new lights. What was unreal has grown real, and what was exciting is insipid. The friends we used to care the world for are shrunken to shadows; the women once so divine, the stars, the woods, and the waters, how now so dull and common!— the young girls that brought an aura of infinity, at present hardly distinguishable existences; the pictures so empty; and as for the books, what *was* there to find so mysteriously significant in Goethe, or in John Mill so full of weight? Instead of all this, more zestful than ever is the work, the work; the fuller and deeper the import of common duties and of common goods.

I am sure that this concrete and total manner of regarding the mind's changes is the only true manner, difficult as it may be to carry it out in detail. If anything seems obscure about it, it will grow clearer as we advance. Meanwhile, if it be true, it is certainly also true that no two "ideas" are ever exactly the same, which is the proposition we started to prove. The proposition is more important theoretically than it at first sight seems. For it makes it already impossible for us to follow obediently in the footprints of either the Lockian or the Herbartian school, schools which have had almost unlimited influence in Germany among ourselves. No doubt it is often *convenient* to formulate the mental facts in an atomistic sort of way, and to treat the higher states of consciousness as if they were all built out of unchanging simple ideas which "pass and turn again." It is convenient often to treat curves as if they were composed of small straight lines, and electricity and nerve-force as if they were fluids. But in the one case as in the other we must never forget that we are talking symbolically, and that there is nothing in nature to answer to our words. *A permanently existing "Idea" which makes its appearance before the footlights of consciousness at periodical intervals is as mythological an entity as the Jack of Spades.*

Within each personal consciousness, thought is sensibly continuous.—I can only define "continuous" as that which is without break, crack, or division. The only breaches that can well be conceived to occur within the limits of a single mind would either be *interruptions, time-gaps* during which the consciousness went out; or they would be breaks in the content of the thought, so abrupt that what followed had no connection whatever with what went before. The proposition that consciousness feel continuous, means two things:

a. That even where there is a time-gap the consciousness after it feels as if it belonged together with the consciousness before it, as another part of the same self;

b. That the changes from one moment to another in the quality of the consciousness are never absolutely abrupt.

The case of the time-gaps, as the simplest, shall be taken first.

a. When Paul and Peter wake up in the same bed, and recognize that they have been asleep, each one of them mentally reaches back and makes connection with but *one* of the two streams of thought which were broken by the sleeping hours. As the current of an electrode buried in the ground unerringly finds its way to its own similarly buried mate, across no matter how much intervening earth; so Peter's present instantly finds out Peter's past, and never by mistake knits itself on to that of Paul. Paul's thought in turn is as little liable to go astray.

The past thought of Peter is appropriated by the present Peter alone. He may have a *knowledge,* and a correct one too, of what Paul's last drowsy states of mind were as he sank into sleep, but it is an entirely different sort of knowledge from that which he has of his own last states. He *remembers his* own states, whilst he only *conceives* Paul's. Remembrance is like direct feeling; its object is suffused with a warmth and intimacy to which no object of mere conception ever attains. This quality of warmth and intimacy and immediacy is what Peter's *present* thought also possesses for itself. So sure as this present is to me, is mine, it says, so sure is anything else that comes with the same warmth and intimacy and immediacy, me and mine. What the qualities called warmth and intimacy may in themselves be will have to be matter for future consideration. But whatever past states appear with those qualities must be admitted to receive the greeting of the present mental state, to be owned by it, and accepted as belonging together with it in a common self. This community of self is what the time-gap cannot break in twain, and is why a present thought, although not ignorant of the time-gap, can still regard itself as continuous with certain chosen portions of the past.

Consciousness, then, does not appear to itself chopped up in bits. Such words as "chain" or "train" do not describe it fitly as it presents itself in the first instance. It is nothing jointed; it flows. A "river" or a "stream" are the metaphors by which it is most naturally described. *In talking of it hereafter, let us call it the stream of thought, of consciousness, or of subjective life.*

b. But now there appears, even within the limits of the same self, and between thoughts all of which alike have this same sense of belonging together, a kind of jointing and separateness among the parts, of which this statement seems to take no account. I refer to the breaks that are produced by sudden *contrasts in the quality* of the successive segments of the stream of thought. If the words "chain" and "train" had no natural fitness in them, how came such words to be used at all? Does not a loud explosion rend the consciousness upon which it abruptly breaks, in twain? No; for even into our awareness of the thunder the awareness of the previous silence creeps and continues; for what we hear when the thunder crashes is not thunder *pure,* but thunder-breaking-upon-silence-and-contrasting-with-it. Our feeling of the same objective thunder, coming in this way, is quite different from what it would be were the thunder a continuation of previous thunder.

The thunder itself we believe to abolish and exclude the silence; but the *feeling* of the thunder is also a feeling of the silence as just gone; and it would be difficult to find in the actual concrete consciousness of man a feeling so limited to the present as not to have an inkling of anything that went before.

"Substantive" and "Transitive" States of mind.—When we take a general view of the wonderful stream of our consciousness, what strikes us first is the different pace of its parts. Like a bird's life, it seems to be an alternation of flights and perchings. The rhythm of language expresses this, where every thought is expressed in a sentence, and every sentence closed by a period. The resting-places are usually occupied by sensorial imaginations of some sort, whose peculiarity is that they can be held before the mind for an indefinite time, and contemplated without changing; the places of flight are filled with thoughts of relations, static or dynamic, that for the most part obtain between the matters contemplated in the periods of comparative rest.

Let us call the resting-places the "substantive parts," and the places of flight the "transitive parts," of the stream of thought. It then appears that our thinking tends at all times towards some other substantive part than the one from which it has just been dislodged. And we may say that the main use of the transitive parts is to lead us from one substantive conclusion to another.

Now it is very difficult, introspectively, to see the transitive parts for what they really are. If they are but flights to a conclusion, stopping them to look at them before the conclusion is reached is really annihilating them. Whilst if we wait till the conclusion *be* reached, it so exceeds them in vigor and stability that it quite eclipses and swallows them up in its glare. Let anyone try to cut a thought across in the middle and get a look at its section, and he will see how difficult the introspective observation of the transitive tracts is. The rush of the thought is so headlong that it almost always brings us up at the conclusion before we can arrest it. Or if our purpose is nimble enough and we do arrest it, it ceases forthwith to be itself. As a snow-flake crystal caught in the warm hand is no longer a crystal but a drop, so, instead of catching the feeling of relation moving to its term, we find we have caught some substantive thing, usually the last word we were pronouncing, statically taken, and with its function, tendency, and particular meaning in the sentence quite evaporated. The attempt at introspective analysis in these cases is in fact like seizing a spinning top to catch its motion, or trying to turn up the gas quickly enough to see how the darkness looks. And the challenge to *produce* these transitive states of consciousness, which is sure to be thrown by doubting psychologists at anyone who contends for their existence, is as unfair as Zeno's treatment of the advocates of motion, when, asking them to point out in what place an arrow *is* when it moves, he argues the falsity of their thesis from their inability to make to so preposterous a question an immediate reply.

The results of this introspective difficulty are baleful. If to hold fast and observe the transitive parts of thought's stream be so hard, then the great blunder to which all schools are liable must be the failure to register them, and the undue emphasizing of the more substantive parts of the stream. Now the blunder has historically worked in two ways. One set of thinkers have been led by it to *Sensationalism.* Unable to lay their hands on any substantive feelings corresponding to the innumerable relations and forms of connection between the sensible things of the world, finding no *named* mental states mirroring such relations, they have for the most part denied that any such states exist; and many of them, like Hume, have gone on to deny the reality of most relations *out* of the mind as well as in it. Simple substantive "ideas," sensations and their copies, juxtaposed like dominoes in a game, but really separate, everything else verbal illusion,—such is the upshot of this view. The *Intellectualists,* on the other hand, unable to give up the reality of relations *extra mentem,* but equally unable to point to any distinct substantive feelings in which they were known, have made the same admission that such feelings do not exist. But they have drawn an opposite conclusion. The relations must be known, they say, in something that is no feeling, no mental "state,"continuous and consubstantial with the subjective tissue out of which sensations and other substantive conditions of consciousness are made. They must be known by something that lies on an entirely different plane, by an *actus purus* of Thought, Intellect, or Reason, all written with capitals and considered to mean something unutterably superior to any passing perishing fact of sensibility whatever.

But from our point of view both Intellectualists and Sensationalists are wrong. If there be such things as feelings at all, *then so surely as relations between objects exist in rerum natura, so surely, and more surely, do feelings exist to which these relations are known.* There is not a conjunction or a preposition, and hardly an adverbial phrase, syntactic form, or inflection of voice, in human speech, that does not express some shading or other of relation which we at some moment actually feel to exist between the larger objects of our thought. If we speak objectively it is the real relations that appear revealed; if we speak subjectively, it is the stream of consciousness that matches each of them by an inward coloring of its own. In either case the relations are numberless, and no existing language is capable of doing justice to all their shades.

We ought to say a feeling of *and*, a feeling of *if*, a feeling of *but*, and a feeling of *by*, quite as readily as we say a feeling of *blue* or a feeling of *cold*. Yet we do not: so inveterate has our habit become of recognizing the existence of the substantive parts alone, that language almost refuses to lend itself to any other use. Consider once again the analogy of the brain. We believe the brain to be an organ whose internal equilibrium is always in a state of change—he change affecting every part. The pulses of change are doubtless more violent in one place than in another, their rhythm more rapid at this time than at that. As in a kaleidoscope revolving at a uniform rate, although the figures are always rearranging themselves, there are instants during which the transformation seems minute and interstitial and almost absent, followed by others when it shoots with magical rapidity, relatively stable forms thus alternating with forms we should not distinguish if seen again; so in the brain the perpetual rearrangement must result in some forms of tension lingering relatively long, whilst others simply come and pass. But if consciousness corresponds to the fact of rearrangement itself, why, if the rearrangement stop not, should the consciousness ever cease? And if a lingering rearrangement brings with it one kind of consciousness, why should not a swift rearrangement bring another kind of consciousness as peculiar as the rearrangement itself?

The object before the mind always has a "fringe."—there are other unnamed modifications of consciousness just as important as the transitive states, and just as cognitive as they. Examples will show what I mean.

Suppose three successive persons say to us: "Wait!" "Hark!" "Look!" Our consciousness is thrown into three quite different attitudes of expectancy, although no definite object is before it in any one of the three cases. Probably no one will deny here the existence of a real conscious affection, a sense of the direction from which an impression is about to come, although no positive impression is yet there.

Meanwhile we have no names for the psychoses in question but the names hark, look, and wait.

Suppose we try to recall a forgotten name. The state of our consciousness is peculiar. There is a gap therein; but no mere gap. It is a gap that is intensely active. A sort of wraith of the name is in it, beckoning us in a given direction, making us at moments tingle with the sense of our closeness, and then letting us sink back without the longed-for term. If wrong names are proposed to us, this singularly definite gap acts immediately so as to negate them. They do not fit into its mold. And the gap of one word does not feel like the gap of another, all empty of content as both might seem necessarily to be when described as gaps. When I vainly try to recall the name of Spalding, my consciousness is far removed from what it is when I vainly try to recall the name of Bowles. There are innumerable consciousnesses of *want*, no one of which taken in itself has a name, but all different from each other. Such feeling of want is *tota coelo* other than a want of feeling: it is an intense feeling. The rhythm of a lost word may be there without a sound to clothe it; or the evanescent sense of something which is the initial vowel or consonant may mock us fitfully without growing more distinct. Everyone must know the tantalizing effect of the blank rhythm of some forgotten verse, restlessly dancing in one's mind, striving to be filled out with words.

What is that first instantaneous glimpse of someone's meaning which we have, when in vulgar phrase we say we "twig" it? Surely an altogether specific affection of our mind. And has the reader never asked himself what kind of a mental fact is his *intention of saying a thing* before he has said it? It is an entirely definite intention, distinct from all other intentions, an absolutely distinct state of consciousness, therefore; and yet how much of it consists of definite sensorial images, either of words or of things? Hardly anything! Linger, and the words and things come into the mind; the anticipatory intention, the divination is there no more. But as the words that replace it arrive, it welcomes them successively and calls them right if they agree with it, it rejects them and calls them wrong if they do not. The intention *to-say-so-and-so* is the only name it can receive. One may admit that a good third of our psychic life consists in these rapid premonitory perspective views of schemes of thought not yet articulate. How comes it about that a man reading something aloud for the first time is able immediately to emphasize all his words aright, unless from the very first he have a sense of at least the form of the sentence yet to come, which sense is fused with his consciousness of the present word, and modifies its emphasis in his mind so as to make him give it the proper accent as he utters it? Emphasis of this kind almost altogether depends on grammatical construction. If we read "no more," we expect presently a "than"; if we read "however," it is a "yet," a "still," or a "nevertheless," that we expect. And this foreboding of the coming verbal and grammatical scheme is so practically accurate that a reader incapable of understanding four ideas of the book he is reading aloud can nevertheless read it with the most delicately modulated expression of intelligence.

It is, the reader will see, the reinstatement of the vague and inarticulate to its proper place in our mental life which I am so anxious to press on the attention. Mr. Galton and Prof. Huxley have, as we shall see in the chapter on Imagination, made one step in advance in exploding the ridiculous theory of Hume and Berkeley that we can have no images but of perfectly definite things. Another is made if we overthrow the equally ridiculous notion that, whilst simple objective qualities are revealed to our knowledge in "states of consciousness," relations are not. But these reforms are not half sweeping and radical enough. What must be admitted is that the definite images of traditional psychology form but the very smallest part of our minds as they actually live. The traditional psychology talks like one who should say a river consists of nothing but pailsful, spoonsful, quartpotsful, barrelsful, and other molded forms of water. Even were the pails and the pots all actually standing in the stream, still between them the free water would continue to flow. It is just this free water of consciousness that psychologists resolutely overlook. Every definite image in the mind is steeped and dyed in the free water that flows round it. With it goes the sense of its relations, near and remote, the dying echo of whence it came to us, the dawning sense of whither it is to lead. The significance, the value, of the image is all in this halo or penumbra that surrounds and escorts it,—-or rather that is fused into one with it and has become bone of its bone and flesh of its flesh; leaving it, it is true, an image of the same *thing* it was before, but making it an image of that thing newly taken and freshly understood.

Let us call the consciousness of this halo of relations around the image by the name of "psychic overtone" or "fringe."

Cerebral Conditions of the "Fringe."—Nothing is easier than to symbolize these facts in terms of brain-action. Just as the echo of the *whence,* the sense of the starting point of our thought, is probably due to the dying excitement of processes but a moment since vividly aroused; so the sense of the whither, the foretaste of the terminus, must be due to the waxing excitement of tracts or processes whose Psychical correlative will a moment hence be the vividly present feature of our thought. Represented by a curve, the neurosis underlying consciousness must at any moment be like this:

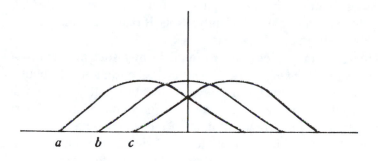

Figure 1

Let the horizontal in Fig. 1 be the line of time, and let the three curves beginning at *a, b,* and *c* respectively stand for the neural processes correlated with the thoughts of those three letters. Each process occupies a certain time during which its intensity waxes, culminates, and wanes. The process for *a* has not yet died out, the process for *c* has already begun, when that for *b* is culminating. At the time-instant represented by the vertical line all three processes are *present,* in the intensities shown by the curve. Those before *c*'s apex *were* more intense a moment ago; those after it *will* be more intense a moment hence. If I recite *a, b, c,* then, at the moment of uttering *b,* neither *a* nor *c* is out of my consciousness altogether, but both, after their respective fashions, "mix their dim lights" with the stronger *b,* because their processes are both awake in some degree.

It is just like "overtones" in music: they are not separately heard by the ear; they blend with the fundamental note, and suffuse it, and alter it; and even so do the waxing and waning brain-processes at every moment blend with and suffuse and alter the psychic effect of the processes which are at their culminating point.

The "Topic" of the Thought.—If we then consider the *cognitive function* of different states of mind, we may feel assured that the difference between those that are mere "acquaintance" and those that are "knowledges-*about*" is reducible almost entirely to the absence or presence of psychic fringes or overtones. Knowledge *about* a thing is knowledge of its relations. Acquaintance with it is limitation to the bare impression which it makes. Of most of its relations we are only aware in the penumbral nascent way of a "fringe" of unarticulated affinities about it. And, before passing to the next topic in order, I must say a little of this sense of affinity, as itself one of the most interesting features of the subjective stream.

Thought may be equally rational in any sort of terms.—*In all our voluntary thinking there is some* TOPIC *or* SUBJECT *about which* all the members of the thought revolve. Relation to this topic or interest is constantly felt in the fringe, and particularly the relation of harmony and discord, of furtherance or hindrance of the topic. Any thought the quality of whose fringe lets us feel "all right," may be considered a thought that furthers the topic. Provided we only feel its object to have a place in the scheme of relations in which the topic also lies, that is sufficient to make of it a relevant and appropriate portion of our train of ideas.

Now we may think about our topic mainly in words, or we may think about it mainly in visual or other images, but this need make no difference as regards the furtherance of our knowledge of the topic. If we only feel in the terms, whatever they be, a fringe of affinity with each other and with the topic, and if we are conscious of approaching a conclusion, we feel that our thought is rational and right. The words in every language have contracted by long association fringes of mutual repugnance or affinity with each other and with the conclusion, which run exactly parallel with like fringes in the visual, tactile, and other ideas. The most important element of these fringes is, I repeat, the mere feeling of harmony or discord, of a right or wrong direction in the thought.

If we know English and French and begin a sentence in French, all the later words that come are French; we hardly ever drop into English. And this affinity of the French words for each other is not something merely operating mechanically as a brain-law, it is something we feel at the time. Our understanding of a French sentence never falls to so low an ebb that we are not aware that the words linguistically belong together. Our attention can hardly so wander that if an English word be suddenly introduced we shall not start at the change. Such a vague sense as this of the words belonging together is the very minimum of fringe that can accompany them, if "thought" at all. Usually the vague perception that all the words we hear belong to the same language and to the same special vocabulary in that language, and that the grammatical sequence is familiar, is practically equivalent to an admission that what we hear is sense. But if an unusual foreign word be introduced, if the grammar trip, or if a term from an incongruous vocabulary suddenly appear, such as "rat-trap" or "plumber's bill" in a philosophical discourse, the sentence detonates as it were, we receive a shock from the incongruity, and the drowsy assent is gone. The feeling of rationality in these cases seems rather a negative than a positive thing, being the mere absence of shock, or sense of discord, between the terms of thought.

Conversely, if words do belong to the same vocabulary, and if the grammatical structure is correct, sentences with absolutely no meaning may be uttered in good faith and pass unchallenged. Discourses at prayer-meetings, reshuffling the same collection of cant phrases, and the whole genus of penny-a-line-isms and newspaper reporter's flourishes give illustrations of this. "The birds filled the tree-tops with their morning song, making the air moist, cool, and pleasant," is a sentence I remember reading once in a report of some athletic exercises in Jerome Park. It was probably written unconsciously by the hurried reporter, and read uncritically by many readers.

We see, then, that it makes little or no difference in what sort of mind-stuff, in what quality of imagery, our thinking goes on. The only images *intrinsically* important are the halting-places, the substantive conclusions, provisional or final, of the thought. Throughout all the rest of the stream, the feelings of relation are everything, and the terms related almost naught. These feelings of relation, these psychic overtones, halos, suffusions, or fringes about the terms, may be the same in very different systems of imagery. A diagram may help to accentuate this indifference of the mental means where the end is the same. Let A be some experience from which a number of thinkers start. Let Z be the practical conclusion rationally inferable from it. One gets to this conclusion by one line, another by another; one follows a course of English, another of German, verbal imagery. With one, visual images predominate; with another tactile. Some trains are tinged with emotions, others not; some are very abridged, synthetic and rapid; others, hesitating and broken into many steps. But when the penultimate terms of all the trains, however differing *inter se,* finally shoot into the same conclusion, we say, and rightly say, that all the thinkers have had sub-stantially the same thought. It would probably astound each of them beyond measure to be let into his neighbor's mind and to find how different the scenery there was from that in his own.

The last peculiarity to which attention is to be drawn in this first rough description of thought's stream is that—

Consciousness is always interested more in one part of its object than in another, and welcomes and rejects, or chooses, all the while it thinks.—The phenomena of selective attention and of deliberative will are of course patent examples of this choosing activity. But few of us are aware how incessantly it is at work in operations not ordinarily called by these names. Accentuation and Emphasis are present in every perception we have. We find it quite impossible to disperse our atten-tion impartially over a number of impressions. A monotonous succes-sion of sonorous strokes is broken up into rhythms, now of one sort, now of another, by the different accent which we place on different strokes. The simplest of these rhythms is the double one, tick-tóck, tick-tóck, tick-tóck. Dots dispersed on a surface are perceived in rows and groups. Lines separate into diverse figures. The ubiquity of the distinctions, *this* and *that, here* and *there, now* and *then,* in our minds

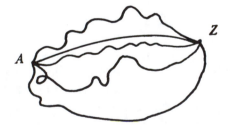

Figure 2

is the result of our laying the same selective emphasis on parts of place and time.

But we do far more than emphasize things, and unite some, and keep others apart. We actually *ignore* most of the things before us. Let me briefly show how this goes.

To begin at the bottom, what are our very senses themselves . . . but organs of selection? Out of the infinite chaos of movements, of which physics teaches us that the outer world consists, each sense-organ picks out those which fall within certain limits of velocity. To these it responds, but ignores the rest as completely as if they did not exist. Out of what is in itself an undistinguishable, swarming *continuum,* devoid of distinction or emphasis, our senses make for us, by attending to this motion and ignoring that, a world full of contrasts, of sharp accents, of abrupt changes, of picturesque light and shade.

If the sensations we receive from a given organ have their causes thus picked out for us by the conformation of the organ's termination, Attention, on the other hand, out of all the sensations yielded, picks out certain ones as worthy of notice and suppresses all the rest. We notice only those sensations which are signs to us of *things* which happen practically or aesthetically to interest us, to which we therefore give substantive names, and which we exalt to this exclusive status of independence and dignity. But in itself, apart from my interest, a particular dust-wreath on a windy day is just as much of an individual *thing,* and just as much or as little deserves an individual name, as my own body does.

And then, among the sensations we get from each separate thing, what happens? The mind selects again. It chooses certain of the sensations to represent the thing most *truly,* and considers the rest as its appearances, modified by the conditions of the moment. Thus my table-top is named *square,* after but one of an infinite number of retinal sensations which it yields, the rest of them being sensations of two acute and two obtuse angles; but I call the latter *perspective* views, and the four right angles the *true* form of the table, and erect the attribute squareness into the table's essence, for aesthetic reasons of my own. In like manner, the real form of the circle is deemed to be the sensation it gives when the line of vision is perpendicular to its center—all its other sensations are *signs* of this sensation. The real sound of the cannon is the sensation it makes when the ear is close by. The real color of the brick is the sensation it gives when the eye looks squarely at it from a near point, out of the sunshine and yet not in the gloom; under other circumstances it gives us other color-sensations which are but signs of this—we then see it looks pinker or bluer than it really is. The reader knows no object which he does not represent to himself by preference as in some typical attitude, of some normal size, at some characteristic distance, of some standard tint, etc., etc. But all these essential characteristics, which together form for us the genuine objectivity of the thing and are contrasted with what we call the subjective sensations it may yield us at a given moment, are mere sensations like the latter. The mind chooses to suit itself, and decides what particular sensation shall be held more real and valid than all the rest.

Next, in a world of objects thus individualized by our mind's selective industry, what is called our "experience" is almost entirely determined by our habits of attention. A thing may be present to a man a hundred times, but if he persistently fails to notice it, it cannot be said to enter into his experience. We are all seeing flies, moths, and beetles by the thousand, but to whom, save an entomologist, do they say anything distinct? On the other hand, a thing met only once in a lifetime may leave an indelible experience in the memory. Let four men make a tour in Europe. One will bring home only picturesque impressions—costumes and colors, parks and views and works of architecture, pictures and statues. To another all this will be non-existent; and distances and prices, populations and drainage-arrangements, door- and window-fastenings, and other useful statistics will take their place. A third will give a rich account of the theaters, restaurants, and public halls, and naught besides; whilst the fourth will perhaps have been so wrapped in his own subjective broodings as to be able to tell little more than a few names of places through which he passed. Each has selected, out of the same mass of presented objects, those which suited his private interest and has made him experience thereby.

If now, leaving the empirical combination of objects, we ask how the mind proceeds *rationally* to connect them, we find selection again to be omnipotent. In a future chapter we shall see that all Reasoning depends on the ability of the mind to break up the totality of the phenomenon reasoned about, into parts, and to pick out from among these the particular one which, in the given emergency, may lead to the proper conclusion. The man of genius is he who will always stick in his bill at the right point, and bring it out with the right element—

"reason" if the emergency be theoretical, "means" if it be practical—transfixed upon it.

If now we pass to the aesthetic department, our law is still more obvious. The artist notoriously selects his items, rejecting all tones, colors, shapes, which do not harmonize with each other and with the main purpose of his work. That unity, harmony, "convergence of characters," as M. Taine calls it, which gives to works of art their superiority over works of nature, is wholly due to *elimination.* Any natural subject will do, if the artist has wit enough to pounce upon some one feature of it as characteristic, and suppress all merely accidental items which do not harmonize with this.

Ascending still higher, we reach the plane of Ethics, where choice reigns notoriously supreme. An act has no ethical quality whatever unless it be chosen out of several, all equally possible. To sustain the arguments for the good course and keep them ever before us, to stifle our longing for more flowery ways, to keep the foot unflinchingly on the arduous path, these are characteristic ethical energies. But more than these; for these but deal with the means of compassing interests already felt by the man to be supreme. The ethical energy *par excellence* has to go farther and choose which *interest* out of several, equally coercive, shall become supreme. The issue here is of the utmost pregnancy, for it decides a man's entire career. When he debates, Shall I commit this crime? choose that profession? accept that office, or marry this fortune?—his choice really lies between one of several equally possible future Characters. What he shall *become* is fixed by the conduct of this moment. Schopenhauer, who enforces his determinism by the argument that with a given fixed character only one reaction is possible under given circumstances, forgets that, in these critical ethical moments, what consciously *seems* to be in question is the complexion of the character itself. The problem with the man is less what act he shall now resolve to do than what being he shall now choose to become.

Taking human experience in a general way, the choosings of different men are to a great extent the same. The race as a whole largely agrees as to what it shall notice and name; and among the noticed parts we select in much the same way for accentuation and preference, or subordination and dislike. There is, however, one entirely extraordinary case in which no two men ever are known to choose alike. One great splitting of the whole universe into two halves is made by each of us; and for each of us almost all of the interest attaches to one of the halves; but we all draw the line of division between them in a different place. When I say that we all call the two halves by the same names, and that those names are "*me*" and "*not-me*" respectively, it will at once be seen what I mean. The altogether unique kind of interest which each human mind feels in those parts of creation which it can call *me* or *mine* may be a moral riddle, but it is a fundamental psychological fact. No mind can take the same interest in his neighbor's me as in his own. The neighbor's *me* falls together with all the rest of things in one foreign mass against which his own *me* stands out in startling relief. Even the trodden worm, as Lotze somewhere says, contrasts his own suffering self with the whole remaining universe, though he have no clear conception either of himself or of what the universe may be. He is for me a mere part of the world; for him it is I who am the mere part. Each of us dichotomizes the Kosmos in a different place.

The Problem of Novelty

The impotence to explain being which we have attributed to all philosophers is, it will be recollected, a conceptual impotence. It is when thinking abstractly of the whole of being at once, as it confronts us ready-made, that we feel our powerlessness so acutely. Possibly, if we followed the empiricist method, considering the parts rather than the whole, and imagining ourselves inside of them perceptually, the subject might defy us less provokingly. We are thus brought back to the problem with which Chapter VII left off. When perceptible amounts of new phenomenal being come to birth, must we hold them to be in all points predetermined and necessary outgrowths of the being already there, or shall we rather admit the possibility that originality may thus instill itself into reality?

If we take concrete perceptual experience, the question can be answered in only one way. "The same returns not, save to bring the different." Time keeps budding into new moments, every one of which presents a content which in its individuality never was before and will never be again. Of no concrete bit of experience was an exact duplicate ever framed. "My youth," writes Delbœuf, "has it not taken flight, carrying away with it love, illusion, poetry, and freedom from care, and leaving with me instead science, austere always, often sad and morose, which sometimes I would willingly forget, which repeats to me hour by hour its grave lessons, or chills me by its threats? Will time, which untiringly piles deaths on births, and births on deaths, ever remake an Aristotle or an Archimedes, a Newton or a Descartes? Can our earth ever cover itself again with those gigantic ferns, those immense equisetaceans, in the midst of which the same antediluvian monsters will crawl and wallow as they did of yore? . . . No, what has been will not, cannot, be again. Time moves on with an unfaltering tread, and never strikes twice an identical hour. The instants of which the existence of the world is composed are all dissimilar—and whatever may be done, something remains that can never be reversed." [1]

---

[1] J. Delbœuf: *Revue philosophique,* Vol. IX, p. 138 (1880). On the infinite variety of reality, compare also W. T. Marvin: *An Introduction to Systematic Philosophy.* New York, 1903, pp. 22–30.

The everlasting coming of concrete novelty into being is so obvious that the rationalizing intellect, bent ever on explaining what is by what was, and having no logical principle but identity to explain by, treats the perceptual flux as a phenomenal illusion, resulting from the unceasing re-combination in new forms of mixture, of unalterable elements, coeval with the world. These elements are supposed to be the only real beings; and, for the intellect once grasped by the vision of them, there can be nothing genuinely new under the sun. The world's history, according to molecular science, signifies only the "redistribution" of the unchanged atoms of the primal fire mist, parting and meeting so as to appear to us spectators in the infinitely diversified configurations which we name as processes and things.[2]

So far as physical nature goes few of us experience any temptation to postulate real novelty. The notion of eternal elements and their mixture serves us in so many ways, that we adopt unhesitatingly the theory that primordial being is inalterable in its attributes as well as in its quantity, and that the laws by which we describe its habits are uniform in the strictest mathematical sense. These are the absolute conceptual foundations, we think, spread beneath the surface of perceptual variety. It is when we come to human lives, that our point of view changes. It is hard to imagine that "really" our own subjective experiences are only molecular arrangements, even though the molecules be conceived as beings of a psychic kind. A material fact may indeed be different from

---

[2] The Atomistic philosophy, which has proved so potent a scientific instrument of explanation, was first formulated by Democritus, who died in 370 B.C. His life overlapped that of Aristotle, who took what on the whole may be called a biological view of the world, and for whom "forms" were as real as elements. The conflict of the two modes of explanation has lasted to our day, for some chemists still defend the Aristotelian tradition which the authority of Descartes had interrupted for so long, and deny our right to say that "water" is not a simple entity, or that oxygen and hydrogen atoms persist in it unchanged. Compare W. Ostwald: *Die Ueberwindung des wissenschaftlichen Materialismus* (1895), p. 12: "The atomic view assumes that when in iron-oxide, for example, all the sensible properties both of iron and oxygen have vanished, iron and oxygen are nevertheless there but now manifest other properties. We are so used to this assumption that it is hard for us to feel its oddity, nay, even its absurdity. When, however, we reflect that all we know of a given kind of matter is its properties, we realize that the assertion that the matter is still there, but without any of those properties, is not far removed from nonsense." Compare the same author's *Principles of Inorganic Chemistry,* English translation, 2d ed. (1904), p. 149 ff. Also P. Duhem: "La Notion de Mixte," in the *Revue de philosophie,* Vol. 1, p. 452ff. (1901). The whole notion of the eternal fixity of elements is melting away before the new discoveries about radiant matter. See for radical statements G. LeBon: *L'Évolution de la matière.*

what we feel it to be, but what sense is there in saying that a feeling, which has no other nature than to be felt, is not as it *is* felt? Psychologically considered, our experiences resist conceptual reduction, and our fields of consciousness, taken simply as such, remain just what they appear, even though facts of a molecular order should prove to be the signals of the appearance. Biography is the concrete form in which all that is is immediately given; the perceptual flux is the authentic stuff of each of our biographies, and yields a perfect effervescence of novelty all the time. New men and women, books, accidents, events, inventions, enterprises, burst unceasingly upon the world. It is vain to resolve these into ancient elements, or to say that they belong to ancient kinds, so long as no one of them in its full individuality ever was here before or will ever come again. Men of science and philosophy, the moment they forget their theoretic abstractions, live in their biographies as much as anyone else, and believe as naively that fact even now is making, and that they themselves, by doing "original work," help to determine what the future shall become.

I have already compared the live or perceptual order with the conceptual order from this point of view. Conception knows no way of explaining save by deducing the identical from the identical, so if the world is to be conceptually rationalized no novelty can really come. This is one of the traits in that general bankruptcy of conceptualism, . . . conceptualism can *name* change and growth, but can translate them into no terms of its own, and is forced to contradict the indestructible sense of life within us by denying that reality grows. . . .

FRIEDRICH NIETZSCHE

Friedrich Wilhelm Nietzsche was born in the village of Röcken, Germany, of devout Christian parents, on October 15, 1844. His father, a Lutheran minister, died when he was five and the family moved to Naumberg. After spending six years at Schulpforta, the most famous boarding school in Germany for classical training, he entered Bonn University but left, after a year, to follow one of his professors, Wilhelm Ritschl, to the University of Leipzig. His four years at Leipzig as a flourishing classical scholar are noteworthy for his appreciative discovery of Schopenhauer's philosophy and his meeting with and eventual inclusion in the circle of Richard Wagner. In 1869, when the chair of classical philology became vacant at the Swiss University of Basel, his mentor Wilhelm Ritschl glowingly recommended him for it. He was hired, changed his citizenship to Swiss, and became a university professor before turning 25. During these years his friendship with Wagner blossomed and then in 1878 abruptly ended, largely because of what he took to be Wagner's growing religiosity, as well as his anti-Semitism and Germanic nationalism, three attitudes with which Nietzsche had no sympathy whatsoever. Nietzsche spent ten years at Basel, but his health declined rapidly after 1871 and he was often on sick leave. In 1879 he resigned his position and took a small pension. For the next ten years, until his collapse into madness in 1889, he wrote and published at a feverish rate, moving constantly from place to place in Switzerland, southern France, and northern Italy, almost always alone, and always plagued with migraines, deteriorating eyesight, and insomnia.

Nietzsche completed his first book, *The Birth of Tragedy*, in 1871 and published it in 1872. It received little notice and what it did receive was unfavorable. During the 17 years from 1871 to the end of 1888, he wrote all of his philosophical work, most of which, when published, often privately or at his own expense, met with the same reception. In spite of this brief span of creativity, there are marked signs of change and development which serve to divide his work into four periods of almost equal length. His lengthy early essays, from his first book through his four *Untimely Meditations*, represent a philosopher who, though clearly creative and original, was still largely under the influence of Schopenhauer and Wagner. With the publication of *Human, All-Too-Human* in the years 1878–1880, followed by *Dawn* and *The Gay Science* in 1881 and 1882, his distance from these early influences becomes obvious. His style became aphoristic, psychologically focused, and bitingly critical of the entire European philosophical tradition from the Greeks to his own time, especially of the assumptions of a transcendent and invariant structure of reality, human nature, and morality. All of the major themes of his later work are foreshadowed: his unrelenting attack upon Christianity and the morality of equality and utility, his celebration of life and the body, his fascination with the notion of eternal recurrence as a device for enshrining the living present, his reading of human experience and motivation in terms of a will to power, his psychological and genealogical reconstruction of human culture, and, most important, his evocation of the continuously self-creating and self-overcoming individual who achieves a separating distance from the herd. Two famous phrases from *The Gay Science*—"God is dead" and "Live dangerously!"—serve as metaphors for most of these themes. The third period of Nietzsche's writing stretches from 1882 through 1885 and is consumed with *Thus Spoke Zarathustra*, the four-part imagistic narrative in which the highest individual becomes the Overman, and the themes of creativity, self-overcoming, eternal recurrence, and the joyful embracing of life are developed and intertwined. For Nietzsche this was his culminating work. Yet it is his last period, comprising the last three and three quarters years of his sanity, which represents the most sustained presentation of his philosophical position, particularly in *Beyond Good and Evil* (1886), *On the Genealogy of Morals* (1887), and *Twilight of the Idols* (1888). It is worth noting that, during these latter years, unknown to Nietzsche, there was developing on the other side of the Atlantic a strikingly similar revolutionary swing away from the traditional metaphysics of transcendence, substance, and necessary invariance and toward an emphasis upon becoming, change, and the concrete, lived experience of everyday life.

In early January 1889 Nietzsche collapsed in the streets of Turin, Italy, while embracing a horse that was being flogged by a coachman. Within hours he had lapsed into a somewhat catatonic state from which he never recovered. He died on August 25, 1900. His sister Elisabeth cared for him after the death of his mother, established the Nietzsche Archives, promoted his philosophy as representing her own anti-Semitic, proto-Nazi predilections, and published in editions from 1901 to 1906 a collection of scraps from Nietzsche's unpublished jottings under the title *The Will to Power*. The misrepresentation of Nietzsche's views thus promulgated, so transparently at odds with his publications and letters, was widely accepted for decades. Fortunately, those who have actually taken the time to read Nietzsche have prevailed.

MAJOR PHILOSOPHICAL WORKS BY NIETZSCHE

1872 *Die Geburt der Tragödie aus dem Geiste der Musik* (The Birth of Tragedy from the Spirit of Music)

1873–1876 *Unzeitgemässe Betrachtungen* (Untimely Meditations.)
I. *David Strauss, der Bekenner und der Schriftsteller* (David Strauss, the Confessor and the Writer.)
II. *Von Nutzen und Nachteil der Historie für das Leben* (On the Usefulness and Disadvantage for Life of History)
III. *Schopenhauer als Erzieher* (Schopenhauer as Educator)
IV. *Richard Wagner in Bayreuth*

1878–1880 *Menschliches, Allzumenschliches. Ein Buch für freie Geister* (Human, All-Too-Human: A Book for Free Spirits)

1881 *Morgenröte. Gedanken über die moralischen Vorurteile* (Dawn. Thoughts on the Prejudices of Morality)

1882 *Die fröhliche Wissenschaft* (The Gay Science). In four books. Book V was published in 1887.

1883–1884 *Also sprach Zarathustra. Ein Buch für Alle und Keinen* (Thus Spoke Zarathustra. A Book for Everyone and No one). In three parts. A fourth part, published privately in 1885, was issued publicly in 1892.

1886 *Jenseits von Gut und Böse. Vorspiel einer Philosophie der Zukunft* (Beyond Good and Evil. Prelude to a Philosophy of the Future)

1887 *Zur Genealogie der Moral. Eine Streitschrift* (On the Genealogy of Morals. A Polemic)

1889 *Götzen-Dämmerung, oder Wie man mit dem Hammer philosophiert* (Twilight of the Idols, or How to Philosophize with a Hammer). Written in 1888.

1895   *Der Antichrist* (The Anti-Christ). Written in 1888.
1908   *Ecce Homo. Wie man wird, was man ist* (Ecce Homo. How One Becomes What One Is). Written in 1888.

Translations into English are available for all of these works. Recommended are those by Walter Kaufmann and R. J. Hollingdale.

IMPORTANT COLLECTIONS OF WORKS BY NIETZSCHE

Kaufmann, Walter (ed. and trans.). *The Portable Nietzsche*. New York: Viking Press, 1954. (Includes selections from writings and letters, as well as the complete *Thus Spoke Zarathustra, Twilight of the Idols,* and *The Anti-Christ.*)

Kaufmann, Walter (ed. and trans). *Basic Writings of Nietzsche*. New York: Random House, 1966. Modern Library edition, 1968. (Includes selections, as well as the complete *The Birth of Tragedy, Beyond Good and Evil, On the Genealogy of Morals,* and *Ecce Homo.*)

RECOMMENDED WORKS ON NIETZSCHE

Clarke, Maudemarie. *Nietzsche on Truth and Philosophy*. Cambridge: Cambridge University Press, 1990.

Hollingdale, R. J. *Nietzsche, the Man and His Philosophy*. Baton Rouge: Louisiana State University Press, 1965.

Kaufmann, Walter. *Nietzsche: Philosopher, Psychologist, Antichrist* 3rd ed., rev. and enlarged. New York: Vintage, 1968.

Magnus, Bernd and Higgins, Kathleen M. *The Cambridge Companion to Nietzsche*. New York: Cambridge University Press, 1996.

Nehamas, Alexander. *Nietzsche: Life as Literature*. Cambridge: Harvard University Press, 1985.

Parkes, Graham. *Composing the Soul*. Chicago: The University of Chicago Press, 1994.

Schacht, Richard. *Nietzsche*. London: Routledge and Kegan Paul, 1983.

Solomon, Robert C. and Higgins, Kathleen M. (eds.). *Reading Nietzsche*. New York: Oxford University Press, 1988.

"Reason" in Philosophy

1

You ask me what all idiosyncrasy is in philosophers? . . . For instance their lack of the historical sense, their hatred even of the idea of Becoming, their Egyptianism. They imagine that they do honour to a thing by divorcing it from history *sub specie æterni,*—when they make a mummy of it. All the ideas that philosophers have treated for thousands of years, have been mummied concepts; nothing real has ever come out of their hands alive. These idolaters of concepts merely kill and stuff things when they worship,—they threaten the life of every thing they adore. Death, change, age, as well as procreation and growth, are in their opinion objections,—even refutations. That which is cannot evolve; that which evolves *is* not. Now all of them believe, and even with desperation, in Being. But, as they cannot lay hold of it, they try to discover reasons why this privilege is withheld from them. "Some merely apparent quality, some deception must be the cause of our not being able to ascertain the nature of Being: where is the deceiver?" "We have him," they cry rejoicing, "it is sensuality!" These senses, *which in other things are so immoral,* cheat us concerning the true world. Moral: we must get rid of the deception of the senses, of Becoming, of history, of falsehood.—History is nothing more than the belief in the senses, the belief in falsehood. Moral: we must say "no" to everything in which the senses believe: to all the rest of mankind: all that belongs to the "people." Let us be philosophers, mummies, monotono-theists, grave-diggers!—And above all, away with the *body,* this wretched *idée fixe* of the senses, infected with all the faults of logic that exist, refuted, even impossible, although it be impudent enough to pose as if it were real!

2

With a feeling of great reverence I except the name of *Heraclitus.* If the rest of the philosophic gang rejected the evidences of the senses, because the latter revealed a state of multifariousness and change, he rejected the same evidence because it revealed things as if they possessed permanence and unity. Even Heraclitus did an injustice to the senses. The latter lie neither as the Eleatics believed them to lie, nor as he believed them to lie,—they do not lie at all. The interpretations we give to their evidence is what first introduces falsehood into it; for instance the lie of unity, the lie of matter, of substance and of permanence. Reason is the cause of our falsifying the evidence of the senses. In so far as the senses show us a state of Becoming, of transiency, and of change, they do not lie. But in declaring that Being was an empty illusion, Heraclitus will remain eternally right. The "apparent" world is the only world: the "true world" is no more than a false adjunct thereto.

3

And what delicate instruments of observation we have in our senses! This human nose, for instance, of which no philosopher has yet spoken with reverence and gratitude, is, for the present, the most finely adjusted instrument at our disposal: it is able to register even such slight changes of movement as the spectroscope would be unable to record. Our scientific triumphs at the present day extend precisely so far as we have accepted the evidence of our senses,—as we have sharpened and armed them, and learned to follow them up to the end. What remains is abortive and not yet science—that is to say, metaphysics, theology, psychology, epistemology, or formal science, or a doctrine of symbols, like logic and its applied form mathematics. In all these things reality does not come into consideration at all, even as a problem; just as little as does the question concerning the general value of such a convention of symbols as logic.

4

The other idiosyncrasy of philosophers is no less dangerous; it consists in confusing the last and the first things. They place that which makes its appearance last—unfortunately! for it ought not to appear at all!— the "highest concept," that is to say, the most general, the emptiest, the last cloudy streak of evaporating reality, at the beginning as the beginning. This again is only their manner of expressing their veneration: the highest thing must not have grown out of the lowest, it must not have grown at all. . . . Moral: everything of the first rank must be *causa sui*. To have been derived from something else, is as good as an objection, it sets the value of a thing in question. All superior values are of the first rank, all the highest concepts—that of Being, of the Absolute, of Goodness, of Truth, and of Perfection; all these things cannot have been evolved, they must therefore be *causa sui*. All these things cannot however be unlike one another, they cannot be opposed to one another. Thus they attain to their stupendous concept "God." The last, most attenuated and emptiest thing is postulated as the first thing, as the absolute cause, as *ens realissimum*. Fancy humanity having to take the brain diseases of morbid cobweb-spinners seriously!— And it has paid dearly for having done so.

5

—Against this let us set the different manner in which we (—you observe that I am courteous enough to say "we") conceive the problem of the error and deceptiveness of things. Formerly people regarded change and evolution in general as the proof of appearance, as a sign of the fact that something must be there that leads us astray. To-day, on the other hand, we realise that precisely as far as the rational bias forces us to postulate unity, identity, permanence, substance, cause, materiality and being, we are in a measure involved in error, driven necessarily to error; however certain we may feel, as the result of a strict examination of the matter, that the error lies here. It is just the same here as with the motion of the sun: In its case it was our eyes that were wrong; in the matter of the concepts above mentioned it is our language itself that pleads most constantly in their favour. In its origin language belongs to an age of the most rudimentary forms of psychology: if we try to conceive of the first conditions of the metaphysics of language, *i.e.,* in plain English, of reason, we immediately find ourselves in the midst of a system of fetishism. For here, the doer and his deed are seen in all circumstances, will is believed in as a cause in general; the ego is taken for granted, the ego as Being, and as substance, and the faith in the ego as substance is projected into all things—in this way, alone, the concept "thing" is created. Being is thought into and insinuated into everything as cause; from the concept "ego," alone, can the concept "Being" proceed. At the beginning stands the tremendously fatal error of supposing the will to be something that actuates,—a faculty. Now we know that it is only a word. Very much later, in a world a thousand times more enlightened, the assurance, the subjective certitude, in the handling of the categories of reason came into the minds of philosophers as a surprise. They concluded that these categories could not be derived from experience,—on the contrary, the whole of experience rather contradicts them. *Whence do they come therefore?* In India, as in Greece, the same mistake was made: "we must already once have lived in a higher world (—instead of in a much lower one, which would have been the truth!), we must have been divine, for we possess reason!" . . . Nothing indeed has exercised a more simple power of persuasion hitherto than the error of Being, as it was formulated by the Eleatics for instance: in its favour are every word and every sentence that we utter!—Even the opponents of the Eleatics succumbed to the seductive powers of their concept of Being. Among others there was Democritus in his discovery of the atom. "Reason" in language!—oh what a deceptive old witch it has been! I fear we shall never be rid of God, so long as we still believe in grammar.

6

People will feel grateful to me if I condense a point of view, which is at once so important and so new, into four theses: by this means I shall facilitate comprehension, and shall likewise challenge contradiction.

Proposition One. The reasons upon which the apparent nature of "this" world have been based, rather tend to prove its reality,—any other kind of reality defies demonstration.

Proposition Two. The characteristics with which man has endowed the "true Being" of things, are the characteristics of non-Being, of *nonentity.* The "true world" has been erected upon a contradiction of the real world; and it is indeed an apparent world, seeing that it is merely a *moralo-optical* delusion.

Proposition Three. There is no sense in spinning yarns about another world, provided, of course, that we do not possess a mighty instinct which urges us to slander, belittle, and cast suspicion upon this life: in this case we should be avenging ourselves on this life with the Phantas-magoria of "another," of a "better" life.

Proposition Four. To divide the world into a "true" and an "appar-ent" world, whether after the manner of Christianity or of Kant (after all a Christian in disguise), is only a sign of decadence,—a symptom of *degenerating* life. The fact that the artist esteems the appearance of a thing higher than reality, is no objection to this statement. For "appearance" signifies once more reality here, but in a selected, strengthened and corrected form. The tragic artist is no pessimist,—he says *Yea* to everything questionable and terrible, he is Dionysian.

The Four Great Errors

1

THE error of the confusion of cause and effect.— There is no more dangerous error than to confound the effect with the cause: I call this error the intrinsic perversion of reason. Nevertheless this error is one of the most ancient and most recent habits of mankind. In one part of the world it has even been canonised; and it bears the name of "Religion" and "Morality." Every postulate formulated by religion and morality contains it. Priests and the promulgators of moral laws are the promoters of this perversion of reason.—Let me give you an example. Everybody knows the book of the famous Cornaro, in which he recommends his slender diet as the recipe for a long, happy and also virtuous life. Few books have been so widely read, and to this day many thousand copies of it are still printed annually in England. I do not doubt that there is scarcely a single book (the Bible of course excepted) that has worked more mischief, shortened more lives, than this well-meant curiosity. The reason of this is the confusion of effect and cause. This worthy Italian saw the cause of his long life in his diet: whereas the prerequisites of long life, which are exceptional slowness of molecular change, and a low rate of expenditure in energy, were the cause of his meagre diet. He was not at liberty to eat a small or a great amount. His frugality was not the result of free choice, he would have been ill had he eaten more. He who does not happen to be a carp, however, is not only wise to eat well, but is also compelled to do so. A scholar of the present day, with his rapid consumption of nervous energy, would soon go to the dogs on Cornaro's diet. *Crede experto.*—

2

The most general principle lying at the root of every religion and morality, is this: "Do this and that and avoid this and that—and thou wilt be happy. Otherwise—." Every morality and every religion is this Imperative—I call it the great original sin of reason,—*immortal unreason.* In my mouth this principle is converted into its opposite—first example of my "Transvaluation of all Values": a well-constituted man, a man who is one of "Nature's lucky strokes," *must* perform certain actions and instinctively fear other actions; he introduces the element of order, of which he is the physiological manifestation, into his relations with men and things. In a formula: his virtue is the consequence of his good constitution. Longevity and plentiful offspring are not the reward of virtue, virtue itself is on the contrary that retardation of the metabolic process which, among other things, results in a long life and in plentiful offspring, in short in *Cornarism.* The Church and morality say: "A race, a people perish through vice and luxury." My reinstated reason says: when a people are going to the dogs, when they are degenerating physiologically, vice and luxury (that is to say, the need of ever stronger and more frequent stimuli such as all exhausted natures are acquainted with) are bound to result. Such and such a young man grows pale and withered prematurely. His friends say this or that illness is the cause of it. I say: the fact that he became ill, the fact that he did not resist illness, was in itself already the outcome of impoverished life, of hereditary exhaustion. The newspaper reader says: such and such a party by committing such an error will meet its death. My superior politics say: a party that can make such mistakes, is in its last agony—it no longer possesses any certainty of instinct. Every mistake is in every sense the sequel to degeneration of the instincts, to disintegration of the will. This is almost the definition of evil. Everything valuable is instinct—and consequently easy, necessary, free. Exertion is an objection, the god is characteristically different from the hero (in my language: light feet are the first attribute of divinity).

3

The error of false causality. In all ages men have believed that they knew what a cause was: but whence did we derive this knowledge, or more accurately, this faith in the fact that we know? Out of the realm of the famous "inner facts of consciousness," not one of which has yet proved itself to be a fact. We believed ourselves to be causes even in the action of the will; we thought that in this matter at least we caught causality red-handed. No one doubted that all the *antecedentia* of an action were to be sought in consciousness, and could be discovered there—as "motive"—if only they were sought. Otherwise we should not be free to perform them, we should not have been responsible for them. Finally who would have questioned that a thought is caused? that the ego causes the thought? Of these three "facts of inner consciousness" by means of which causality seemed to be guaranteed, the first and most convincing is that of the will as cause; the conception of consciousness ("spirit") as a cause, and subsequently that of the ego (the "subject") as a cause, were merely born afterwards, once the causality of the will stood established as "given," as a fact of experience. Meanwhile we have come to our senses. To-day we no longer believe a word of all this. The "inner world" is full of phantoms and will-o'-the-wisps: the will is one of these. The will no longer actuates, consequently it no longer explains anything—all it does is to accompany processes; it may even be absent. The so-called "motive" is another error. It is merely a ripple on the surface of consciousness, a side issue of the action, which is much more likely to conceal than to reveal the *antecedentia* of the latter. And as for the ego! It has become legendary, fictional, a play upon words: it has ceased utterly and completely from thinking, feeling, and willing! What is the result of it all? There are no such things as spiritual causes. The whole of popular experience on this subject went to the devil! That is the result of it all. For we had blissfully abused that experience, we had built the world upon it as a world of causes, as a world of will, as a world of spirit. The most antiquated and most traditional psychology has been at work here, it has done nothing else: all phenomena were deeds in the light of this psychology, and all deeds were the result of will; according to it the world was a complex mechanism of agents, an agent (a "subject") lay at the root of all things. Man projected his three "inner facts of consciousness," the will, the spirit, and the ego in which he believed most firmly, outside himself. He first deduced the concept Being out of the concept Ego, he supposed "things" to exist as he did himself, according to his notion of the ego as cause. Was it to be wondered at that later on he always found in things only that which he had laid in them?—The thing itself, I repeat, the concept thing was merely a reflex of the belief in the ego as cause. And even your atom, my dear good Mechanists and Physicists, what an amount of error, of rudimentary psychology still adheres to it!—Not to speak of the "thing-in-itself," of the *horrendum pudendum* of the metaphysicians! The error of spirit regarded as a cause, confounded with reality! And made the measure of reality! And called *God!*

4

The Error of imaginary Causes. Starting out from dreamland, we find that to any definite sensation, like that produced by a distant cannon shot for instance, we are wont to ascribe a cause after the fact (very often quite a little romance in which the dreamer himself is, of course, the hero). Meanwhile the sensation becomes protracted like a sort of continuous echo, until, as it were, the instinct of causality allows it to come to the front rank, no longer however as a chance occurrence, but as a thing which has some meaning. The cannon shot presents itself in *a causal* manner, by means of an apparent reversal in the order of time. That which occurs last, the motivation, is experienced first, often with a hundred details which flash past like lightning, and the shot is the *result.* What has happened? The ideas suggested by a particular state of our senses, are misinterpreted as the cause of that state. As a matter of fact we proceed in precisely the same manner when we are awake. The greater number of our general sensations—every kind of obstacle, pressure, tension, explosion in the interplay of the organs, and more particularly the condition of the *nervus sympathicus*—stimulate our instinct of causality: we will have a reason which will account for our feeling thus or thus,—for feeling ill or well. We are never satisfied by merely ascertaining the fact that we feel thus or thus: we admit this fact—we become conscious of it—only when we have attributed it to some kind of motivation. Memory, which, in such circumstances unconsciously becomes active, adduces former conditions of a like kind, together with the causal interpretations with which the are associated,—but not their real cause. The belief that the ideas, the accompanying processes of consciousness, have been the causes, is certainly produced by the agency of memory. And in this way we become *accustomed* to a particular interpretation of causes which, truth to tell, actually hinders and even utterly prevents the investigation of the proper cause.

5

The Psychological Explanation of the above Fact. To trace something unfamiliar back to something familiar, is at once a relief, a comfort and a satisfaction, while it also produces a feeling of power. The unfamiliar involves danger, anxiety and care,—the fundamental instinct is to get rid of these painful circumstances. First principle: any explanation is better than none at all. Since, at bottom, it is only a question of shaking one's self free from certain oppressive ideas, the means employed to this end are not selected with overmuch punctiliousness: the first idea by means of which the unfamiliar is revealed as familiar, produces a feeling of such comfort that it is "held to be true." The proof of happiness ("of power") as the criterion of truth. The instinct of causality is therefore conditioned and stimulated by the feeling of fear. Whenever possible, the question "why?" should not only educe the cause as cause, but rather a certain kind of cause—a comforting, liberating and reassuring cause. The first result of this need is that something known or already experienced, and recorded in the memory, is posited as the cause. The new factor, that which has not been experienced and which is unfamiliar, is excluded from the sphere of causes. Not only do we try to find a certain kind of explanation as the cause, but those kinds of explanations are selected and preferred which dissipate most rapidly the sensation of strangeness, novelty and unfamiliarity,—in fact the most ordinary explanations. And the result is that a certain manner of postulating causes tends to predominate ever more and more, becomes concentrated into a system, and finally reigns supreme, to the complete exclusion of all other causes and explanations. The banker thinks immediately of business, the Christian of "sin," and the girl of her love affair.

6

The whole Domain of Morality and Religion may be classified under the Rubric "Imaginary Causes." The "explanation" of general unpleasant sensations. These sensations are dependent upon certain creatures who are hostile to us (evil spirits: the most famous example of this—the mistaking of hysterical women for witches). These sensations are dependent upon actions which are reprehensible (the feeling of "sin," "sinfulness" is a manner of accounting for a certain physiological disorder—people always find reasons for being dissatisfied with themselves). These sensations depend upon punishment, upon compensation for something which we ought not to have done, which we ought not to have been (this idea was generalised in a more impudent form by Schopenhauer, into that principle in which morality appears—in its real colours,—that is to say, as a veritable poisoner and slanderer of life: "all great suffering, whether mental or physical, reveals what we deserve: for it could not visit us if we did not deserve it,"—"The World as Will and Idea," vol. 2, p. 666). These sensations are the outcome of ill-considered actions, having evil consequences, (—the passions, the senses, postulated as causes, as guilty. By means of other calamities distressing physiological conditions are interpreted as "merited").— The "explanation" of pleasant sensations. These sensations are dependent upon a trust in God. They may depend upon our consciousness of having done one or two good actions (a so-called "good conscience" is a physiological condition, which may be the outcome of good digestion). They may depend upon the happy issue of certain undertakings (—an ingenuous mistake: the happy issue of an undertaking certainly does not give a hypochondriac or a Pascal any general sensation of pleasure). They may depend upon faith, love and hope,—the Christian virtues. As a matter of fact all these pretended explanations are but the results of certain states, and as it were translations of feelings of pleasure and pain into a false dialect: a man is in a condition of hopefulness because the dominant physiological sensation of his being is again one of strength and wealth; he trusts in God because the feeling of abundance and power gives him a peaceful state of mind. Morality and religion are completely and utterly parts of the psychology of error: in every particular case cause and effect are confounded; as truth is confounded with the effect of that which is believed to be true or a certain state of consciousness is confounded with the chain of causes which brought it about.

7

The Error of Free-Will. At present we no longer have any mercy upon the concept "free-will": we know only too well what it is—the most egregious theological trick that has ever existed for the purpose of making mankind "responsible" in a theological manner,—that is to say, to make mankind dependent upon theologians. I will now explain to you only the psychology of the whole process of inculcating the sense of responsibility. Wherever men try to trace responsibility home to anyone, it is the instinct of punishment and of the desire to judge which is active. Becoming is robbed of its innocence when any particular condition of things is traced to a will, to intentions and to responsible actions. The doctrine of the will was invented principally for the purpose of punishment—that is to say, with the intention of tracing guilt. The whole of ancient psychology, or the psychology of the will, is the outcome of the fact that its originators, who were the priests at the head of ancient communities, wanted to create for themselves a right to administer punishments—or the right for God to do so. Men were thought of as "free" in order that they might be judged and punished—in order that they might be held guilty: consequently every action had to be regarded as voluntary, and the origin of every action had to be imagined as lying in consciousness (—in this way the most fundamentally fraudulent character of psychology was established as the very principle of psychology itself). Now that we have entered upon the opposite movement, now that we immoralists are trying with all our power to eliminate the concepts of guilt and punishment from the world once more, and to cleanse psychology, history, nature and all social institutions and customs of all signs of those two concepts, we recognise no more radical opponents than the theologians, who with their notion of "a moral order, of things," still continue to pollute the innocence of Becoming with punishment and guilt. Christianity is the metaphysics of the hangman.

8

What then, alone, can our teaching be?—That no one gives man his qualities, neither God, society his parents, his ancestors, nor himself (—this nonsensical idea which is at last refuted here, was taught as "intelligible freedom" by Kant, and perhaps even as early as Plato himself). No one is responsible for the fact that he exists at all, that he is constituted as he is, and that he happens to be in certain circumstances and in a particular environment. The fatality of his being cannot be divorced from the fatality of all that which has been and will be.

This is not the result. of an individual intention, of a will, of an aim, there is no attempt at attaining to any "ideal man," or "ideal happiness" or "ideal morality" with him,—it is absurd to wish him to be careering towards some sort of purpose. *We* invented the concept "purpose"; in reality purpose is altogether lacking. One is necessary, one is a piece of fate, one belongs to the whole, one is in the whole,—there is nothing that could judge, measure, compare, and condemn our existence, for that would mean judging, measuring, comparing and condemning the whole. *But there is nothing outside the whole!* The fact that no one shall any longer be made responsible, that the nature of existence may not be traced to a *causa prima,* that the world is an entity neither as a sensorium nor as a spirit—*this alone is the great deliverance,*—thus alone is the innocence of Becoming restored. . . . The concept "God" has been the greatest objection to existence hitherto. . . . We deny God, we deny responsibility in God: thus alone do we save the world.—

SAMUEL ALEXANDER

Samuel Alexander (1859–1938) was born of Jewish parents in Sydney, Australia. After studying at Melbourne and Oxford, he became a Fellow of Lincoln College, Oxford, in 1882. From 1893 until his retirement in 1924 he was Professor of Philosophy at Victoria University, Manchester, in which capacity he taught psychology as well. He remained a bachelor throughout his life, but his circle of friends was large and fiercely loyal, and it was said that he was much admired by the ladies. He first became known in philosophy as one of the most articulate of those numerous champions of epistemological realism whose writings dominated the journals in England and America during the first two decades of the century. Yet his statement in the Arthur Davis Memorial Lecture of 1921 that the distinguishing mark of contemporary philosophy is that it "takes time seriously" is more revealing of his fundamental commitment. His greatest work and one of the monuments of philosophical system is *Space, Time and Deity,* published in 1920 in two volumes. In his later years at Manchester he became a fixture of local color because of his habit of dressing in extremely shabby clothes, which he used on occasion, instead of an eraser, to clean his classroom blackboard; his attachment to his bicycle, which was his one means of transportation throughout the whole of England; and his near deafness, so pronounced that he used an ear-trumpet, forcing those who wished to question him to approach within a few feet and shout. However, he was widely known for his melodious voice and his oratorical genius.

MAJOR PHILOSOPHICAL WORKS BY ALEXANDER

1889   *Moral Order and Progress: An Analysis of Ethical Conceptions.* London: Trübner & Co.

1909   *Locke.* London: Constable.

1914   "The Basis of Realism," *Proceedings of the British Academy,* January.

1920   *Space, Time and Deity.* Two volumes. London: Macmillan. (Gifford Lectures.)
1921   *Spinoza and Time.* London: Allen & Unwin. (Arthur Davis Memorial Lecture.)
1933   *Beauty and Other Forms of Value.* London: Macmillan.
1939   *Philosophical and Literary Pieces.* Edited by John Laird. London: Macmillan. (Contains fourteen previously published essays, including "Artistic Creation and Cosmic Creation," "Natural Piety," and "Spinoza and Time," and a lengthy memoir by John Laird.)

RECOMMENDED WORK ON ALEXANDER

McCarthy, John W. *The Naturalism of Samuel Alexander.* New York: King's Crown Press, 1948.

Natural Piety

I do not mean by natural piety exactly what Wordsworth meant by it—the reverent joy in nature, by which he wished that his days might be bound to each other—though there is enough connection with his interpretation to justify me in using his phrase. The natural piety I am going to speak of is that of the scientific investigator, by which he accepts with loyalty the mysteries which he cannot explain in nature and has no right to try to explain. I may describe it as the habit of knowing when to stop in asking questions of nature. The limits to the right of asking questions are drawn differently for different purposes. They are not the same in science as in ordinary intercourse between men in conversation. I may recall an incident in the life of Dr. Johnson. "I was once present," says Boswell, "when a gentleman [perhaps it was Boswell himself] asked so many [questions], as 'What did you do, sir?' 'What did you say, sir?' that at last he grew enraged, and said, 'I will not be put to the *question*. Don't you consider, sir, that these are not the manners of a gentleman? I will not be baited with *what* and *why*. What is this? What is that? Why is a cow's tail long? Why is a fox's tail bushy?'" Boswell adds that the gentleman, who was a good deal out of countenance, said, "Why, sir, you are so good, that I venture to trouble you." *JOHNSON*—"Sir, my being so *good* is no reason why you should be so ill." The questions which Johnson regarded as typically offensive in conversation about the cow's and the fox's tail might quite legitimately be asked in science, and, I fancy, answered by a naturalist without any particular difficulty. There is a mental disease known as the questioning or metaphysical mania, which cannot accept anything, even the most trivial, without demanding explanation. Why do I stand here where I stand? Why is a glass a glass, a chair a chair? How is it that men are only of the size they are? Why not as big as houses? etc. (I quote from William James.) Now the very life of knowledge depends on asking questions. Is it not called inquiry? And its limits are not drawn by considerations of politeness or by shrinking from insanity. But it does recognize that, however far it may push its explanations, the world presents characters which must be accepted reverently as beyond explanation, though they do not pass understanding. And I call this habit of acceptance of nature by the name of natural piety, because simple-minded religion is accustomed to speak of events for which it can find no reason as the will of God.

I will illustrate my meaning from human matters, before passing on to the proper subject of nature. Familiar with the style of Shakespeare, we might with sufficient knowledge of his antecedents, his physiological inheritance, the influences upon him of the company in which he lived, the common speech of the time, and its literature, persuade ourselves that we can understand how he came to write as he did. But the distinctive flavor of it we could not with any amount of knowledge predict, as possibly we might predict with a style such as that of R. L. Stevenson, which carries with it the traces of its origin; we can but acknowledge it as a new creation and confine ourselves to inquiring into its conditions. The same thing may perhaps be said of the style of Plato or of Pascal. The French Revolution introduced into political and social life a conception which, however hard to define, was new and gave a new direction to the political thought of Europe, inspiring even those who in the end overthrew the revolutionary regime. That a change was about to occur could have been foreseen by those who considered the evils of the aristocratic polity of France and the direction of the thinking of political writers. But that the change would be the new idea of democracy could not have been foretold. A new feeling had arisen in men's minds of the claims of the common man. Even at the present moment, when the sanguine hopes which were entertained of a regenerated world which was to arise from the war seem to be swept away by the recrudescence of evil passions of domination, or terror, or selfishness, it can hardly be doubted that the world has suffered a political change, which we are too near the event to describe, which owes something to the ideals of the conquered as well as of the conquerors, a new flavor of political life, of which we can understand the conditions but can only feel the presence. We can tell how it has come about, but we do not explain why it should be what it is, and we hardly as yet realize what it is. Compare the teaching of Jesus with what we know of the Judaism of the first century of our era. If our authorities are to be trusted the difference appears to be far smaller than accounts for the immense consequences of the new teaching. That there was novelty, a new conception introduced into morality and the relations between man and God, it would be impossible to deny, and it provided the material when the organization of Christianity by Paul came about. A religion had come into existence, not put forward by its founder as more than a reform of Judaism, and yet possessing a flavor of its own which was the mark of its originality. What may seem a mere difference of emphasis, a brighter flame of passion (I believe I am taking these phrases from Mr. Montefiore)—all these things, for which the historian can note the antecedents, were fused and welded into a new and distinctive idea. All great historical transformations might be used to supply further examples—the marvel which was born when men of Dorian birth adopted the civilization and the arts of Egypt and Phoenicia; the limited idea of constitutional liberty for which the Great Rebellion in our own country was fought; the Reformation itself; and a hundred such great changes, of which once more we can understand with sufficient knowledge how they came to be, but not how they should have taken the particular coloring or flavor which actually they possessed.

In these critical changes, further, there is a constant feature. The new creation inherits the ancient ways out of which it grows, but it simplifies the old complexity. There was a chaos of conflicting forces; men's minds were groping confusedly in a tangle of divergent and intercrossing interests; there was a vast unrest; the old habits were lingering on though they had lost their convincingness and bred dissatisfaction; experiment after experiment upon the traditional lines had failed; yet the newer thoughts that were abroad had reached as yet no more than the condition of subterranean and indistinct rebellion. Suddenly, at the bidding of some great single mind, or oftener perhaps of some conspiration of many minds, stirred to their depths with obscure foreboding of the future birth of time, and finely if still vaguely touched to the fine issues, a light has arisen; the discordant elements fall into their places, and the complexity gives way to simplicity. The synthesis is no mere reconciliation; it is creative. So the historians have traced for us the birth of democratic freedom out of the turmoil of the eighteenth century, when once its complacence had broken down; or the preparation of the world to receive the Gentile gospel, when the dull universalizing regime of the Roman Empire was fired with the deeper thinking of the Palestinian prophet. So, too, we may feel today that our minds are moving this way and that in a sheer confusion of old with new; the complexity and disorganization of the world are more patent than its unification; and yet we doubt not, or at least we hope, that we have not passed through the ordeal in vain, and that some time and somehow the tangled skein of our present condition will be unraveled, and our conflicting ways may be found convergent towards a simpler and clearer ideal of national and international life. Hence it is, because the creative simplicity is conditioned by so immense a confusion and welter of interests, that it is sometimes more plainly revealed away from the place of its more immediate origin; that the smaller peoples may exhibit more definitely the principle for which larger and better organized nations have striven.

Nor is it only in political and industrial affairs that the creative simplicity emerges from the chaos of complexity. The same feature is even more palpable in science and all pursuit of knowledge. Simple and illuminating discoveries presuppose an immense labor, conducted upon older lines, of material which remains, till the new creation, in-coordinated and blind. The new thought or theory reduces the old material to order, while it emancipates us from its confusion. The physical science of today uses a language singularly unlike that of the nineteenth century, which it half seems to forget; considered more closely, it is at once the continuance of that work and the discovery of a new and simpler world. Other sciences may not have reached this fulfillment so soon. In history I am told the vast accumulation of detailed investigations awaits as yet the constructive thought which is to give it coherence and simplicity. Philosophy exhibits at the moment all the signs of approaching creation, but is for the time a chaos of discordant doctrines, all of them containing their measure of truth, testifying the awakening of philosophy from its complacent dream, but none as yet completely binding experience into its desired unity. The extreme forms of idealism and realism, the traditional idealism and the antagonist ideas inspired by the revolt against intellect taken alone, or rather by the passion for seeing in the world the fulfillment of man's practical or aesthetic or religious ends; Bradley and Bergson, Croce and William James with his later followers, James Ward and Bertrand Russell; the 'discovery' of Time and the invasion of our ideas by the march of relativity, with its meaning and issues as yet half understood and certainly undecided; the breaking down of the older literary conception of philosophy and its return to its ancient unity and kinship with science, physical and biological; here is a picture of a world distraught by its own complex and abundant vitality. Yet the philosophic believer in philosophy never doubts the imminent birth of a more satisfying thought for which these labors have supplied the favoring marriage of unlikes feeling out towards their blending, and which once attained will set the mind free, as the older idealism has done for a century, to explore with a new guiding thread the vast provinces of special philosophical inquiry.

These features which have been traced in human affairs; new creations which lend an unexplained and strange flavor to existing institutions and remodel them; external habits and ways of life retained but their inward meaning transformed; immense complexities of elements, hitherto chaotic, now gathering themselves together and as it were flowering into some undreamed simplicity; these features are found in the nature of which man is but the latest stage. Nature is "stratified," and if we apply to it our customary conceptions of growth and development, we can regard it as a geological formation with a history. But the comparison is still inadequate; for new geological strata are but fresh deposits laid down upon the subjacent ones, not drawing from them their new life. Nature is rather a history of organic growth of species, in which the new type of organism is the outgrowth of the older type, and continues the earlier life into a form at once more complex and more highly simplified. As there is in the animal world or the plant world a hierarchy of forms, so in nature there is a hierarchy of qualities which are characteristics of various levels of development. There are, if I may borrow a metaphor used by Mr. Sellars of Michigan in his recent book,[1] "critical points" in the unfolding of nature when she gathers up her resources for a new experiment and breeds a new quality of existence. The earliest of these qualities of being which is familiar to us is that of physical matter, whatever we are to suppose it is that materiality consists in. Other well marked levels are those of chemical structure and behavior, and life, which is the quality of things which behave physiologically.

I am not concerned to offer a complete enumeration of these levels of existence with their distinguishing qualities. The three qualities mentioned are but a selection. Every attempt at completeness raises questions of difficulty. Certain, however, it is now that mere physical materiality is a highly developed stage, late in the history of the world: that there are forms of submaterial being, and the line between the

---

[1] *Evolutionary Naturalism,* R. W. Sellars, Open Court, Chicago, 1922.

submaterial and the material is not for me to draw. Neither is it for me to say whether electrons are the lowest existence in the scale. Again, beyond life, some have maintained that mind is itself a new quality which arises out of life, while others treat consciousness merely as a function of all life, and for them consciousness and life are one, and accordingly all the knowing on which we pride ourselves so much is in the end only a special form of vital behavior. There is another debatable question. To me, colors and sounds and tastes and all the sensible characters of material things appear to be resident in things themselves; and colored existence to be a critical point in nature. When a physical body is such that the light which it sends out to our eyes has a determinate wave length, that body is red. To others, and they are the majority, the color depends upon the possession by the percipient of eyes. These questions I need not raise in this place because they take us away from the central theme into historic problems which have occupied physics and philosophy from the days of Galileo and before. There is still another matter I leave open. Life is without doubt such a critical point in nature. Are the various gradations of life, first of all the difference of plants and animals as a whole, and next the marked differences of kinds among animals and plants themselves, to be regarded likewise? The differences which part a humble amoeba or hydra from the monkey, or even from the lizard or crab, are vast. Are they critical differences? All I need answer is that if they are not, at least the outgrowth of the higher from the lower forms of life helps us mightily to understand the outgrowth at the critical point of the higher level of quality from the lower. Further, if it is right to treat colors as real qualities, not dependent for existence on the physiological organs; which are but instruments in that case for apprehending, not for creating them; if this is so, the different kinds of colors—red, green, and the rest—are comparable to the species of animals or plants, and if they do not mark a change of level they mark differences upon that level. All these matters of debate I leave aside, in order to insist on the vital feature of nature that she does exhibit critical changes of quality, which mark new syntheses, that we can but note. We may and must observe with care out of what previous conditions these new creations arise. We cannot tell why they should assume these qualities. We can but accept them as we find them, and this acceptance is natural piety.

These bodies with new qualities, these "creative syntheses," which arise at critical points from a lower level of existence, are therefore no mere mechanical resultants of their lower conditions. If they were they would have merely the quality of their antecedents or components, as the component pulls upon a body along the sides of a parallelogram are equivalent to a resultant pull along the diagonal. Even the chemical combination of sodium and sulphuric acid, though it leads to something new and its process is not purely mechanical, does but issue in a new chemical body, just as the pairing of two living beings may lead to a new variety, but still a variety of living being. They are, therefore, after the usage of the late George Henry Lewes, described as emergents by Mr. Lloyd Morgan, with whom I have for many years shared this conception of things, which he has expounded with a simplicity and lucidity beyond my powers in a chapter of his book, *Instinct and Experience,* and with particular force in the address with which he inaugurated the independent section of Psychology at the recent meeting of the British Association at Edinburgh (1921).

Without attempting to take in the whole field of nature, I will confine myself here to life, considered as an emergent from the realm of physico-chemical bodies. A living body is, according to this conception, a physico-chemical body of a certain degree and kind of complexity, whose actions may severally be viewed as physical or chemical, but taken in their integration, or entirety (to borrow a word of Lord Haldane's), have the quality of life. Life is therefore resoluble without remainder into physico-chemical processes; but it cannot be treated as *merely* physico-chemical. Certain of its functions may be referred to physical or chemical laws, but it is not these separable processes which constitute life. Life exists only when we have that particular collocation of such physico-chemical actions which we know as living. It is the special coordination which conditions the appearance or creation of the new quality of life. We might therefore be disposed to describe the living body indifferently as being a physico-chemical body which is *also* vital, or as being vital and *also* physico-chemical. In reality only the second designation is satisfactory. The first would imply that a certain grouping of such processes remains no more than physical and chemical, that life is not something new but a name for this integration, whereas it is a new quality conditioned by and equivalent to the particular complexity of integration. Given life, we can hope to resolve it into its physico-chemical equivalent. We can even hope to reproduce partially or wholly by artificial means the existence of life. It is well known, for instance, that certain foams or emulsions of oil have exhibited streaming movements like those of living protoplasm. But life has been already attained, and it is our clue to the invention of the necessary machinery. Given merely physical and chemical processes, we can only generate life when we have hit upon the required form of integration. Thus life is *also* physico-chemical, because in its separable activities it is comparable with other physico-chemical processes. But it is not *merely* physico-chemical, because merely physico-chemical processes are not alive, and they do not give us life until the requisite complexity of integration is attained. So important is it to remember that besides elements there is the form of their combination, and that the form is as much a reality as the elements and gives them their significance; that it is not the patches of color alone which make the picture, but their selection and arrangement which make the separate patches contribute to the expressiveness of the picture; that a melody is not merely the notes by which it is conveyed, but the choice and order which the musician has introduced into them; that in the choice and combination of the parts the whole receives a meaning which does not belong to the several components; and that while a combination of sounds is still a sound, and the blending of male and female elements in a human being is still human, there is still room at critical points for the combination to carry us into a new quality of being. Even where there is no such new quality of being, the change that is due to form may shadow forth these greater and more creative changes; as when, to revert to former illustrations, the choice of words generates the indescribable flavor of style, or, in music, to quote the often quoted words:

> Consider it well: each tone in our scale in itself is nought;
> It is everywhere in the world—loud, soft, and all is said:
> Give it to me to use! I mix it with two in my thought
> And, there! ye have heard and seen: consider and bow the head!

That attitude is an illustration of what I am calling natural piety.

It is here that we are brought face to face with the long-drawn-out dispute between the so-called mechanistic explanation of life and vitalism. The latest contribution to the controversy is to be found in the highly interesting work on "the mechanism of life,"[2] by Mr. Johnstone, the professor of Oceanography at Liverpool. I do not mention his work

---

[2] *The Mechanism of Life,* London (Arnold), 1921. Cp. W. M'Dougall, *Body and Mind,* p. 245.

in order to discuss his own explanation of life. He distinguishes the vital and the material mechanism in this way. All material mechanisms expend a part of the energy supplied to them not in doing work but in the form of heat which is no longer available for work; in the technical phrase they increase the sum of entropy or unavailing energy, and they represent a progression towards the condition of general dissipation of available energy. Living machines, on the contrary, delay or reverse the accumulation of entropy. It is beyond my competence to inquire into the correctness of this view. Rather I wish to direct your attention to the point that there is upon this doctrine such a "mechanism" of life, because it suggests that the sharp distinction of the mechanical from the vital is unfounded and that life may be a mechanism and yet have, as I have said, a new quality (though this view I am not attributing to Mr. Johnstone himself), and that while there is no new entity life, there is a new quality life, with which certain combinations of matter may be endowed. Vitalism supposed that there was an actual vital force, nonphysical, which interfered with and directed the physical behavior of the organism, and it has been reintroduced in our day by Mr. Hans Driesch under the guise of a presiding psychoid or entelechy, as he names it, a distinguishable principle, not resoluble into chemical or physical action. In this controversy a middle position is occupied by Mr. J. S. Haldane, who has called attention to a number of delicate adjustments performed by the organism which cannot be accounted for, he thinks, by the separate chemical processes of the body. Thus the respiratory actions under the guidance of the nervous center are so delicate that they preserve the pressure of carbonic acid in the air in the lungs and therefore in the blood vessels, and restore it to the normal when the amount of it has been disturbed even in the slightest degree, as by taking deeper breath and so diluting the carbonic acid. The arterial blood has, as he otherwise puts it, a normal faint alkalinity, and if this is disturbed, however slightly, by defect of carbonic acid, the pressure is restored. In the same way the blood has a normal salinity, which is kept constant in the face of the slightest changes by delicate reactions on the part of the kidneys. Mr. Haldane takes this delicacy of adjustment to mean that physiological action can only be understood by including in any function the organization of the whole creature. Here we might seem to have a matter upon which only a physiologist has the right to speak. Still, a mere philosopher may be allowed to consider the wider issue raised. If this concept of organization means only that vital action implies, and is not rightly described without, it, a philosopher must declare Mr. Haldane right. If he means that vital action precludes the resolution of life without remainder into chemical and physical action, he is open to the charge that, in his zeal for this new fact of life, he is forgetting that the whole make-up of the organism is itself, as Mr. Lloyd Morgan has pointed out, a factor in the chemical and physical processes in question. The moral which I draw from his work is not his own, but precisely the statement made at the beginning, that that organization which is alive is not merely physico-chemical, though completely resoluble into such terms, but has the new quality of life. No appeal is needed, so far as I can see, to a vital force or even an *élan vital.* It is enough to note the emergence of the quality, and try to describe what is involved in its conditions. That task will be, I imagine, difficult enough, and Mr. Johnstone's own account[3] may be valued as an attempt towards performing it.

The emergence of life with this new collocation of conditions implies that life is continuous with chemical, physical, and mechanical action. To be more explicit, the living body is also physical and chemical. It surrenders no claim to be considered a part of the physical world. But the new quality of fife which it possesses is neither chemical nor mechanical, but something new. Thus the parts of the living body have color but life is not colored, and they are material but life itself is not material, but only the body which is alive is material. The lower conditions out of whose collocations life emerges supply a body as it were to a new soul. The specific characters which they possess are not continued into the new soul. The continuity which exists between life and the material does not mean that the material is carried over into life. There would not in that case be continuity between the living body as a new emergent and its predecessors; the living body would be nothing more than an elaborate material mechanism, which would illustrate material action, but could not claim a position of privilege. The characters which *are* continued from the lower level into life are not the specific qualities of the lower level; they are rather those characters which all existence shares in common, such as existence in time and space, intensity, capacity of affecting other existences, all of which belong to life as much as to matter.

---

[3] *The Mechanism of Life,* chapter xi.

From this it will be clear that when we draw a sharp contrast between life and mechanism, as too often we do, we are guilty of exaggeration if not of confusion.[4] It is more to the purpose to indicate their differences after we have assured ourselves of a fundamental continuity or resemblance. What is salient in mechanical bodies is their general uniformity of response, the routine character of their behavior. What is salient in life is its capacity of fine adjustment to varying conditions, a capacity such as no merely material body possesses, not even any machine made as yet by human design. This capacity of variation in its response may seem even to amount in certain cases to an originality which has led some to credit life with genuine freedom from determination by previous conditions, with indetermination, such as is supposed to appear in human beings as free will—not in the ordinary sense in which we are undoubtedly free, as directing ourselves consciously to foreseen ends, but in the sense of making new departures without determining reasons. How, then, we may ask, if life is resoluble without remainder into mechanical, physical, and chemical elements, can a living body be other than the automaton which Descartes declared it to be? (Descartes, observe in passing, would, if I am right, have been justified, if he had only realized that an automaton of sufficient complexity would cease to be a mere automaton.) Now these questions are put because of confusing the determinate with the purely mechanical. All behavior, it is safe to assert, is determinate, and its fine capacity of variation and spontaneity are determined by its delicately complex organization. But not all determinate action is therefore mechanical. The mechanical is simple and its responses broadly constant; the vital is highly complex and its responses, though definite, may vary according to circumstances; and that is all. If one thing is appearing more clearly than another from recent science, it is that material action is not so much that from which vital action diverges, as a first approximation towards vital action. The idea of life tends in our day to be extended downwards towards more primitive kinds of existence. Not that material existence is to be regarded as a form of life, but that it exhibits features which correspond to life; so that the transition from matter to life is no longer the passage to something absolutely heterogeneous but the manifestation of a single principle operating under conditions of

---

[4] Compare on this subject chapter vi and vii of Mr. R. F. A. Hoernle's *Studies in Contemporary Metaphysics,* New York and London, 1920.

various complexity, and generating emergents with distinctive qualities, and yet retaining them all in one linked progression of affinity.

We are to combine in our thoughts this fundamental unity with the recognition of emergent qualities which can only be accepted but cannot be accounted for. One difficulty in the way of effecting this combination in our thought is the idea that if the world is a determinate growth, each new creation determined by its predecessors on a lower level, the history of the world must be capable of prediction, according to the famous assertion of Laplace. But this conclusion does not follow. Laplace's calculator might foresee that at a certain point a certain complexity might arise, whose actions were capable of measurement and would be those of living things. He could never affirm that this form of action would have the quality of life, unless he lived to see. He might predict ethereal waves but could not predict them to be light; still less that a material body would be material or when touched by light would be red, or even merely look red to a living body with eyes. All known forms of action could be predicted in their measurable characters, but never in their emergent ones. Not even God, if we suppose a God presiding over the birth of the world, in accordance with the conception of the crudest theism, could predict what these emergent qualities would be; he could only accept them like ourselves when the world he made had originated them.

I have chosen as illustrating the attitude of natural piety our acceptance of the emergence of these qualities. They remain forever a mysterious fact. But they are after all only a part of the mystery which encompasses us and which we have no right to ask to penetrate. They are themselves related to simpler conditions, which it is the object of science to discover. Some persons have even supposed, following the precedent of the early Greek philosophers, and in particular of the chief Pythagorean speaker in Plato's great dialogue, the *Timaeus,* that all these features in the world are but specifications of some ultimate stuff of which the world is made. If this were true, it might be repugnant to the feelings of some, but natural piety would accept it, as it accepts the law of gravitation, or the law of the progression in the forms of life according to evolution, whatever the law of evolution may turn out to be; or as it would accept, if we are compelled to think so, that the four-dimensional space-time in which we live is bent in the neighborhood of matter. All science attempts to connect the variegated phenomena of the world by expressing them in terms of measurable motions. It seems to take the color and richness from the world of secondary sensible qualities and express them in terms of primary qualities which in the end are terms of space and time. It does not, nor does it pretend to, remove the mystery of the secondary qualities, and in all its explanations it does but bring us in face of other mysteries which we must needs accept.

We are thus forever in presence of miracles; and as old Nathan said, the greatest of all miracles is that the genuine miracles should be so familiar. And here I interpolate a remark, not altogether irrelevant to my subject, upon the uses of great men. The emergence of qualities is the familiar miracle, but great men, and in particular great men of science, are forever enlarging our mysteries, simplifying them and extending their scope, as when they record the law of attraction, or the idea which lies at the basis of the notion of relativity. And thus with their fresher insight they keep for us our sense of piety to nature alive. Compared with other men they are like the springs of a river. Perhaps some of you may have shared with me the exquisite experience of seeing the springs of the Aberdeenshire Dee below the top of Brae Riach in the Grampians. There the clear water bubbles to the surface through mosses pink and yellow and green with all the varying shades of green; and as it gathers to the edge it falls in tiny trickles which unite with one another into rills, and these with like rills from other portions of the plateau, until in the end they combine to form the river which you see at the foot, already a considerable stream. The stream is discolored in its course by the soil through which it flows or the products of human labor, and is put to the service of man before it reaches the sea. And as its springs are fed by the sea into which it falls, whose vapors are drawn up and fall in rain so that a continuous life is maintained between the ocean and the fresh waters on the heights, so it is that the thoughts of great men keep up for general mankind our communion with the circumambient mystery.

The mystery of facts, whether these facts are the individual facts of experience or the larger universal facts which are scientific laws, or such facts, more comprehensive still, as may be discovered by a prudent and scientific philosophy, is the last word of knowledge. The reverent temper which accepts them is the mood of natural piety.

HENRI BERGSON

Henri Bergson was born in Paris on October 18, 1859, of Jewish parents. His mother was British and his father, an accomplished musician, was Polish. It was an auspicious year in which to begin the business of life, for it also saw the birth of John Dewey, Samuel Alexander, and Edmund Husserl and the publication of Darwin's *Origin of Species.* In 1878 Bergson entered the École Normale Supérieure and received his *agrégé de philosophie* in 1881 and *docteur ès lettres* in 1889. He taught from 1881 to 1898 in various *lycées* in and about Paris. Indeed, Bergson's education and the development of his academic career were steady and uneventful until the publication in 1889 of his thesis, *Essai sur les données immédiates de la conscience,* which brought him immediate recognition. There followed a series of brilliant academic and philosophical successes. In 1898 he was appointed a professor at the École Normale Supérieure and two years later he was awarded the Chair of Philosophy at the Collège de France. From 1896 to 1922 he published five books and numerous articles, each of which met with popular acclaim. By the turn of the century Bergson was already a figure of international eminence and there is no doubt that in the few years preceding the First World War he reigned unchallenged as the world's best known and most respected living philosopher. But when Europe and the world emerged from the prolonged distraction of the war, different concerns and distinctive ways of doing philosophy became fashionable and Bergson's fame rapidly faded. Much of his time was now devoted to the cultural mission of the League of Nations. In 1921 he was forced to resign his professorship at the Collège de France due to ill health. And though he received the Nobel Prize for literature in 1927 and published a final book in 1932, these and other events of his later life passed virtually unnoticed. In the last decade of his life Bergson turned increasingly toward Roman Catholicism, which he saw as the culmination of Judaism. However, he was never officially converted, choosing rather, as he put it, to remain with those who were to be persecuted. Nevertheless, when he died in 1941, a priest was called, prayers were said, and the sign of the cross was made over his head. He was a man of consummate artistry, courage, and philosophical dedication. His influence as a founding member of contemporary process philosophy cannot be overestimated.

MAJOR PHILOSOPHICAL WORKS BY BERGSON

1889   *Essai sur les données immédiates de la conscience.* Paris: Alcan.
        Authorized translation under the title *Time and Free Will* by F. L. Pogson. London: George Allen & Unwin, 1910.
1896   *Matiére et Mèmoire, essai sur la relation du corps á l'esprit.* Paris: Alcan.
        Authorized translation as *Matter and Memory by* N. M. Paul and W. S. Palmer. London: George Allen & Unwin, 1911.
1900   *Le Rire, essai sur la signification du comique.* Paris: Alcan.
        Authorized translation as *Laughter* by C. Brereton and F. Rothwell. New York: Macmillan, 1911.
1903   "Introduction à la Métaphysique." *Revue de métaphysique et de morale,* January.
        Authorized translation by T. E. Hulme as *An Introduction to Metaphysics.* New York: G. P. Putnam's Sons, 1912.
1907   L'*Évolution créatrice.* Paris: Alcan.
        Authorized translation under the title *Creative Evolution* by A. Mitchell. New York: Holt, 1911.
1919   *L'Énergie spirituelle.* Paris: Alcan.
        Translated by H. Wildon Carr as *Mind-Energy.* London: Macmillan, 1920.
        (Contains seven very important articles and lectures written from 1901 to 1913, the most significant of which are probably "Dreams" and "Intellectual Effort.")
1922   *Durée et Simultanéité.* Paris: Alcan.
1932   *Les Deux Sources de la morale et de la religion.* Paris: Alcan.
        Authorized translation as *The Two Sources of Morality and Religion* by R. Ashley Audra, Cloudesley Brereton, and W. Horsfall Carter. New York: Holt, 1935.
1934   *La Pensée et le Mouvant.* Paris: Alcan.
        Translated by Mabelle L. Andison as *The Creative Mind.* New York: Philosophical Library, 1946.

(Contains two lengthy and excellent introductions and seven other previously published articles and lectures, including "The Introduction to Metaphysics," "The Possible and the Real," and "Philosophical Intuition.")

RECOMMENDED WORKS ON BERGSON

Alexander, Ian W. *Bergson, Philosopher of Reflection.* London: Bowes & Bowes, 1957.

James, William. "Bergson and His Critique of Intellectualism," Lecture VI in *A Pluralistic Universe.* (Originally published in 1909.) Cambridge: Harvard University Press, 1977.

Papanicolaou, A. C. and Gunter, P. A. Y. (eds.). *Bergson and Modern Thought: Towards a Unified Science.* New York: Harwood Academic Publishers, 1987.

The Idea of Duration

Number may be defined in general as a collection of units, or, speaking more exactly, as the synthesis of the one and the many. Every number is one, since it is brought before the mind by a simple intuition and is given a name; but the unity which attaches to it is that of a sum, it covers a multiplicity of parts which can be considered separately. Without attempting for the present any thorough examination of these conceptions of unity and multiplicity, let us inquire whether the idea of number does not imply the representation of something else as well.

It is not enough to say that a number is a collection of units; we must add that these units are identical with one another, or at least that they are assumed to be identical when they are counted. No doubt we can count the sheep in a flock and say that there are fifty, although they are all different from one another and are easily recognized by the shepherd: but the reason is that we agree in that case to neglect their individual differences and to take into account only what they have in common. On the other hand, as soon as we fix our attention on the particular features of objects or individuals, we can of course make an enumeration of them, but not a total. We place ourselves at these two very different points of view when we count the soldiers in a battalion and when we call the roll. Hence we may conclude that the idea of number implies the simple intuition of a multiplicity of parts or units, which are absolutely alike.

And yet they must be somehow distinct from one another, since otherwise they would merge into a single unit. Let us assume that all the sheep in the flock are identical; they differ at least by the position which they occupy in space, otherwise they would not form a flock. But now let us even set aside the fifty sheep themselves and retain only the idea of them. Either we include them all in the same image, and it follows as a necessary consequence that we place them side by side in an ideal space, or else we repeat fifty times in succession the image of a single one, and in that case it does seem, indeed, that the series lies in duration rather than in space. But we shall soon find out that it cannot be so. For if we picture to ourselves each of the sheep in the flock in succession and separately, we shall never have to do with more than a single sheep. In order that the number should go on increasing in proportion as we advance, we must retain the successive images and set them alongside each of the new units which we picture to ourselves: now, it is in space that such a juxtaposition takes place and not in pure duration. In fact, it will be easily granted that counting material objects means thinking all these objects together, thereby leaving them in space. But does this intuition of space accompany every idea of number, even of an abstract number?

Anyone can answer this question by reviewing the various forms which the idea of number has assumed for him since his childhood. It will be seen that we began by imagining, e.g., a row of balls, that these balls afterwards became points, and, finally, this image itself disappeared, leaving behind it, as we say, nothing but *abstract* number. But at this very moment we ceased to have an image or even an idea of it; we kept only the symbol which is necessary for reckoning and which is the conventional way of *expressing* number. For we can confidently assert that 12 is half of 24 without thinking either the number 12 or the number 24: indeed, as far as quick calculation is concerned, we have everything to gain by not doing so. But as soon as we wish to picture *number* to ourselves, and not merely figures or words, we are compelled to have recourse to an extended image. What leads to misunderstanding on this point seems to be the habit we have fallen into of counting in time rather than in space. In order to imagine the number 50, for example, we repeat all the numbers starting from unity, and when we have arrived at the fiftieth, we believe we have built up the number in duration and in duration only. And there is no doubt that in this way we have counted moments of duration rather than points in space; but the question is whether we have not counted the moments of duration by means of points in space. It is certainly possible to perceive in time, and in time only, a succession which is nothing but a succession, but not an addition, i.e., a succession which culminates in a sum. For though we reach a sum by taking into account a succession of different terms, yet it is necessary that each of these terms should remain when we pass to the following, and should wait, so to speak, to be added to the others: how could it wait, if it were nothing but an instant of duration? We involuntarily fix at a point in space each of the moments which we count, and it is only on this condition that the abstract units come to form a sum. No doubt it is possible, as we shall show later, to conceive the successive moments of time independently of space; but when we add to the present moment those which have preceded it, as is the case when we are adding up units, we are not dealing with these moments themselves, since they have vanished forever, but with the lasting traces which they seem to have left in space on their passage through it. It is true that we generally dispense with this mental image, and that, after having used it for the first two or three numbers, it is enough to know that it would serve just as well for the mental picturing of the others, if we needed it. But every clear idea of number implies a visual image in space; and the direct study of the units which go to form a discrete multiplicity will lead us to the same conclusion on this point as the examination of number itself.

Every number is a collection of units, as we have said, and on the other hand every number is itself a unit, in so far as it is a synthesis of the units which compose it. But is the word unit taken in the same sense in both cases? When we assert that number is a *unit,* we understand by this that we master the whole of it by a simple and indivisible intuition of the mind; this unity thus includes a multiplicity, since it is the unity of a whole. But when we speak of the units which go to form number, we no longer think of these units as sums, but as pure, simple, irreducible units, intended to yield the natural series of numbers by an indefinitely continued process of accumulation. It seems, then, that there are two kinds of units, the one ultimate, out of which a number is formed by a process of addition, and the other provisional, the number so formed, which is multiple in itself, and owes its unity to the simplicity of the act by which the mind perceives it. And there is no doubt that, when we picture the units which make up number, we believe that we are thinking of indivisible components: this belief has a great deal to do with the idea that it is possible to conceive number independently of space. Nevertheless, by looking more closely into the matter, we shall see that all unity is the unity of a simple act of the mind, and that, as this is an act of unification, there must be some multiplicity for it to unify. No doubt, at the moment at which I think each of these units separately, I look upon it as indivisible, since I am determined to think of its unity alone. But as soon as I put it aside in order to pass to the next, I objectify it, and by that very deed I make it a thing, that is to say, a multiplicity. To convince oneself of this, it is enough to notice that the units by means of which arithmetic forms numbers are *provi-*

sional units, which can be subdivided without limit, and that each of them is the sum of fractional quantities as small and as numerous as we like to imagine. How could we divide the unit, if it were here that ultimate unity which characterizes a simple act of the mind? How could we split it up into fractions whilst affirming its unity, if we did not regard it implicitly as an extended object, one in intuition but multiple in space? You will never get out of an idea which you have formed anything which you have not put into it; and if the unity by means of which you make up your number is the unity of an act and not of an object, no effort of analysis will bring out of it anything but unity pure and simple. No doubt, when you equate the number 3 to the sum of 1 + 1 + 1, nothing prevents you from regarding the units which compose it as indivisible: but the reason is that you do not choose to make use of the multiplicity which is enclosed within each of these units. Indeed, it is probable that the number 3 first assumes to our mind this simpler shape, because we think rather of the way in which we have obtained it than of the use which we might make of it. But we soon perceive that, while all multiplication implies the possibility of treating any number whatever as a provisional unit which can be added to itself, inversely the units in their turn are true numbers which are as big as we like, but are regarded as provisionally indivisible for the purpose of compounding them with one another. Now, the very admission that it is possible to divide the unit into as many parts as we like, shows that we regard it as extended.

For we must understand what is meant by the *discontinuity* of number. It cannot be denied that the formation or construction of a number implies discontinuity. In other words, as we remarked above, each of the units with which we form the number 3 seems to be indivisible while we are dealing with it, and we pass abruptly from one to the other. Again, if we form the same number with halves, with quarters, with any units whatever, these units, in so far as they serve to form the said number, will still constitute elements which are provisionally indivisible, and it is always by jerks, by sudden jumps, so to speak, that we advance from one to the other. And the reason is that, in order to get a number, we are compelled to fix our attention successively on each of the units of which it is compounded. The indivisibility of the act by which we conceive any one of them is then represented under the form of a mathematical point which is separated from the following point by an interval of space. But, while a series of mathematical points arranged in empty space expresses fairly well the process by which we form the idea of number, these mathematical points have a tendency to develop into lines in proportion as our attention is diverted from them, as if they were trying to reunite with one another. And when we look at number in its finished state, this union is an accomplished fact: the points have become lines, the divisions have been blotted out, the whole displays all the characteristics of continuity. This is why number, although we have formed it according to a definite law, can be split up on any system we please. In a word, we must distinguish between the unity which we think of and the unity which we set up as an object after having thought of it, as also between number in process of formation and number once formed. The unit is irreducible while we are thinking it and number is discontinuous while we are building it up. But as soon as we consider number in its finished state, we objectify it, and it then appears to be divisible to an unlimited extent. In fact, we apply the term *subjective* to what seems to be completely and adequately known, and the term *objective* to what is known in such a way that a constantly increasing number of new impressions could be substituted for the idea which we actually have of it. Thus a complex feeling will contain a fairly large number of simple elements; but, as long as these elements do not stand out with perfect clearness, we cannot say that they were completely realized, and, as soon as consciousness has a distinct perception of them, the psychic state which results from their synthesis will have changed for this very reason. But there is no change in the general appearance of a body, however it is analyzed by thought, because these different analyses, and an infinity of others, are already visible in the mental image which we form of the body, though they are not realized: this actual and not merely virtual perception of subdivisions in what is undivided is just what we call objectivity. It then becomes easy to determine the exact part played by the subjective and the objective in the idea of number. What properly belongs to the mind is the indivisible process by which it concentrates attention successively on the different parts of a given space; but the parts which have thus been isolated remain in order to join with the others, and, once the addition is made, they may be broken up in any way whatever. They are therefore parts of space, and space is, accordingly, the material with which the mind builds up number, the medium in which the mind places it.

Properly speaking, it is arithmetic which teaches us to split up without limit the units of which number consists. Common sense is very much inclined to build up number with indivisibles. And this is easily understood, since the provisional simplicity of the component units is just what they owe to the mind, and the latter pays more attention to its own acts than to the material on which it works. Science confines itself, here, to drawing our attention to this material: if we did not already localize number in space, science would certainly not succeed in making us transfer it thither. From the beginning, therefore, we must have thought of number as of a juxtaposition in space. This is the conclusion which we reached at first, basing ourselves on the fact that all addition implies a multiplicity of parts simultaneously perceived.

Now, if this conception of number is granted, it will be seen that everything is not counted in the same way, and that there are two very different kinds of multiplicity. When we speak of material objects, we refer to the possibility of seeing and touching them; we localize them in space. In that case, no effort of the inventive faculty or of symbolical representation is necessary in order to count them; we have only to think them; at first separately, and then simultaneously, within the very medium in which they come under our observation. The case is no longer the same when we consider purely affective psychic states, or even mental images other than those built up by means of sight and touch. Here, the terms being no longer given in space, it seems, *a priori,* that we can hardly count them except by some process of symbolical representation. In fact, we are well aware of a representation of this kind when we are dealing with sensations the cause of which is obviously situated in space. Thus, when we hear a noise of steps in the street, we have a confused vision of somebody walking along: each of the successive sounds is then localized at a point in space where the passer-by might tread: we count our sensations in the very space in which their tangible causes are ranged. Perhaps some people count the successive strokes of a distant bell in a similar way, their imagination pictures the bell coming and going; this spatial sort of image is sufficient for the first two units, and the others follow naturally. But most people's minds do not proceed in this way. They range the successive sounds in an ideal space and then fancy that they are counting them in pure duration. Yet we must be clear on this point. The sounds of the bell certainly reach me one after the other; but one of two alternatives must be true. Either I retain each of these successive sensations in order to combine it with the others and form a group which reminds me of

an air or rhythm which I know: in that case I do not *count* the sounds,
I limit myself to gathering, so to speak, the qualitative impression produced by the whole series. Or else I intend explicitly to count them,
and then I shall have to separate them, and this separation must take
place within some homogeneous medium in which the sounds, stripped
of their qualities, and in a manner emptied, leave traces of their presence which are absolutely alike. The question now is, whether this
medium is time or space. But a moment of time, we repeat, cannot
persist in order to be added to others. If the sounds are separated, they
must leave empty intervals between them. If we count them, the intervals must remain though the sounds disappear: how could these intervals remain, if they were pure duration and not space? It is in space,
therefore, that the operation takes place. It becomes, indeed, more and
more difficult as we penetrate further into the depths of consciousness.
Here we find ourselves confronted by a confused multiplicity of sensations and feelings which analysis alone can distinguish. Their number
is identical with the number of the moments which we take up when
we count them; but these moments, as they can be added to one another, are again points in space. Our final conclusion, therefore, is that
there are two kinds of multiplicity: that of material objects, to which
the conception of number is immediately applicable; and the multiplicity of states of consciousness, which cannot be regarded as numerical
without the help of some symbolical representation, in which a necessary element is *space.*

As a matter of fact, each of us makes a distinction between these
two kinds of multiplicity whenever he speaks of the impenetrability of
matter. We sometimes set up impenetrability as a fundamental property
of bodies, known in the same way and put on the same level as, e.g.,
weight or resistance. But a purely negative property of this kind cannot
be revealed by our senses; indeed, certain experiments in mixing and
combining things might lead us to call it in question if our minds were
not already made up on this point. Try to picture one body penetrating
another: you will at once assume that there are empty spaces in the one
which will be occupied by the particles of the other; these particles in
their turn cannot penetrate one another unless one of them divides in
order to fill up the interstices of the other; and our thought will prolong
this operation indefinitely in preference to picturing two bodies in the
same place. Now, if impenetrability were really a quality of matter
which was known by the senses, it is not at all clear why we should

experience more difficulty in conceiving two bodies merging into one another than a surface devoid of resistance or a weightless fluid. In reality, it is not a physical but a logical necessity which attaches to the proposition: "Two bodies cannot occupy the same place at the same time." The contrary assertion involves an absurdity which no conceivable experience could succeed in dispelling. In a word, it implies a contradiction. But does not this amount to recognizing that the very idea of the number 2, or, more generally, of any number whatever, involves the idea of juxtaposition in space? If impenetrability is generally regarded as a quality of matter, the reason is that the idea of number is thought to be independent of the idea of space. We thus believe that we are adding something to the idea of two or more objects by saying that they cannot occupy the same place: as if the idea of the number 2, even the abstract number, were not already, as we have shown, that of two different positions in space! Hence to assert the impenetrability of matter is simply to recognize the interconnection between the notions of number and space, it is to state a property of number rather than of matter.—Yet, it will be said, do we not count feelings, sensations, ideas, all of which permeate one another, and each of which, for its part, takes up the whole of the soul?—Yes, undoubtedly; but, just because they permeate one another, we cannot count them unless we represent them by homogeneous units which occupy separate positions in space and consequently no longer permeate one another. Impenetrability thus makes its appearance at the same time as number; and when we attribute this quality to matter in order to distinguish it from everything which is not matter, we simply state under another form the distinction established above between extended objects, to which the conception of number is immediately applicable, and states of consciousness, which have first of all to be represented symbolically in space.

It is advisable to dwell on the last point. If, in order to count states of consciousness, we have to represent them symbolically in space, is it not likely that this symbolical representation will alter the normal conditions of inner perception? Let us recall what we said a short time ago about the intensity of certain psychic states. Representative sensation, looked at in itself, is pure quality; but, seen through the medium of extensity, this quality becomes in a certain sense quantity, and is called intensity. In the same way, our projection of our psychic states into space in order to form a discrete multiplicity is likely to influence these states themselves and to give them in reflective consciousness a new form, which immediate perception did not attribute to them. Now, let us notice that when we speak of *time,* we generally think of a homogeneous medium in which our conscious states are ranged alongside one another as in space, so as to form a discrete multiplicity. Would not time, thus understood, be to the multiplicity of our psychic states what intensity is to certain of them—a sign, a symbol, absolutely distinct from true duration? Let us ask consciousness to isolate itself from the external world, and, by a vigorous effort of abstraction, to become itself again. We shall then put this question to it: does the multiplicity of our conscious states bear the slightest resemblance to the multiplicity of the units of a number? Has true duration anything to do with space? Certainly, our analysis of the idea of number could not but make us doubt this analogy, to say no more. For if time, as the reflective consciousness represents it, is a medium in which our conscious states form a discrete series so as to admit of being counted, and if on the other hand our conception of number ends in spreading out in space everything which can be directly counted, it is to be presumed that time, understood in the sense of a medium in which we make distinctions and count, is nothing but space. That which goes to confirm this opinion is that we are compelled to borrow from space the images by which we describe what the reflective consciousness feels about time and even about succession; it follows that pure duration must be something different. Such are the questions which we have been led to ask by the very analysis of the notion of discrete multiplicity. But we cannot throw any light upon them except by a direct study of the ideas of space and time in their mutual relations.

We shall not lay too much stress on the questions of the absolute reality of space: perhaps we might as well ask whether space is or is not in space. In short, our senses perceive the qualities of bodies and space along with them: the great difficulty seems to have been to discover whether extensity is an aspect of these physical qualities—a quality of quality—or whether these qualities are essentially unextended, space coming in as a later addition, but being self-sufficient and existing without them. On the first hypothesis, space would be reduced to an abstraction, or, speaking more correctly, an extract; it would express the common element possessed by certain sensations called representative. In the second case, space would be a reality as solid as the sensations themselves, although of a different order. We owe the exact formulation of this latter conception to Kant: the theory which he works out in the "Transcendental Aesthetic" consists in endowing space with an existence independent of its content, in laying down as *de jure* separable what each of us separates *de facto,* and in refusing to regard extensity as an abstraction like the others. In this respect the Kantian conception of space differs less than is usually imagined from the popular belief. Far from shaking our faith in the reality of space, Kant has shown what it actually means and has even justified it.

Moreover, the solution given by Kant does not seem to have been seriously disputed since his time: indeed, it has forced itself, sometimes without their knowledge, on the majority of those who have approached the problem anew, whether nativists or empiricists. Psychologists agree in assigning a Kantian origin to the nativistic explanation of Johann Müller; but Lotze's hypothesis of local signs, Bain's theory, and the more comprehensive explanation suggested by Wundt, may seem at first sight quite independent of the Transcendental Aesthetic. The authors of these theories seem indeed to have put aside the problem of the nature of space, in order to investigate simply by what process our sensations come to be situated in space and to be set, so to speak, alongside one another: but this very question shows that they regard sensations as inextensive and make a radical distinction, just as Kant did, between the matter of representation and its form. The conclusion to be drawn from the theories of Lotze and Bain, and from Wundt's attempt to reconcile them, is that the sensations by means of which we come to form the notion of space are themselves unextended and simply qualitative: extensity is supposed to result from their synthesis, as water from the combination of two gases. The empirical or genetic explanations have thus taken up the problem of space at the very point where Kant left it: Kant separated space from its contents: the empiricists ask how these contents, which are taken out of space by our thought, manage to get back again. It is true that they have apparently disregarded the activity of the mind, and that they are obviously inclined to regard the extensive form under which we represent things as produced by a kind of alliance of the sensations with one another: space, without being extracted from the sensations, is supposed to result from their co-existence. But how can we explain such an origination without the active intervention of the mind? The extensive differs by hypothesis from the inextensive: and even if we assume that extension is nothing but a relation between inextensive terms, this relation must still be established by a mind capable of thus associating several terms. It is no use quoting the example of chemical combinations, in which the whole seems to assume, of its own accord a form and qualities which did not belong to any of the elementary atoms. This form and these qualities owe their origin just to the fact that we gather up the multiplicity of atoms in a single perception: get rid of the mind which carries out this synthesis and you will at once do away with the qualities, that is to say, the aspect under which the synthesis of elementary parts is presented to our consciousness. Thus inextensive sensations will remain what they are, viz., inextensive sensations, if nothing be added to them. For their co-existence to give rise to space, there must be an act of the mind which takes them in all at the same time and sets them in juxtaposition: this unique act is very like what Kant calls an *a priori* form of sensibility.

If we now seek to characterize this act, we see that it consists essentially in the intuition, or rather the conception, of an empty homogeneous medium. For it is scarcely possible to give any other definition of space: space is what enables us to distinguish a number of identical and simultaneous sensations from one another; it is thus a principle of differentiation other than that of qualitative differentiation, and consequently it is a reality with no quality. Someone may say, with the believers in the theory of local signs, that simultaneous sensations are never identical, and that, in consequence of the diversity of the organic elements which they affect, there are no two points of a homogeneous surface which make the same impression on the sight or the touch. We are quite ready to grant it, for if these two points affected us in the same way, there would be no reason for placing one of them on the right rather than on the left. But, just because we afterwards interpret this difference of quality in the sense of a difference of situation, it follows that we must have a clear idea of a homogeneous medium, i.e., of a simultaneity of terms which, although identical in quality, are yet distinct from one another. The more you insist on the difference between the impressions made on our retina by two points of a homogeneous surface, the more do you thereby make room for the activity of the mind, which perceives under the form of extensive homogeneity what is given it as qualitative heterogeneity. No doubt, though the representation of a homogeneous space grows out of an effort of the mind, there must be within the qualities themselves which differentiate two sensations some reason why they occupy this or that definite position in space. We must thus distinguish between the perception of extensity and the conception of space: they are no doubt implied in one another, but the higher we rise in the scale of intelligent beings, the more clearly do we meet with the independent idea of a homogeneous space. It is therefore doubtful whether animals perceive the external world quite as we do, and especially whether they represent externality in the same way as ourselves. Naturalists have pointed out, as a remarkable fact, the surprising ease with which many vertebrates, and even some insects, manage to find their way through space. Animals have been seen to return almost in a straight line to their old home, pursuing a path which was hitherto unknown to them over a distance which may amount to several hundreds of miles. Attempts have been made to explain this feeling of direction by sight or smell, and, more recently, by the perception of magnetic currents which would enable the animal to take its bearings like a living compass. This amounts to saying that space is not so homogeneous for the animal as for us, and that determinations of space, or directions, do not assume for it a purely geometrical form. Each of these directions might appear to it with its own shade, its peculiar quality. We shall understand how a perception of this kind is possible if we remember that we ourselves distinguish our right from our left by a natural feeling, and that these two parts to our own extensity do then appear to us as if they bore a different *quality*; in fact, this is the very reason why we cannot give a proper definition of right and left. In truth, qualitative differences exist everywhere in nature, and I do not see why two concrete directions should not be marked in immediate perception as two colors. But the conception of an empty homogeneous medium is something far more extraordinary, being a kind of reaction against that heterogeneity which is the very ground of our experience. Therefore, instead of saying that animals have a special sense of direction, we may as well say that men have a special faculty of perceiving or conceiving a space without quality. This faculty is not the faculty of abstraction: indeed, if we notice that abstraction assumes clean-cut distinctions and a kind of externality of the concepts or their symbols with regard to one another, we shall find that the faculty of abstraction already implies the intuition of a homogeneous medium. What we must say is that we have to do with two different kinds of reality, the one heterogeneous, that of sensible qualities, the other homogeneous, namely space. This latter, clearly conceived by the human intellect, enables us to use clean-cut distinctions, to count, to abstract, and perhaps also to speak.

Now, if space is to be defined as the homogeneous, it seems that inversely every homogeneous and unbounded medium will be space. For, homogeneity here consisting in the absence of every quality, it is hard to see how two forms of the homogeneous could be distinguished from one another. Nevertheless it is generally agreed to regard time as an unbounded medium, different from space but homogeneous like the latter: the homogeneous is thus supposed to take two forms, according as its contents co-exist or follow one another. It is true that, when we make time a homogeneous medium in which conscious states unfold themselves, we take it to be given all at once, which amounts to saying that we abstract it from duration. This simple consideration ought to warn us that we are thus unwittingly falling back upon space, and really, giving up time. Moreover, we can understand that material objects, being exterior to one another and to themselves, derive both exteriorities from the homogeneity of a medium which inserts intervals between them and sets off their outlines: but states of consciousness, even when successive, permeate one another, and in the simplest of them the whole soul can be reflected. We may therefore surmise that time, conceived under the form of a homogeneous medium, is some spurious concept, due to the trespassing of the idea of space upon the field of pure consciousness. At any rate we cannot finally admit two forms of the homogeneous, time and space, without first seeking whether one of them cannot be reduced to the other. Now, externality is the distinguishing mark of things which occupy space, while states of consciousness are not essentially external to one another, and become so only by being spread out in time, regarded as a homogeneous medium. If, then, one of these two supposed forms of the homogeneous, namely time and space, is derived from the other, we can surmise *a priori* that the idea of space is the fundamental datum. But, misled by the apparent simplicity of the idea of time, the philosophers who have tried to reduce one of these ideas to the other have thought that they could make extensity out of duration. While showing how they have been misled, we shall see that time, conceived under the form of an unbounded and homogeneous medium, is nothing but the ghost of space haunting the reflective consciousness.

The English school tries, in fact, to reduce relations of extensity to more or less complex relations of succession in time. When, with our eyes shut, we run our hands along a surface, the rubbing of our fingers against the surface, and especially the varied play of our joints, provide a series of sensations, which differ only by their *qualities* and which exhibit a certain order in time. Moreover, experience teaches us that this series can be reversed, that we can, by an effort of a different kind (or, as we shall call it later, *in an opposite direction),* obtain the same sensations over again in an inverse order: relations of position in space might then be defined as reversible relations of succession in time. There are, indeed, as we shall show a little later, two possible conceptions of time, the one free from all alloy, the other surreptitiously bringing in the idea of space. Pure duration is the form which the succession of our conscious states assumes when our ego lets itself *live,* when it refrains from separating its present state from its former states. For this purpose it need not be entirely absorbed in the passing sensation or idea; for then, on the contrary, it would no longer *endure.* Nor need it forget its former states: it is enough that in recalling these states, it does not set them alongside its actual state as one point alongside another, but forms both the past and the present states into an organic whole, as happens when we recall the notes of a tune, melting, so to speak, into one another. Might it not be said that, even if these notes succeed one another, yet we perceive them in one another, and that their totality may be compared to a living being whose parts, although distinct, permeate one another just because they are so closely connected? The proof is that, if we interrupt the rhythm by dwelling longer than is right on one note of the tune, it is not its exaggerated length, as length, which will warn of our mistake, but the qualitative change thereby caused in the whole of the musical phrase. We can thus conceive of succession without distinction, and think of it as a mutual penetration, an interconnection and organization of elements, each one of which represents the whole, and cannot be distinguished or isolated from it except by abstract thought. Such is the account of duration which would be given by a being who was ever the same and ever changing, and who had no idea of space. But, familiar with the latter idea and indeed beset by it, we introduce it unwittingly into our feeling of pure succession; we set our states of consciousness side by side in such a way as to perceive them simultaneously, no longer in one another, but alongside one another; in a word, we project time into space, we express duration in terms of extensity, and succession thus takes the form of a continuous line or a chain, the parts of which touch without penetrating one another. Note that the mental image thus shaped implies the perception, no longer successive, but simultaneous, of a *before* and *after,* and that it would be a contradiction to suppose a succession which was only a succession, and which nevertheless was contained in one and the same instant. Now, when we speak of an *order* of succession in duration, and of the reversibility of this order, is the succession we are dealing with pure succession, such as we have just defined it, without any admixture of extensity, or is it succession developing in space, in such a way that we can take in at once a number of elements which are both distinct and set side by side? There is no doubt about the answer: we could not introduce *order* among terms without first distinguishing them and then comparing the places which they occupy; hence we must perceive them as multiple, simultaneous and distinct; in a word, we set them side by side, and if we introduce an order in what is successive, the reason is that succession is converted into simultaneity and is projected into space. In short, when the movement of my finger along a surface or a line provides me with a series of sensations of different qualities, one of two things happens: either I picture these sensations to myself as in duration only, and in that case they succeed one another in such a way that I cannot at a given moment perceive a number of them as simultaneous and yet distinct; or else I make out an order of succession, but in that case I display the faculty not only of perceiving a succession of elements, but also of setting them out in line after having distinguished them: in a word, I already possess the idea of space. Hence the idea of a reversible series in duration, or even simply of a certain *order* of succession in time, itself implies the representation of space, and cannot be used to define it.

To give this argument a stricter form, let us imagine a straight line of unlimited length, and on this line a material point A, which moves, If this point were conscious of itself, it would feel itself change, since it moves: it would perceive a succession; but would this succession assume for it the form of a line? No doubt it would, if it could rise, so to speak, above the line which it traverses, and perceive simultaneously several points of it in juxtaposition: but by doing so it would form the idea of space, and it is in space and not in pure duration that it would see displayed the changes which it undergoes. We here put our finger on the mistake of those who regard pure duration as something similar to space, but of a simpler nature. They are fond of setting psychic states side by side, of forming a chain or a line of them, and do not imagine that they are introducing into this operation the idea of space properly so called, the idea of space in its totality, because space is a medium of three dimensions. But how can they fail to notice that, in order to perceive a line as a line, it is necessary to take up a position outside it, to take account of the void which surrounds it, and consequently to think a space of three dimensions? If our conscious point A does not yet possess the idea of space—and this is the hypothesis which we have agreed to adopt—the succession of states through which it passes cannot assume for it the form of a line; but its sensations will add themselves dynamically to one another and will organize themselves, like the successive notes of a tune by which we allow ourselves to be lulled and soothed. In a word, pure duration might well be nothing but a succession of qualitative changes, which melt into and permeate one another, without precise outlines, without any tendency to externalize themselves in relation to one another, without any affiliation with number: it would be pure heterogeneity. But for the present we shall not insist upon this point; it is enough for us to have shown that, from the moment when you attribute the least homogeneity to duration, you surreptitiously introduce space.

It is true that we count successive moments of duration, and that, because of its relations with number, time at first seems to us to be a measurable magnitude, just like space. But there is here an important distinction to be made. I say, e.g., that a minute has just elapsed, and I mean by this that a pendulum, beating the seconds, has completed sixty oscillations. If I picture these sixty oscillations to myself all at once by a single mental perception, I exclude by hypothesis the idea of a succession. I do not think of sixty strokes which succeed one another, but of sixty points on a fixed line, each one of which symbolizes, so to speak, an oscillation of the pendulum. If, on the other hand, I wish to picture these sixty oscillations in succession, but without altering the way they are produced in space, I shall be compelled to think of each oscillation to the exclusion of the recollection of the preceding one, for space has preserved no trace of it; but by doing so I shall condemn myself to remain forever in the present; I shall give up the attempt to think a succession or a duration. Now if, finally, I retain the recollection of the preceding oscillation together with the image of the present oscillation, one of two things will happen. Either I shall set the two images side by side, and we then fall back on our first hypothesis, or I shall perceive one in the other, each permeating the other and organizing themselves like the notes of a tune, so as to form what we shall call a continuous or qualitative multiplicity with no resemblance to number. I shall thus get the image of pure duration; but I shall have entirely got rid of the idea of a homogeneous medium or a measurable quantity. By carefully examining our consciousness we shall recognize that it proceeds in this way whenever it refrains from representing duration symbolically. When the regular oscillations of the pendulum make us sleepy, is it the last sound heard, the last movement perceived, which produces this effect? No, undoubtedly not, for why then should not the first have done the same? Is it the recollection of the preceding sounds or movements, set in juxtaposition to the last one? But this same recollection, if it is later on set in juxtaposition to a single sound or movement, will remain without effect. Hence we must admit that the sounds combined with one another and acted, not by their quantity as quantity, but by the quality which their quantity exhibited, i.e., by the rhythmic organization of the whole. Could the effect of a slight but continuous stimulation be understood in any other way? If the sensation remained always the same, it would continue to be indefinitely slight and indefinitely bearable. But the fact is that each increase of stimulation is taken up into the preceding stimulations, and that the whole produces on us the effect of a musical phrase which is constantly on the point of ending and constantly altered in its totality by the addition of some new note. If we assert that it is always the *same* sensation, the reason is that we are thinking, not of the sensation itself, but of its objective cause situated in space. We then set it out in space in its turn, and in place of an organism which develops, in place of changes which permeate one another, we perceive one and the same sensation stretching itself out lengthwise, so to speak, and setting itself in juxtaposition to itself without limit. Pure duration, that which consciousness perceives, must thus be reckoned among the so-called intensive magnitudes, if intensities can be called magnitudes: strictly speaking, however, it is not a quantity, and as soon as we try to measure it, we unwittingly replace it by space.

But we find it extraordinarily difficult to think of duration in its original purity; this is due, no doubt, to the fact that we do not *endure* alone; external objects, it seems, *endure* as we do, and time, regarded from this point of view, has every appearance of a homogeneous medium. Not only do the moments of this duration seem to be external to one another, like bodies in space, but the movement perceived by our senses is the, so to speak, palpable sign of a homogeneous and measurable duration. Nay more, time enters into the formulae of mechanics, into the calculations of the astronomer, and even of the physicist, under the form of a quantity. We measure the velocity of a movement, implying that time itself is a magnitude. Indeed, the analysis which we have just attempted requires to be completed, for if duration properly so-called cannot be measured, what is it that is measured by the oscillation of the pendulum? Granted that inner duration, perceived by consciousness, is nothing else but the melting of states of consciousness into one another, and the gradual growth of the ego, it will be said, notwithstanding, that the time which the astronomer introduces into his formulae, the time which our clocks divide into equal portions, this time, at least, is something different: it must be a measurable and therefore homogeneous magnitude.—It is nothing of the sort, however, and a close examination will dispel this last illusion.

When I follow with my eyes on the dial of a clock the movement of the hand which corresponds to the oscillation of the pendulum, I do not measure duration, as seems to be thought; I merely count simultaneities, which is very different. Outside of me, in space, there is never more than a single position of the hand and the pendulum, for nothing is left of the past positions. Within myself a process of organization or interpenetration of conscious states is going on, which constitutes true duration. It is because I *endure in* this way that I picture to myself what I call the past oscillations of the pendulum at the same time as I perceive the present oscillation. Now, let us withdraw for a moment the ego which thinks these so-called successive oscillations: there will never be more than a single oscillation, and indeed only a single position, of the pendulum, and hence no duration. Withdraw, on the other hand, the pendulum and its oscillations; there will no longer be anything but the heterogeneous duration of the ego, without moments external to one another, without relation to number. Thus, within our ego, there is succession without mutual externality; outside the ego, in pure space, mutual externality without succession: mutual externality, since the present oscillation is radically distinct from the previous oscillation, which no longer exists; but no succession, since succession exists solely for a conscious spectator who keeps the past in mind and sets the two oscillations or their symbols side by side in an auxiliary space. Now, between this succession without externality and this externality without succession, a kind of exchange takes place, very similar to what physicists call the phenomenon of endosmosis. As the successive phases of our conscious life, although interpenetrating, correspond individually to an oscillation of the pendulum which occurs at the same time, and as, moreover, these oscillations are sharply distinguished from one another, we get into the habit of setting up the same distinction between the successive moments of our conscious life: the oscillations of the pendulum break it up, so to speak, into parts external to one another: hence the mistaken idea of a homogeneous inner duration, similar to space, the moments of which are identical and follow, without penetrating, one another. But, on the other hand, the oscillations of the pendulum, which are distinct only because one has disappeared when the other appears on the scene, profit, as it were, from the influence which they have thus exercised over our conscious life. Owing to the fact that our consciousness has organized them as a whole in memory, they are first preserved and afterwards disposed in a series: in a word, we create for them a fourth dimension of space, which we call homogeneous time, and which enables the movement of the pendulum, although taking place at one spot, to be continually set in juxtaposition to itself. Now, if we try to determine the exact part played by the real and the imaginary in this very complex process, this is what we find. There is a real space, without duration, in which phenomena appear and disappear simultaneously with our states of consciousness. There is a real duration, the heterogeneous moments of which permeate one another; each moment, however, can be brought into relation with a state of the external world which is contemporaneous with it, and can be separated from the other moments in consequence of this very process. The comparison of these two realities gives rise to a symbolical representation of duration, derived from space. Duration thus assumes the illusory form of a homogeneous medium, and the connecting link between these two terms, space and duration, is simultaneity, which might be defined as the intersection of time and space.

If we analyze in the same way the concept of motion, the living symbol of this seemingly homogeneous duration, we shall be led to make a distinction of the same kind. We generally say that a movement takes place *in* space, and when we assert that motion is homogeneous and divisible, it is of the space traversed that we are thinking, as if it were interchangeable with the motion itself. Now, if we reflect further, we shall see that the successive positions of the moving body really do occupy space, but that the process by which it passes from one position to the other, a process which occupies duration and which has no reality except for a conscious spectator, eludes space. We have to do here not with an *object* but with a *progress:* motion, in so far as it is a passage from one point to another, is a mental synthesis, a psychic and therefore unextended process. Space contains only parts of space, and at whatever point of space we consider the moving body, we shall get only a position. If consciousness is aware of anything more than positions, the reason is that it keeps the successive positions in mind and synthesizes them. But how does it carry out a synthesis of this kind? It cannot be by a fresh setting out of these same positions in a homogeneous medium, for a fresh synthesis would be necessary to connect the positions with one another, and so on indefinitely. We are thus compelled to admit that we have here to do with a synthesis which is, so to speak, qualitative, a gradual organization of our successive sensations, a unity resembling that of a phrase in a melody. This is just the idea of motion which we form when we think of it by itself, when, so to speak, from motion we extract mobility. Think of what you experience on suddenly perceiving a shooting star: in this extremely rapid motion there is a natural and instinctive separation between the space traversed, which appears to you under the form of a line of fire, and the absolutely indivisible sensation of motion or mobility. A rapid gesture, made with one's eyes shut, will assume for consciousness the form of a purely qualitative sensation as long as there is no thought of the space traversed. In a word, there are two elements to be distinguished in motion, the space traversed and the act by which we traverse it, the successive positions and the synthesis of these positions. The first of these elements is a homogeneous quantity: the second has no reality except in a consciousness: it is a quality or an intensity, whichever you prefer. But here again we meet with a case of endosmosis, an intermingling of the purely intensive sensation of mobility with the extensive representation of the space traversed. On the one hand we attribute to the motion the divisibility of the space which it traverses, forgetting that it is quite possible to divide an *object* but not an *act:* and on the other hand we accustom ourselves to projecting this act itself into space, to applying it to the whole of the line which the moving body traverses, in a word, to solidifying it: as if this localizing of a *progress* in space did not amount to asserting that even outside consciousness, the past coexists along with the present!

It is to this confusion between motion and the space traversed that
the paradoxes of the Eleatics are due; for the interval which separates
two points is infinitely divisible, and if motion consisted of parts like
those of the interval itself, the interval would never be crossed. But the
truth is that each of Achilles' steps is a simple indivisible act, and that,
after a given number of these acts, Achilles will have passed the tortoise. The mistake of the Eleatics arises from their identification of this
series of acts, each of which is of *a definite kind* and *indivisible,* with
the homogeneous space which underlies them. As this space can be
divided and put together again according to any law whatever, they
think they are justified in reconstructing Achilles' whole movement,
not with Achilles' kind of step, but with the tortoise's kind: in place of
Achilles pursuing the tortoise they really put two tortoises, regulated
by each other, two tortoises which agree to make the same kind of
steps or simultaneous acts, so as never to catch one another. Why does
Achilles outstrip the tortoise? Because each of Achilles' steps and each
of the tortoise's steps are indivisible acts in so far as they are movements, and are different magnitudes in so far as they are space: so that
additions will soon give a greater length for the space traversed by
Achilles than is obtained by adding together the space traversed by the
tortoise and the handicap with which it started. This is what Zeno
leaves out of account when he reconstructs the movement of Achilles
according to the same law as the movement of the tortoise, forgetting
that space alone can be divided and put together again in any way we
like, and thus confusing space with motion. Hence we do not think it
necessary to admit, even after the acute and profound analysis of a
contemporary thinker, that the meeting of the two moving bodies implies a discrepancy between real and imaginary motion, between *space
in itself* and indefinitely divisible space, between concrete time and
abstract time. Why resort to a metaphysical hypothesis, however ingenious, about the nature of space, time, and motion, when immediate
intuition shows us motion within duration, and duration outside space?
There is no need to assume a limit to the divisibility of concrete space;
we can admit that it is infinitely divisible, provided that we make a
distinction between the simultaneous positions of the two moving bodies, which are in fact in space, and their movements, which cannot
occupy space, being duration rather than extent, quality and not quantity. To measure the velocity of a movement, as we shall see, is simply
to ascertain a simultaneity; to introduce this velocity into calculations

is simply to use a convenient means of anticipating a simultaneity. Thus mathematics confines itself to its own province as long as it is occupied with determining the simultaneous positions of Achilles and the tortoise at a given moment, or when it admits *a priori* that the two moving bodies meet at a point X—a meeting which is itself a simultaneity. But it goes beyond its province when it claims to reconstruct what takes place in the interval between two simultaneities; or rather it is inevitably led, even then, to consider simultaneities once more, fresh simultaneities, the indefinitely increasing number of which ought to be a warning that we cannot make movement out of immobilities, nor time out of space. In short, just as nothing will be found homogeneous in duration except a symbolical medium with no duration at all, namely space, in which simultaneities are set out in line, in the same way no homogeneous element will be found in motion except that which least belongs to it, the traversed space, which is motionless.

Now, just for this reason, science cannot deal with time and motion except on condition of first eliminating the essential and qualitative element—of time, duration, and of motion, mobility. We may easily convince ourselves of this by examining the part played in astronomy and mechanics by considerations of time, motion, and velocity.

Treatises on mechanics are careful to announce that they do not intend to define duration itself but only the equality of two durations. "Two intervals of time are equal when two identical bodies, in identical conditions at the beginning of each of these intervals and subject to the same actions and influences of every kind, have traversed the same space at the end of these intervals." In other words, we are to note the exact moment at which the motion begins, i.e., the coincidence of an external change with one of our psychic states; we are to note the moment at which the motion ends, that is to say, another simultaneity; finally we are to measure the space traversed, the only thing, in fact, which is really measurable. Hence there is no question here of duration, but only of space and simultaneities. To announce that something will take place at the end of a time t is to declare that consciousness will note between now and then a number t of simultaneities of a certain kind. And we must not be led astray by the words "between now and then," for the interval of duration exists only for us and on account of the interpenetration of our conscious states. Outside ourselves we should find only space, and consequently nothing but simultaneities, of which we could not even say that they are objectively successive, since succession can only be thought through *comparing* the present with the past.—That the interval of duration itself cannot be taken into account by science is proved by the fact that, if all the motions of the universe took place twice or thrice as quickly, there would be nothing to alter either in our formulae or in the figures which are to be found in them. Consciousness would have an indefinable and as it were qualitative impression of the change, but the change would not make itself felt outside consciousness, since the same number of simultaneities would go on taking place in space. We shall see, later on, that when the astronomer predicts, e.g., an eclipse, he does something of this kind: he shortens infinitely the intervals of duration, as these do not count for science, and thus perceives in a very short time—a few seconds at the most—a succession of simultaneities which may take up several centuries for the concrete consciousness, compelled to live through the intervals instead of merely counting their extremities.

A direct analysis of the notion of velocity will bring us to the same conclusion. Mechanics gets this notion through a series of ideas, the connection of which it is easy enough to trace. It first builds up the idea of uniform motion by picturing, on the one hand, the path AB of a certain moving body, and, on the other, a physical phenomenon which is repeated indefinitely under the same conditions, e.g., a stone always falling from the same height on to the same spot. If we mark on the path AB the points M, N, P . . . reached by the moving body at each of the moments when the stone touches the ground, and if the intervals AM, MN and NP are found to be equal to one another, the motion will be said to be uniform: and any one of these intervals will be called the velocity of the moving body, provided that it is agreed to adopt as unit of duration the physical phenomenon which has been chosen as the term of comparison. Thus, the velocity of a uniform motion is defined by mechanics without appealing to any other notions than those of space and simultaneity. Now let us turn to the case of a variable motion, that is, to the case when the elements AM, MN, NP . . . are found to be unequal. In order to define the velocity of the moving body A at the point M, we shall only have to imagine an unlimited number of moving bodies A_1, A_2, A_3, . . . all moving uniformly with velocities v_1, v_2, v_3. . . . which are arranged, e.g., in an ascending scale and which correspond to all possible magnitudes. Let us then consider on the path of the moving body A two points M' and M'', situated on either side of the point M but very near it. At the same time as this moving body reaches the points M′, M, M″, the other moving bodies reach points M′$_1$ M$_1$ M″$_1$ M′$_2$ M$_2$ M″$_2$ . . . on their respective paths; and there must be two moving bodies A$_h$ and A$_p$ such that we have on the one hand M′M = M′$_h$M$_h$, and on the other hand MM″ = M$_p$M″$_p$. We shall then agree to say that the velocity of the moving body A at the point M lies between v_h and v_p. But nothing prevents our assuming that the points M′ and M″ are still nearer the point M, and it will then be necessary to replace v_h, and v_p by two fresh velocities v_i and v_n, the one greater than v_h and the other less than v_p. And in proportion as we reduce the two intervals M′M and MM″, we shall lessen the difference between the velocities of the uniform corresponding movements. Now, the two intervals being capable of decreasing right down to zero, there evidently exists between v_i and v_n a certain velocity v_m, such that the difference between this velocity and v_h, v_i . . . on the one hand, and v_p, v_n . . . on the other, can become smaller than any given quantity. It is this common limit v_m which we shall call the velocity of the moving body A at the point M. Now, in this analysis of variable motion, as in that of uniform motion, it is a question only of spaces once traversed and of simultaneous positions once reached. We were thus justified in saying that, while all that mechanics retains of time is simultaneity, all that it retains of motion itself—restricted, as it is, to a *measurement* of motion—is immobility.

This result might have been foreseen by noticing that mechanics necessarily deals with equations, and that an algebraic equation always expresses something already done. Now, it is of the very essence of duration and motion, as they appear to our consciousness, to be something that is unceasingly being done; thus algebra can represent the results gained at a certain moment of duration and the positions occupied by a certain moving body in space, but not duration and motion themselves. Mathematics may, indeed, increase the number of simultaneities and positions which it takes into consideration by making the intervals very small; it may even, by using the differential instead of the difference, show that it is possible to increase without limit the number of these intervals of duration. Nevertheless, however small the interval is supposed to be, it is the extremity of the interval at which mathematics always places itself. As for the interval itself, as for the duration and the motion, they are necessarily left out of the equation. The reason is that duration and motion are mental syntheses, and not objects; that, although the moving body occupies, one after the other, points on a line, motion itself has nothing to do with a line; and finally that, although the positions occupied by the moving body vary with the different moments of duration, though it even creates distinct moments by the mere fact of occupying different positions, duration properly so called has no moments which are identical or external to one another, being essentially heterogeneous, continuous, and with no analogy to number.

It follows from this analysis that space alone is homogeneous, that objects in space form a discrete multiplicity, and that every discrete multiplicity is got by a process of unfolding in space. It also follows that there is neither duration nor even succession in space, if we give to these words the meaning in which consciousness takes them: each of the so-called successive states of the external world exists alone; their multiplicity is real only for a consciousness that can first retain them and then set them side by side by externalizing them in relation to one another. If it retains them, it is because these distinct states of the external world give rise to states of consciousness which permeate one another, imperceptibly organize themselves into a whole, and bind the past to the present by this very process of connection. If it externalizes them in relation to one another, the reason is that, thinking of their radical distinctness (the one having ceased to be when the other appears on the scene), it perceives them under the form of a discrete multiplicity, which amounts to setting them out in line, in the space in which each of them existed separately. The space employed for this purpose is just that which is called homogeneous time.

But another conclusion results from this analysis, namely, that the multiplicity of conscious states, regarded in its original purity, is not at all like the discrete multiplicity which goes to form a number. In such a case there is, as we said, a qualitative multiplicity. In short, we must admit two kinds of multiplicity, two possible senses of the word "distinguish," two conceptions, the one qualitative and the other quantitative, of the difference between *same* and *other*. Sometimes this multiplicity, this distinctness, this heterogeneity contains number only potentially, as Aristotle would have said. Consciousness, then, makes a qualitative discrimination without any further thought of counting the qualities or even of distinguishing them as *several*. In such a case we have multiplicity without quantity. Sometimes, on the other hand, it is a question of a multiplicity of terms which are counted or which are conceived as capable of being counted; but we think then of the possibility of externalizing them in relation to one another, we set them out in space. Unfortunately, we are so accustomed to illustrate one of these two meanings of the same word by the other, and even to perceive the one in the other, that we find it extraordinarily difficult to distinguish between them or at least to express this distinction in words. Thus I said that several conscious states are organized into a whole, permeate one another, gradually gain a richer content, and might thus give any-one ignorant of space the feeling of pure duration; but the very use of the word "several" shows that I had already isolated these states, externalized them in relation to one another, and, in a word, set them side by side; thus, by the very language which I was compelled to use, I betrayed the deeply ingrained habit of setting out time in space. From this spatial setting out, already accomplished, we are compelled to bor-row the terms which we use to describe the state of a mind which has not yet accomplished it: these terms are thus misleading from the very beginning, and the idea of a multiplicity without relation to number or space, although clear for pure reflective thought, cannot be translated into the language of common sense. And yet we cannot even form the idea of discrete multiplicity without considering at the same time a qualitative multiplicity. When we explicitly count units by stringing them along a spatial line, is it not the case that, alongside this addition of identical terms standing out from a homogeneous background, an organization of these units is going on in the depths of the soul, a wholly dynamic process, not unlike the purely qualitative way in which an anvil, if it could feel, would realize a series of blows from a ham-mer? In this sense we might almost say that the numbers in daily use have each their emotional equivalent. Tradesmen are well aware of it, and instead of indicating the price of an object by a round number of shillings, they will mark the next smaller number, leaving themselves to insert afterwards a sufficient number of pence and farthings. In a word, the process by which we count units and make them into a dis-crete multiplicity has two sides; on the one hand we assume that they are identical, which is conceivable only on condition that these units are ranged alongside each other in a homogeneous medium; but on the other hand the third unit, for example, when added to the other two alters the nature, the appearance and, as it were, the rhythm of the whole; without this interpenetration and this, so to speak, qualitative progress, no addition would be possible. Hence it is through the quality of quantity that we form the idea of quantity without quality.

It is therefore obvious that, if it did not betake itself to a symbolical substitute, our consciousness would never regard time as a homogeneous medium, in which the terms of a succession remain outside one another. But we naturally reach this symbolical representation by the mere fact that, in a series of identical terms, each term assumes a double aspect for our consciousness: one aspect which is the same for all of them, since we are thinking then of the sameness of the external object, and another aspect which is characteristic of each of them, because the supervening of each term brings about a new organization of the whole. Hence the possibility of setting out in space, under the form of numerical multiplicity, what we have called a qualitative multiplicity, and of regarding the one as the equivalent of the other. Now, this twofold process is nowhere accomplished so easily as in the perception of the external phenomenon which takes for us the form of motion. Here we certainly have a series of identical terms, since it is always the same moving body; but, on the other hand, the synthesis carried out by our consciousness between the actual position and what our memory calls the former positions, causes these images to permeate, complete, and, so to speak, continue one another. Hence, it is principally by the help of motion that duration assumes the form of a homogeneous medium, and that time is projected into space. But, even if we leave out motion, any repetition of a well-marked external phenomenon would suggest to consciousness the same mode of representation. Thus, when we hear a series of blows of a hammer, the sounds form an indivisible melody in so far as they are pure sensations, and, here again, give rise to a dynamic progress; but, knowing that the same objective cause is at work, we cut up this progress into phases which we then regard as identical; and this multiplicity of elements no longer being conceivable except by being set out in space, since they have now become identical, we are necessarily led to the idea of a homogeneous time, the symbolical image of real duration. In a word, our ego comes in contact with the external world at its surface; our successive sensations, although dissolving into one another, retain something of the mutual externality which belongs to their objective causes; and thus our superficial psychic life comes to be pictured without any great effort as set out in a homogeneous medium. But the symbolical character of such a picture becomes more striking as we advance further into the depths of consciousness: the deep-seated self which ponders and decides, which heats and blazes up, is a self whose states and changes permeate one another and undergo a deep alteration as soon as we separate them from one another in order to set them out in space. But as this deeper self forms one and the same person with the superficial ego, the two seem to *endure* in the same way. And as the repeated picture of one identical objective phenomenon, ever recurring, cuts up our superficial psychic life into parts external to one another, the moments which are thus determined determine in their turn distinct segments in the dynamic and undivided progress of our more personal conscious states. Thus the mutual externality which material objects gain from the juxtaposition in homogeneous space reverberates and spreads in the depths of consciousness: little by little our sensations are distinguished from one another like the external causes which gave rise to them, and our feelings or ideas come to be separated like the sensations with which they are contemporaneous.

That our ordinary conception of duration depends on a gradual incursion of space into the domain of pure consciousness is proved by the fact that, in order to deprive the ego of the faculty perceiving a homogeneous time, it is enough to take away from it this outer circle of psychic states which it uses as a balance-wheel. These conditions are realized when we dream; for sleep, by relaxing the play of the organic functions, alters the communicating surface between the ego and external objects. Here we no longer measure duration, but we feel it; from quantity it returns to the state of quality; we no longer estimate past time mathematically: the mathematical estimate gives place to a confused instinct capable, like all instincts, of committing gross errors, but also of acting at times with extraordinary skill. Even in the waking state daily experience ought to teach us to distinguish between duration as quality, that which consciousness reaches immediately and which is probably what animals perceive, and time so to speak materialized, time that has become quantity by being set out in space. Whilst I am writing these lines, the hour strikes on a neighboring clock, but my inattentive ear does not perceive it until several strokes have made themselves heard. Hence I have not counted them; and yet I only have to turn my attention backwards to count up the four strokes which have already sounded and add them to those which I hear. If, then, I question myself carefully on what has just taken place, I perceive that the first four sounds had struck my ear and even affected my consciousness, but that the sensations produced by each one of them, instead of being set side by side, had melted into one another in such a way as to give the whole a peculiar quality, to make a kind of musical phrase out of it. In order, then, to estimate retrospectively the number of strokes sounded, I tried to reconstruct this phrase in thought: my imagination made one stroke, then two, then three, and as long as it did not reach the exact number four, my feeling, when consulted, answered that the total effect was qualitatively different. It had thus ascertained in its own way the succession of four strokes, but quite otherwise than by a process of addition, and without bringing in the image of a juxtaposition of distinct terms. In a word, the number of strokes was perceived as a quality and not as a quantity: it is thus that duration is presented to immediate consciousness, and it retains this form so long as it does not give place to a symbolical representation derived from extensity.

We should therefore distinguish two forms of multiplicity, two very different ways of regarding duration, two aspects of conscious life. Below homogeneous duration, which is the extensive symbol of true duration, a close psychological analysis distinguishes a duration whose heterogeneous moments permeate one another; below the numerical multiplicity of conscious states, a qualitative multiplicity; below the self with well-defined states, a self in which *succeeding each other* means *melting into one another* and forming an organic whole. But we are generally content with the first, i.e., with the shadow of the self projected into homogeneous space. Consciousness, goaded by an insatiable desire to separate, substitutes the symbol for the reality, or perceives the reality only through the symbol. As the self thus refracted and thereby broken to pieces, is much better adapted to the requirements of social life in general and language in particular, consciousness prefers it, and gradually loses sight of the fundamental self.

In order to recover this fundamental self, as the unsophisticated consciousness would perceive it, a vigorous effort of analysis is necessary, which will isolate the fluid inner states from their image, first refracted, then solidified in homogeneous space. In other words, our perceptions, sensations, emotions, and ideas occur under two aspects: the one clear and precise, but impersonal; the other confused, ever changing, and inexpressible, because language cannot get hold of it without arresting its mobility or fit it into its commonplace forms without making it into public property. If we have been led to distinguish two forms of multiplicity, two forms of duration, we must expect each conscious state, taken by itself, to assume a different aspect according as we consider it within a discrete multiplicity or a confused multiplicity, in the time as quality, in which it is produced, or in the time as quantity, into which it is projected.

When, e.g., I take my first walk in a town in which I am going to live, my environment produces on me two impressions at the same time, one of which is destined to last while the other will constantly change. Every day I perceive the same houses, and as I know that they are the same objects, I always call them by the same name and I also fancy that they always look the same to me. But if I recur, at the end of a sufficiently long period, to the impression which I experienced during the first few years, I am surprised at the remarkable, inexplicable, and indeed inexpressible change which has taken place. It seems that these objects, continually perceived by me and constantly impressing themselves on my mind, have ended by borrowing from me something of my own conscious existence; like myself they have lived, and like myself they have grown old. This is not a mere illusion; for if today's impression were absolutely identical with that of yesterday, what difference would there be between perceiving and recognizing, between learning and remembering? Yet this difference escapes the attention of most of us; we shall hardly perceive it, unless we are warned of it and then carefully look into ourselves. The reason is that our outer and, so to speak, social life is more practically important to us than our inner and individual existence. We instinctively tend to solidify our impressions in order to express them in language. Hence we confuse the feeling itself, which is in a perpetual state of becoming, with its permanent external object, and especially with the word which expresses this object. In the same way as the fleeting duration of our ego is fixed by its projection in homogeneous space, our constantly changing impressions, wrapping themselves round the external object which is their cause, take on its definite outlines and its immobility.

Our simple sensations, taken in their natural state, are still more fleeting. Such and such a flavor, such and such a scent, pleased me when I was a child though I dislike them today. Yet I still give the same name to the sensation experienced, and I speak as if only my taste had changed, whilst the scent and the flavor have remained the same. Thus I again solidify the sensation; and when its changeableness becomes so obvious that I cannot help recognizing it, I abstract this changeableness to give it a name of its own and solidify it in the shape of a *taste*. But in reality there are neither identical sensations nor multiple tastes: for sensations and tastes seem to me to be *objects* as soon as I isolate and name them, and in the human soul there are only *processes*. What I ought to say is that every sensation is altered by repetition, and that if it does not seem to me to change from day to day, it is because I perceive it through the object which is its cause, through the word which translates it. This influence of language on sensation is deeper than is usually thought. Not only does language make us believe in the unchangeableness of our sensations, but it will sometimes deceive us as to the nature of the sensation felt. Thus, when I partake of a dish that is supposed to be exquisite, the name which it bears, suggestive of the approval given to it, comes between my sensation and my consciousness; I may believe that the flavor pleases me when a slight effort of attention would prove the contrary. In short, the word with well-defined outlines, the rough and ready word, which stores up the stable, common, and consequently impersonal element in the impressions of mankind, overwhelms or at least covers over the delicate and fugitive impressions of our individual consciousness. To maintain the struggle on equal terms, the latter ought to express themselves in precise words; but these words, as soon as they were formed, would turn against the sensation which gave birth to them, and, invented to show that the sensation is unstable, they would impose on it their own stability.

This overwhelming of the immediate consciousness is nowhere so striking as in the case of our feelings. A violent love or a deep melancholy takes possession of our soul: here we feel a thousand different elements which dissolve into and permeate one another without any precise outlines, without the least tendency to externalize themselves in relation to one another; hence their originality. We distort them as soon as we distinguish a numerical multiplicity in their confused mass: what will it be, then, when we set them out, isolated from one another, in this homogeneous medium which may be called either time or space, whichever you prefer? A moment ago each of them was borrowing an indefinable color from its surroundings: now we have it colorless, and ready to accept a name. The feeling itself is a being which lives and develops and is therefore constantly changing; otherwise how could it gradually lead us to form a resolution? Our resolution would be immediately taken. But it lives because the duration in which it develops is a duration whose moments permeate one another. By separating these moments from each other, by spreading out time in space, we have caused this feeling to lose its life and its color. Hence, we are now standing before our own shadow: we believe that we have analyzed our feeling, while we have really replaced it by a juxtaposition of lifeless states which can be translated into words, and each of which constitutes the common element, the impersonal residue, of the impressions felt in a given case by the whole of society. And this is why we reason about these states and apply our simple logic to them: having set them up as genera by the mere fact of having isolated them from one another, we have prepared them for use in some future deduction. Now, if some bold novelist, tearing aside the cleverly woven curtain of our conventional ego, shows us under the appearance of logic a fundamental absurdity, under this juxtaposition of simple states an infinite permeation of a thousand different impressions which have already ceased to exist the instant they are named, we commend him for having known us better than we knew ourselves. This is not the case, however, and the very fact that he spreads out our feeling in a homogeneous time, and expresses its elements by words, shows that he in his turn is only offering us its shadow: but he has arranged this shadow in such a way as to make us suspect the extraordinary and illogical nature of the object which projects it; he has made us reflect by giving outward expression to something of that contradiction, that interpenetration, which is the very essence of the elements expressed. Encouraged by him, we have put aside for an instant the veil which we interposed between our consciousness and ourselves. He has brought us back into our own presence.

We should experience the same sort of surprise if we strove to seize our ideas themselves in their natural state, as our consciousness would perceive them if it were no longer beset by space. This breaking up of the constituent elements of an idea, which issues in abstraction, is too convenient for us to do without it in ordinary life and even in philosophical discussion. But when we fancy that the parts thus artificially separated are the genuine threads with which the concrete idea was woven, when, substituting for the interpenetration of the real terms the juxtaposition of their symbols, we claim to make duration out of space, we unavoidably fall into the mistakes of associationism. We shall not insist on the latter point, which will be the subject of a thorough examination in the next chapter. Let it be enough to say that the impulsive zeal with which we take sides on certain questions shows how our intellect has its instincts—and what can an instinct of this kind be if not an impetus common to all our ideas, i.e., their very interpenetration? The beliefs to which we most strongly adhere are those of which we should find it most difficult to give an account, and the reasons by which we justify them are seldom those which have led us to adopt them. In a certain sense we have adopted them without any reason, for what makes them valuable in our eyes is that they match the color of all our other ideas, and that from the very first we have seen in them something of ourselves. Hence they do not take in our minds that common-looking form which they will assume as soon as we try to give expression to them in words; and, although they bear the same name in other minds, they are by no means the same thing. The fact is that each of them has the same kind of life as a cell in an organism: everything which affects the general state of the self affects it also. But while the cell occupies a definite point in the organism, an idea which is truly ours fills the whole of our self. Not all our ideas, however, are thus incorporated in the fluid mass of our conscious states. Many float on the surface, like dead leaves on the water of a pond: the mind, when it thinks them over and over again, finds them ever the same, as if they were external to it. Among these are the ideas which we receive ready-made, and which remain in us without ever being properly assimilated, or again the ideas which we have omitted to cherish and which have withered in neglect. If, in proportion as we get away from the deeper strata of the self, our conscious states tend more and more to assume the form of a numerical multiplicity, and to spread out in a homogeneous space, it is just because these conscious states tend to become more and more lifeless, more and more impersonal. Hence we need not be surprised if only those ideas which least belong to us can be adequately expressed in words: only to these, as we shall see, does the associationist theory apply. External to one another, they keep up relations among themselves in which the inmost nature of each of them counts for nothing, relations which can therefore be classified. It may thus be said that they are associated by contiguity or for some logical reason. But if, digging below the surface of contact between the self and external objects, we penetrate into the depths of the organized and living intelligence, we shall witness the joining together or rather the blending of many ideas which, when once dissociated, seem to exclude one another as logically contradictory terms. The strangest dreams, in which two images overlie one another and show us at the same time two different persons, who yet make only one, will hardly give us an idea of the interweaving of concepts which goes on when we are awake. The imagination of the dreamer, cut off from the external world, imitates with mere images, and parodies in its own way, the process which constantly goes on with regard to ideas in the deeper regions of the intellectual life.

Thus may be verified, thus, too, will be illustrated by a further study of deep-seated psychic phenomena, the principle from which we started: conscious life displays two aspects according as we perceive it directly or by refraction through space. Considered in themselves, the deep-seated conscious states have no relation to quantity, they are pure quality; they intermingle in such a way that we cannot tell whether they are one or several, nor even examine them from this point of view without at once altering their nature. The duration which they thus create is a duration whose moments do not constitute a numerical multiplicity: to characterize these moments by saying that they encroach on one another would still be to distinguish them. If each of us lived a purely individual life, if there were neither society nor language, would our consciousness grasp the series of inner states in this unbroken form? Undoubtedly it would not quite succeed, because we should still retain the idea of a homogeneous space in which objects are sharply distinguished from one another, and because it is too convenient to set out in such a medium the somewhat cloudy states which first attract the attention of consciousness, in order to resolve them into simpler terms. But mark that the intuition of a homogeneous space is already a step toward social life. Probably animals do not picture to themselves, beside their sensations, as we do, an external world quite distinct from themselves, which is the common property of all conscious beings. Our tendency to form a clear picture of this externality of things and the homogeneity of their medium is the same as the impulse which leads us to live in common and to speak. But, in proportion as the conditions of social life are more completely realized, the current which carries our conscious states from within outwards is strengthened; little by little these states are made into objects or things; they break off not only from one another, but from ourselves. Henceforth, we no longer perceive them except in the homogeneous medium in which we have set their image, and through the word which lends them its commonplace color. Thus a second self is formed which obscures the first, a self whose existence is made up of distinct moments, whose states are separated from one another and easily expressed in words. I do not mean, here, to split up the personality, nor to bring back in another form the numerical multiplicity which I shut out at the beginning. It is the same self which perceives distinct states at first, and which, by afterwards concentrating its attention, will see these states melt into one another like the crystals of a snow-flake when touched for some time with the finger. And, in truth, for the sake of language, the self has everything to gain by not bringing back confusion where order reigns, and in not upsetting this ingenious arrangement of almost impersonal states by which it has ceased to form "a kingdom within a kingdom." An inner life with well distinguished moments and with clearly characterized states will answer better the requirements of social life. Indeed, a superficial psychology may be content with describing it without thereby falling into error, on condition, however, that it restricts itself to the study of what has taken place and leaves out what is going on. But if, passing from statics to dynamics, this psychology claims to reason about things in the making as it reasoned about things made, if it offers us the concrete and living self as an association of terms which are distinct from one another and are set side by side in a homogeneous medium, it will see difficulty after difficulty rising in its path. And these difficulties will multiply the greater the efforts it makes to overcome them, for all its efforts will only bring into clearer light the absurdity of the fundamental hypothesis by which it spreads out time in space and puts succession at the very center of simultaneity. We shall see that the contradictions implied in the problems of causality, freedom, personality, spring from no other source, and that, if we wish to get rid of them, we have only to go back to the real and concrete self and give up its symbolical substitute.

The Possible and the Real

I should like to come back to a subject on which I have already spoken, the continuous creation of unforeseeable novelty which seems to be going on in the universe. As far as I am concerned, I feel I am experiencing it constantly. No matter how I try to imagine in detail what is going to happen to me, still how inadequate, how abstract and stilted is the thing I have imagined in comparison to what actually happens! The realization brings along with it an unforeseeable nothing which changes everything. For example, I am to be present at a gathering; I know what people I shall find there, around what table, in what order, to discuss what problem. But let them come, be seated, and chat as I expected, let them say what I was sure they would say: the whole gives me an impression at once novel and unique, as if it were but now designed at one original stroke by the hand of an artist. Gone is the image I had conceived of it, a mere prearrangeable juxtaposition of things already known! I agree that the picture has not the artistic value of a Rembrandt or a Velasquez: yet it is just as unexpected and, in this sense, quite as original. It will be alleged that I did not know the circumstances in detail, that I could not control the persons in question, their gestures, their attitudes, and that if the thing as a whole provided me with something new it was because they produced additional factors. But I have the same impression of novelty before the unrolling of my inner life. I feel it more vividly than ever, before the action I willed and of which I was sole master. If I deliberate before acting, the moments of deliberation present themselves to my consciousness like the successive sketches a painter makes of his pictures, each one unique of its kind; and no matter whether the act itself in its accomplishment realizes something willed and consequently foreseen, it has none the less its own particular form in all its originality.—Granted, someone will say; there is perhaps something original and unique in a state of soul; but matter is repetition; the external world yields to mathematical laws; a superhuman intelligence which would know the position, the direction, and the speed of all the atoms and electrons of the material universe at a given moment could calculate any future state of this universe as we do in the case of an eclipse of the sun or the moon.—I admit all this for the sake of argument, if it concerns only the inert world and at least with regard to elementary phenomena, although this is beginning to be a much debated question. But this "inert" world is only an abstraction. Concrete reality comprises those living, conscious beings enframed in inorganic matter. I say living and conscious, for I believe that the living is conscious by right; it becomes unconscious in fact where consciousness falls asleep, but even in the regions where consciousness is in a state of somnolence, in the vegetable kingdom for example, there is regulated evolution, definite progress, aging; in fact, all the external signs of the duration which characterizes consciousness. And why must we speak of an inert matter into which life and consciousness would be inserted as in a frame? By what right do we put the inert first? The ancients had imagined a World Soul supposed to assure the continuity of existence of the material universe. Stripping this conception of its mythical element, I should say that the inorganic world is a series of infinitely rapid repetitions or quasi-repetitions which, when totaled, constitute visible and previsible changes. I should compare them to the swinging of the pendulum of a clock: the swingings of a spring linking them together and whose unwinding they mark; the repetitions of the inorganic world constitute rhythm in the life of conscious beings and measure their duration. Thus the living being essentially has duration; it has duration precisely because it is continuously elaborating what is new and because there is no elaboration without searching, no searching without groping. Time is this very hesitation, or it is nothing. Suppress the conscious and the living (and you can do this only through an artificial effort of abstraction, for the material world once again implies perhaps the necessary presence of consciousness and of life), you obtain in fact a universe whose successive states are in theory calculable in advance, like the images placed side by side along the cinematographic film, prior to its unrolling. Why, then, the unrolling? Why does reality unfurl? Why is it not spread out? What good is time? (I refer to real, concrete time, and not to that abstract time which is only a fourth dimension of space.) This, in days gone by, was the starting-point of my reflections. Some fifty years ago I was very much attached to the philosophy of Spencer. I perceived one fine day that, in it, time served no purpose, did nothing. Nevertheless, I said to myself, time is something. Therefore it acts.

What can it be doing? Plain common sense answered: time is what hinders everything from being given at once. It retards, or rather it is retardation. It must, therefore, be elaboration. Would it not then be a vehicle of creation and of choice? Would not the existence of time prove that there is indetermination in things? Would not time be that indetermination itself?

If such is not the opinion of most philosophers, it is because human intelligence is made precisely to take things by the other end. I say intelligence, I do not say thought, I do not say mind. Alongside of intelligence there is in effect the immediate perception by each of us of his own activity and of the conditions in which it is exercised. Call it what you will; it is the feeling we have of being creators of our intentions, of our decisions, of our acts, and by that, of our habits, our characters, ourselves. Artisans of our life, even artists when we so desire, we work continually, with the material furnished us by the past and present, by heredity and opportunity, to mold a figure unique, new, original, as unforeseeable as the form given by the sculptor to the clay. Of this work and what there is unique about it we are warned, no doubt, even while it is being done, but the essential thing is that we do it. It is up to us to go deeply into it; it is not even necessary that we be fully conscious of it, any more than the artist needs to analyze his creative ability; he leaves that to the philosopher to worry about, being content, himself, simply to create. On the other hand, the sculptor must be familiar with the technique of his art and know everything that can be learned about it: this technique deals especially with what his work has in common with other works; it is governed by the demands of the material upon which he operates and which are imposed upon him as upon all artists; it concerns in art what is repetition or fabrication, and has nothing to do with creation itself. On it is concentrated the attention of the artist, what I should call his intellectuality. In the same way, in the creation of our character, we know very little about our creative ability: in order to learn about it we should have to turn back upon ourselves, to philosophize, and to climb back up the slope of nature; for nature desired action, it hardly thought about speculation. The moment it is no longer simply a question of feeling an impulse within oneself and of being assured that one can act, but of turning thought upon itself in order that it may seize this ability and catch this impulse, the difficulty becomes great, as if the whole normal direction of consciousness had to be reversed. On the contrary we have a supreme interest in familiarizing ourselves with the technique of our action, that is to say, in extracting from the conditions in which it is exercised, all that can furnish us with recipes and general rules upon which to base our conduct. There will be novelty in our acts thanks only to the repetition we have found in things. Our normal faculty of knowing is then essentially a power of extracting what stability and regularity there is in the flow of reality. Is it a question of perceiving? Perception seizes upon the infinitely repeated shocks which are light or heat, for example, and contracts them into relatively invariable sensations: trillions of external vibrations are what the vision of a color condenses in our eyes in the fraction of a second. Is it a question of conceiving? To form a general idea is to abstract from varied and changing things a common aspect which does not change or at least offers an invariable hold to our action. The invariability of our attitude, the identity of our eventual or virtual reaction to the multiplicity and variability of the objects represented is what first marks and delineates the generality of the idea. Finally, is it a question of understanding? It is simply finding connections, establishing stable relations between transitory facts, evolving laws; an operation which is much more perfect as the relation becomes more definite and the law more mathematical. All these functions are constitutives of the intellect. And the intellect is in the line of truth so long as it attaches itself, in its penchant for regularity and stability, to what is stable and regular in the real, that is to say, to materiality. In so doing it touches one of the sides of the absolute, as our consciousness touches another when it grasps within us a perceptual efflorescence of novelty or when, broadening out, it comes into sympathy with that effort of nature which is constantly renewing. Error begins when the intellect claims to think one of the aspects as it thought the other, directing its powers on something for which it was not intended.

I believe that the great metaphysical problems are in general badly stated, that they frequently resolve themselves of their own accord when correctly stated, or else are problems formulated in terms of illusion which disappear as soon as the terms of the formula are more closely examined. They arise in fact from our habit of transposing into fabrication what is creation. Reality is global and undivided growth, progressive invention, duration: it resembles a gradually expanding rubber balloon assuming at each moment unexpected forms. But our intelligence imagines its origin and evolution as an arrangement and rearrangement of parts which supposedly merely shift from one place to another; in theory, therefore, it should be able to foresee any one state of the whole: by positing a definite number of stable elements one has, predetermined, all their possible combinations. That is not all. Reality, as immediately perceived, is fullness constantly swelling out, to which emptiness is unknown. It has extension just as it has duration; but this concrete extent is not the infinite and infinitely divisible space the intellect takes as a place in which to build. Concrete space has been extracted from things. They are not in it; it is space which is in them. Only, as soon as our thought reasons about reality, it makes space a receptacle. As it has the habit of assembling parts in a relative vacuum, it imagines that reality fills up some absolute kind of vacuum. Now, if the failure to recognize radical novelty is the original cause of those badly stated metaphysical questions, the habit of proceeding from emptiness to fullness is the source of problems which are nonexistent. Moreover, it is easy to see that the second mistake is already implied in the first. But I should like first of all to define it more precisely.

I say that there are pseudo-problems, and that they are the agonizing problems of metaphysics. I reduce them to two. One gave rise to theories of being, the other to theories of knowledge. The first false problem consists in asking oneself why there is being, why something or someone exists. The nature of what is is of little importance; say that it is matter, or mind, or both, or that matter and mind are not self-sufficient and manifest a transcendent Cause: in any case, when existences and causes are brought into consideration and the causes of these causes, one feels as if pressed into a race—if one calls a halt, it is to avoid dizziness. But just the same one sees, or thinks one sees, that the difficulty still exists, that the problem is still there and will never be solved. It will never, in fact, be solved, but it should never have been raised. It arises only if one posits a nothingness which supposedly precedes being. One says: "There could be nothing," and then is astonished that there should be something—or someone. But analyze that sentence: "There could be nothing." You will see you are dealing with words, not at all with ideas, and that "nothing" here has no meaning. "Nothing" is a term in ordinary language which can only have meaning in the sphere, proper to man, of action and fabrication. "Nothing" designates the absence of what we are seeking, we desire, expect. Let us suppose that absolute emptiness was known to our experience: it would be limited, have contours, and would therefore be something. But in reality there is no vacuum. We perceive and can perceive only occupied space. One thing disappears only because another replaces it. Suppression thus means substitution. We say "suppression," however, when we envisage, in the case of substitution, only one of its two halves, or rather the one of its two sides which interests us; in this way we indicate a desire to turn our attention to the object which is gone, and away from the one replacing it.

We say then that there is nothing more, meaning by that, that what exists does not interest us, that we are interested in what is no longer there or in what might have been there. The idea of absence, or of nothingness, or of nothing, is therefore inseparably bound to that of suppression, real or eventual, and the idea of suppression is itself only an aspect of the idea of substitution. Those are the ways of thinking we use in practical life; it is particularly essential to our industry that our thought should be able to lag behind reality and remain attached, when need be, to what was or to what might be, instead of being absorbed by what is. But when we go from the domain of fabrication to that of creation, when we ask ourselves why there is being, why something or someone, why the world or God, exists and why not nothingness, when, in short, we set ourselves the most agonizing of metaphysical problems, we virtually accept an absurdity; for if all suppression is a substitution, if the idea of a suppression is only the truncated idea of a substitution, then to speak of a suppression of everything is to posit a substitution which would not be one, that is, to be self-contradictory. Either the idea of a suppression of everything has just about as much existence as that of a round square—the existence of a sound, *flatus vocis*—or else, if it does represent something, it translates a movement of the intellect from one object to another, preferring the one it has just left to the object it finds before it, and designates by "absence of the first" the presence of the second. We have posited the whole, then made each of its parts disappear one by one, without consenting to see what replaced it; it is therefore the totality of presences, simply arranged in a new order, that one has in mind in attempting to total up the absences. In other words, this so-called representation of absolute emptiness is, in reality, that of universal fullness in a mind which leaps indefinitely from part to part, with the fixed resolution never to consider anything but the emptiness of its dissatisfaction instead of the fullness of things. All of which amounts to saying that the idea of Nothing, when it is not that of a simple word, implies as much matter as the idea of All, with, in addition, an operation of thought.

I should say as much of the idea of disorder. Why is the universe well-ordered? How is rule imposed upon what is without rule, and form upon matter? How is it that our thought recognizes itself in things? This problem, which among the moderns has become the problem of knowledge after having been, among the ancients, the problem of being, was born of an illusion of the same order. It disappears if one considers that the idea of disorder has a definite meaning in the domain of human industry or, as we say, of fabrication, but not in that of creation. Disorder is simply the order we are not looking for. You cannot suppress one order even by thought, without causing another to spring up. If there is not finality or will, it is because there is mechanism; if the mechanism gives way, so much the gain for will, caprice, finality. But when you expect one of these two orders and you find the other, you say there is disorder, formulating what is in terms of what might or should be, and objectifying your regret. All disorder thus includes two things: outside us, one order; within us, the representation of a different order which alone interests us. Suppression therefore again signifies substitution, And the idea of a suppression of all order, that is to say, the idea of an absolute disorder, then contains a veritable contradiction, because it consists in leaving only a single aspect to the operation which, by hypothesis, embraced two. Either the idea of an absolute disorder represents no more than a combination of sounds, *flatus vocis,* or else, if it corresponds to something, it translates a movement of the mind which leaps from mechanism to finality, from finality to mechanism, and which, in order to mark the spot where it is, prefers each time to indicate the point where it is not. Therefore, in wishing to suppress order, you find yourself with two or more "orders." This is tantamount to saying that the conception of an order which is superadded to an "absence of order" implies an absurdity, and that the problem disappears.

The two illusions I have just mentioned are in reality only one. They consist in believing that there is *less* in the idea of the empty than in the idea of the full, *less* in the concept of disorder than in that of order. In reality, there is more intellectual content in the ideas of disorder and nothingness when they represent something than in those of order and existence, because they imply several orders, several existences and, in addition, a play of wit which unconsciously juggles with them.

Very well then, I find the same illusion in the case in point. Underlying the doctrines which disregard the radical novelty of each moment of evolution there are many misunderstandings, many errors. But there is especially the idea that the possible is *less* than the real, and that, for this reason, the possibility of things precedes their existence. They would thus be capable of representation beforehand; they could be thought of before being realized. But it is the reverse that is true. If we leave aside the closed systems, subjected to purely mathematical laws, isolable because duration does not act upon them, if we consider the totality of concrete reality or simply the world of life, and still more that of consciousness, we find there is more and not less in the possibility of each of the successive states than in their reality. For the possible is only the real with the addition of an act of mind which throws its image back into the past, once it has been enacted. But that is what our intellectual habits prevent us from seeing.

During the great war certain newspapers and periodicals sometimes turned aside from the terrible worries of the day to think of what would happen later once peace was restored. They were particularly preoccupied with the future of literature. Someone came one day to ask me my ideas on the subject. A little embarrassed, I declared I had none. "Do you not at least perceive," I was asked, "certain possible directions? Let us grant that one cannot foresee things in detail; you as a philosopher have at least an idea of the whole. How do you conceive, for example, the great dramatic work of tomorrow?" I shall always remember my interlocutor's surprise when I answered, "If I knew what was to be the great dramatic work of the future, I should be writing it." I saw distinctly that he conceived the future work as being already stored up in some cupboard reserved for possibles; because of my longstanding relations with philosophy, I should have been able to obtain from it the key to the storehouse. "But," I said, "the work of which you speak is not yet possible."—"But it must be, since it is to take place."—"No, it is not. I grant you, at most, that it *will have been possible*." "What do you mean by that?"—"It's quite simple. Let a man of talent or genius come forth, let him create a work: it will then be real, and by that very fact it becomes retrospectively or retroactively possible. It would not be possible, it would not have been so, if this man had not come upon the scene. That is why I tell you that it will have been possible today, but that it is not yet so." "You're not serious! You are surely not going to maintain that the future has an effect upon the present, that the present brings something into the past, that action works back over the course of time and imprints its mark afterwards?"—"That depends. That one can put reality into the past and thus work backwards in time is something I have never claimed. But that one can put the possible there, or rather that the possible may put itself there at any moment, is not to be doubted. As reality is created as something unforeseeable and new, its image is reflected behind it into the indefinite past; thus it finds that it has from all time been possible, but it is at this precise moment that it begins to have been always possible, and that is why I said that its possibility, which does not precede its reality, will have preceded it once the reality has appeared. The possible is therefore the mirage of the present in the past; and as we know the future will finally constitute a present and the mirage effect is continually being produced, we are convinced that the image of tomorrow is already contained in our actual present, which will be the past of tomorrow, although we did not manage to grasp it. That is precisely the illusion. It is as though one were to fancy, in seeing his reflection in the mirror in front of him, that he could have touched it had he stayed behind it. Thus in judging that the possible does not presuppose the real, one admits that the realization adds something to the simple possibility: the possible would have been there from all time, a phantom awaiting its hour; it would therefore have become reality by the addition of something, by some transfusion of blood or life. One does not see that the contrary is the case, that the possible implies the corresponding reality with, moreover, something added, since the possible is the combined effect of reality once it has appeared and of a condition which throws it back in time. The idea immanent in most philosophies and natural to the human mind, of possibles which would be realized by an acquisition of existence, is therefore pure illusion. One might as well claim that the man in flesh and blood comes from the materialization of his image seen in the mirror, because in that real man is everything found in this virtual image with, in addition, the solidity which makes it possible to touch it. But the truth is that more is needed here to obtain the virtual than is necessary for the real, more for the image of the man than for the man himself, for the image of the man will not be portrayed if the man is not first produced, and in addition one has to have the mirror."

That is what my interlocutor was forgetting as he questioned me on the theater of tomorrow. Perhaps too he was unconsciously playing on the meaning of the word "possible." *Hamlet* was doubtless possible before being realized, if that means that there was no insurmountable obstacle to its realization. In this particular sense one calls possible what is not impossible; and it stands to reason that this non-impossibility of a thing is the condition of its realization. But the possible thus understood is in no degree virtual, something ideally pre-existent. If you close the gate you know no one will cross the road; it does not follow that you can predict who will cross when you open it. Nevertheless, from the quite negative sense of the term "impossible" you pass surreptitiously, unconsciously to the positive sense. Possibility signified "absence of hindrance" a few minutes ago: now you make of it a "pre-existence under the form of an idea," which is quite another thing. In the first meaning of the word it was a truism to say that the possibility of a thing precedes its reality: by that you meant simply that obstacles, having been surmounted, were surmountable. But in the second meaning it is an absurdity, for it is clear that a mind in which the *Hamlet* of Shakespeare had taken shape in the form of possible would by that fact have created its reality: it would thus have been, by definition, Shakespeare himself. In vain do you imagine at first that this mind could have appeared before Shakespeare; it is because you are not thinking then of all the details in the play. As you complete them the predecessor of Shakespeare finds himself thinking all that Shakespeare will think, feeling all he will feel, knowing all he will know, perceiving therefore all he will perceive, and consequently occupying the same point in space and time, having the same body and the same soul: it is Shakespeare himself.

But I am putting too much stress on what is self-evident. We are forced to these considerations in discussing a work of art. I believe in the end we shall consider it evident that the artist in executing his work is creating the possible as well as the real. Whence comes it then that one might hesitate to say the same thing for nature? Is not the world a work of art incomparably richer than that of the greatest artist? And is there not as much absurdity, if not more, in supposing, in the work of nature, that the future is outlined in advance, that possibility existed before reality? Once more let me say I am perfectly willing to admit that the future states of a closed system of material points are calculable and hence visible in its present state. But, and I repeat, this system is extracted, or abstracted, from a whole which, in addition to inert and unorganized matter, comprises organization. Take the concrete and complete world, with the life and consciousness it encloses; consider nature in its entirety, nature the generator of new species as novel and original in form as the design of any artist: in these species concentrate upon individuals, plants, or animals, each of which has its own charac-ter—I was going to say its personality (for one blade of grass does not resemble another blade of grass any more than a Raphael resembles a Rembrandt); lift your attention above and beyond individual man to societies which disclose actions and situations comparable to those of any drama: how can one still speak of possibles which would precede their own realization? How can we fail to see that if the event can always be explained afterwards by an arbitrary choice of antecedent events, a completely different event could have been equally well ex-plained in the same circumstances by another choice of antecedent—nay, by the same antecedents otherwise cut out, otherwise distributed, otherwise perceived—in short, by our retrospective attention? Back-wards over the course of time a constant remodeling of the past by the present, of the cause by the effect is being carried out.

We do not see it, always for the same reason, always a prey to the same illusion, always because we treat as the more what is the less, as the less what is the more. If we put the possible back into its proper place, evolution becomes something quite different from the realization of a program: the gates of the future open wide; freedom is offered an unlimited field. The fault of those doctrines—rare indeed in the history of philosophy—which have succeeded in leaving room for indetermi-nation and freedom in the world, is to have failed to see what their affirmation implied. When they spoke of indetermination, of freedom, they meant by indetermination a competition between possibles, by freedom a choice between possibles—as if possibility was not created by freedom itself! As if any other hypothesis, by affirming an ideal pre-existence of the possible to the real, did not reduce the new to a mere rearrangement of former elements! As if it were not thus to be led sooner or later to regard that rearrangement as calculable and fore-seeable! By accepting the premiss [*sic*] of the contrary theory one was letting the enemy in. We must resign ourselves to the inevitable: it is the real which makes itself possible, and not the possible which be-comes real.

But the truth is that philosophy has never frankly admitted this con-tinuous creation of unforeseeable novelty. The ancients already re-volted against it because, Platonists to a greater or less degree, they imagined that Being was given once and for all, complete and perfect, in the immutable system of Ideas: the world which unfolds before our eyes could therefore add nothing to it; it was, on the contrary, only diminution or degradation: its successive states measured as it were the increasing or decreasing distance between what is, a shadow projected in time, and what ought to be, Idea set in eternity; they would outline the variations of a deficiency, the changing form of a void. It was Time which, according to them, spoiled everything. The modems, it is true, take a quite different point of view. They no longer treat Time as an intruder, a disturber of eternity; but they would very much like to reduce it to a simple appearance. The temporal is, then, only the confused form of the rational. What we perceive as being a succession of states is conceived by our intellect, once the fog has settled, as a system of relations. The real becomes once more the eternal, with this single difference, that it is the eternity of the Laws in which the phenomena are resolved instead of being the eternity of the Ideas which serve them as models. But in each case, we are dealing with theories. Let us stick to the facts. Time is immediately given. That is sufficient for us, and until its inexistence or perversity is proved to us we shall merely register that there is effectively a flow of unforeseeable novelty.

Philosophy stands to gain in finding some absolute in the moving world of phenomena. But we shall gain also in our feeling of greater joy and strength. Greater joy because the reality invented before our eyes will give each one of us, unceasingly, certain of the satisfactions which art at rare intervals procures for the privileged; it will reveal to us, beyond the fixity and monotony which our senses, hypnotized by our constant needs, at first perceived in it, ever-recurring novelty, the moving originality of things. But above all we shall have greater strength, for we shall feel we are participating, creators of ourselves, in the great work of creation which is the origin of all things and which goes on before our eyes. By getting hold of itself, our faculty for acting will become intensified. Humbled heretofore in an attitude of obedience, slaves of certain vaguely-felt natural necessities, we shall once more stand erect, masters associated with a greater Master. To such a conclusion will our study bring us. In this speculation on the relation between the possible and the real, let us guard against seeing a simple game. It can be a preparation for the art of living.

JOHN DEWEY

John Dewey was born in Burlington, Vermont, on October 20, 1859. Upon graduation from high school at the age of fifteen, he entered the University of Vermont, which at that time had a faculty of eight and a student body of less than a hundred. For several years after receiving his bachelor's degree there in 1879, Dewey taught such subjects as Latin and algebra in public schools in Pennsylvania and Vermont. It was during this time (in 1882) that he began his extremely prolific career of philosophical publication when two of his articles were accepted by the *Journal of Speculative Philosophy*. Later that year he entered the newly founded Johns Hopkins Graduate School, where he took courses under George S. Morris and Charles Sanders Peirce, among others. He received his Ph.D. in 1884 with a thesis entitled "The Psychology of Kant" and then accompanied Morris to the University of Michigan. There he remained for ten years, with the exception of one year at the University of Minnesota (1890), rising to Chairman of the Department, raising a family, spending most of his summers in Europe, and writing many books and articles. In 1894 Dewey accepted the position of Chairman of the Department of Philosophy, Psychology, and Pedagogy at the University of Chicago, where he remained until his resignation in 1904 over matters concerning the administration of his famous elementary "Laboratory School." It was during this period that Dewey's fame as a philosopher of education spread throughout the world. Upon leaving Chicago, Dewey became Professor of Philosophy at Columbia University, a position he held until his retirement over thirty years later. It should be mentioned that Dewey was one of the founders and the first president of the American Association of University Professors in 1915

Generally thought of as a provincial thinker, John Dewey was undoubtedly one of the most widely traveled and internationally sensitive of all philosophers. For a year beginning in 1918 he lectured at the Tokyo Imperial University (those lectures were subsequently published as *Reconstruction in Philosophy*), then moved immediately to China for two years, giving extremely well received and influential lectures in Peking, Nanking, and other cities throughout the country. There followed extensive travels in Turkey in 1924, Mexico in 1926, and Russia in 1928, each of which involved educational consultation as well as lectures. In 1929 he delivered the Gifford Lectures (*The Quest for Certainty*) in Edinburgh, Scotland. In 1937 he returned to Mexico as chairman of a commission inquiring into charges which had been made against Leon Trotsky in the Moscow trials. His first wife had died in 1927, and in 1946 Dewey remarried. Though retired from academic duties in these last years, Dewey continued writing and publishing until his death on June 1, 1952.

Dewey's philosophical development can be divided into three phases. Prior to 1903 his work was characterized by a slow extrication from the domination of Hegel and various post-Hegelian British idealists. The outstanding work of this time is his *Psychology,* published in 1887. The publication in 1903 of his contributions in *Studies in Logical Theory* signaled the onset of a period devoted largely to the development of an instrumentalist methodology, though he also continued to write extensively in the fields of ethics and the philosophy of education. Turning his back upon the traditional concerns of system construction, metaphysics, and epistemology, Dewey at this time sought merely to fashion a method for dealing with the problems of men. However, this abstention from the traditional pursuits came to an end in 1925 with the publication of a work in process metaphysics, *Experience and Nature.* Dewey now entered upon his third and final phase wherein he attempted to frame a comprehensive system and a general philosophy of culture. Volumes in epistemology, value theory, aesthetics, philosophy of religion, political and social philosophy, and (as always) philosophy of education followed rapidly. By 1940 he was willing to say that ". . . I have a system. In so far I have to retract disparaging remarks I have made in the past about the need for system in philosophy." ("Nature in Experience," LW 14.)

MAJOR PUBLISHED PHILOSOPHICAL WORKS BY DEWEY

In 1990, the Southern Illinois University Press completed their 23-year project of publishing *The Collected Works of John Dewey* in 37 volumes under the general editorship of Jo Ann Boydston. These volumes now serve as the standard edition. This collection is divided into three groups: *The Early Works (1882–1898)* (Five Volumes, abbr. EW), *The Middle Works (1899–1924)* (15 Volumes, abbr. MW), and *The Later Works (1925–1953)* (17 Volumes, abbr. LW). The following divisions of Dewey's work into three phases corresponds closely to these divisions.

Phase One: Pre-instrumentalism (1882–1902).

1887   *Psychology*, EW2.

1888   *Leibniz's New Essays Concerning Human Understanding*, EW1.

1891   *Outlines of a Critical Theory of Ethics*, EW3.

1894   *The Study of Ethics: A Syllabus*, EW4.

1896   "The Reflex Arc Concept in Psychology," EW5.

1899   *The School and Society*, MW1.

1902   *The Child and the Curriculum*, (Pamphlet), MW2.

Phase Two: Instrumentalism (1903–1924).

1903   *Studies in Logical Theory* (with others), MW2.

1908   *Ethics* (with James Tufts), MW5.

1909   *Moral Principles in Education*, MW4.

1910   *How We Think*, MW6.

1913   *Interest and Effort in Education*, MW7.

1915   *German Philosophy and Politics*, MW8.

1915   *Schools of Tomorrow* (with Evelyn Dewey), MW8.

1916   *Democracy and Education*, MW9.

1916   *Essays in Experimental Logic* (a collection of previously published essays).

1917   "The Need for a Recovery of Philosophy," MW10.

1920   *Reconstruction in Philosophy*, MW12.

1922   *Human Nature and Conduct*, MW14.

Phase Three: Process-philosophy (1925–1953).

1925   *Experience and Nature* (Carus Lectures), LW1.

1927   *The Public and Its Problems*, LW2.

1929   *The Quest for Certainty*, LW4.

1930   *Individualism Old and New*, LW5.

1930   *Construction and Criticism*, LW5.

1931   *Philosophy and Civilization*. (A collection of 18 previously published essays, including "Qualitative Thought" and "Philosophies of Freedom.")

1931　　"Context and Thought," LW6.

1932　　*Ethics*, LW7. (A complete revision of the 1908 *Ethics*.)

1933　　*How We Think*, LW8. (A complete revision of the 1910 version.)

1934　　*Art as Experience*, LW10.

1934　　*A Common Faith*, LW9.

1935　　*Liberalism and Social Action*, LW11.

1938　　*Experience and Education*, LW13.

1938　　*Logic: The Theory of Inquiry*, LW12.

1939　　*Freedom and Culture*, LW13.

1939　　*Theory of Valuation*, LW13.

1940　　"Time and Individuality," LW14.

1946　　*Problems of Men.* (A collection of previously published essays).

1949　　*Knowing and the Known*, LW16.

IMPORTANT COLLECTIONS OF WORKS BY DEWEY

Hickman, Larry A. and Thomas Alexander (eds.). *The Essential Dewey*. Bloomington: Indiana University Press, 1998.

McDermott, John J. (ed.). *The Philosophy of John Dewey*. Chicago: The University of Chicago Press, 1981.

RECOMMENDED COMMENTARIES AND RELATED READING

Alexander, Thomas: *John Dewey's Theory of Art, Experience and Nature: The Horizons of Feeling*. Albany: SUNY Press, 1987.

Bernstein, Richard J. *John Dewey*. New York: Washington Square Press, 1966.

Burke, Tom. *Dewey's New Logic: A Reply to Russell*. Chicago: The University of Chicago Press, 1994.

Geiger, George R. *John Dewey in Perspective*. Westport, Conn.: Greenwood Publishing Group, Inc., 1974.

Hickman, Larry A. *John Dewey's Pragmatic Technology*. Bloomington: Indiana University Press, 1990.

(ed.). *Reading Dewey: Interpretations for a Postmodern Generation*. Bloomington: Indiana University Press, 1998.

Schilpp, P. A. (ed.). *The Philosophy of John Dewey*. La Salle, Ill.: Open
  Court Publishing Co., 1970.
Sleeper, R. W. *The Necessity of Pragmatism*. New Haven: Yale Univer-
  sity Press, 1986.
Westbrook, Robert. *John Dewey and American Democracy*. Ithaca,
  N.Y: Cornell University Press, 1991.

Qualitative Thought

The world in which we immediately live, that in which we strive, succeed, and are defeated is preeminently a qualitative world. What we act for, suffer, and enjoy are things in their qualitative determinations. This world forms the field of characteristic modes of thinking, characteristic in that thought is definitely regulated by qualitative considerations. Were it not for the double and hence ambiguous sense of the term "common-sense," it might be said that common-sense thinking, that concerned with action and its consequences, whether undergone in enjoyment or suffering, is qualitative. But since "common-sense" is also used to designate accepted traditions and is appealed to in support of them, it is safe at the outset to refer simply to that thought which has to do with objects involved in the concerns and issues of living.

The problem of qualitative objects has influenced metaphysics and epistemology but has not received corresponding attention in logical theory. The propositions significant in physical science are oblivious of qualitative considerations as such; they deal with "primary qualities" in distinction from secondary and tertiary; in actual treatment, moreover, these primary qualities are not qualities but relations. Consider the difference between movement as qualitative alteration, and motion as $F = ma;$ between stress as involving effort and tension, and as force per unit surface; between the red of the blood issuing from a wound, and red as signifying 400 trillion vibrations per time unit. Metaphysics has been concerned with the existential status of qualitative objects as contrasted with those of physical science, while epistemology, having frequently decided that qualities are subjective and Psychical, has been concerned with their relation in knowing to the properties of "external" objects defined in non-qualitative terms.

But a logical problem remains. What is the relation or lack of relations between the two types of propositions, one which refers to objects of physical science and the other to qualitative objects? What, if any, are the distinguishing logical marks of each kind? If it were true that things as things, apart from interaction with an organism, are quality-less, the logical problem would remain. For the truth would concern the mode of production and existence of qualitative things. It is irrelevant to their logical status. Logic can hardly admit that it is concerned only with objects having one special mode of production and existence, and yet claim universality. And it would be fatal to the claims of logic to say that because qualities are psychical—supposing for the moment that they are—therefore logical theory has nothing to do with forms of thought characteristic of qualitative objects. It is even possible that some of the difficulties of metaphysical and epistemological theory about scientific and ordinary objects spring from neglect of a basic logical treatment.

A preliminary introduction to the topic may be found in the fact that Aristotelian logic, which still passes current nominally, is a logic based upon the idea that qualitative objects are existential in the fullest sense. To retain logical principles based on this conception along with the acceptance of theories of existence and knowledge based on an opposite conception is not, to say the least, conducive to clearness—a consideration that has a good deal to do with the existing dualism between traditional and the newer relational logics. A more obviously pertinent consideration is the fact that the interpretation of classic logic treats qualitative determinations as fixed properties of objects, and thus is committed to either an attributive or a classificatory doctrine of the import of propositions. Take the proposition: "The red Indian is stoical." This is interpreted either as signifying that the Indian in question is characterized by the property of stoicism in addition to that of redness, or that he belongs to the class of stoical objects. The ordinary direct sense of the proposition escapes recognition in either case. For this sense expresses the fact that the indigenous American was permeated throughout by a certain quality, instead of being an object possessing a certain quality along with others. He lived, acted, endured stoically.

If one thinks that the difference between the two meanings has no logical import, let him reflect that the whole current subject-predication theory of propositions is affected by the "property" notion, whether the theory speaks in the language of attribution or classification. A subject is "given"—ultimately apart from thinking—and then thought adds to what is given a further determination or else assigns it to a ready-made class of things. Neither theory can have any place for the integral development and reconstruction of subject-matter effected by the thought expressed in propositions. In effect it excludes thought from any share in the determination of the subject-matter of knowledge, confining it to setting forth the results (whether conceived as attributive or classificatory) of knowledge already attained in isolation from the method by which it is attained.

Perhaps, however, the consideration that will appeal to most people is the fact that the neglect of qualitative objects and considerations leaves thought in certain subjects without any logical status and control. In esthetic matters, in morals and politics, the effect of this neglect is either to deny (implicitly at least) that they have logical foundation or else, in order to bring them under received logical categories, to evacuate them of their distinctive meaning—a procedure which produces the myth of the "economic man" and the reduction of esthetics and morals, as far as they can receive any intellectual treatment at all, to quasi-mathematical subjects.

Consider for example a picture that is a work of art and not just a chromo or other mode of mechanical product. Its quality is not a property which it possesses in addition to its other properties. It is something which externally demarcates it from other paintings, and which internally pervades, colors, tones, and weights every detail and every relation of the work of art. The same thing is true of the "quality" of a person or of historic events. We follow, with apparently complete understanding, a tale in which a certain quality or character is ascribed to a certain man. But something said causes us to interject, "Oh, you are speaking of Thomas Jones, I supposed you meant John Jones." Every detail related, every distinction set forth remains just what it was before. Yet the significance, the color and weight, of every detail is altered. For the quality that runs through them all, that gives meaning to each and binds them together, is transformed.

Now my point is that unless such underlying and pervasive qualitative determinations are acknowledged in a distinct logical formulation, one or other of two results is bound to follow. Either thought is denied to the subject-matter in question, and the phenomena are attributed to "intuition" or "genius" or "impulse" or "personality" as ultimate and unanalyzable entities; or, worse yet, intellectual analysis is reduced to a mechanical enumeration of isolated items or "properties." As a matter of fact, such intellectual definiteness and coherence as the objects and criticisms of esthetic and moral subjects possess is due to their being controlled by the quality of subject-matter as a whole. Consideration of the meaning of regulation by an underlying and pervasive quality is the theme of this article.

What is intended may be indicated by drawing a distinction between something called a "situation" and something termed an "object." By the term situation in this connection is signified the fact that the subject-matter ultimately referred to in existential propositions is a complex existence that is held together in spite of its internal complexity by the fact that it is dominated and characterized throughout by a single quality. By "object" is meant some element in the complex whole that is defined in abstraction from the whole of which it is a distinction. The special point made is that the selective determination and relation of objects in thought is controlled by reference to a situation—to that which is constituted by a pervasive and internally integrating quality, so that failure to acknowledge the situation leaves, in the end, the logical force of objects and their relations inexplicable.

Now in current logical formulations, the beginning is always made with "objects." If we take the proposition "the stone is shaly," the logical import of the proposition is treated as if something called "stone" had complete intellectual import in and of itself and then some property, having equally a fixed content in isolation, "shaly" is attributed to it. No such self-sufficient and self-enclosed entity can possibly lead anywhere nor be led to; connection among such entities is mechanical and arbitrary, not intellectual. Any proposition about "stone" or "shaly" would have to be analytic in the Kantian sense, merely stating part of the content already known to be contained in the meaning of the terms. That a tautological proposition is a proposition only in name is well recognized. In fact, "stone," "shaly" (or whatever are subject and predicate) are determinations or distinctions instituted within the total subject-matter to which thought refers. When such propositions figure in logical textbooks, the actual subject-matter referred to is some branch of logical theory which is exemplified in the proposition.

This larger and inclusive subject-matter is what is meant by the term "situation." Two further points follow. The situation as such is not and cannot be stated or made explicit. It is taken for granted, "understood," or implicit in all propositional symbolization. It forms the universe of discourse of whatever is expressly stated or of what appears as a term in a proposition. The situation cannot present itself as an element in a proposition any more than a universe of discourse can appear as a member of discourse within that universe. To call it "implicit" does not signify that it is implied. It is present throughout as that of which whatever is explicitly stated or propounded is a distinction. A quart bowl cannot be held within itself or in any of its contents. It may, however, be contained in another bowl, and similarly what is the "situation" in one proposition may appear as a term in *another* proposition—that is, in connection with some *other* situation to which thought now refers.

Secondly, the situation controls the terms of thought, for they are *its* distinctions, and applicability to it is the ultimate test of their validity. It is this phase of the matter which is suggested by the earlier use of the idea of a pervasive and underlying quality. If the quart container affected the import of everything held within it, there would be a physical analogy, a consideration that may be awkwardly hinted at by the case of a person protesting to a salesman that he has not received a full quart; the deficiency affects everything that he has purchased. A work of art provides an apter illustration. In it, as we have already noted, the quality of the whole permeates, affects, and controls every detail. There are paintings, buildings, novels, arguments, in which an observer notes an inability of the author to sustain a unified attention throughout. The details fall to pieces; they are not distinctions of one subject-matter, because there is no qualitative unity underlying them. Confusion and incoherence are always marks of lack of control by a single pervasive quality. The latter alone enables a person to keep track of what he is doing, saying, hearing, reading, in whatever explicitly appears. The underlying unity of qualitativeness regulates pertinence or relevancy and force of every distinction and relation; it guides selection and rejection and the manner of utilization of all explicit terms. This quality enables us to keep thinking about one problem without our having constantly to stop to ask ourselves what it is after all that we are thinking about. We are aware of it not by itself but as the background, the thread, and the directive clue in what we do expressly think of. For the latter things are *its* distinctions and relations.[1]

If we designate this permeating qualitative unity in psychological language, we say it is felt rather than thought. Then, if we hypostatize

---

[1] The "fringe" of James seems to me to be a somewhat unfortunate way of expressing the role of the underlying qualitative character that constitutes a situation—unfortunate because the metaphor tends to treat it as an additional element instead of an all-pervasive influence in determining other contents.

it, we call it *a* feeling. But to term it a feeling is to reverse the actual state of affairs. The existence of unifying qualitativeness in the subject-matter defines the meaning of "feeling." The notion that "a feeling" designates a ready-made independent psychical entity is a product of a reflection which presupposes the direct presence of quality as such. "Feeling" and "felt" are names for a *relation* of quality. When, for example, anger exists, it is the pervading tone, color, and quality of persons, things, and circumstances, or of a situation. When angry we are not aware of anger but of these objects in their immediate and unique qualities. In another situation, anger may appear as a distinct term, and analysis may then call it a feeling or emotion. But we have now shifted the universe of discourse, and the validity of the terms of the later one depends upon the existence of the direct quality of the whole in a former one. That is, in saying that something was *felt* not thought of, we are analyzing in a new situation, having its own immediate quality, the subject-matter of a prior situation; we are making anger an object of analytic examination, not being angry.

When it is said that I have a feeling, or impression, or "hunch," that things are thus and so, what is actually designated is primarily the presence of a dominating quality in a situation as a whole, not just the existence of a feeling as a psychical or psychological fact. To say I have a feeling or impression that so and so is the case is to note that the quality in question is not yet resolved into determinate terms and relations; it marks a conclusion without statement of the reasons for it, the grounds upon which it rests. It is the first stage in the development of explicit distinctions. All thought in every subject begins with just such an unanalyzed whole. When the subject-matter is reasonably familiar, relevant distinctions speedily offer themselves, and sheer qualitativeness may not remain long enough to be readily recalled. But it often persists and forms a haunting and engrossing problem. It is a commonplace that a problem *stated* is well on its way to solution, for statement of the nature of a problem signifies that the underlying quality is being transformed into determinate distinctions of terms and relations or has become an object of articulate thought. But something presents itself as problematic before there is recognition of *what* the problem is. The problem is had or experienced before it can be stated or set forth; but it is had as an immediate quality of the whole situation. The sense of something problematic, of something perplexing and to be resolved, marks the presence of something pervading all elements and considerations. Thought is the operation by which it is converted into pertinent and coherent terms.

The word "intuition" has many meanings. But in its popular, as distinct from refined philosophic, usage it is closely connected with the single qualitativeness underlying all the details of explicit reasoning. It may be relatively dumb and inarticulate and yet penetrating; unexpressed in definite ideas which form reasons and justifications and yet profoundly right. To my mind, Bergson's contention that intuition precedes conception and goes deeper is correct. Reflection and rational elaboration spring from and make explicit a prior intuition. But there is nothing mystical about this fact, and it does not signify that there are two modes of knowledge, one of which is appropriate to one kind of subject-matter, and the other mode to the other kind. Thinking and theorizing about physical matters set out from an Intuition, and reflection about affairs of life and mind consists in an ideational and conceptual transformation of what begins as an intuition. Intuition, in short, signifies the realization of a pervasive quality such that it regulates the determination of relevant distinctions or of whatever, whether in the way of terms or relations, becomes the accepted object of thought.

While some ejaculations and interjections are merely organic responses, there are those which have an intellectual import, though only context and the total situation can decide to which class a particular ejaculation belongs. "Alas," "Yes," "No," "Oh" may each of them be the symbol of an integrated attitude toward the quality of a situation as a whole; that it is thoroughly pitiful, acceptable, to be rejected, or is a matter of complete surprise. In this case, they characterize the existent situation and as such have a cognitive import. The exclamation "Good!" may mark a deep apprehension of the quality of a piece of acting on the stage, of a deed performed, or of a picture in its wealth of content. The actual judgment may find better expression in these symbols than in a long-winded disquisition. To many persons there is something artificial and repellent in discoursing about any consummatory event or object. It speaks so completely for itself that words are poor substitutes—not that thought fails, but that thought so completely grasps the dominant quality that translation into explicit terms gives a partial and inadequate result.

Such ejaculatory judgments supply perhaps the simplest example of qualitative thought in its purity. While they are primitive, it does not follow that they are always superficial and immature. Sometimes, indeed, they express an infantile mode of intellectual response. But they may also sum up and integrate prolonged previous experience and training, and bring to a unified head the results of severe and consecutive reflection. Only the situation symbolized and not the formal and propositional symbol can decide which is the case. The full content of meaning is best appprehended in case of the judgment of the esthetic expert in the presence of a work of art. But they come at the beginning and at the close of every scientific investigation. These open with the "Oh" of wonder and terminate with the "Good" of a rounded-out and organized situation. Neither the "Oh" nor the "Good" expresses a mere state of personal feeling. Each characterizes a subject-matter. "How beautiful" symbolizes neither a state of feeling nor the supervening of an external essence upon a state of existence but marks the realized appreciation of a pervading quality that is now translated into a system of definite and coherent terms. Language fails not because thought fails, but because no verbal symbols can do justice to the fullness and richness of thought. If we are to continue talking about "data" in any other sense than as reflective distinctions, the original datum is always such a qualitative whole.

The logic of artistic construction is worth more than a passing notice, whether its product be a painting, a symphony, a statue, a building, a drama, or a novel. So far as it is not evidence of conceit on the part of a specialized class, refusal to admit thought and logic on the part of those who make these constructions is evidence of the breakdown of traditional logic. There are (as we previously noted) alleged works of art in which parts do not hang together and in which the quality of one part does not reinforce and expand the quality of every other part. But this fact is itself a manifestation of the defective character of the thought involved in their production. It illustrates by contrast the nature of such works as are genuine intellectual and logical wholes. In the latter, the underlying quality that defines the work, that circumscribes it externally and integrates it internally, controls the thinking of the artist; his logic is the logic of what I have called qualitative thinking.

Upon subsequent analysis, we term the properties of a work of art by such names as symmetry, harmony, rhythm, measure, and proportion. These may, in some cases at least, be formulated mathematically. But the apprehension of these formal relationships is not primary for either the artist or the appreciative spectator. The subject-matter formulated by these terms is primarily qualitative, and is apprehended qualita-

tively. Without an independent qualitative apprehension, the characteristics of a work of art can be translated into explicit harmonies,
symmetries, etc., only in a way which substitutes mechanical formulae
for esthetic quality. The value of any such translation in esthetic criticism is measured, moreover, by the extent to which the propositional
statements return to effect a heightening and deepening of a qualitative
apprehension. Otherwise, esthetic appreciation is replaced by judgment
of isolated technique.

The logic of artistic construction and esthetic appreciation is peculiarly significant because they exemplify in accentuated and purified
form the control of selection of detail and of mode of relation, or integration, by a qualitative whole. The underlying quality demands certain
distinctions, and the degree in which the demand is met confers upon
the work of art that necessary or inevitable character which is its mark.
Formal necessities, such as can be made explicit, depend upon the material necessity imposed by the pervasive and underlying quality. Artistic thought is not however unique in this respect but only shows an
intensification of a characteristic of all thought. In a looser way, it is a
characteristic of all non-technical, non-"scientific" thought. Scientific
thought is, in its turn, a specialized form of art, with its own qualitative
control. The more formal and mathematical science becomes, the more
it is controlled by sensitiveness to a special kind of qualitative considerations. Failure to realize the qualitative and artistic nature of formal
scientific construction is due to two causes. One is conventional, the
habit of associating art and esthetic appreciation with a few popularly
recognized forms. The other cause is the fact that a student is so concerned with the mastery of symbolic or propositional forms that he
fails to recognize and to repeat the creative operations involved in their
construction. Or, when they are mastered, he is more concerned with
their further application than with realization of their intrinsic intellectual meaning.

The foregoing remarks are intended to suggest the significance to be
attached to the term "qualitative thought." But as statements they are
propositions and hence symbolic. Their meaning can be apprehended
only by going beyond them, by using them as clues to call up qualitative situations. When an experience of the latter is had and they are re-
lived, the realities corresponding to the propositions laid down may be
had. Assuming that such a realization has been experienced, we pro-

ceed to consider some further questions upon which qualitative thought throws light.

First as to the nature of the predication. The difficulties connected with the problem of predication are of long standing. They were recognized in Greek thought, and the scepticism they induced was a factor in developing the Platonic theory of the same-and-the-other and the Aristotelian conception of potentiality-and-actuality. The sceptical difficulty may be summed up in the statement that predication is either tautological and so meaningless, or else falsifying or at least arbitrary. Take the proposition "that thing is sweet." If "sweet" already qualifies the meaning of "that thing," the predication is analytic in the Kantian sense, or forms a trivial proposition in the sense of Locke. But if "sweet" does not already qualify "that thing" what ground is there for tacking it on? The most that can be said is that some one who did not know before that it was sweet has now learned it. But such a statement refers only to an episode in the some one's intellectual biography. It has no logical force; it does not touch the question of predication that has objective reference and possible validity.

When, however, it is recognized that predication—any proposition having subject—predicate form-marks an attempt to make a qualitative whole which is directly and non-reflectively experienced into an object of thought for the sake of its own development, the case stands otherwise. What is "given" is not an object by itself nor a term having a meaning of its own. The "given," that is to say the existent, is precisely an undetermined and dominant complex quality. "Subject" and "predicate" are correlative determinations of this quality. The "copula" stands for the fact that one term is predicated of the other, and is thus a sign of the development of the qualitative whole by means of their distinction. It is, so to speak, the assertion of the fact that the distinctions designated in subject and predicate are correlative and work together in a common function of determination.

A certain quality is experienced. When it is inquired into or thought (judged), it differentiates into "that thing" on the one hand, and "sweet" on the other. Both "that thing" and "sweet" are analytic of the quality, but are additive, synthetic, ampliative, with respect to each other. The copula "is" marks just the effect of this distinction upon the correlative terms. They mark something like a division of labor, and the copula marks the function or work done by the structures that exhibit the division of labor. To say that "that thing is sweet" means "that thing" will *sweeten* some other object, say coffee, or a batter of milk and eggs. The intent of sweetening something formed the ground for converting a dumb quality into an articulate object of thought.

The logical force of the copula is always that of an active verb. It is merely a linguistic peculiarity, not a logical fact, that we say "that is red" instead of "that reddens," either in the sense of growing, becoming red, or in the sense of making something else red. Even linguistically our "is" is a weakened form of an active verb signifying "stays" or "stands." But the nature of any act (designated by the true verbal form) is best apprehended in its effect and issue; we say "is sweet" rather than "sweetens," "is red" rather than "reddens" because we define the active change by its anticipated or attained outcome. To say "the dog is ugly" is a way of setting forth what he is likely to do, namely to snarl and bite. "Man is mortal" indicates what man does or what actively is done to him, calling attention to a consequence. If we convert its verbal form into "men die," we realize the transitive and additive force of predication and escape the self-made difficulties of the attributive theory.

The underlying pervasive quality in the last instance, when it is put in words, involves care or concern for human destiny. But we must remember that this exists as a dumb quality until it is symbolized in an intellectual and propositional form. Out of this quality there emerges the idea of man and of mortality and of their existential connection with each other. No one of them has any meaning apart from the others, neither the distinctions, the terms, nor their relation, the predication. All the difficulties that attend the problem of predication spring from supposing that we can take the terms and their connection as having meaning by themselves. The sole alternative to this supposition is the recognition that the object of thought, designated propositionally, is a quality that is first directly and unreflectively experienced or had.

One source of the difficulty and the error in the classic theory lies in a radical misconception of the treacherous idea of the "given." The only thing that is unqualifiedly given is the total pervasive quality; and the objection to calling it "given" is that the word suggests something *to* which it is given, mind or thought or consciousness or whatever, as well possibly as something that gives. In truth "given" in this connection signifies only that the quality immediately exists, or is brutely there. In this capacity, it forms that to which all objects of thought refer, although, as we have noticed, it is never part of the manifest subject-matter of thought. In itself, it is the big, buzzing, blooming confusion of which James wrote. This expresses not only the state of a baby's experience but the first stage and background of all thinking on any subject. There is, however, no inarticulate quality which is merely buzzing and blooming. It buzzes to some effect; it blooms toward some fruitage. That is, the quality, although dumb, has as a part of its complex quality a movement or transition in some direction. It can, therefore, be intellectually symbolized and converted into an object of thought. This is done by statement of limits and of direction of transition between them. "That" and "sweet" define the limits of the moving quality, the copula "tastes" (the real force of "is") defines the direction of movement between these limits. Putting the nature of the two limits briefly and without any attempt to justify the statement here, the subject represents the pervasive quality as means or condition and the predicate represents it as outcome or end.

These considerations define not only the subject-predicate structure of categorical propositions but they explain why the selective character of all such propositions with respect to the fullness of existence is not falsifying in character. Idealistic logicians, in calling attention to the partial or selective character of particular judgments, have used the fact to cast logical aspersion upon them, and to infer their need of correction first by transformation into conditional propositions and then finally into a judgment coextensive with the whole universe, arguing that only the latter can be truly true. But enough is always enough, and the underlying quality is itself the test of the "enough" for any particular case. All that is needed is to determine this quality by indicating the limits between which it moves and the direction or tendency of its movement. Sometimes the situation is simple and the most meagre indications serve, like the "safe" or "out" of a baseball umpire. At other times, a quality is complex and prolonged, and a multitude of distinctions and subordinate relations are required for its determinate statement. It would have been logically vicious on one occasion to propound more than "my kingdom for a horse," while under other circumstances it may need a volume to set forth the quality of the situation so as to make It comprehensible. Any proposition that serves the purpose for which it is made is logically adequate; the idea that it is inadequate until the whole universe has been included is a consequence of giving judgment a wrong office—an error that has its source in failure to see the domination of every instance of thought by a qualitative whole needing statement in order that it may function.

At this point a reference to what is termed association of ideas is in place. For while the subject is usually treated as psychological in nature, thinking as an existential process takes place through association; existentially, thinking *is* association as far as the latter is controlled. And the mechanics of thinking can hardly be totally irrelevant to its *logical* structure and function. I shall assume without much argument that "ideas" here signify objects, not psychical entities; objects, that is to say, as meanings to which reference may be made. When one, seeing smoke, thinks of fire he is associating objects, not just states in his own mind. And so when thinking of a hand, one thinks of grasping or of an organism. Thus, when association takes the form of thought, or is controlled and not loose day-dreaming, association is a name for a connection of objects or their elements in the total situation having a qualitative unity. This statement signifies something different than does a statement that associated objects are physical parts of a physical whole. It happens to hold in the case of "hand-organism" and with some qualifications in the case of "smoke-fire." But a philosophical student might be led by the thought of hand to the thought of Aristotle on the ground of a remark made by Aristotle.

In any case an original contiguity (or similarity) is not the *cause* of an association. We do not associate *by* contiguity, for recognition of a whole in which elements are juxtaposed in space or in temporal sequence is the *result* of suggestion. The absurdity of the preposition "by" when applied to similarity is still more obvious. It is the reason why some writers reduce similarity to identity in differences, a position that will be examined later. That by which association is effected, by which suggestion and evocation of a distinct object of thought is brought about, is some acquired modification of the organism, usually designated habit. The conditioning mechanism may not be known at present in detail, but it cannot be an original contiguity because that contiguity is apprehended only in consequence of association. It may well be an organic attitude formed in consequence of a responsive act to things once coexistent or sequential. But this act was unitary; reference to it only accentuates the fact that the quality attending it was spread over and inclusive of the two things in question. That is, it was a response to a *situation* within which objects were related in space or time.

Given the conditions, the real problem is to say why objects once conjoined in a whole are now distinguished as two objects, one that which suggests, and the other that which is suggested. If I think of a chiffonier, the thought does not call up that of drawers as a distinct idea. For the drawers are a part of the object thought of. So when I originally saw, say a bird-in-a-nest, I saw a single total object. Why then does the sight or thought of a bird now call up that of a nest as a distinct idea? In general, the reason is that I have so often seen birds without seeing a nest and nests without birds. Moreover, it must be remembered that a person often sees a bird or nest, and instead of thinking of any other object, he reacts to it directly, as a man does when shooting at a bird or a boy climbing a tree to get the nest. While there is no association without habit, the natural tendency of habit is to produce an immediate reaction, not to evoke another distinct object of thought or idea. As the *dis*association of birds and nests in experience shows, this additional factor is some resistance to the attitude formed by the sight of nest-with-a-bird-in-it. Otherwise we should have the case over again of chiffonier and its drawers, or any object and its constitutive parts. Without the resistant or negative factor, there would be no tension to effect the change from a direct response, an immediate act, to an indirect one, a distinct object of thought.

Not only then is there no association *by* contiguity, but association is not *of* two objects separated yet contiguous in a prior experience. Its characteristic nature is that it presents as distinct but connected objects what originally were either two parts of one situational object, or (in the case that a man had previously always seen birds and nests separately from each other) that it presents in coexistence or sequence with one another objects previously separated in space and time. This consideration is fatal to the notion that the associated objects account by themselves or in their own isolated nature for association. It indicates that coexistence or sequence as a physical existential fact is not the ground of association. What alternative remains save that the quality of a situation as a whole operates to produce a functional connection? Acceptance of this alternative implies that association is an *intellectual* connection, thus aligning association with thought, as we shall now see.

There is nothing intellectual or logical in contiguity, in mere juxtaposition in space and time. If association were, then, either *of* or *by* contiguity, association would not have any logical force, any connection with thought.[2] But in fact association of bare contiguities is a myth. There is an indefinite number of particulars contiguous to one another in space and time. When I think of a nest, why does a bird come into my mind? As a matter of contiguity, there are multitudinous leaves and twigs which are more frequently and more obviously juxtaposed than is a bird. When I think of a hammer, why is the idea of nail so likely to follow? Such questions suggest, I hope, that even in seemingly casual cases of association, there is an underlying quality which operates to control the connection of objects thought of. It takes something else than contiguity to effect association; there must be relevancy of both ideas to a situation defined by unity of quality. There is coherence of some sort because of mutual pertinency of both ideas (or of all ideas in train) to a basis beyond any of them and beyond mere juxtaposition of objects in space and time.

The usual notion that association is merely *de facto* receives a still more obvious shock in the case of similarity. When I associate bird with nest, there may have been at least some previous conjunction in experience of the two objects, even though that conjunction is not by itself a sufficient condition of the later association. But when troublesome thought suggests the sting of an insect, or when change of fortune suggests the ebb and flow of the sea, there is *no* physical conjunction in the past to which appeal can be made. To try to explain the matter by saying that two objects are associated *because* they are similar is either to offer the problem as a solution or to attribute causal efficacy to "similarity"—which is to utter meaningless words. So-called association "by" similarity is a striking example of the influence of an underlying pervasive quality in determining the connection essential in thought.

There is, as far as I am aware, but one serious attempt to explain such association on some other basis. This is found in the view that there is in what is called similarity an actual existential identity among differences and that this identity works and then reinstates differences by contiguity. I fail to see how the explanation applies in many cases— such as that of the troublesome thought and the sting of an insect, or Socrates and a gadfly. "Identity" seems to be the result rather than

---

[2] The assumption that in the case of contiguity association is of merely *de facto* or existential nature is the root of Lotze's (and other's) theory that *a priori* logical forms are necessary in order to change juxtaposition of things into coherence of meaning.

the antecedent of the association. But I shall confine the discussion to instances in which it is claimed to work. Bradley has stated the theory in question most clearly and I shall use his illustration.[3]

Walking on the shore of England, one sees a promontory and re-marks how like it is to one in Wales. Bradley's explanation is that there is an actual identity of form in both and that this identical form sug-gests by contiguity in space certain elements which cannot be referred to the promontory now seen (size, color, etc., being incompatible) and thus constitutes in connection with identical form the content of the idea of the promontory in Wales. The seeming plausibility of this ex-planation is shattered by the fact that form is not one isolated element among others, but is an arrangement or pattern of elements. Identity of pattern, arrangement of form is something that can be apprehended only *after* the other promontory has been suggested, by comparison of the two objects.

The only way that form or pattern can operate as an immediate link is by the mode of a directly experienced *quality,* something present and prior to and independent of all reflective analysis, something of the same nature which controls artistic construction. In psychological lan-guage, it is felt, and the feeling is made explicit or a term of thought in the idea of another promontory. What operates is not an external exis-tential identity between two things, but a present immediate qual-ity—an explanation which is the only one applicable to some cases already cited, and to being reminded of blotting paper by a certain voice. The priority of regulative quality of the situation as a whole is especially obvious in the case of esthetic judgments. A man sees a picture and says at first sight that it is by Goya or by some one influ-enced by him. He passes the judgment long before he has made any analysis or any explicit identification of elements. It is the quality of the picture as a whole that operates. With a trained observer such a judgment based on pervasive quality may lead later to definite analysis of elements and details; the result of the analysis may confirm or may lead to rejection of the original ascription. But the basic appreciation of quality as a whole is a more dependable basis of such point by point analysis and its conclusion than is an external analysis performed by a critic who knows history and mechanical points of brushwork but who is lacking in sensitiveness to pervasive quality.

---

[3] *Logic,* Vol. I, Book II, Part 2, Ch. I, Sec. 30.

Another instance of Bradley's refers to Mill's denial that the suggestion of another triangle by a given triangle can be reduced to contiguity. For, Mill says, "the form of a triangle is not one single feature among others." Bradley thinks such a view absurd; he cannot, he says, even tell what is meant. The use of the term "feature" may be unfortunate. For when we speak of a nose as a feature of a face, we have in mind one element or part among others. Now triangularity is not such an isolable element. It is a characteristic of the disposition, arrangement, or pattern of all elements, and it must be capable of immediate realization. Even a nose as a feature of a man's face is not completely isolable. For it is characterized by the whole face as well as characterizing that face. A better instance is found, however, when we speak of a man's *expression.* That assuredly is a total effect of all elements in their relation to one another, not a "single feature among others." And so is triangularity. Family resemblances are often detected, and yet one is totally unable to specify the points of resemblance. Unanalyzed quality of the whole accounts for the identification as a *result,* and it is a radically different thing from identification of a man by finger prints.

The outcome of this brief discussion, in revealing the significance of dominant qualitativeness in suggestion and connection of ideas, shows why thinking as an existential process is all one with controlled association.[4] For the latter is not explained by any merely external conjunction or any external identity in things. If it were, association would itself be merely another case of existential sequence, coexistence, or identity and would be lacking in intellectual and logical import. But selection and coherence determined by an immediate quality that constitutes and delimits a situation are characteristics of "association." These traits are different in kind from existential conjunction and physical sameness, and identical with those of thought. The case of similarity or resemblance is almost uniquely significant. The problem of its nature is a crux of philosophies. The difficulty of dealing with it leads one on the one hand to thinking of it as purely psychical in nature, and, on the other hand, to the idealistic identification of the ontological and

---

[4] Were I to venture into speculative territory, I might apply this conception to the problem of "thinking" in animals, and what the *Gestalt* psychologists call "insight." That total quality operates with animals and sometimes secures, as with monkeys, results like those we obtain by reflective analysis cannot, it seems to me, be doubted. But that this operation of quality in effecting results then goes out into symbolization and analysis is quite another matter.

the logical *via* the principle of identity in difference. The recognition of pervasive quality enables us to avoid both extremes. By its means a voice is assimilated to blotting paper, and in more serious intellectual matters analogy becomes a guiding principle of scientific thought. On the basis of *assimilation* a further explicit recognition of similarity takes place. For assimilation is not itself the perception or judgment of similarity; the latter requires a further act made possible by symbols. It involves a proposition. The saying that there is a "tide in the affairs of men, etc." does not of itself involve any direct comparison of human affairs with the ocean and an explicit judgment of likeness. A pervasive quality has resulted in an assimilation. If symbols are at hand, this assimilation may lead to a further act—the judgment of similarity. But *de facto* assimilation comes first and need not eventuate in the express conception of resemblance.[5]

"Assimilation" denotes the efficacious operation of pervasive quality; "similarity" denotes a *relation*. *Sheer* assimilation results in the presence of a single object of apprehension. To identify a seen thing *as* a promontory is a case of assimilation. By some physiological process, not exactly understood at present but to which the name "habit" is given, the net outcome of prior experiences gives a dominant quality, designated "promontory" to a perceived existence. Passage from this object to some other implies resistance to mere assimilation and results in making distinctions. The pervasive quality is differentiated while at the same time these differentiations are connected. The result is an explicit statement or proposition.

I have touched, as I am well aware, only upon the fringes of a complex subject. But in view of the general neglect of the subject, I shall be satisfied if I have turned the attention of those interested in thought and its workings to an overlooked field. Omitting reference to ramifications, the gist of the matter is that the immediate existence of quality, and of dominant and pervasive quality, is the background, the point of departure, and the regulative principle of all thinking. Thought which denies the existential reality of qualitative things is therefore bound to end in self-contradiction and in denying itself. "Scientific" thinking, that expressed in physical science, never gets away from qualitative

---

[5] Thus, to recur to Bradley's example, one may pass directly from the promontory in England to one in Wales and become absorbed into the latter without any judgment of the likeness of the two.

existence. Directly, it always has its own qualitative background; indirectly, it has that of the world in which the ordinary experience of the common man is lived. Failure to recognize this fact is the source of a large part of the artificial problems and fallacies that infect our theory of knowledge and our metaphysics, or theories of existence. With this general conclusion goes another that has been emphasized in the preceding discussion. Construction that is artistic is as much a case of genuine thought as that expressed in scientific and philosophical matters, and so is all genuine esthetic appreciation of art, since the latter must in some way, to be vital, retrace the course of the creative process. But the development of this point in its bearing upon esthetic judgment and theory is another story.

Time and Individuality

The Greeks had a saying, "Count no man happy till after his death." The adage was a way of calling attention to the uncertainties of life. No one knows what a year or even a day may bring forth. The healthy become ill; the rich poor; the mighty are cast down; fame changes to obloquy. Men live at the mercy of forces they cannot control. Belief in fortune and luck, good or evil, is one of the most widespread and persistent of human beliefs. Chance has been deified by many peoples. Fate has been set up as an overlord to whom even the Gods must bow. Belief in a Goddess of Luck is in ill repute among pious folk but their belief in providence is a tribute to the fact no individual controls his own destiny.

The uncertainty of life and one's final lot has always been associated with mutability, while unforeseen and uncontrollable change has been linked with time. Time is the tooth that gnaws; it is the destroyer; we are born only to die and every day brings us one day nearer death. This attitude is not confined to the ignorant and vulgar. It is the root of what is sometimes called the instinctive belief in immortality. Everything perishes in time but men are unable to believe that perishing is the last word. For centuries poets made the uncertainty which time brings with it the theme of their discourse—read Shakespeare's sonnets. Nothing stays; life is fleeting and all earthly things are transitory.

It was not then for metaphysical reasons that classic philosophy maintained that change, and consequently time, are marks of inferior reality, holding that true and ultimate reality is immutable and eternal. Human reasons, all too human, have given birth to the idea that over and beyond the lower realm of things that shift like the sands on the seashore there is the kingdom of the unchanging, of the complete, the perfect. The grounds for the belief are couched in the technical language of philosophy, but the cause for the grounds is the heart's desire for surcease from change, struggle, and uncertainty. The eternal and immutable is the consummation of mortal man's quest for certainty.

It is not strange then that philosophies which have been at odds on every other point have been one in the conviction that the ultimately real is fixed and unchanging, even though they have been as far apart as the poles in their ideas of its constitution. The idealist has found it in a realm of rational ideas; the materialist in the laws of matter. The mechanist pins his faith to eternal atoms and to unmoved and unmoving space. The teleologist finds that all change is subservient to fixed ends and final goals, which are the one steadfast thing in the universe, conferring upon changing things whatever meaning and value they possess. The typical realist attributes to unchanging essences a greater degree of reality than belongs to existences; the modem mathematical realist finds the stability his heart desires in the immunity of the realm of possibilities from vicissitude. Although classic rationalism looked askance at experience and empirical things because of their continual subjection to alteration, yet strangely enough traditional sensational empiricism relegated time to a secondary role. Sensations appeared and disappeared but in their own nature they were as fixed as were Newtonian atoms—of which indeed they were mental copies. Ideas were but weakened copies of sensory impressions and had no inherent forward power and application. The passage of time dimmed their vividness and caused their decay. Because of their subjection to the tooth of time, they were denied productive force.

In the late eighteenth and the greater part of the nineteenth centuries appeared the first marked cultural shift in the attitude taken toward change. Under the names of indefinite perfectability, progress, and evolution, the movement of things in the universe itself and of the universe as a whole began to take on a beneficent instead of a hateful aspect. Not every change was regarded as a sign of advance but the general trend of change, cosmic and social, was thought to be toward the better. Aside from the Christian idea of a millennium of good and bliss to be finally wrought by supernatural means, the Golden Age for the first time in history was placed in the future instead of at the beginning, and change and time were assigned a benevolent role.

Even if the new optimism was not adequately grounded, there were sufficient causes for its occurrence as there are for all great changes in intellectual climate. The rise of new science in the seventeenth century laid hold upon general culture in the next century. Its popular effect was not great, but its influence upon the intellectual elite, even upon those who were not themselves engaged in scientific inquiry, was prodigious. The enlightenment, the *éclaircissement,* the *Aufklärung*—

names which in the three most advanced countries of Europe testified to the widespread belief that at last light had dawned, that dissipation of the darkness of ignorance, superstition, and bigotry was at hand, and the triumph of reason was assured—for reason was the counterpart in man of the laws of nature which science was disclosing. The reign of law in the natural world was to be followed by the reign of law in human affairs. A vista of the indefinite perfectibility of man was opened. It played a large part in that optimistic theory of automatic evolution which later found its classic formulation in the philosophy of Herbert Spencer. The faith may have been pathetic but it has its own nobility.

At last, time was thought to be working on the side of the good instead of as a destructive agent. Things were moving to an event which was divine, even if far off.

This new philosophy, however, was far from giving the temporal an inherent position and function in the constitution of things. Change was working on the side of man but only because of *fixed* laws which governed the changes that take place. There was hope in change just because the laws that govern it do not change. The locus of the immutable was shifted to scientific natural law, but the faith and hope of philosophers and intellectuals were still tied to the unchanging. The belief that "evolution" is identical with progress was based upon trust in laws which, being fixed, worked automatically toward the final end of freedom, justice, and brotherhood, the natural consequences of the reign of reason.

Not till the late nineteenth century was the doctrine of the subordination of time and change seriously challenged. Bergson and William James, animated by different motives and proceeding by different methods, then installed change at the very heart of things. Bergson took his stand on the primacy of life and consciousness, which are notoriously in a state of flux. He assimilated that which is completely real in the natural world to them, conceiving the static as that which life leaves behind as a deposit as it moves on. From this point of view he criticized mechanistic and teleological theories on the ground that both are guilty of the same error, although from opposite points. Fixed laws which govern change and fixed ends toward which changes tend are both the products of a backward look, one that ignores the forward movement of life. They apply only to that which life has produced and has then left behind in its ongoing vital creative course, a course whose behavior and outcome are unpredictable both mechanistically and from the standpoint of ends. The intellect is at home in that which is fixed only because it is done and over with, for intellect is itself just as much a deposit of past life as is the matter to which it is congenial. Intuition alone articulates in the forward thrust of life and alone lays hold of reality.

The animating purpose of James was, on the other hand, primarily moral and artistic. It is expressed in his phrase, "block universe," employed as a term of adverse criticism. Mechanism and idealism were abhorrent to him because they both hold to a closed universe in which there is no room for novelty and adventure. Both sacrifice individuality and all the values, moral and aesthetic, which hang upon individuality; for according to absolute idealism, as to mechanistic materialism, the individual is simply a part determined by the whole of which he is a part. Only a philosophy of pluralism, of genuine indetermination, and of change which is real and intrinsic gives significance to individuality. It alone justifies struggle in creative activity and gives opportunity for the emergence of the genuinely new.

It was reserved, however, for the present century to give birth to the out-and-out assertion in systematic form that reality *is* process, and that laws as well as things develop in the processes of unceasing change. The modem Heraclitean is Alfred North Whitehead, but he is Heraclitus with a change. The doctrine of the latter, while it held that all things flow like a river and that change is so continuous that a man cannot step into the same river even once (since it changes as he steps), nevertheless also held that there is a fixed order which controls the ebb and flow of the universal tide.

My theme, however, is not historical, nor is it to argue in behalf of any one of the various doctrines regarding time that have been advanced. The purpose of the history just roughly sketched is to indicate that the nature of time and change has now become in its own right a philosophical problem of the first importance. It is of time as a problem that I wish to speak. The aspect of the problem that will be considered is the connection of time with individuality, as the latter is exemplified in the living organism and especially in human beings.

Take the account of the life of any person, whether the account is a biography or an autobiography. The story begins with birth, a temporal incident; it extends to include the temporal existence of parents and ancestry. It does not end with death, for it takes in the influence upon subsequent events of the words and deeds of the one whose life is told. Everything recorded is an historical event; it is something temporal. The individual whose life history is told, be it Socrates or Nero, St. Francis or Abraham Lincoln, is an extensive event; or, if you prefer, it is a course of events each of which takes up into itself something of what went before and leads on to that which comes after. The skill, the art, of the biographer is displayed in his ability to discover and portray the subtle ways, hidden often from the individual himself, in which one event grows out of those which preceded and enters into those which follow. The human individual is himself a history, a career, and for this reason his biography can be related only as a temporal event. That which comes later explains the earlier quite as truly as the earlier explains the later. Take the individual Abraham Lincoln at one year, at five years, at ten years, at thirty years of age, and imagine everything later wiped out, no matter how minutely his life is recorded up to the date set. It is plain beyond the need of words that we then have not his biography but only a fragment of it, while the significance of that fragment is undisclosed. For he did not just exist in a time which externally surrounded him, but time was the heart of his existence.

Temporal seriality is the very essence, then, of the human individual. It is impossible for a biographer in writing, say, the story of the first thirty years of the life of Lincoln, not to bear in mind his later career. Lincoln as an individual is a history; any particular event cut off from that history ceases to be a part of his life as an individual. As Lincoln is a particular development in time, so is every other human individual. Individuality is the uniqueness of the history, of the career, not something given once for all at the beginning which then proceeds to unroll as a ball of yarn may be unwound. Lincoln made history. But it is just as true that he made himself as an individual in the history he made.

I have been speaking about human individuality. Now an important part of the problem of time is that what is true of the human individual does not seem to be true of physical individuals. The common saying "as like as two peas" is a virtual denial to one kind of vegetable life of the kind of individuality that marks human beings. It is hard to conceive of the individuality of a given pea in terms of a unique history or career; such individuality as it appears to possess seems to be due in part to spatial separateness and in part to peculiarities that are externally caused. The same thing holds true of lower forms of animal life. Most persons would resent denial of some sort of unique individuality to their own dogs, but would be slow to attribute it to worms, clams, and bees. Indeed, it seems to be an exclusive prerogative of the romantic novelist to find anything in the way of a unique career in animal lives in general.

When we come to inanimate elements, the prevailing view has been that time and sequential change are entirely foreign to their nature. According to this view they do not have careers; they simply change their relations in space. We have only to think of the classic conception of atoms. The Newtonian atom, for example, moved and was moved, thus changing its position in space, but it was unchangeable in its own being. What it was at the beginning or without any beginning it is always and forever. Owing to the impact of other things it changes its direction and velocity of motion so that it comes closer and further away from other things. But all this was believed to be external to its own substantial being. It had no development, no history, because it had no potentialities. In itself it was like a God, the same yesterday, today, and forever. Time did not enter into its being either to corrode or to develop it. Nevertheless, as an ultimate element it was supposed to have some sort of individuality, to be itself and not something else. Time, in physical science, has been simply a measure of motion in space.

Now, this apparently complete unlikeness in kind between the human and the physical individual is a part of the problem of time. Some philosophers have been content to note the difference and to make it the ground for affirming a sheer dualism between man and other things, a ground for assigning to man a spiritual being in contrast with material things. Others, fewer in numbers, have sought to explain away the seeming disparity, holding that the apparent uniqueness of human individuality is specious, being in fact the effect of the vast number of physical molecules, themselves complex, which make up his being, so that what looks like genuine temporal change or development is really but a function of the number and complexity of changes of constituent fixed elements. Of late, there have been a few daring souls who have held that temporal quality and historical career are a mark of everything, including atomic elements, to which individuality may be attributed.

I shall mention some of the reasons from the side of physical science that have led to this third idea. The first reason is the growing recognition that scientific objects are purely relational and have nothing to do with the intrinsic qualities of individual things and nothing to say about them. The meaning of this statement appears most clearly in the case of scientific laws. It is now a commonplace that a physical law states a correlation of changes or of ways and manners of change. The law of gravitation, for example, states a relation which holds between bodies with respect to distance and mass. It needs no argument to show that distance is a relation. Mass was long regarded as an inherent property of ultimate and individual elements. But even the Newtonian conception was obliged to recognize that mass could be defined only in terms of inertia and that inertia could be defined only in terms, on the one hand, of the resistance it offered to the impact of other bodies, and, on the other hand, of its capacity to exercise impact upon them, impact being measured in terms of motion with respect to acceleration. The idea that mass is an inherent property which caused inertia and momentum was simply a holdover from an old metaphysical idea of force. As far as the findings of science are concerned, independent of the intrusion of metaphysical ideas, mass is inertia-momentum and these are strictly measures and relations. The discovery that mass changes with velocity, a discovery made when minute bodies came under consideration, finally forced surrender of the notion that mass is a fixed and inalienable possession of ultimate elements or individuals, so that time is now considered to be their fourth dimension.

It may be remarked incidentally that the recognition of the relational character of scientific objects completely eliminates an old metaphysical issue. One of the outstanding problems created by the rise of modern science was due to the fact that scientific definitions and descriptions are framed in terms in which qualities play no part. Qualities were wholly superfluous. As long as the idea persisted (an inheritance from Greek metaphysical science) that the business of knowledge is to penetrate into the inner being of objects, the existence of qualities like colors, sounds, etc., was embarrassing. The usual way of dealing with them is to declare that they are merely subjective, existing only in the consciousness of individual knowers. Given the old idea that the purpose of knowledge (represented at its best in science) is to penetrate into the heart of reality and reveal its "true" nature, the conclusion was a logical one. The discovery that the objects of scientific knowledge are purely relational shows that the problem is an artificial one. It was "solved" by the discovery that it needed no solution, since fulfillment of the function and business of science compels disregard of qualities.

Using the older language, it was seen that so-called primary qualities are no more inherent properties of ultimate objects than are so-called secondary qualities of odors, sounds, and colors, since the former are also strictly relational; or, as Locke stated in his moments of clear insight, are "retainers" of objects in their connections with other things. The discovery of the nonscientific because of the empirically unverifiable and unnecessary character of absolute space, absolute motion, and absolute time gave the final *coup de grace* to the traditional idea that solidity, mass, size, etc., are inherent possessions of ultimate individuals.

The revolution in scientific ideas just mentioned is primarily logical. It is due to recognition that the very method of physical science, with its primary standard units of mass, space, and time, is concerned with measurement of relations of change, not with individuals as such. This acknowledgment brought with it a further idea which, in spite of the resistance made to it by adherents of older metaphysical views, is making constant headway. This idea is that laws which purport to be statements of what actually occurs are statistical in character as distinct from so-called dynamic laws that are abstract and mathematical, and disguised definitions. Recognition of the statistical nature of physical laws was first effected in the case of gases when it became evident that generalizations regarding the behavior of swarms of molecules were not descriptions or predictions of the behavior of any individual particle. A single molecule is not and cannot be a gas. It is consequently absurd to suppose that a scientific law is about the elementary constituents of a gas. It is a statement of what happens when a very large number of such constituents interact with one another under certain conditions.

Statistical statements are of the nature of probability formulations. No insurance company makes any prediction as to what will happen to any given person in respect to death, or to any building with respect to destruction by fire. Insurance is conducted upon the basis of observation that out of a large number of persons of a given age such and such a proportionate number will probably live one year more, another proportionate number two years, and so on, while premiums are adjusted on the basis of these probability estimates. The validity of the estimates depends, as in the case of a swarm of molecules, upon the existence of a sufficiently large number of individuals, a knowledge which is a matter of the relative frequency of events of a certain kind to the total number of events which occur. No statement is made about what will take place in the case of an *individual*. The application to scientific formulations of the principle of probability statistically determined is thus a logical corollary of the principle already stated, that the subject matter of scientific findings is relational, not individual. It is for this reason that it is safe to predict the ultimate triumph of the statistical doctrine.

The third scientific consideration is found in Heisenberg's principle of uncertainty or indeterminacy, which may be regarded as a generalization of the ideas already stated. In form, this principle seems to be limited in its application. Classical science was based upon the belief that it is possible to formulate both the position and the velocity at one time of any given particle. It followed that knowledge of the position and velocity of a given number of particles would enable the future behavior of the whole collection to be accurately predicted. The principle of Heisenberg is that given the determination of position, its velocity can be stated only as of a certain order of probability, while if its velocity is determined the correlative factor of position can be stated only as of a certain order of probability. Both cannot be determined at once, from which it follows necessarily that the future of the whole collection cannot possibly be foretold except in terms of some order of probability.

Because of the fundamental place of the conception of position and velocity in physical science the principle is not limited in scope but is of the broadest possible significance.

Given the classic conception, Laplace stated its logical outcome when he said, "We may conceive the present state of the universe as the effect of its past and the cause of its future. An intellect who at any given instant knew all the forces of animate nature and the mutual position of the beings who compose it . . . could condense into a single formula the movement both of the greatest body in [the] universe and of its lightest atom. Nothing would be uncertain to such an intellect, for the future, even as the past would be ever present before his eyes." No more sweeping statement of the complete irrelevancy of time to the physical world and of the complete unreality for individuals of time could well be uttered. But the principle of indeterminacy annihilates the premises from which the conclusion follows. The principle is thus a way of acknowledging the pertinency of real time to physical beings. The utmost possible regarding an individual is a statement as to some order of probability about the future. Heisenberg's principle has been seized upon as a basis for wild statements to the effect that the doctrine of arbitrary free will and totally uncaused activity are now scientifically substantiated. Its actual force and significance is generalization of the idea that the individual is a temporal career whose future cannot logically be deduced from its past.

As long as scientific knowledge was supposed to be concerned with individuals in their own intrinsic nature, there was no way to bridge the gap between the career of human individuals and that of physical individuals, save by holding that the seeming fundamental place of development and hence of time in the life histories of the former is only seeming or specious. The unescapable conclusion is that as human individuality can be understood only in terms of time as fundamental reality, so for physical individuals time is not simply a measure of predetermined changes in mutual positions, but is something that enters into their being. Laws do not "govern" the activity of individuals. They are a formulation of the frequency distributions of the behavior of large numbers of individuals engaged in interactions with one another.

This statement does not mean that physical and human individuality are identical, nor that the things which appear to us to be nonliving have the distinguishing characteristic of organisms. The difference between the inanimate and the animate is not so easily wiped out. But it does show that there is no fixed gap between them. The conclusion which most naturally follows, without indulging in premature speculations, is that the principle of a developing career applies to all things in nature, as well as to human beings—that they are born, undergo qualitative changes, and finally die, giving place to other individuals. The idea of development applied to nature involves differences of forms and qualities as surely as it rules out absolute breaches of continuity. The differences between the amoeba and the human organism are genuinely there even if we accept the idea of organic evolution of species. Indeed, to deny the reality of the differences and their immense significance would be to deny the very idea of development. To wipe out differences because of denial of complete breaks and the need for intervention of some outside power is just as surely a way to deny development as is assertion of gaps which can be bridged only by the intervention of some supernatural force. It is then in terms of development, or if one prefers the more grandiose term, evolution, that I shall further discuss the problem of time.

The issue involved is perhaps the most fundamental one in philosophy at the present time. Are the changes which go on in the world simply external redistributions, rearrangements in space of what previously existed, or are they genuine qualitative changes such as apparently take place in the physiological development of an organism, from the union of ovum and sperm to maturity, and as apparently take place in the personal life career of individuals? When the question is raised, certain misapprehensions must be first guarded against. Development and evolution have historically been eulogistically interpreted. They have been thought of as necessarily proceeding from the lower to the higher, from the relatively worse to the relatively better. But this property was read in from outside moral and theological preoccupations. The real issue is that stated above: Is what happens simply a spatial rearrangement of what existed previously or does it involve something qualitatively new? From this point of view, cancer is as genuinely a physiological development as is growth in vigor; criminals as well as heroes are a social development; the emergence of totalitarian states is a social evolution out of constitutional states independently of whether we like or approve them.

If we accept the intrinsic connection of time with individuality, they are not mere redistributions of what existed before.

Since it is a *problem* I am presenting, I shall assume that genuine transformations occur, and consider its implications. First and negatively, the idea (which is often identified with the essential meaning of evolution) is excluded that development is a process of unfolding what was previously implicit or latent. Positively it is implied that potentiality is a category of existence, for development cannot occur unless an individual has powers or capacities that are not actualized at a given time. But it also means that these powers are not unfolded from within, but are called out through interaction with other things. While it is necessary to revive the category of potentiality as a characteristic of individuality, it has to be revived in a different form from that of its classic Aristotelian formulation. According to that view, potentialities are connected with a *fixed* end which the individual endeavors by its own nature or essence to actualize, although its success in actualization depended upon the cooperation of external things and hence might be thwarted by the "accidents" of its surroundings—as not every acorn becomes a tree and few if any acorns become the typical oak.

When the idea that development is due to some indwelling end which tends to control the series of changes passed through is abandoned, potentialities must be thought of in terms of consequences of interactions with other things. Hence potentialities cannot be *known* till *after* the interactions have occurred. There are at a given time unactualized potentialities in an individual because and in as far as there are in existence other things with which it has not as yet interacted. Potentialities of milk are known today, for example, that were not known a generation ago, because milk has been brought into interaction with things other than organisms, and hence now has other than furnishing nutriment consequence. It is now predicted that in the future human beings will be wearing clothes made of glass and that the clothes will be cleaned by throwing them into a hot furnace. Whether this particular prediction is fulfilled or not makes no difference to its value as an illustration. Every new scientific discovery leads to some mode of technology that did not previously exist. As things are brought by new procedures into new contacts and new interactions, new consequences are produced and the power to produce these new consequences is a recognized potentiality of the thing in question. The idea that potentialities are inherent and fixed by relation to a predetermined end was a product of a highly restricted state of technology. Because of this restriction, the only potentialities recognized were those consequences which were customary in the given state of culture and were accordingly taken to be "natural." When the only possible use of milk was as an article of food, it was "natural" to suppose that it had an inherent tendency to serve that particular need. With the use of milk as a plastic, and with no one able to tell what future consequences may be produced by new techniques which bring it into new interactions, the only reasonable conclusion is that potentialities are not fixed and intrinsic, but are a matter of an indefinite range of interactions in which an individual may engage.

Return for a moment to the human individual. It is impossible to think of the historical career, which is the special individuality constituting Abraham Lincoln, apart from the particular conditions in which he lived. He did not create, for example, the conditions that formed the issues of states' rights and of slavery, the issues that influenced his development. What his being as an individual would have been without these interacting conditions it is idle to speculate upon. The conditions did not form him from without as wax is supposed to be shaped by external pressure. There is no such thing as interaction that is merely a one-way movement. There were many other persons living under much the same conditions whose careers were very different, because conditions acted upon them and were acted upon by them in different ways. Hence there is no account possible of Lincoln's life that does not portray him interacting day by day with special conditions, with his parents, his wife and children, his neighbors, his economic conditions, his school facilities, the incidents of his profession as a lawyer, and so on. The career which is his unique individuality is the series of interactions in which he was created to be what he was by the ways in which he responded to the occasions with which he was presented. One cannot leave out either conditions as *opportunities* nor yet unique ways of responding to them. An occasion is an opportunity only when it is an evocation of a specific event, while a response is not a necessary effect of a cause but is a way of using an occasion to render it a constituent of an ongoing unique history.

Individuality conceived as a temporal development involves uncertainty, indeterminacy, or contingency. Individuality is the source of whatever is unpredictable in the world. The indeterminate is not change in the sense of violation of law, for laws state probable correlations of change and these probabilities exist no matter what the source of change may be. When a change occurs, *after* it has occurred it belongs to the observable world and is connected with other changes. The nomination of Lincoln for the presidency, his election, his Emancipation Proclamation, his assassination, after they took place can be shown to be related to other events; they can also be shown to have a certain connection with Lincoln's own past. But there was nothing in Lincoln's own life to cause by itself the conjunction of circumstances which brought about any one of these events. As far as he as an individual was concerned, the events were contingent, and as far as the conjunction of circumstances was concerned, his behavior at any given time in response to them was also contingent, or if you please fortuitous.

At critical junctures, his response could not be predicted either from his own past or from the nature of the circumstances, except as a probability. To say this is not arbitrarily to introduce mere chance into the world. It is to say that genuine individuality exists; that individuality is pregnant with new developments; that time is real. If we knew enough about Shakespeare's life we could doubtless show *after Hamlet* was produced how it is connected with other things. We could link it with sources; we could connect its mood with specific experiences of its author, and so on. But no one with the fullest knowledge of Shakespeare's past could have predicted the drama as it stands. If they could have done so, they would have been able to write it. Not even Shakespeare himself could have told in advance just what he was going to say—not if he was an individual, not a nodal point in the spatial redistribution of what already existed.

The mystery of time is thus the mystery of the existence of real individuals. It is a mystery because it is a mystery that anything which exists is just what it is. We are given to forgetting, with our insistence upon causation and upon the necessity of things happening as they do happen, that things exist as just what they qualitatively are. We can account for a change by relating it to other changes, but existences we have to accept for just what they are. Given a butterfly or an earthquake as an event, as a change, we can at least in theory find out and state its connection with other changes. But the individual butterfly or earthquake remains just the unique existence which it is. We forget in explaining its occurrence that it is only the *occurrence* that is explained, not the thing itself. We forget that in explaining the occurrence we are compelled to fall back on other individual things that have just the unique qualities they do have. Go as far back as we please in accounting for present conditions and we still come upon the mystery of things being just what they are.

Their occurrence, their manifestation, may be accounted for in terms of other occurrences, but their own quality of existence is final and opaque. The mystery is that the world is as it is—a mystery that is the source of all joy and all sorrow, of all hope and fear, and the source of development both creative and degenerative. The contingency of all into which time enters is the source of pathos, comedy, and tragedy. Genuine time, if it exists as anything else except the measure of motions in space, is all one with the existence of individuals as individuals, with the creative, with the occurrence of unpredictable novelties. Everything that can be said contrary to this conclusion is but a reminder that an individual may lose his individuality, for individuals become imprisoned in routine and fall to the level of mechanisms. Genuine time then ceases to be an integral element in their being. Our behavior becomes predictable, because it is but an external rearrangement of what went before.

In conclusion, I would like to point out two considerations that seem to me to follow, two morals, if you wish to give them that name. I said earlier that the traditional idea of progress and evolution was based upon belief that the fixed structure of the universe is such as automatically brings it about. This optimistic and fatalistic idea is now at a discount. It is easy in the present state of the world to deny all validity whatever to the idea of progress, since so much of the human world seems bent on demonstrating the truth of the old theological doctrine of the fall of man. But the real conclusion is that, while progress is not inevitable, it is up to men as individuals to bring it about. Change is going to occur anyway, and the problem is the control of change in a given direction. The direction, the quality of change, is a matter of individuality. Surrender of individuality by the many to someone who is taken to be a superindividual explains the retrograde movement of society. Dictatorships and totalitarian states, and belief in the inevitability of this or that result coming to pass are, strange as it may sound, ways of denying the reality of time and the creativeness of the individual. Freedom of thought and of expression are not mere rights to be claimed. They have their roots deep in the existence of individuals as developing careers in time. Their denial and abrogation is an abdication of individuality and a virtual rejection of time as opportunity.

The ground of democratic ideas and practices is faith in the potentialities of individuals, faith in the capacity for positive developments if proper conditions are provided. The weakness of the philosophy originally advanced to justify the democratic movement was that it took individuality to be something given ready-made, that is, in abstraction from time, instead of as a power to develop.

The other conclusion is that art is the complement of science. Science as I have said is concerned wholly with relations, not with individuals. Art, on the other hand, is not only the disclosure of the individuality of the artist but is also a manifestation of individuality as creative of the future, in an unprecedented response to conditions as they were in the past. Some artists in their vision of what might be but is not have been conscious rebels. But conscious protest and revolt is not the form which the labor of the artist in creation of the future must necessarily take. Discontent with things as they are is normally the expression of vision of what may be and is not, art in being the manifestation of individuality is this prophetic vision. To regiment artists, to make them servants of some particular cause does violence to the very springs of artistic creation. But it does more than that. It betrays the very cause of a better future it would serve, for in its subjection of the individuality of the artist it annihilates the source of that which is genuinely new. Were the regimentation successful, it would cause the future to be but a rearrangement of the past.

The artist in realizing his own individuality reveals potentialities hitherto unrealized. This revelation is the inspiration of other individuals to make the potentialities real, for it is not sheer revolt against things as they are which stirs human endeavor to its depths, but vision of what might be and is not. Subordination of the artists to any special cause no matter how worthy does violence not only to the artist but to the living source of a new and better future. Art is not the possession of the few who are recognized writers, painters, musicians; it is the authentic expression of any and all individuality. Those who have the gift of creative expression in unusually large measure disclose the meaning of the individuality of others to those others. In participating in the work of art, they become artists in their activity. They learn to know and honor individuality in whatever form it appears. The fountains of creative activity are discovered and released. The free individuality which is the source of art is also the final source of creative development in time.

Existence as Precarious and Stable

A feature of existence which is emphasized by cultural phenomena is the precarious and perilous. Sumner refers to Grimm as authority for the statement that the Germanic tribes had over a thousand distinct sayings, proverbs, and apothegms concerning luck. Time is brief, and this statement must stand instead of the discourse which the subject deserves. Man finds himself living in an aleatory world; his existence involves, to put it baldly, a gamble. The world is a scene of risk; it is uncertain, unstable, uncannily unstable. Its dangers are irregular, inconstant, not to be counted upon as to their times and seasons. Although persistent, they are sporadic, episodic. It is darkest just before dawn; pride goes before a fall; the moment of greatest prosperity is the moment most charged with ill-omen, most opportune for the evil eye. Plague, famine, failure of crops, disease, death, defeat in battle, are always just around the comer, and so are abundance, strength, victory, festival, and song. Luck is proverbially both good and bad in its distributions. The sacred and the accursed are potentialities of the same situation; and there is no category of things which has not embodied the sacred and accursed: persons, words, places, times, directions in space, stones, winds, animals, stars.

Anthropologists have shown incontrovertibly the part played by the precarious aspect of the world in generating religion with its ceremonies, rites, cults, myths, magic; and it has shown the pervasive penetration of these affairs into morals, law, art, and industry. Beliefs and dispositions connected with them are the background out of which philosophy and secular morals slowly developed, as well as more slowly those late inventions, art for art's sake, and business is business. Interesting and instructive as is this fact, it is not the ramifications which here concern us. We must not be diverted to consider the consequences for philosophy, even for doctrines reigning today, of facts concerning the origin of philosophies. We confine ourselves to one outstanding fact: the evidence that the world of empirical things includes the uncertain, unpredictable, uncontrollable, and hazardous.

It is an old saying that the gods were born of fear. The saying is only too likely to strengthen a misconception bred by confirmed subjective habits. We first endow man in isolation with an instinct of fear and then we imagine him irrationally ejecting that fear into the environment, scattering broadcast as it were, the fruits of his own purely personal limitations, and thereby creating superstition. But fear, whether an instinct or an acquisition, is a function of the environment. Man fears because he exists in a fearful, an awful world. The *world* is precarious and perilous. It is as easily accessible and striking evidence of this fact that primitive experience is cited. The voice is that of early man; but the hand is that of nature, the nature in which we still live. It was not fear of gods that created the gods.

For if the life of early man is filled with expiations and propitiations, if in his feasts and festivals what is enjoyed is gratefully shared with his gods, it is not because a belief in supernatural powers created a need for expiatory, propitiatory, and communal offerings. Everything that man achieves and possesses is got by actions that may involve him in other and obnoxious consequences in addition to those wanted and enjoyed. His acts are trespasses upon the domain of the unknown; and hence atonement, if offered in season, may ward off direful consequences that haunt even the moment of prosperity—or that most haunt that moment. While unknown consequences flowing from the past dog the present, the future is even more unknown and perilous; the present by that fact is ominous. If unknown forces that decide future destiny can be placated, the man who will not study the methods of securing their favor is incredibly flippant. In enjoyment of present food and companionship, nature, tradition, and social organization have cooperated, thereby supplementing our own endeavors so petty and so feeble without this extraneous reinforcement. Goods are by grace not of ourselves. He is a dangerous churl who will not gratefully acknowledge by means of free-will offerings the help that sustains him.

These things are as true today as they were in the days of early culture. It is not the facts which have changed, but the methods of insurance, regulation, and acknowledgment. Herbert Spencer sometimes colored his devotion to symbolic experiences with a fact of dire experience. When he says that every fact has two opposite sides, "the one its near or visible side and the other its remote or invisible side," he expresses a persistent trait of every object in experience. The visible is set in the invisible; and in the end what is unseen decides what happens in the seen; the tangible rests precariously upon the untouched and ungrasped. The contrast and the potential maladjustment of the immediate, the conspicuous and focal phase of things, with those indirect and hidden factors which determine the origin and career of what is present, are indestructible features of any and every experience. We may term the way in which our ancestors dealt with the contrast superstitious, but the contrast is no superstition. It is a primary datum in any experience.

We have substituted sophistication for superstition, at least measurably so. But the sophistication is often as irrational and as much at the mercy of words as the superstition it replaces. Our magical safeguard against the uncertain character of the world is to deny the existence of chance, to mumble universal and necessary law, the ubiquity of cause and effect, the uniformity of nature, universal progress, and the inherent rationality of the universe. These magic formulae borrow their potency from conditions that are not magical. Through science we have secured a degree of power of prediction and of control; through tools, machinery, and an accompanying technique we have made the world more conformable to our needs, a more secure abode. We have heaped up riches and means of comfort between ourselves and the risks of the world. We have professionalized amusement as an agency of escape and forgetfulness. But when all is said and done, the fundamentally hazardous character of the world is not seriously modified, much less eliminated. Such an incident as the last war and preparations for a future war remind us that it is easy to overlook the extent to which, after all, our attainments are only devices for blurring the disagreeable recognition of a fact, instead of means of altering the fact itself.

What has been said sounds pessimistic. But the concern is not with morals but with metaphysics, with, that is to say, the nature of the existential world in which we live. It would have been as easy and more comfortable to emphasize good luck, grace, unexpected and unwon joys, those unsought-for happenings which we so significantly call happiness. We might have appealed to good fortune as evidence of this important trait of hazard in nature. Comedy is as genuine as tragedy. But it is traditional that comedy strikes a more superficial note than tragedy. And there is an even better reason for appealing to misfortunes and mistakes as evidence of the precarious nature of the world. The problem of evil is a well recognized problem, while we rarely or never hear of a problem of good. Goods we take for granted; they are as they should be; they are natural and proper. The good is a recognition of our deserts. When we pull out a plum we treat it as evidence of the *real* order of cause and effect in the world. For this reason it is difficult for the goods of existence to furnish as convincing evidence of the uncertain character of nature as do evils. It is the latter we term accidents, not the former, even when their adventitious character is as certain.

What of it all, it may be asked? In the sense in which an assertion is true that uncontrolled distribution of good and evil is evidence of the precarious, uncertain nature of existence, it is a truism, and no problem is forwarded by its reiteration. But it is submitted that just this predicament of the inextricable mixture of stability and uncertainty gives rise to philosophy, and that it is reflected in all its recurrent problems and issues. If classic philosophy says so much about unity and so little about unreconciled diversity, so much about the eternal and permanent, and so little about change (save as something to be resolved into combinations of the permanent), so much about necessity and so little about contingency, so much about the comprehending universal and so little about the recalcitrant particular, it may well be because the ambiguousness and ambivalence of reality are actually so pervasive. Since these things form the problem, solution is more apparent (although not more actual) in the degree in which whatever of stability and assurance the world presents is fastened upon and asserted.

Upon their surface, the reports of the world which form our different philosophies are various to the point of stark contrariness. They range from spiritualism to materialism, from absolutism to relativistic phenomenalism, from transcendentalism to positivism, from rationalism to sensationalism, from idealism to realism, from subjectivism to bald objectivism, from Platonic realism to nominalism. The array of contradictions is so imposing as to suggest to skeptics that the mind of man has tackled an impossible job, or that philosophers have abandoned themselves to vagary. These radical oppositions in philosophers suggest however another consideration. They suggest that all their different philosophies have a common premise, and that their diversity is due to acceptance of a common premise. Variant philosophies may be looked at as different ways of supplying recipes for denying to the universe the character of contingency which it possesses so integrally that its denial leaves the reflecting mind without a clew, and puts subsequent philosophizing at the mercy of temperament, interest, and local surroundings.

Quarrels among conflicting types of philosophy are thus family quarrels. They go on within the limits of a too domestic circle, and can be settled only by venturing further afield, and out of doors. Concerned with imputing complete, finished, and sure character to the world of real existence, even if things have to be broken into two disconnected pieces in order to accomplish the result, the character desiderated can plausibly be found in reason or in mechanism; in rational conceptions like those of mathematics, or brute things like sensory data; in atoms or in essences; in consciousness or in a physical externality which forces and overrides consciousness.

As against this common identification of reality with what is sure, regular, and finished, experience in unsophisticated forms gives evidence of a different world and points to a different metaphysics. We live in a world which is an impressive and irresistible mixture of sufficiencies, tight completenesses, order, recurrences which make possible prediction and control and singularities, ambiguities, uncertain possibilities, processes going on to consequences as yet indeterminate. They are mixed not mechanically but vitally like the wheat and tares of the parable. We may recognize them separately but we cannot divide them, for unlike wheat and tares they grow from the same root. Qualities have defects as necessary conditions of their excellencies; the instrumentalities of truth are the causes of error; change gives meaning to permanence and recurrence makes novelty possible. A world that was wholly risky would be a world in which adventure is impossible, and only a living world can include death. Such facts have been celebrated by thinkers like Heraclitus and Laotze; they have been greeted by theologians as furnishing occasions for exercise of divine grace; they have been elaborately formulated by various schools under a principle of relativity, so defined as to become itself final and absolute. They have rarely been frankly recognized as fundamentally significant for the formation of a naturalistic metaphysics.

Aristotle perhaps came the nearest to a start in that direction. But his thought did not go far on the road, though it may be used to suggest the road which he failed to take. Aristotle acknowledged contingency, but he never surrenders his bias in favor of the fixed, certain, and finished. His whole theory of forms and ends is a theory of the superiority in Being of rounded-out fixities. His physics is a fixation of ranks or grades of necessity and contingency so sorted that necessity measures dignity and equals degree of reality, while contingency and change measure degrees of deficiency of Being. The empirical impact and sting of the mixture of universality and singularity and chance is evaded by parcelling out the regions of space so that they have their natural abode in different portions of nature. His logic is one of definition and classification, so that its task is completed when changing and contingent things are distinguished from the necessary, universal, and fixed, by attribution to inferior species of things. Chance appears in thought not as a calculus of probabilities in predicting the observable occurrence of any and every event, but as marking an inferior type of syllogism. Things that move are intrinsically different from things that exhibit eternal regularity. Change is honestly recognized as a genuine feature of *some* things, but the point of the recognition is avoided by imputing alternation to inherent deficiency of Being over against complete Being which never changes. Changing things belong to a purgatorial realm, where they wander aimlessly until redeemed by love of finality of form, the acquisition of which lifts them to a paradise of self-sufficient Being. With slight exaggeration, it may be said that the thoroughgoing way in which Aristotle defined, distinguished, and classified rest and movement, the finished and the incomplete, the actual and potential, did more to fix tradition, *the* genteel tradition one is tempted to add, which identifies the fixed and regular with reality of Being and the changing and hazardous with deficiency of Being than ever was accomplished by those who took the shorter path of asserting that change is illusory.

His philosophy was closer to empirical facts than most modern philosophies, in that it was neither monistic nor dualistic but openly pluralistic. His plurals fall, however, within a grammatical system, to each portion of which a corresponding cosmic status is allotted. Thus his pluralism solved the problem of how to have your cake and eat it too, for a classified and hierarchically ordered set of pluralities, of variants, has none of the sting of the miscellaneous and uncoordinated plurals of our actual world. In this classificatory scheme of separation he has been followed, though perhaps unwittingly, by many philosophers of different import. Thus Kant assigns all that is manifold and chaotic to one realm, that of sense, and all that is uniform and regular to that of reason. A single and all-embracing dialectic problem of the combination of sense and thought is thereby substituted for the concrete problems that arise through the mixed and varied union in existence of the variable and the constant, the necessary and that which proceeds uncertainly.

The device is characteristic of a conversion such as has already been commented upon of a moral insight to be made good in action into an antecedent metaphysics of existence or a general theory of knowledge. The striving to make stability of meaning prevail over the instability of events is the main task of intelligent human effort. But when the function is dropped from the province of art and treated as a property of given things, whether cosmological or logical, effort is rendered useless, and a premium is put upon the accidental good fortune of a class that happens to be furnished by the toil of another class with products that give to life its dignity and leisurely stability.

The argument is not forgetful that there are, from Heraclitus to Bergson, philosophies, metaphysics, of change. One is grateful to them for keeping alive a sense of what classic, orthodox philosophies have whisked out of sight. But the philosophies of flux also indicate the intensity of the craving for the sure and fixed. They have deified change by making it universal, regular, sure. To say this is not, I hope, verbal by-play. Consider the wholly eulogistic fashion in which Hegel and Bergson, and the professedly evolutionary philosophers of becoming, have taken change. With Hegel becoming is a rational process which defines logic, although a new and strange logic, and an absolute, although new and strange, God. With Spencer, evolution is but the transitional process of attaining a fixed and universal equilibrium of harmonious adjustment. With Bergson, change is the creative operation of God, or *is* God—one is not quite sure which. The change of change is not only cosmic pyrotechnics, but is a process of divine, spiritual, energy. We are here in the presence of prescription, not description. Romanticism is an evangel in the garb of metaphysics. It sidesteps the painful, toilsome labor of understanding and of control which change sets us, by glorifying it for its own sake. Flux is made something to revere, something profoundly akin to what is best within ourselves, will and creative energy. It is not, as it is in experience, a call to effort, a challenge to investigation, a potential doom of disaster and death.

If we follow classical terminology, philosophy is love of wisdom, while metaphysics is cognizance of the generic traits of existence. In this sense of metaphysics, incompleteness and precariousness is a trait that must be given footing of the same rank as the finished and fixed. Love of wisdom is concerned with finding its implications for the conduct of life, in devotion to what is good. On the cognitive side, the issue is largely that of measure, of the ratio one bears to others in the situations of life. On the practical side, it is a question of the use to be made of each, of turning each to best account. Man is naturally philosophic, rather than metaphysical or coldly scientific, noting and describing. Concerned with prudence if not with what is honorifically called wisdom, man naturally prizes knowledge only for the sake of its bearing upon success and failure in attaining goods and avoiding evils. This is a fact of our structure and nothing is gained by recommending it as an ideal truth, and equally nothing is gained by attributing to intellect an intrinsic relationship to pure truth for its own sake or bare fact on its own account. The first method encourages dogma, and the second expresses a myth. The love of knowledge for its own sake is an ideal of morals; it is an integral condition of the wisdom that rightly conceives and effectually pursues the good. For wisdom as to ends depends upon acquaintance with conditions and means, and unless the acquaintance is adequate and fair, wisdom becomes a sublimated folly of self-deception.

Denial of an inherent relation of mind to truth or fact for its own sake, apart from insight into what the fact or truth exacts of us in behavior and imposes upon us in joy and suffering; and simultaneous affirmation that devotion to fact, to truth, is a necessary moral demand, involves no inconsistency. Denial relates to natural events as independent of choice and endeavor; affirmation relates to choice and action. But choice and the effective effort involved in it are themselves such contingent events and so bound up with the precarious uncertainty of other events, that philosophers have too readily assumed that metaphysics and science of fact and truth are themselves wisdom, thinking thus to avoid the necessity of either exercising or recognizing choice. The consequence is that conversion of unavowed morals or wisdom into cosmology, and into a metaphysics of nature, which was termed in the last chapter the philosophic fallacy. It supplies the formula of the technique by which thinkers have relegated the uncertain and unfinished to an invidious state of unreal being, while they have systematically exalted the assured and complete to the rank of true Being.

Upon the side of wisdom, as human beings interested in good and bad things in their connection with human conduct, thinkers are concerned to mitigate the instability of life, to introduce moderation, temper, and economy, and when worst comes to worst to suggest consolations and compensations. They are concerned with rendering more stable good things, and more unstable bad things; they are interested in how changes may be turned to account in the consequences to which they contribute. The facts of the ungoing, unfinished, and ambiguously potential world give point and poignancy to the search for absolutes and finalities. Then when philosophers have hit in reflection upon a thing which is stably good in quality and hence worthy of persistent and continued choice, they hesitate, and withdraw from the effort and struggle that choice demands—namely from the effort to give it some such stability in observed existence as it possesses in quality when thought of. Thus it becomes a refuge, an asylum for contemplation, or a theme for dialectical elaboration, instead of an ideal to inspire and guide conduct.

Since thinkers claim to be concerned with knowledge of existence, rather than with imagination, they have to make good the pretensions to knowledge. Hence they transmute the imaginative perception of the stably good object into a definition and description of true reality in contrast with lower and specious existence, which, being precarious and incomplete, alone involves us in the necessity of choice and active struggle. Thus they remove from actual existence the very traits which generate philosophic reflection and which give point and bearing to its conclusions. In briefest formula, "reality" becomes what we wish existence to be, after we have analyzed its defects and decided upon what would remove them; "reality" is what existence would be if our reasonably justified preferences were so completely established in nature as to exhaust and define its entire being and thereby render search and struggle unnecessary. What is left over (and since trouble, struggle, conflict, and error still empirically exist, something *is* left over), being excluded by definition from full reality is assigned to a grade or order of being which is asserted to be metaphysically inferior; an order variously called appearance, illusion, mortal mind, or the merely empirical, against what really and truly is. Then the problem of metaphysics alters: instead of being a detection and description of the generic traits of existence, it becomes an endeavor to adjust or reconcile to each other two separate realms of being. Empirically we have just what we started with: the mixture of the precarious and problematic with the assured and complete. But a classificatory device, based on desire and elaborated in reflective imagination, has been introduced by which the two traits are tom apart, one of them being labeled reality and the other appearance. The genuinely moral problem of mitigating and regulating the troublesome factor by active employment of the stable factor then drops out of sight. The dialectic problem of logical reconciliation of two notions has taken its place.

The most widespread of these classificatory devices, the one of greatest popular appeal, is that which divides existence into the supernatural and the natural. Men may fear the gods but it is axiomatic that the gods have nothing to fear. They lead a life of untroubled serenity, the life that pleases them. There is a long step between the primitive forms of this division of objects of experience and the dialectical imputation to the divine of omnipotence, omniscience, eternity, and infinity, in contrast with the attribution to man and experienced nature of finitude, weakness, limitation, struggle, and change. But in the make-up of human psychology, the later history is implicit in the early crude division. One realm is the home of assured appropriation and possession; the other of striving, transiency, and frustration. How many persons are there today who conceive that they have disposed of ignorance, struggle, and disappointment by pointing to man's "finite" nature—as if finitude signifies anything else but an abstract classificatory naming of certain concrete and discriminative traits of nature itself—traits of nature which generate ignorance, arbitrary appearance and disappearance, failure and striving. It pleases man to substitute the dialectic exercise of showing how the "finite" can exist with or within the "infinite" for the problem of dealing with the contingent, thinking to solve the problem by distinguishing and naming its factors. Failure of the exercise is certain, but the failure can be flourished as one more proof of the finitude of man's intellect, and the needlessness because impotency of endeavor of "finite" creatures to attack ignorance and oppressive fatalities. Wisdom then consists in administration of the temporal, finite, and human in its relation to the eternal and infinite, by means of dogma and cult, rather than in regulation of the events of life by understanding of actual conditions.

It does not demand great ingenuity to detect the inversion here. The starting point is precisely the existing mixture of the regular and dependable and the unsettled and uncertain. There are a multitude of recipes for obtaining a vicarious possession of the stable and final without getting involved in the labor and pain of intellectual effort attending regulation of the conditions upon which these fruits depend.

This situation is worthy of remark as an exemplification of how easy it is to arrive at a description of existence via a theory of wisdom, of reflective insight into goods. It has a direct bearing upon a metaphysical doctrine which is not popular, like the division into the supernatural and natural, but which is learned and technical. The philosopher may have little esteem for the crude forms assumed by the popular metaphysics of earth and heaven, of God, nature, and man. But the philosopher has often proceeded in a manner analogous to that which resulted in this popular metaphysics; some of the most cherished metaphysical distinctions seem to be but learned counterparts, dependent upon an elaborate intellectual technique, for these rough, crude notions of supernatural and natural, divine and human, in popular belief. I refer to such things as the Platonic division into ideal archetypes and physical events; the Aristotelian division into form which is actuality and matter which is potential, when that is understood as a distinction of ranks of reality; the noumenal things, things-in-themselves of Kant in contrast with natural objects as phenomenal; the distinction, current among contemporary absolute idealists, of reality and appearance.

The division however is not confined to philosophers with leanings toward spiritualistic philosophies. There is some evidence that Plato got the term Idea, as a name for essential form, from Democritus. Whether this be the case or no, the Idea of Democritus, though having a radically diverse structure from the Platonic Idea, had the same function of designating a finished, complete, stable, wholly unprecarious reality. Both philosophers craved solidity and both found it; corresponding to the Platonic phenomenal flux are the Democritean things as they are in custom or ordinary experience: corresponding to the ideal archetypes are substantial indivisible atoms. Corresponding again to the Platonic theory of Ideas is the modern theory of mathematical structures which are alone independently real, while the empirical impressions and suggestions to which they give rise is the counterpart of his realm of phenomena.

Apart from the materialistic and spiritualistic schools, there is the Spinozistic division into attributes and modes; the old division of essence and existence, and its modern counterpart subsistence and existence. It is impossible to force Mr. Bertrand Russell into any of the pigeonholes of the cabinet of conventional philosophic schools. But moral, or philosophical, motivation is obvious in his metaphysics when he says that mathematics take us "into the region of absolute necessity, to which not only the actual world but every possible world must conform." Indeed with his usual lucidity, he says, mathematics "finds a habitation eternally standing, where our ideals are fully satisfied and our best hopes are not thwarted." When he adds that contemplation of such objects is the "chief means of overcoming the terrible sense of impotence, of weakness, of exile amid hostile power, which is too apt to result from acknowledging the all but omnipotence of alien forces," the presence of moral origin is explicit.

No modern thinker has pointed out so persuasively as Santayana that "every phase of the ideal world emanates from the natural," that "sense, art, religion, society express nature exuberantly." And yet unless one reads him wrong, he then confounds his would-be disciples and confuses his critics by holding that nature is *truly* presented only in an esthetic contemplation of essences reached by physical science, an envisagement reached through a dialectic which "is a transubstantiation of matter, a passage from existence to eternity." This passage moreover is so utter that there is no road back. The stable ideal meanings which are the fruit of nature are forbidden, in the degree in which they are its highest and truest fruits, from dropping seeds in nature to its further fructification.

The perception of genetic continuity between the dynamic flux of nature and an eternity of static ideal forms thus terminates in a sharp division, in reiteration of the old tradition. Perhaps it is a caricature to say that the ultimate of reason is held to be ability to behold nature as a complete mechanism which generates and sustains the beholding of the mechanism, but the caricature is not willful. If the separation of contingency and necessity is abandoned, what is there to exclude a belief that science, while it is grasp of the regular and stable mechanism of nature, is also an organ of regulating and enriching, through its own expansion, the more exuberant and irregular expressions of nature in human intercourse, the arts, religion, industry, and politics?

To follow out the latter suggestion would take us to a theme reserved for later consideration. We are here concerned with the fact that it is the intricate mixture of the stable and the precarious, the fixed and the unpredictably novel, the assured and the uncertain, in existence which sets mankind upon that love of wisdom which forms philosophy. Yet too commonly, although in a great variety of technical modes, the result of the search is converted into a metaphysics which denies or conceals from acknowledgment the very characters of existence which initiated it, and which give significance to its conclusions. The form assumed by the denial is, most frequently, that striking division into a superior true realm of being and lower illusory, insignificant, or phenomenal realm which characterizes metaphysical systems as unlike as those of Plato and Democritus, St. Thomas and Spinoza, Aristotle and Kant, Descartes and Comte, Haeckel and Mrs. Eddy.

The same jumble of acknowledgment and denial attends the conception of Absolute Experience: as if any experience could be more absolutely experience than that which marks the life of humanity. This conception constitutes the most recent device for first admitting and then denying the combinedly stable and unstable nature of the world, Its plaintive recognition of our experience as finite and temporal, as full of error, conflict, and contradiction, is an acknowledgment of the precarious uncertainty of the objects and connections that constitute nature as it emerges in history. Human experience however has also the pathetic longing for truth, beauty, and order. There is more than the longing: there are moments of achievement. Experience exhibits ability to possess harmonious objects. It evinces an ability, within limits, to safeguard the excellent objects and to deflect and reduce the obnoxious ones. The concept of an absolute experience which is only and always perfect and good, first explicates these desirable implications of things of actual experience, and then asserts that they alone are real. The experienced occurrences which give poignancy and pertinency to the longing for a better world, the experimental endeavors and plans which make possible actual betterments within the objects of actual experience, are thus swept out of real Being into a limbo of appearances.

The notion of Absolute Experience thus serves as a symbol of two facts. One is the ineradicable union in nature of the relatively stable and the relatively contingent. The division of the movement and readings of things which are experienced into two parts, such that one set constitutes and defines absolute and eternal experience, while the other set constitutes and defines finite experience, tells us nothing about absolute experience. It tells us a good deal about experience as it exists: namely, that it is such as to involve permanent and general objects of reference as well as temporally changing events; the possibility of truth as well as error; conclusive objects and goods as well as things whose purport and nature is determinable only in an indeterminate future. Nothing is gained—except the delights of a dialectic problem—in labeling one assortment absolute experience and the other finite experience. Since the appeal of the adherents of the philosophy of absolute and phenomenal experience is to a logical criterion, namely, to the implication in every judgment, however erroneous, of a standard of consistency which excludes any possibility of contradictoriness, the inherent logical contradictions in the doctrine itself are worth noting.

In the first place, the contents as well as the form of ultimate Absolute Experience are derived from and based upon the features of actual experience, the very experience which is then relegated to unreality by the supreme reality derived from its unreality. It is "real" just long enough to afford a springboard into ultimate reality and to afford a hint of the essential contents of the latter and then it obligingly dissolves into mere appearance. If we start from the standpoint of the Absolute Experience thus reached, the contradiction is repeated from its side. Although absolute, eternal, all-comprehensive, and pervasively integrated into a whole so logically perfect that no separate patterns, to say nothing of seams and holes, can exist in it, it proceeds to play a tragic joke upon itself—for there is nothing else to be fooled—by appearing in a queer combination of rags and glittering gewgaws, in the garb of the temporal, partial and conflicting things, mental as well as physical, of ordinary experience. I do not cite these dialectic contradictions as having an inherent importance. But the fact that a doctrine which avowedly takes logical consistence for its method and criterion, whose adherents are noteworthy for dialectic acumen in specific issues, should terminate in such thoroughgoing contradictions may be cited as evidence that after all the doctrine is merely engaged in an arbitrary sorting out of characters of things which in nature are always present in conjunction and interpenetration.

The union of the hazardous and the stable, of the incomplete and the recurrent, is the condition of all experienced satisfaction as truly as of our predicaments and problems. While it is the source of ignorance, error, and failure of expectation, it is the source of the delight which fulfillments bring. For if there were nothing in the way, if there were no deviations and resistances, fulfillment would be at once, and in so being would fulfill nothing, but merely be. It would not be in connection with desire or satisfaction. Moreover, when a fulfillment comes and is pronounced good, it is *judged* good, distinguished and asserted, simply because it is in jeopardy, because it occurs amid indifferent and divergent things. Because of this mixture of the regular and that which cuts across stability, a good object once experienced acquires ideal quality and attracts demand and effort to itself. A particular ideal may be an illusion, but having ideals is no illusion. It embodies features of existence. Although imagination is often fantastic it is also an organ of nature; for it is the appropriate phase of indeterminate events moving toward eventualities that are now but possibilities. A purely stable world permits of no illusions, but neither is it clothed with ideals. It just exists. To be good is to be better than; and there can be no better except where there is shock and discord combined with enough assured order to make attainment of harmony possible. Better objects when brought into existence are existent not ideal; they retain ideal quality only retrospectively as commemorative of issue from prior conflict and prospectively, in contrast with forces which make for their destruction. Water that slakes thirst, or a conclusion that solves a problem have ideal character as long as thirst or problem persists in a way which qualifies the result. But water that is not a satisfaction of need has no more ideal quality than water running through pipes into a reservoir; a solution ceases to be a solution and becomes a bare incident of existence when its antecedent generating conditions of doubt, ambiguity, and search are lost from its context. While the precarious nature of existence is indeed the source of all trouble, it is also an indispensable condition of ideality, becoming a sufficient condition when conjoined with the regular and assured.

We long, amid a troubled world, for perfect being. We forget that what gives meaning to the notion of perfection is the events that create longing, and that, apart from them, a "perfect" world would mean just an unchanging brute existential thing. The ideal significance of esthetic objects is no exception to this principle. Their satisfying quality, their power to compose while they arouse, is not dependent upon definite prior desire and effort as is the case with the ideally satisfying quality of practical and scientific objects. It is part of their peculiar satisfying quality to be gratuitous, not purchased by endeavor. The contrast to other things of this detachment from toil and labor in a world where most realizations have to be bought, as well as the contrast to trouble and uncertainty, give esthetic objects their peculiar traits. If all things came to us in the way our esthetic objects do, none of them would be a source of esthetic delight.

Some phases of recent philosophy have made much of need, desire, and satisfaction. Critics have frequently held that the outcome is only recurrence to an older subjective empiricism, though with substitution of affections and volitional states for cognitive sensory states. But need and desire are exponents of natural being. They are, if we use Aristotelian phraseology, actualizations of its contingencies and incompletenesses; as such nature itself is wistful and pathetic, turbulent and passionate. Were it not, the existence of wants would be a miracle. In a world where everything is complete, nothing requires anything else for its completion. A world in which events can be carried to a finish only through the coinciding assistance of other transitory events, is already necessitous, a world of begging as well as of beggarly elements. If human experience is to express and reflect this world, it must be marked by needs; in becoming aware of the needful and needed quality of things it must project satisfactions or completions. For irrespective of whether a satisfaction is conscious, a satisfaction or non-satisfaction is an objective thing with objective conditions. It means fulfillment of the demands of objective factors. Happiness may *mark* an awareness of such satisfaction, and it may *be* its culminating form. But satisfaction is not subjective, private or personal: it is conditioned by objective partialities and defections and made real by objective situations and completions.

By the same logic, necessity implies the precarious and contingent. A world that was all necessity would not be a world of necessity; it would just be. For in its being, nothing would be necessary for anything else. But where some things are indigent, other things are necessary if demands are to be met. The common failure to note the fact that a world of complete being would be a world in which necessity is meaningless is due to a rapid shift from one universe of discourse to another. First we postulate a whole of Being; then we shift to a part; now since a "part" is logically dependent as such in its existence and its properties, it is necessitated by other parts. But we have unwittingly introduced contingency in the very fact of marking off something as just a part. If the logical implications of the original notion are held to firmly, a part is already a part-of-a-whole. Its being what it is, is not necessitated by the whole or by other parts: its being what it is, is just a name for the whole being what it is. Whole and parts alike are but names for existence there as just what it is. But wherever we can say *if* so-and-so, then something else, there is necessity, because partialities are implied which are not just parts-of-a-whole. A world of "ifs" is alone a world of "musts"—the "ifs" express real differences; the "musts" real connections. The stable and recurrent is needed for the fulfillment of the possible; the doubtful can be settled only through its adaptations to stable objects. The necessary is always necessary for, not necessary in and of itself; it is conditioned by the contingent, although itself a condition of the full determination of the latter.

One of the most striking phases of the history of philosophic thought is the recurrent grouping together of unity, permanence (or "the eternal"), completeness, and rational thought, while upon another side fall multiplicity, change, and the temporal, the partial, defective, sense and desire. This division is obviously but another case of violent separation of the precarious and unsettled from the regular and determinate. One aspect of it, however, is worthy of particular attention: the connection of thought and unity. Empirically, all reflection sets out from the problematic and confused. Its aim is to clarify and ascertain. When thinking is successful, its career closes in transforming the disordered into the orderly, the mixed up into the distinguished or placed, the unclear and ambiguous into the defined and unequivocal, the disconnected into the systematized. It is empirically assured that the goal of thinking does not remain a mere ideal, but is attained often enough so as to render reasonable additional efforts to achieve it.

In these facts we have, I think, the empirical basis of the philosophic doctrines which assert that reality is really and truly a rational system, a coherent whole of relations that cannot be conceived otherwise than in terms of intellect. Reflective inquiry moves in each particular case from differences toward unity; from indeterminate and ambiguous position to clear determination, from confusion and disorder to system. When thought in a given case has reached its goal of organized totality, of definite relations of distinctly placed elements, its object is the accepted starting point, the defined subject-matter, of further experiences; antecedent and outgrown conditions of darkness and of unreconciled differences are dismissed as a transitory state of ignorance and inadequate apprehensions. Retain connection of the goal with the thinking by which it is reached, and then identify it with true reality in contrast with the merely phenomenal, and the outline of the logic of rational and "objective" idealisms is before us. Thought, like Being, has two forms; one real, the other phenomenal. It is compelled to take on *reflective* form, it involves doubt, inquiry, and hypothesis, because it sets out from a subject-matter conditioned by sense, a fact which proves that thought, intellect, is not pure in man, but restricted by an animal organism that is but one part linked with other parts of nature. But the conclusion of reflection affords us a pattern and guarantee of thought which is *constitutive;* one with the system of objective reality. Such in outline is the procedure of all ontological logics.

A philosophy which accepts the denotative or empirical method accepts at full value the fact that reflective thinking transforms confusion, ambiguity, and discrepancy into illumination, definiteness, and consistency. But it also points to the contextual situation in which thinking occurs. It notes that the starting point is the actually *problematic,* and that the problematic phase resides in some actual and specifiable situation.

It notes that the means of converting the dubious into the assured, and the incomplete into the determinate, is use of assured and established things, which are just as empirical and as indicative of the nature of experienced things as is the uncertain. It thus notes that thinking is no different in kind from the use of natural materials and energies, say fire and tools, to refine, re-order, and shape other natural materials, say ore. In both cases, there are matters which as they stand are unsatisfactory and there are also adequate agencies for dealing with them and connecting them. At no point or place is there any jump outside empirical, natural objects and their relations. Thought and reason are not specific powers. They consist of the procedures intentionally employed in the application to each other of the unsatisfactorily confused and indeterminate on one side and the regular and stable on the other. Generalizing from such observations, empirical philosophy perceives that thinking is a continuous process of temporal re-organization within one and the same world of experienced things, not a jump from the latter world into one of objects constituted once for all by thought. It discovers thereby the empirical basis of rational idealism, and the point at which it empirically goes astray. Idealism fails to take into account the specified or concrete character of the uncertain situation in which thought occurs; it fails to note the empirically concrete nature of the subject-matter, acts, and tools by which determination and consistency are reached; it fails to note that the conclusive eventual objects having the latter properties are themselves as many as the situations dealt with. The conversion of the logic of reflection into an ontology of rational being is thus due to arbitrary conversion of an eventual natural function of unification into a causal antecedent reality; this in turn is due to the tendency of the imagination working under the influence of emotion to carry unification from an actual, objective, and experimental enterprise, limited to particular situations where it is needed, into an unrestricted, wholesale movement which ends in an all-absorbing dream.

The occurrence of reflection is crucial for dualistic metaphysics as well as for idealistic ontologies. Reflection occurs only in situations qualified by uncertainty, alternatives, questioning, search, hypotheses, tentative trials or experiments which test the worth of thinking. A naturalistic metaphysics is bound to consider reflection as itself a natural event occurring *within* nature because of traits of the latter. It is bound to inference from the empirical traits of thinking in precisely the same way as the sciences make inferences from the happening of suns, radioactivity, thunderstorms, or any other natural event. Traits of reflection are as truly indicative or evidential of the traits of *other* things as are the traits of these events. A theory of the nature of the occurrence and career of a sun reached by denial of the obvious traits of the sun, or by denial that these traits are so connected with the traits of other natural events that they can be used as evidence concerning the nature of these other things, would hardly possess scientific standing. Yet philosophers, and strangely enough philosophers who call themselves realists, have constantly held that the traits which are characteristic of thinking, namely, uncertainty, ambiguity, alternatives, inquiring, search, selection, experimental re-shaping of external conditions, do not possess the same existential character as do the objects of valid knowledge. They have denied that these traits are evidential of the character of the world within which thinking occurs. They have not, as realists, asserted that these traits are mere appearances; but they have often asserted and implied that such things are only personal or psychological in contrast with a world of objective nature. But the interests of empirical and denotative method and of naturalistic metaphysics wholly coincide. The world must actually be such as to generate ignorance and inquiry; doubt and hypothesis; trial and temporal conclusions; the latter being such that they develop out of existences which while wholly "real" are not as satisfactory, as good, or as significant, as those into which they are eventually re-organized. The ultimate evidence of genuine hazard, contingency, irregularity, and indeterminateness in nature is thus found in the occurrence of thinking. The traits of natural existence which generate the fears and adorations of superstitious barbarians generate the scientific procedures of disciplined civilization. The superiority of the latter does not consist in the fact that they are based on "real" existence, while the former depend wholly upon a human nature different from nature in general. It consists in the fact that scientific inquiries reach *objects* which are better, because reached by method which controls them and which adds greater control to life itself, method which mitigates accident, turns contingency to account, and releases thought and other forms of endeavor.

The conjunction of problematic and determinate characters in nature renders every existence, as well as every idea and human act, an experiment in fact, even though not in design. To be intelligently experimental is but to be conscious of this intersection of natural conditions so as to profit by it instead of being at its mercy. The Christian idea of this world and this life as a probation is a kind of distorted recognition of the situation; distorted because it applied wholesale to one stretch of existence in contrast with another, regarded as original and final. But in truth anything which can exist at any place and at any time occurs subject to tests imposed upon it by surroundings, which are only in part compatible and reinforcing. These surroundings test its strength and measure its endurance. As we can discourse of change only in terms of velocity and acceleration which involve relations to other things, so assertion of the permanent and enduring is comparative. The stablest thing we can speak of is not free from conditions set to it by other things. That even the solid earth mountains, the emblems of constancy, appear and disappear like the clouds is an old theme of moralists and poets. The fixed and unchanged being of the Democritean atom is now reported by inquirers to possess some of the traits of his non-being, and to embody a temporary equilibrium in the economy of nature's compromises and adjustments. A thing may endure *saecula saeculorum* and yet not be everlasting; it will crumble before the gnawing tooth of time, as it exceeds a certain measure. Every existence is an event.

This fact is nothing at which to repine and nothing to gloat over. It is something to be noted and used. If it is discomfiting when applied to good things, to our friends, possessions, and precious selves, it is consoling also to know that no evil endures forever; that the longest lane turns sometime, and that the memory of loss of nearest and dearest grows dim in time. The eventful character of all existences is no reason for consigning them to the realm of mere appearance any more than it is a reason for idealizing flux into a deity. The important thing is measure, relation, ratio, knowledge of the comparative tempos of change. In mathematics some variables are constants in some problems; so it is in nature and life. The rate of change of some things is so slow, or is so rhythmic, that these changes have all the advantages of stability in dealing with more transitory and irregular happenings—if we know enough. Indeed, if any one thing that concerns us is subject to change, it is fortunate that all other things change. A thing "absolutely" stable and unchangeable would be out of the range of the principle of action and reaction, of resistance and leverage as well as of friction. Here it would have no applicability, no potentiality of use as measure and control of other events. To designate the slower and the regular rhythmic events structure, and more rapid and irregular ones process, is sound practical sense. It expresses the function of one in respect to the other.

But spiritualistic idealism and materialism alike treat this relational and functional distinction as something fixed and absolute. One doctrine finds structure in a framework of ideal forms, the other finds it in matter. They agree in supposing that structure has some superlative reality. This supposition is another form taken by preference for the stable over the precarious and uncompleted. The fact is that all structure is structure of something; anything defined as structure is a character of *events*, not something intrinsic and *per se.* A set of traits is called structure, because of its limiting function in relation to other traits of events. A house has a structure; in comparison with the disintegration and collapse that would occur without its presence, this structure is fixed. Yet it is not something external to which the changes involved in building and using the house have to submit. It is rather an arrangement of changing events such that properties which change slowly, limit and direct a series of quick changes and give them an order which they do not otherwise possess. Structure is constancy of means, of things used for consequences, not of things taken by themselves or absolutely. Structure is what makes construction possible and cannot be discovered or defined except in some realized construction, construction being, of course, an evident order of changes. The isolation of structure from the changes whose stable ordering it is, renders it mysterious—something that is metaphysical in the popular sense of the word, a kind of ghostly queerness.

The "matter" of materialists and the "spirit" of idealists is a creature similar to the constitution of the United States in the minds of unimaginative persons. Obviously the real constitution is certain basic relationships among the activities of the citizens of the country; it is a property or phase of these processes, so connected with them as to influence their rate and direction of change. But by literalists it is often conceived of as something external to them; in itself fixed, a rigid framework to which all changes must accommodate themselves. Similarly what we call matter is that character of natural events which is so tied up with changes that are sufficiently rapid to be perceptible as to give the latter a characteristic rhythmic order, the causal sequence. It is no cause or source of events or processes; no absolute monarch; no principle of explanation; no substance behind or underlying changes—save in that sense of substance in which a man well fortified with this world's goods, and hence able to maintain himself through vicissitudes of surroundings, is a man of substance. The name designates a character in operation, not an entity.

That structure, whether of the kind called material or of the kind summed up in the word mental, is stable or permanent relationally and in its office, may be shown in another way. There is no action without reaction; there is no exclusively one-way exercise of conditioning power, no mode of regulation that operates wholly from above to below or from within outwards or from without inwards. Whatever influences the changes of other things is itself changed. The idea of an activity proceeding only in one direction, of an unmoved mover, is a survival of Greek physics. It has been banished from science, but remains to haunt philosophy. The vague and mysterious properties assigned to mind and matter, the very conceptions of mind and matter in traditional thought, are ghosts walking underground. The notion of matter actually found in the practice of science has nothing in common with the matter of materialists—and almost everybody is still a materialist as to matter, to which he merely adds a second rigid structure which he calls mind. The matter of science is a character of natural events and changes as they change; their character of regular and stable order.

Natural events are so complex and varied that there is nothing surprising in their possession of different characterizations, characters so different that they can be easily treated as opposites.

Nothing but unfamiliarity stands in the way of thinking of both mind and matter as different characters of natural events, in which matter expresses their sequential order, and mind the order of their meanings in their logical connections and dependencies. Processes may be eventful for functions which taken in abstract separation are at opposite poles, just as physiological processes eventuate in both anabolic and catabolic functions. The idea that matter and mind are two sides or "aspects" of the same things, like the convex and the concave in a curve, is literally unthinkable.

A curve is an intelligible object and concave and convex are defined in terms of this object; they are indeed but names for properties involved in its meaning. We do not start with convexity and concavity as two independent things and then set up an unknown *tertium quid* to unite two disparate things. In spite of the literal absurdity of the comparison, it may be understood however in a way which conveys an inkling of the truth. That to which both mind and matter belong is the complex of events that constitute nature. This becomes a mysterious *tertium quid,* incapable of designation, only when mind and matter are taken to be static structures instead of functional characters. It is a plausible prediction that if there were an interdict placed for a generation upon the use of mind, matter, consciousness as nouns, and we were obliged to employ adjectives and adverbs, conscious and consciously, mental and mentally, material and physically, we should find many of our problems much simplified.

We have selected only a few of the variety of the illustrations that might be used in support of the idea that the significant problems and issues of life and philosophy concern the rate and mode of the conjunction of the precarious and the assured, the incomplete and the finished, the repetitious and the varying, the safe and sane and the hazardous. If we trust to the evidence of experienced things, these traits, and the modes and tempos of their interaction with each other, are fundamental features of natural existence. The experience of their various consequences, according as they are relatively isolated, unhappily or happily combined, is evidence that wisdom, and hence that love of wisdom which is philosophy, is concerned with choice and administration of their proportioned union. Structure and process, substance and accident, matter and energy, permanence and flux, one and many, continuity and discreteness, order and progress, law and liberty, uniformity and growth, tradition and innovation, rational will and impelling desires, proof and discovery, the actual and the possible, are names given to various phases of their conjunction, and the issue of living depends upon the art with which these things are adjusted to each other.

While metaphysics may stop short with noting and registering these traits, man is not contemplatively detached from them. They involve him in his perplexities and troubles, and are the source of his joys and achievements. The situation is not indifferent to man, because it forms man as a desiring, striving, thinking, feeling creature. It is not egotism that leads man from contemplative registration of these traits to interest in managing them, to intelligence and purposive art. Interest, thinking, planning, striving, consummation, and frustration are a drama enacted by these forces and conditions. A particular choice may be arbitrary; this is only to say that it does not approve itself to reflection. But choice is not arbitrary, not in a universe like this one, a world which is not finished and which has not consistently made up its mind where it is going and what it is going to do. Or, if we call it arbitrary, the arbitrariness is not ours but that of existence itself. And to call existence arbitrary or by any moral name, whether disparaging or honorific, is to patronize nature. To assume an attitude of condescension toward existence is perhaps a natural human compensation for the straits of life. But it is an ultimate source of the covert, uncandid, and cheap in philosophy. This compensatory disposition it is which forgets that reflection exists to guide choice and effort. Hence its love of wisdom is but an unlaborious transformation of existence by dialectic, instead of an opening and enlarging of the ways of nature in man. A true wisdom, devoted to the latter task, discovers in thoughtful observation and experiment the method of administering the unfinished processes of existence so that frail goods shall be substantiated, secure goods be extended, and the precarious promises of good that haunt experienced things be more liberally fulfilled.

Nature, Life and Body-Mind

Empirically speaking, the most obvious difference between living and non-living things is that the activities of the former are characterized by needs, by efforts which are active demands to satisfy needs, and by satisfactions. In making this statement, the terms need, effort and satisfaction are primarily employed in a biological sense. By need is meant a condition of tensional distribution of energies such that the body is in a condition of uneasy or unstable equilibrium. By demand or effort is meant the fact that this state is manifested in movements which modify environing bodies in ways which react upon the body, so that its characteristic pattern of active equilibrium is restored. By satisfaction is meant this recovery of equilibrium pattern, consequent upon the changes of environment due to interactions with the active demands of the organism.

A plant needs water, carbon dioxide; upon occasion it needs to bear seeds. The need is neither an immaterial psychic force superimposed upon matter, nor is it merely a notional or conceptual distinction, introduced by thought after comparison of two different states of the organism, one of emptiness and one of repletion. It denotes a concrete state of events: a condition of tension in the distribution of energies such as involves pressure from points of high potential to those of low potential, which in turn effects distinctive changes such that the connection with the environment is altered, so that it acts differently upon the environment and is exposed to different influences from it. In this fact, taken by itself, there is nothing which marks off the plant from the physico-chemical activity of inanimate bodies. The latter also are subject to conditions of disturbed inner equilibrium, which lead to activity in relation to surrounding things, and which terminate after a cycle of changes—a terminus termed saturation, corresponding to satisfaction in organic bodies.

The difference between the animate plant and the inanimate iron molecule is not that the former has something in addition to physico-chemical energy; it lies in the *way* in which physicochemical energies are interconnected and operate, whence different *consequences* mark inanimate and animate activity respectively. For with animate bodies, recovery or restoration of the equilibrium pattern applies to the complex integrated course or history. In inanimate bodies as such, "saturation" occurs indifferently, not in such a way as to tend to maintain a temporal pattern of activity. The interactions of the various constituent parts of a plant take place in such ways as to tend to continue a characteristically organized activity; they tend to utilize conserved consequences of past activities so as to adapt subsequent changes to the needs of the integral system to which they belong. Organization is a fact, though it is not an original organizing force. Iron as such exhibits characteristics of bias or selective reactions, but it shows no bias in favor of remaining simple iron; it had just as soon, so to speak, become iron-oxide. It shows no tendency in its interaction with water to modify the interaction so that consequences will perpetuate the characteristics of pure iron. If it did, it would have the marks of a living body, and would be called an organism. Iron as a genuine constituent of an *organized* body acts so as to tend to maintain the type of activity of the organism to which it belongs.

If we identify, as common speech does, the physical as such with the inanimate we need another word to denote the activity of organisms as such. Psycho-physical is an appropriate term. Thus employed, "psycho-physical" denotes the conjunctive presence in activity of need-demand-satisfaction, in the sense in which these terms have been defined. In the compound word, the prefix "psycho" denotes that physical activity has acquired additional properties, those of ability to procure a peculiar kind of interactive support of needs from surrounding media. Psycho-physical does not denote an abrogation of the physico-chemical; nor a peculiar mixture of something physical and something psychical (as a centaur is half man and half horse); it denotes the possession of certain qualities and efficacies not displayed by the inanimate.

Thus conceived there is no problem of the relation of physical *and* psychic. There are specifiable empirical events marked by distinctive qualities and efficacies. There is first of all, *organization* with all which is implied thereby. The problem involved is one of definite factual inquiry. Under exactly what conditions does organization occur, and just what are its various modes and their consequences? We may not be able to answer these questions satisfactorily; but the difficulties are not those of a philosophical mystery, but such as attend any inquiry into highly complex affairs. Organization is an empirical trait of some events, no matter how speculative and dubious theories about it may be; especially no matter how false are certain doctrines about it which have had great vogue—namely, those doctrines which have construed it as evidence of a special force or entity called life or soul. Organization is so characteristic of the nature of some events in their sequential linkages that no theory about it can be as speculative or absurd as those which ignore or deny its genuine existence. Denial is never based on empirical evidence, but is a dialectical conclusion from a preconception that whatever appears later in time must be metaphysically unreal as compared with what is found earlier, or from a preconception that since the complex is controlled by means of the simpler, the latter is more "real."

Whenever the activities of the constituent parts of an organized pattern of activity are of such a nature as to conduce to the perpetuation of the patterned activity, there exists the basis of sensitivity. Each "part" of an organism is itself organized, and so of the "parts" of the part. Hence its selective bias in interactions with environing things is exercised so as to maintain *itself,* while also maintaining the whole of which it is a member. The root-tips of a plant interact with chemical properties of the soil in such ways as to serve organized life activity; and in such ways as to exact from the rest of the organism their own share of requisite nutrition. This pervasive operative presence of the whole in the part and of the part in the whole constitutes susceptibility—the capacity of feeling—whether or no this potentiality be actualized in plant-life. Responses are not merely selective, but are discriminatory, in behalf of some results rather than others. This discrimination is the essence of sensitivity. Thus with organization, bias becomes interest, and satisfaction a good or value and not a mere satiation of wants or repletion of deficiencies.

However it may be with plants and lower animals, in animals in which locomotion and distance-receptors exist, sensitivity and interest are realized as feeling, even though only as vague and massive uneasiness, comfort, vigor and exhaustion. A sessile organism requires no premonitions of what is to occur, nor cumulative embodiments of what has occurred. An organism with locomotion is vitally connected with the remote as well as with the nearby; when locomotor organs are accompanied by distance-receptors, response to the distant in space becomes increasingly prepotent and equivalent in effect to response to the future in time. A response toward what is distant is in effect an expectation or prediction of a later contact. Activities are differentiated into the preparatory, or anticipatory, and the fulfilling or consummatory. The resultant is a peculiar tension in which each immediate preparatory response is suffused with the consummatory tone of sex or food or security to which it contributes. Sensitivity, the capacity, is then actualized as feeling; susceptibility to the useful and harmful in surroundings becomes premonitory, an occasion of eventual consequences within life.

On the other hand, a consummation or satisfaction carries with it the continuation, in allied and reinforcing form, of preparatory or anticipatory activities. It is not only a culmination out of them, but is an integrated cumulation, a funded conservation *of* them. Comfort or discomfort, fatigue or exhilaration, implicitly sum up a history, and thereby unwittingly provide a means whereby, (when other conditions become present) the past can be unravelled and made explicit. For it is characteristic of feeling that while it may exist in a formless condition, or without configured distinctions, it is capable of receiving and bearing distinctions without end. With the multiplication of sensitive discriminatory reactions to different energies of the environment (the differentiation of sense-organs, extero-ceptors and proprio-ceptors) and with the increase in scope and delicacy of movements (the development of motor-organs, to which internal glandular organs for effecting a requisite redistribution of energy correspond), feelings vary more and more in quality and intensity.

Complex and active animals *have,* therefore, feelings which vary abundantly in quality, corresponding to distinctive directions and phases—initiating, mediating, fulfilling or frustrating—of activities, bound up in distinctive connections with environmental affairs. They *have* them, but they do not know they have them. Activity is psychophysical, but not "mental," that is, not aware of meanings. As life is a character of events in a peculiar condition of organization, and "feeling" is a quality of life-forms marked by complexly mobile and discriminating responses, so "mind" is an added property assumed by a feeling creature, when it reaches that organized interaction with other living creatures which is language, communication. Then the qualities of feeling become significant of objective differences in external things and of episodes past and to come. This state of things in which qualitatively different feelings are not just had but are significant of objective differences, is mind. Feelings are no longer just felt. They have and they make *sense;* record and prophesy.

That is to say, differences in qualities (feelings) of acts when employed as indications of acts performed and to be performed and as signs of their consequences, *mean* something. And they mean it directly; the meaning is had as their own character. Feelings make sense; as immediate meanings of events and objects, they are sensations, or, more properly, sensa. Without language, the qualities of organic action that are feelings are pains, pleasures, odors, colors, noises, tones, only potentially and proleptically. With language they are discriminated and identified. They are then "objectified"; they are immediate traits of things. This "objectification" is not a miraculous ejection from the organism or soul into external things, nor an illusory attribution of Psychical entities to physical things. The qualities never were "in" the organism; they always were qualities of interactions in which both extra-organic things and organisms partake. When named, they enable identification and discrimination of things to take place as means in a further course of inclusive interaction. Hence they are as much qualities of the things engaged as of the organism. For purposes of control they may be referred specifically to either the thing or to the organism or to a specified structure of the organism. Thus color which turns out not to be a reliable sign of external events becomes a sign of, say, a defect in visual apparatus. The notion that sensory affections discriminate and identify themselves, apart from discourse, as being colors and sounds, etc., and thus *ipso facto* constitute certain elementary modes of knowledge, even though it be only knowledge of their own existence, is inherently so absurd that it would never have occurred to any one to entertain it, were it not for certain preconceptions about mind and knowledge. Sentiency in itself is anoetic; it exists as any immediate quality exists, but nevertheless it is an indispensable means of any noetic function.

For when, through language, sentience is taken up into a system of signs, when for example a certain quality of the active relationship of organism and environment is named hunger, it is seen as an organic demand for an extra-organic object. To term a quality "hunger," to name it, is to refer to an object, to food, to that which will satisfy it, towards which the active situation moves. Similarly, to name another quality "red," is to direct an interaction between an organism and a thing to some object which fulfills the demand or need of the situation. It requires but slight observation of mental growth of a child to note that organically conditioned qualities, including those special sense-organs, are discriminated only as they are employed to designate objects; red, for instance, as the property of a dress or toy. The difficulty in the way of identifying the qualities of acts conditioned by proprio-ceptor organs is notoriously enormous. They just merge in the general situation. If they entered into communication as shared means to social consequences they would acquire the same objective distinctiveness as do qualities conditioned by the extero-ceptor organs. On the other hand, the qualities of the latter are just shades of the general tone of situations until they are used, in language, as common or shared means to common ends. Then they are identified as traits of objects. The child has to learn through social intercourse that certain qualities of action mean greediness or anger or fear or rudeness; the case is not otherwise with those qualities which are identified as red, musical tone, a foul odor. The latter may have instigated nausea, and "red" may have excited uneasiness (as blood makes some persons faint); but discrimination of the nauseating object *as* foul odor, and of the excitation *as* red occurs only when they are designated as signs.

The qualities of situations in which organisms and surrounding conditions interact, when discriminated, make sense. Sense is distinct from feeling, for it has a recognized reference; it is the qualitative characteristic of something, not just a submerged unidentified quality or tone. Sense is also different from signification. The latter involves use of a quality as a sign or index of something else, as when the red of a light signifies danger, and the need of bringing a moving locomotive to a stop. The sense of a thing, on the other hand, is an immediate and immanent meaning; it is meaning which is itself felt or directly had. When we are baffled by perplexing conditions, and finally hit upon a clew, and everything falls into place, the whole thing suddenly, as we say, "makes sense." In such a situation, the clew has signification in virtue of being an indication, a guide to interpretation. But the meaning of the *whole* situation as apprehended is sense. This idiomatic usage of the word sense is much nearer the empirical facts than is the ordinary restriction of the word in psychological literature to a single simple recognized quality, like sweet or red: the latter simply designates a case of *minimum* sense, deliberately limited for purposes of intellectual safety-first. Whenever a situation has this double function of meaning, namely signification and sense, mind, intellect is definitely present.

The distinction between physical, psycho-physical, and mental is thus one of levels of increasing complexity and intimacy of interaction among natural events. The idea that matter, life and mind represent separate kinds of Being is a doctrine that springs, as so many philosophic errors have sprung, from a substantiation of eventual functions. The fallacy converts consequences of interaction of events into causes of the occurrence of these consequences—a reduplication which is significant as to the *importance* of the functions, but which hopelessly confuses understanding of them. "Matter," or the physical, is a character of events when they occur at a certain level of interaction. It is not itself an event or existence; the notion that while "mind" denotes essence, "matter" denotes existence is superstition. It is more than a bare essence; for it is a property of a particular field of interacting events. But as it figures in *science* it is as much an essence as is acceleration, or the square root of minus one; which meanings also express derivative characters of events in interaction. Consequently, while the theory that life, feeling and thought are never independent of physical events may be deemed materialism, it may also be considered just the opposite. For it is reasonable to believe that the most adequate definition of the basic traits of natural existence can be had only when its properties are most fully displayed—a condition which is met in the degree of the scope and intimacy of interactions realized.

In any case, genuine objection to metaphysical materialism is neither moral nor esthetic. Historically speaking, materialism and mechanistic metaphysics—as distinct from mechanistic science—designate the doctrine that matter is the efficient cause of life and mind, and that "cause" occupies a position superior in reality to that of "effect." Both parts of this statement are contrary to fact. As far as the conception of causation is to be introduced at all, not matter but the natural events having matter as a character, "cause" life and mind. "Effects," since they mark the release of potentialities, are more adequate indications of the nature of nature than are just "causes." Control of the occurrence of the complex depends upon its analysis into the more elementary; the dependence of life, sentiency and mind upon "matter" is thus practical or instrumental. Lesser, more external fields of interaction are more manageable than are wider and more intimate ones, and only through managing the former can we direct the occurrence of the latter.

Thus it is in virtue of the character of events which is termed matter that psycho-physical and intellectual affairs can be differentially determined. Every discovery of concrete dependence of life and mind upon physical events is therefore an addition to our resources. If life and mind had no mechanism, education, deliberate modification, rectification, prevention and constructive control would be impossible. To damn "matter" because of honorific interest in spirit is but another edition of the old habit of eulogizing ends and disparaging the means on which they depend.

This, then, is the significance of our introductory statement that the "solution" of the problem of mind-body is to be found in a revision of the preliminary assumptions about existence which generate the problem. As we have already noted, fruitful science of nature began when inquirers neglected immediate qualities, the "sense" of events, wet and dry, hot and cold, light and heavy, up and down, in behalf of "primary," namely, signifying, qualities, and when they treated the latter, although called qualities, not as such but as relations. This device made possible a totally different dialectical treatment. Classic science operated in terms of properties already attached to qualitative phenomena of sense and custom. Hence it could only repeat these phenomena in a changed vocabulary;—the vocabulary of sensory forms and forces which were, after all nothing but the already given meanings of things reduplicated. But the new dialectic was that of mathematical equations and functions. It started from meanings which ignored obvious characters or meanings of phenomena; hence it could lead to radically new relationships and generalizations—new in kind, and not merely in detail. No longer was the connection or classification of one color simply with other colors, but with all events involving rhythmic rates of change. Thus events hitherto disjoined were brought together under principles of inclusive formulation and prediction. Temporal qualities were stated as spatial velocities; thereby mathematical functions directly applicable to spatial positions, directions and distances, made it possible to reduce sequence of events into calculable terms. Neglect of temporal qualities as such centered thought upon *order* of succession, an order convertible into one of coexistence.

All this in effect is equivalent to seizing upon relations of events as the proper objects of knowledge. The surrender of immediate qualities, sensory and significant, as objects of science, and as proper forms of classification and understanding, left in reality these immediate qualities just as they were; since they are *had* there is no need to *know* them. But, as we have had frequent occasion to notice, the traditional view that the object of knowledge is reality *par excellence* led to the conclusion that the proper object of science was preeminently metaphysically real. Hence immediate qualities, being extruded from the object of science, were left thereby hanging loose from the "real" object. Since their *existence* could not be denied, they were gathered together into a psychic realm of being, set over against the object of physics. Given this premise, all the problems regarding the relation of mind and matter, the psychic and the bodily, necessarily follow. Change the metaphysical premise; restore, that is to say, immediate qualities to their rightful position as qualities of inclusive situations, and the problems in question cease to be epistemological problems. They become specifiable scientific problems: questions, that is to say, of how such and such an event having such and such qualities actually occurs.

Greek science imputed efficacy to qualities like wet and dry, hot and cold, heavy and light and to such qualitative differences in movement as up and down, to and fro, around and around. The world was formulated and explained on the basis of the causal efficacy of these qualities. The scientific revolution of the seventeenth century took its departure from a denial of causal status (and hence of significance for science) of these and all other direct qualities. On account, however, of the conversion of this fact about scientific procedure into a denial of the existence of qualities outside of mind and consciousness, psycho-physical and mental functions became inexplicable anomalies, supernatural in the literal sense of the word. The error of Greek science lay not in assigning qualities to natural existence, but in misconceiving the locus of their efficacy. It attributed to qualities apart from organic action efficiencies which qualities possess only through the medium of an organized activity of life and mind. When life and mind are recognized to be characters of the highly complex and extensive interaction of events, it is possible to give natural existential status to qualities, without falling into the mistake of Greek science. Psycho-physical phenomena and higher mental phenomena may be admitted in their full empirical reality, without recourse to dualistic breach in historic, existential continuity.

When knowing inanimate things, qualities as such may be safely disregarded. They present themselves as intensities and vector directions of movement capable of statement in mathematical terms. Thus

their immediate individuality is got around; it is impertinent for science, concerned as the latter is with relationships. The most that can
be said about qualities in the inanimate field is that they mark the
limit of the contact of historical affairs, being abrupt ends or termini,
boundaries of beginning and closing where a particular interaction
ceases. They are like a line of foam marking the impact of waves of
different directions of movement. They have to be noted and accepted
in order to delimit a field of inquiry, but they do not enter into the
inquiry as factors or terms.

In life and mind they play an active role. The delimitation or individ-
ualization they constitute on this level is not external to events. It is all
one with the organization which permeates them, and which in permeating them, converts prior limitations of intensity and direction of energy into actual and intrinsic qualities, or sentient differences. For in
feeling a quality exists as quality, and not merely as an abrupt, discrete,
unique delimitation of interaction. Red differs from green for purposes
of physical science as that which gives specific meaning to two sets of
numbers applied to vibrations, or to two different placements of lines
in a spectrum. The difference is proleptically qualitative; it refers to a
unique difference of potentiality in the affairs under consideration. But
as far as calculation and prediction are concerned these differences
remain designable by non-qualitative indices of number and form. But
in an organic creature sensitive to light, these differences of potentiality
may be realized as differences in immediate sentiency. To say that they
are *felt,* is to say that they come to independent and intrinsic existence
on their own account. The proposition does not mean that feeling has
been extraneously superadded to something else, or that a mode of
extrinsic cognitive access to a purely physical thing has entered intru-
sively into a world of Psychical things. "Feeling" is in general a name
for the newly actualized quality acquired by events previously occurring upon a physical level, when these events come into more extensive
and delicate relationships of interaction. More specifically, it is a name
for the coming to existence of those ultimate differences in affairs
which mark them off from one another and give them discreteness;
differences which upon the physical plane can be spoken of only in
anticipation of subsequent realization, or in terms of different numerical formulae, and different space-time positions and contiguities.

Thus qualities characteristic of sentiency are qualities *of* cosmic
events. Only because they are such, is it possible to establish the one

to one correspondence which natural science does establish between series of numbers and spatial positions on one hand and the series and spectra of sensory qualities on the other. The notion that the universe is split into two separate and disconnected realms of existence, one psychical and the other physical, and then that these two realms of being, in spite of their total disjunction, specifically and minutely correspond to each other—as a serial order of numbered vibrations corresponds to the immediately felt qualities of vision of the prismatic spectrum—presents the acme of incredibility. The one-to-one agreement is intelligible only as a correspondence of properties and relations in one and the same world, which is first taken upon a narrower and more external level of interaction, and then upon a more inclusive and intimate level. When we recall that by taking natural events on these two levels and instituting point to point correspondence (or "parallelism") between them, the richer and more complex display of characters is rendered amenable to prediction and deliberate guidance, the intelligibility of the procedure becomes concretely sensible.

Thus while modern science is correct in denying direct efficacy and position in the described sequence of events to say, red, or dry; yet Greek science was correct in its underlying naive assumption that qualities count for something highly important. Apart from sentiency and life, the career of an event can indeed be fully described without any reference to its having red as a quality,—though even in this case, since description is an event which happens only through mental events, dependence upon an overt or actualized quality of red is required in order to delimit the phenomenon of which a mathematical-mechanical statement is made. Qualities actually become specifically effective however, in psycho-physical situations. Where animal susceptibility exists, a red or an odor or sound may instigate a determinate mode of action; it has selective power in maintenance of a certain pattern of energy-organization. So striking is this fact that we might even define the difference between an inanimate body and a vital and psycho-physical one, by saying that the latter responds to qualities while the former does not. In this response, qualities become productive of results, and hence potentially significant. That is, in achieving effects, they become connected with consequences, and hence capable of meaning, knowable if not known. This explains the fact that while we are forced to ascribe qualities to events on the physical level, we cannot *know* them on this level; they have when assigned strictly to that level no consequences.

But through the medium of living things, they generate effects, which, when qualities are used as means to produce them, are consequences. Thus qualities become intelligible, knowable.

In the higher organisms, those with distance-receptors of ear and eye and, in lesser degree, of smelling, qualities further achieve a difference which is the material basis or substratum of a distinction into activities having preparatory and having consummatory status. "Ends" are not necessarily fulfillments or consummations. They may be mere closures, abrupt cessations, as a railway line may by force of external conditions come to an end, although the end does not fulfill antecedent activities. So there are starts, beginnings which are in no sense preparatory, being rather disturbances and interferences. Events of the physical type have such ends and beginnings which mark them off qualitatively and individually. But as such they are not in any true sense possessed of instrumental nor fulfilling character. They neither initiate nor complete. But when these qualities are realized through organic action, giving rise to acts of utilization, of adaptation (response to quality), they are converted into a series, in which some acts are preparatory and others consummatory. An original contact-activity (including intra-organic disturbances or needs) renders distance receptors open to stimulation; the responses which take place in consequence tend to occur in such a way as to terminate in a further contact-activity in which original need is satisfied.

This series forms the immediate material of thought when social communication and discourse supervene. The beginning not only *is* the initial term in a *series* (as distinct from a *succession),* but it gains the *meaning* of subsequent activity moving toward a consequence of which it is the first member. The concluding term conserves within itself the meaning of the entire preparatory process. Thereby the original status of contact and distance activities is reversed. When activity is directed by distant things, contact activities must be inhibited or held in. They become instrumental; they function only as far as is needed to direct the distance-conditioned activities. The result is nothing less than revolutionary. Organic activity is liberated from subjection to what is closest at hand in space and time. Man is led or drawn rather than pushed. The immediate is significant in respect to what has occurred and will occur; the organic basis of memory and expectation is supplied. The subordination of contact-activity to distance-activity is equivalent to possibility of release from submergence in the merely given, namely, to abstraction, generalization, inference. It institutes both a difference and a connection between matters that prepare the way for other events and the affairs finally appropriated; it furnishes the material for the relation of thing signifying and thing signified—a relation that is actualized when discourse occurs. When this juncture of events is reached, there comes about the distinction mentioned between sense and signification. The latter denotes the possibility of a later fulfilling sense of things in immediate appropriations and enjoyments. But meanwhile there is a sentience that has to be transformed by subordination to the distance-conditioned activity; which till it is thus transformed is vacant, confused, demanding but lacking meaning. Meanwhile also the distance-conditioned activities acquire as an integral part of their own quality the consequences of their prior fulfillments. They have *significance* with respect to their consequences; but they have perspicuous and coherent *sense* of their own. Thus they become final, and the qualities of contact-activity instrumental. In short, hearing and vision are notoriously the intellectual *and* esthetic senses—an undeniable fact which throws much light on the doctrine of those theorists about value who attempt to divide thought and enjoyable liking from each other in their definitions of value, and who also—quite logically on this premise-sharply separate values into contributory and intrinsic.

The foregoing discussion is both too technical and not elaborately technical enough for adequate comprehension. It may be conceived as an attempt to contribute to what has come to be called an "emergent" theory of mind. But every word that we can use, organism, feeling, psycho-physical, sensation and sense, "emergence" itself, is infected by the associations of old theories, whose import is opposite to that here stated. We may, however attempt a recapitulation by premising that while there is no isolated occurrence in nature, yet interaction and connection are not wholesale and homogenous. Interacting events have tighter and looser ties, which qualify them with certain beginnings and endings, and which mark them off from other fields of interaction. Such relatively closed fields come into conjunction at times so as to interact with each other, and a critical alteration is effected. A new larger field is formed, in which new energies are released, and to which new qualities appertain. Regulation, conscious direction and science imply ability to smooth over the rough junctures, and to form by translation and substitution a homogenous medium. Yet these functions do not abrogate or deny qualitative differences and unlike fields or ranges of operation, from atoms to solar systems. They do just what they are meant to do: give facility and security in utilizing the simpler manageable field to predict and modify the course of the more complete and highly organized.

In general, three plateaus of such fields may be discriminated. The first, the scene of narrower and more external interactions, while qualitatively diversified in itself, is physical; its distinctive properties are those of the mathematical-mechanical system discovered by physics and which define matter as a general character. The second level is that of life. Qualitative differences, like those of plant and animal, lower and higher animal forms, are here even more conspicuous; but in spite of their variety they have qualities in common which define the psychophysical. The third plateau is that of association, communication, participation. This is still further internally diversified, consisting of individualities. It is marked throughout its diversities, however, by common properties, which define mind as intellect; possession of and response to meanings.

Each one of these levels having its own characteristic empirical traits has its own categories. They are however categories of description, conceptions required to state the fact in question. They are not "explanatory" categories, as explanation is sometimes understood; they do not designate, that is, the operation of forces as "causes." They stick to empirical facts noting and denoting characteristic qualities and consequences peculiar to various levels of interaction. Viewed from this standpoint, the traditional "mechanical" and "teleological" theories both suffer from a common fallacy, which may be suggested by saying that they both purport to be explanatory in the old, non-historical sense of causality. One theory makes matter account for the existence of mind; the other regards happenings that precede the appearance of mind as preparations made for the sake of mind in a sense of preparation that is alleged to explain the occurrence of these antecedents.

Mechanistic metaphysics calls attention to the fact that the latter occurrence could not have taken place without the earlier; that given the earlier, the latter was bound to follow. Spiritualistic metaphysics calls attention to the fact that the earlier, material affairs, prepare the way for vital and ideal affairs, lead up to them; promote them. Both statements are equally true descriptively; neither statement is true in the explanatory and metaphysical meaning imputed to it.

The notion of causal explanation involved in both conceptions implies a breach in the continuity of historic process; the gulf created has then to be bridged by an emission or transfer of force. If one starts with the assumption that mind and matter are two separate things, while the evidence forces one to see that they are connected, one has no option save to attribute the power to make the connection, to carry from one to the other, to one or the other of the two things involved. The one selected is then "cause"; it accounts for the existence of the other. One person is struck by such affairs as that when a match is struck and paper is near-by the paper catches fire, whether any one wished or intended it to do so or not. He is struck by a compulsory power exercised by the earlier over the later; given the lighted match and contiguous paper and the latter *must* burst into flame. Another person is struck by the fact that matches and paper exist only because somebody has use for them; that the intent and purpose of use preceded the coming into being of match and paper. So he concludes that thought, purpose, starts an emission and transfer of force which brought things into existence in order to accomplish the object of thought. Or, if a little less devoted to human analogies, one notes the cunning continuity of nature, how neatly one thing leads up to another, and how elegantly the later registers and takes advantage of what has gone before, and, beholding that the later is the more complex and the more significant, decides that what goes before occurs for the sake of the later, in its behalf, on its account. The eventual has somehow been there from the start, "implicitly," "potentially," but efficaciously enough to attend to its own realization by using material conditions at every stage.

The gratuitous nature of both assumptions is seen if we set out with any acknowledged historic process—say, the growth from infancy to maturity, or the development of a melodic theme. There are those who regard childhood as merely getting ready for the supreme dignity of adulthood, and there are those who seem quite sure that adult life is merely an unrolling by way of mechanical effects of the "causal" forces found in childhood. One of the theories makes youth a preliminary and intrinsically insignificant journey toward a goal; the other makes adulthood a projection, on a supernumerary screen, of a plate and pattern previously inserted in the projecting apparatus of childhood or of prenatal condition, or of heredity, or wherever the fixed and separated antecedent be located. Nevertheless the notion of growth makes it easy, I think, to detect the fallacy residing in both views: namely, the breaking up of a continuity of historical change into two separate parts, together with the necessity which follows from the breaking-in-two for some device by which to bring them together again.

The reality *is* the growth-process itself; childhood and adulthood are phases of a continuity, in which just because it is a history, the later cannot exist until the earlier exists ("mechanistic materialism" in germ); and in which the later makes use of the registered and cumulative outcome of the earlier—or, more strictly, *is* its utilization ("spiritualistic teleology" in germ). The real existence is the history in its entirety, the history as just what it is. The operations of splitting it up into two parts and then having to unite them again by appeal to causative power are equally arbitrary and gratuitous. Childhood is the childhood *of* and *in* a certain serial process of changes which is just what it is, and so is maturity. To give the traits of either phase a kind of independent existence, and then to use the form selected to account for or explain the rest of the process is a silly reduplication; reduplication, because we have after all only parts of one and the same original history; silly because we fancy that we have accounted for the history on the basis of an arbitrary selection of part of itself.

Substitute for such growth a more extensive history of nature and call it the evolution of mind from matter, and the conclusion is not different. In the old dispute as to whether a stag runs because he has long and slender legs, or has the legs in order that he may run, both parties overlook the natural descriptive statement; namely, that it is of the nature of what goes on in the world that the stag has long legs and that having them he runs. When mind is said to be implicit, involved, latent, or potential in matter, and subsequent change is asserted to be an affair of making it explicit, evolved, manifest, actual, what happens is that a natural history is first cut arbitrarily and unconsciously in two, and then the severance is consciously and arbitrarily cancelled. It is simpler not to start by engaging in such manoeuvers.

The discussion gives an understanding of the adaptation of nature and life and mind to one another. A mystery has not seldom been made of the fact that objective nature lends itself to man's sense of fitness, order and beauty; or, in another region of discourse, that objective nature submits to mental operations sufficiently to be known. Or, the mystery is conceived from the other end: it seems wonderful that man should be possessed of a sense of order, beauty and rightness; that he should have a capacity of thinking and knowing, so that man is elevated far above nature and seated with angels. But the wonder and mystery do not seem to be other than the wonder and mystery that there should be such a thing as nature, as existential events, at all, and that in being they should be what they are. The wonder should be transferred to the whole course of things. Only because an arbitrary breach has previously been introduced by which the world is first conceived as something quite different from what it demonstrably is, does it then appear passing strange that after all it should be just what it is. The world is subject-matter for knowledge, because mind has developed *in* that world; a body-mind, whose structures have developed according to the structures of the world in which it exists, will naturally find some of its structures to be concordant and congenial with nature, and some phases of nature with itself. The latter are beautiful and fit, and others ugly and unfit. Since mind cannot evolve except where there is an organized process in which the fulfillments of the past are conserved and employed, it is not surprising that mind when it evolves should be mindful of the past and future, and that it should use the structures which are biological adaptations of organism and environment as its own and its only organs. In ultimate analysis the mystery that mind should use a body, or that a body should have a mind, is like the mystery that a man cultivating plants should use the soil; or that the soil which grows plants at all should grow those adapted to its own physico-chemical properties and relations.

ALFRED NORTH WHITEHEAD

Alfred North Whitehead was born in Ramsgate, Isle of Thanet, Kent, on February 15, 1861. While Alfred was still a child, his father gave up his position as master of a local private school to become an Anglican clergyman. In 1875 the boy was sent to school at Sherborne in Dorsetshire, one of England's most ancient educational institutions, where the lessons were largely in Greek and Latin and where Whitehead's firm grounding in history and the humanities began. He entered Trinity College, Cambridge, in 1880, attending only mathematics lectures until his graduation, though his discussions in literature and philosophy with other young men of high intellectual capability and attainment were lengthy and thorough. In 1885 he became a Fellow of Trinity College, where he remained until 1910. He married Evelyn Willoughby Wade in 1890, and between 1891 and 1898 his three children were born. The youngest son was a casualty of the First World War. Whitehead tells us that for sixteen years during this time he was plagued by insomnia and that many times he seriously considered giving up his teaching career because of it. Another interesting note from this period is that for eight years he read extensively in theology, building up a large library which he sold in one lot to a local bookseller when his interest was exhausted. During his later years at Cambridge he participated in political activities on behalf of the Liberal Party.

It was during the early 1890s that Bertrand Russell became first his student and then his colleague. After 1903 there began the famous collaboration toward the production of a joint work on the foundations of mathematics, but their ambitions for the project expanded and it was not until 1910 that the first volume of *Principia Mathematica* was finally published. The third and final volume of the work came from the presses three years later. By this time the views of Whitehead and Russell on many philosophical and social matters had diverged greatly and they never again worked together.

Already internationally famous as a mathematician and logician, Whitehead now entered upon a new phase of his life. In 1910 he gave up his Cambridge position and moved to London without the promise of an academic post of any sort. It was a gamble. Fortunately, in 1911 he secured an appointment teaching mathematical physics at the Imperial College of Science and Technology of the University of London. When he terminated his tenure there in 1924, he was serving as Dean of the Faculty of Science. This London period was characterized by a deepening of his interest in epistemology and the philosophy of science and the diminishing of interest in mathematics and logic. The publishing of his *Principles of Natural Knowledge* in 1919 established him as the darling of the British realists.

In 1924, at the age of 63, Whitehead accepted the position of Professor of Philosophy at Harvard University. This was not to be a period of graceful retirement. Released from heavy teaching and administrative duties, Whitehead found time to develop his profound but long-contained love of metaphysics and cosmology. The invitation to deliver the Gifford Lectures at the University of Edinburgh for the term of 1927–1928 provided the opportunity to put together a comprehensive picture of his vision of the universe. The outcome was the book that represents the culmination of process metaphysics, *Process and Reality,* published in 1929. Whitehead was 68 years old. He continued the elaboration of his position through the publication of a number of important books and articles during the following twelve years. He died on December 30, 1947.

MAJOR PHILOSOPHICAL WORKS BY WHITEHEAD

Phase One: Mathematics and Logic (1898–1914).

1898 *A Treatise on Universal Algebra.* Cambridge: Cambridge University Press.

1906 *The Axioms of Projective Geometry.* Cambridge: Cambridge University Press.

1906 "On Mathematical Concepts of the Material World," *Philosophical Transactions,* Royal Society of London, Series A, Vol. 205.

1907 *The Axioms of Descriptive Geometry.* Cambridge: Cambridge University Press.

1910–1913 *Principia Mathematica* (with Bertrand Russell). Three volumes. Cambridge: Cambridge University Press.

1911 *An Introduction to Mathematics.* London: Williams and Norgate.

Phase Two: Epistemology and Philosophy of Science (1915–1923).

1917 *The Organization of Thought.* London: Williams and Norgate. (A collection of eight essays, including "Space, Time, and Relativity," "The Organization of Thought," and "The Anatomy of Some Scientific Ideas.")

1919 *An Inquiry Concerning the Principles of Natural Knowledge.* Cambridge: Cambridge University Press.

1920 *The Concept of Nature.* (Tamer Lectures.) Cambridge: Cambridge University Press.

1922 *The Principle of Relativity.* Cambridge: Cambridge University Press.

1922 "Uniformity and Contingency," *Proceedings, Aristotelian Society, n.s.,* Vol. 23.

Phase Three: Metaphysics and Philosophy of Culture (1924–1947)

1925 *Science and the Modern World.* (Lowell Institute Lectures.) New York: Macmillan.

1926 *Religion in the Making.* (Lowell Institute Lectures.) New York: Macmillan.

1926 *"Time,"* Proceedings, Sixth International Congress of Philosophy. New York: Longmans, Green.

1927 *Symbolism.* (Barbour-Page Lectures.) New York: Macmillan.

1929 *Process and Reality.* An essay in Cosmology. (Gifford Lectures.) New York: Macmillan.

1929 *The Function of Reason.* Princeton: Princeton University Press.

1929 *The Aims of Education and Other Essays.* New York: Macmillan. (Ten previously published essays, including the three mentioned above in the note on *The Organization of Thought.)*

1933 *Adventures of Ideas.* New York: Macmillan.

1938 *Modes of Thought.* New York: Macmillan.

1941 "Mathematics and the Good," *The Philosophy of Alfred North Whitehead,* edited by Paul Schilpp. Evanston, Ill.: The Library of Living Philosophers.

1941 "Immortality," *The Philosophy of Alfred North Whitehead,* edited by Paul Schilpp. Evanston, Ill.: The Library of Living Philosophers.

1947 *Essays in Science and Philosophy.* New York: Philosophical Library. (A collection of twenty-four previously published articles.)

RECOMMENDED COMMENTARIES AND DISCUSSIONS
ABOUT WHITEHEAD

Christian, William A. *An Interpretation of Whitehead's Metaphysics.*
New Haven: Yale University Press, 1959.

Emmet, D. M. *Whitehead's Philosophy of Organism.* London: Macmillan, 1932.

Ford, Lewis S. *The Emergence of Whitehead's Metaphysics, 1925–1929.* Albany: SUNY Press, 1982.

Franklin, Stephen. *Speaking from the Depths: Alfred N. Whitehead's Hermeneutical Metaphysics of Propositions, Experience, Symbolism, Language and Religion.* Grand Rapids, Mich.: W. B. Eerdmans Pub. Co., 1990.

Hartshorne, Charles. *Whitehead's Philosophy: Selected Essays, 1935–1970.* Lincoln: University of Nebraska Press, 1972.

Hosinski, Thomas E. *Stubborn Fact and Creative Advance: An Introduction to the Metaphysics of Alfred North Whitehead.* Lanham, Md.: Rowan and Littlefield, 1993.

Kline, George L. (ed.). *Alfred North Whitehead.* Englewood Cliffs, N.J.: Prentice–Hall, 1963. (Twenty articles and documents by various authors.)

Lawrence, Nathaniel. *Whitehead's Philosophical Development.* Berkeley: University of California Press, 1956.

Leclerc, Ivor (ed.). *The Relevance of Whitehead.* London: George Allen and Unwin, 1961.

————. *Whitehead's Metaphysics.* London: George Allen and Unwin, 1958.

Lowe, Victor. *Alfred North Whitehead: The Man and His Work.* Baltimore: Johns Hopkins University Press, 1985–1990 (in 2 vols.).

Lucas, George. *The Rehabilitation of Whitehead: An Analytic and Historical Assessment of Process Philosophy.* Albany: SUNY Press, 1989.

Mays, W. *The Philosophy of Whitehead.* London: George Allen and Unwin, 1959.

Miller, D. L., Gentry, G. V. *The Philosophy of A. N. Whitehead.* Minneapolis: Burgess Publishing Co., 1938.

Nobo, Jorge L. *Whitehead's Metaphysics of Extension and Solidarity.* Albany: SUNY Press, 1986.

Palter, Robert M. *Whitehead's Philosophy of Science.* Chicago: The University of Chicago Press, 1960.

Price, Lucien (ed.). *Dialogues of Alfred North Whitehead.* New York: Little, Brown, 1954.

Ross, Stephen David. *Perspective in Whitehead's Metaphysics.* Albany: SUNY Press, 1983.

Schilpp, P. A. (ed.). *The Philosophy of Alfred North Whitehead.* Evanston, Ill.: The Library of Living Philosophers, 1941. Second edition, New York: Tudor, 1951. (Includes a complete bibliography of Whitehead's writings.)

Sherburne, Donald. *A Whiteheadian Aesthetic.* New Haven: Yale University Press, 1961.

Critique of Scientific Materialism

I shall trace the successes and the failures of the particular conceptions of cosmology with which the European intellect has clothed itself in the last three centuries. General climates of opinion persist for periods of about two to three generations, that is to say, for periods of sixty to a hundred years. There are also shorter waves of thought, which play on the surface of the tidal movement. We shall find, therefore, transformations in the European outlook, slowly modifying the successive centuries. There persists, however, throughout the whole period the fixed scientific cosmology which presupposes the ultimate fact of an irreducible brute matter, or material, spread throughout space in a flux of configurations. In itself such a material is senseless, valueless, purposeless. It just does what it does do, following a fixed routine imposed by external relations which do not spring from the nature of its being. It is this assumption that I call 'scientific materialism.' Also it is an assumption which I shall challenge as being entirely unsuited to the scientific situation at which we have now arrived. It is not wrong, if properly construed. If we confine ourselves to certain types of facts, abstracted from the complete circumstances in which they occur, the materialistic assumption expresses these facts to perfection. But when we pass beyond the abstraction, either by more subtle employment of our senses, or by the request for meanings and for coherence of thoughts, the scheme breaks down at once. The narrow efficiency of the scheme was the very cause of its supreme methodological success. For it directed attention to just those groups of facts which, in the state of knowledge then existing, required investigation.

*   *   *

. . . When you are criticizing the philosophy of an epoch, do not chiefly direct your attention to those intellectual positions which its exponents feel it necessary explicitly to defend. There will be some fundamental assumptions which adherents of all the various systems within the epoch unconsciously presuppose. Such assumptions appear so obvious that people do not know what they are assuming because no other way of putting things has ever occurred to them. With these assumptions a certain limited number of types of philosophic systems are possible, and this group of systems constitutes the philosophy of the epoch.

One such assumption underlies the whole philosophy of nature during the modern period. It is embodied in the conception which is supposed to express the most concrete aspect of nature. The Ionian philosophers asked, What is nature made of? The answer is couched in terms of stuff, or matter, or material—the particular name chosen is indifferent—which has the property of simple location in space and time, or, if you adopt the more modem ideas, in space-time. What I mean by matter, or material, is anything which has this property of *simple location*. By simple location I mean one major characteristic which refers equally both to space and to time, and other minor characteristics which are diverse as between space and time.

The characteristic common both to space and time is that material can be said to be *here* in space and *here* in time, or *here* in space-time, in a perfectly definite sense which does not require for its explanation any reference to other regions of space-time. Curiously enough this character of simple location holds whether we look on a region of space-time as determined absolutely or relatively. For if a region is merely a way of indicating a certain set of relations to other entities, then this character, which I shall call simple location, is that material can be said to have just these relations of position to the other entities without requiring for its explanation any reference to other regions constituted by analogous relations of position to the same entities. In fact, as soon as you have settled, however you do settle, what you mean by a definite place in space-time, you can adequately state the relation of a particular material body to space-time by saying that it is just there, in that place; and, so far as simple location is concerned, there is nothing more to be said on the subject.

There are, however, some subordinate explanations to be made which bring in the minor characteristics which I have already mentioned. First, as regards time, if material has existed during any period, it has equally been in existence during any portion of that period. In other words, dividing the time does not divide the material. Secondly, in respect to space, dividing the volume does divide the material. Accordingly, if material exists throughout a volume, there will be less of that material distributed through any definite half of that volume. It is from this property that there arises our notion of density at a point of space. Anyone who talks about density is not assimilating time and space to the extent that some extremists of the modern school of relativists very rashly desire. For the division of time functions, in respect to material, quite differently from the division of space.

Furthermore, this fact that the material is indifferent to the division of time leads to the conclusion that the lapse of time is an accident, rather than of the essence, of the material. The material is fully itself in any sub-period however short. Thus the transition of time has nothing to do with the character of the material. The material is equally itself at an instant of time. Here an instant of time is conceived as in itself without transition, since the temporal transition is the succession of instants.

The answer, therefore, which the seventeenth century gave to the ancient question of the Ionian thinkers, "What is the world made of?" was that the world is a succession of instantaneous configurations of matter—or of material, if you wish to include stuff more subtle than ordinary matter, the ether for example.

We cannot wonder that science rested content with this assumption as to the fundamental elements of nature. The great forces of nature, such as gravitation, were entirely determined by the configurations of masses. Thus the configurations determined their own changes, so that the circle of scientific thought was completely closed. This is the famous mechanistic theory of nature, which has reigned supreme ever since the seventeenth century. It is the orthodox creed of physical science. Furthermore, the creed justified itself by the pragmatic test. It worked. Physicists took no more interest in philosophy. They emphasized the anti-rationalism of the Historical Revolt. But the difficulties of this theory of materialistic mechanism very soon became apparent. The history of thought in the eighteenth and nineteenth centuries is governed by the fact that the world had got hold of a general idea which it could neither live with nor live without.

This simple location of instantaneous material configurations is what Bergson has protested against, so far as it concerns time and so far as it is taken to be the fundamental fact of concrete nature. He calls it a distortion of nature due to the intellectual 'spatialization' of things. I agree with Bergson in his protest: but I do not agree that such distortion is a vice necessary to the intellectual apprehension of nature. I shall in subsequent lectures endeavor to show that this spatialization is the expression of more concrete facts under the guise of very abstract logical constructions. There is an error; but it is merely the accidental error of mistaking the abstract for the concrete. It is an example of what I will call the 'Fallacy of Misplaced Concreteness.' This fallacy is the occasion of great confusion in philosophy. It is not necessary for the intellect to fall into the trap, though in this example there has been a very general tendency to do so.

It is at once evident that the concept of simple location is going to make great difficulties for induction. For, if in the location of configurations of matter throughout a stretch of time there is no inherent reference to any other times, past or future, it immediately follows that nature within any period does not refer to nature at any other period. Accordingly, induction is not based on anything which can be observed as inherent in nature. Thus we cannot look to nature for the justification of our belief in any law such as the law of gravitation. In other words, the order of nature cannot be justified by the mere observation of nature. For there is nothing in the present fact which inherently refers either to the past or to the future. It looks, therefore, as though memory, as well as induction, would fail to find any justification within nature itself.

I have been anticipating the course of future thought, and have been repeating Hume's argument. This train of thought follows so immediately from the consideration of simple location that we cannot wait for the eighteenth century before considering it. The only wonder is that the world did in fact wait for Hume before noting the difficulty. Also it illustrates the anti-rationalism of the scientific public that, when Hume did appear, it was only the religious implications of his philosophy which attracted attention. This was because the clergy were in principle rationalists, whereas the men of science were content with a simple faith in the order of nature. Hume himself remarks, no doubt scoffingly, 'Our holy religion is founded on faith.' This attitude satisfied the Royal Society but not the Church. It also satisfied Hume and has satisfied subsequent empiricists.

There is another presupposition of thought which must be put beside the theory of simple location. I mean the two correlative categories of substance and quality. There is, however, this difference. There were different theories as to the adequate description of the status of space. But whatever its status, no one had any doubt but that the connection with space enjoyed by entities, which are said to be in space, is that of simple location. We may put this shortly by saying that it was tacitly assumed that space is the locus of simple locations. Whatever is in space is *simpliciter* in some definite portion of space. But in respect to substance and quality the leading minds of the seventeenth century were definitely perplexed; though, with their usual genius, they at once constructed a theory which was adequate for their immediate purposes.

Of course, substance and quality, as well as simple location, are the most natural ideas for the human mind. It is the way in which we think of things, and without these ways of thinking we could not get our ideas straight for daily use. There is no doubt about this. The only question is, How concretely are we thinking when we consider nature under these conceptions? My point will be, that we are presenting ourselves with simplified editions of immediate matters of fact. When we examine the primary elements of these simplified editions, we shall find that they are in truth only to be justified as being elaborate logical constructions of a high degree of abstraction. Of course, as a point of individual psychology, we get at the ideas by the rough and ready method of suppressing what appear to be irrelevant details. But when we attempt to justify this suppression of irrelevance, we find that, though there are entities left corresponding to the entities we talk about, yet these entities are of a high degree of abstraction.

Thus I hold that substance and quality afford another instance of the fallacy of misplaced concreteness. Let us consider how the notions of substance and quality arise. We observe an object as an entity with certain characteristics. Furthermore, each individual entity is apprehended through its characteristics. For example, we observe a body; there is something about it which we note. Perhaps it is hard, and blue, and round, and noisy. We observe something which possesses these qualities: apart from these qualities we do not observe anything at all. Accordingly, the entity is the substratum, or substance, of which we predicate qualities. Some of the qualities are essential, so that apart from them the entity would not be itself; while other qualities are accidental and changeable. In respect to material bodies, the qualities of having a quantitative mass, and of simple location somewhere, were held by John Locke at the close of the seventeenth century to be essential qualities. Of course, the location was changeable, and the unchangeability of mass was merely an experimental fact except for some extremists.

So far, so good. But when we pass to blueness and noisiness a new situation has to be faced. In the first place, the body may not be always blue, or noisy. We have already allowed for this by our theory of accidental qualities, which for the moment we may accept as adequate. But in the second place, the seventeenth century exposed a real difficulty. The great physicists elaborated transmission theories of light and sound, based upon their materialistic views of nature. There were two hypotheses as to light: either it was transmitted by the vibratory waves of a materialistic ether, or—according to Newton—it was transmitted by the motion of incredibly small corpuscles of some subtle matter. We all know that the wave theory of Huyghens held the field during the nineteenth century, and at present physicists are endeavoring to explain some obscure circumstances attending radiation by a combination of both theories. But whatever theory you choose, there is no light or color as a fact in external nature. There is merely motion of material. Again, when the light enters your eyes and falls on the retina, there is merely motion of material. Then your nerves are affected and your brain is affected, and again this is merely motion of material. The same line of argument holds for sound, substituting waves in the air for waves in the ether, and ears for eyes.

We then ask in what sense are blueness and noisiness qualities of the body. By analogous reasoning, we also ask in what sense is its scent a quality of the rose.

Galileo considered this question, and at once pointed out that, apart from eyes, ears, or noses, there would be no colors, sounds, or smells. Descartes and Locke elaborated a theory of primary and secondary qualities. For example Descartes in his "Sixth Meditation" says:[1] "And indeed, as I perceive different sorts of colors, sounds, odors, tastes, heat, hardness, etc., I safely conclude that there are in the bodies from which the diverse perceptions of the senses proceed, certain varieties corresponding to them, although, perhaps, not in reality like them; . . ."

Also in his *Principles of Philosophy,* he says: "That by our senses we know nothing of external objects beyond their figure [or situation], magnitude, and motion."

Locke, writing with a knowledge of Newtonian dynamics, places mass among the primary qualities of bodies. In short, he elaborates a theory of primary and secondary qualities in accordance with the state

---

[1] Translation by Professor John Veitch.

of physical science at the close of the seventeenth century. The primary qualities are the essential qualities of substances whose spatio-temporal relationships constitute nature. The orderliness of these relationships constitutes the order of nature. The occurrences of nature are in some way apprehended by minds, which are associated with living bodies. Primarily, the mental apprehension is aroused by the occurrences in certain parts of the correlated body, the occurrences in the brain, for instance. But the mind in apprehending also experiences sensations which, properly speaking, are qualities of the mind alone. These sensations are projected by the mind so as to clothe appropriate bodies in external nature. Thus the bodies are perceived as with qualities which in reality do not belong to them, qualities which in fact are purely the offspring of the mind. Thus nature gets credit which should in truth be reserved for ourselves: the rose for its scent: the nightingale for his song: and the sun for his radiance. The poets are entirely mistaken. They should address their lyrics to themselves, and should turn them into odes of self-congratulation on the excellency of the human mind. Nature is a dull affair, soundless, scentless, colorless; merely the hurrying of material, endlessly, meaninglessly.

However you disguise it, this is the practical outcome of the characteristic scientific philosophy which closed the seventeenth century.

In the first place, we must note its astounding efficiency as a system of concepts for the organization of scientific research. In this respect, it is fully worthy of the genius of the century which produced it. It has held its own as the guiding principle of scientific studies ever since. It is still reigning. Every university in the world organizes itself in accordance with it. No alternative system of organizing the pursuit of scientific truth has been suggested. It is not only reigning, but it is without a rival.

And yet—it is quite unbelievable. This conception of the universe is surely framed in terms of high abstractions, and the paradox only arises because we have mistaken our abstraction for concrete realities. . . .

*   *   *

No epoch is homogeneous; whatever you may have assigned as the dominant note of a considerable period, it will always be possible to produce men, and great men, belonging to the same time, who exhibit themselves as antagonistic to the tone of their age. This is certainly the case with the eighteenth century. For example, the names of John Wesley and of Rousseau must have occurred to you while I was drawing the character of that time. But I do not want to speak of them, or of others. The man whose ideas I must consider at some length is Bishop Berkeley. Quite at the commencement of the epoch, he made all the right criticisms, at least in principle. It would be untrue to say that he produced no effect. He was a famous man. The wife of George II was one of the few queens who, in any country, have been clever enough, and wise enough, to patronise learning judiciously; accordingly, Berkeley was made a bishop, in days when bishops in Great Britain were relatively far greater men than they are now. Also, what was more important than his bishopric, Hume studied him, and developed one side of his philosophy in a way which might have disturbed the ghost of the great ecclesiastic. Then Kant studied Hume. So, to say that Berkeley was uninfluential during the century, would certainly be absurd. But all the same, he failed to affect the main stream of scientific thought. It flowed on as if he had never written. Its general success made it impervious to criticism, then and since. The world of science has always remained perfectly satisfied with its peculiar abstractions. They work, and that is sufficient for it.

The point before us is that this scientific field of thought is now, in the twentieth century, too narrow for the concrete facts which are before it for analysis. This is true even in physics, and is more especially urgent in the biological sciences. Thus, in order to understand the difficulties of modern scientific thought and also its reactions on the modern world, we should have in our minds some conception of a wider field of abstraction, a more concrete analysis, which shall stand nearer to the complete concreteness of our intuitive experience. Such an analysis should find itself a niche for the concepts of matter and spirit, as abstractions in terms of which much of our physical experience can be interpreted. It is in the search for this wider basis for scientific thought that Berkeley is so important. He launched his criticism shortly after the schools of Newton and Locke had completed their work, and laid his finger exactly on the weak spots which they had left. I do not propose to consider either the subjective idealism which has been derived from him, or the schools of development which trace their descent from Hume and Kant respectively. My point will be that—whatever the final metaphysics you may adopt—there is another line of development embedded in Berkeley, pointing to the analysis which we are in search of. Berkeley overlooked it, partly by reason of the overintellectualism of philosophers, and partly by his haste to have recourse to an idealism with its objectivity grounded in the mind of God. You will remember that I have already stated that the key of the problem lies in the notion of simple location. Berkeley, in effect, criticises this notion. He also raises the question, What do we mean by things being realised in the world of nature?

In Sections 23 and 24 of his *Principles of Human Knowledge,* Berkeley gives his answer to this latter question. I will quote some detached sentences from those Sections:

'23. But, say you, surely there is nothing easier than for me to imagine trees, for instance, in a park, or books existing in a closet, and nobody by to perceive them. I answer, you may so, there is no difficulty in it; but what is all this, I beseech you, more than framing in your mind certain ideas which you call books and trees, and at the same time omitting to frame the idea of any one that may perceive them? . . .

'When we do our utmost to conceive the existence of external bodies, we are all the while only contemplating our own ideas. But the mind *taking no notice of itself,* is deluded to think it can and does conceive bodies existing unthought of or without the mind, though at the same time they are apprehended by or exist in itself. . . .

'24. It is very obvious, upon the least inquiry into our thoughts, to know whether it be possible for us to understand what is meant by the *absolute existence of sensible objects in themselves, or without the mind.* To me it is evident those words mark out either a direct contradiction, or else nothing at all. . . .'

Again there is a very remarkable passage in Section 10, of the fourth Dialogue of Berkeley's *Alciphron.* I have already quoted it, at greater length, in my *Principles of Natural Knowledge:*

'*Euphranor.* Tell me, Alciphron, can you discern the doors, window and battlements of that same castle?

'*Alciphron.* I cannot. At this distance it seems only a small round tower.

'*Euph.* But I, who have been at it, know that it is no small round tower, but a large square building with battlements and turrets, which it seems you do not see.

'*Alc.* What will you infer from thence?

'*Euph.* I would infer that the very object which you strictly and properly perceive by sight is not that thing which is several miles distant.

'*Alc.* Why so?

'*Euph.* Because a little round object is one thing, and a great square object is another. Is it not so? . . .'

Some analogous examples concerning a planet and a cloud are then cited in the dialogue, and this passage finally concludes with:

'*Euphranor.* Is it not plain, therefore, that neither the castle, the planet, nor the cloud, *which you see here,* are those real ones which you suppose exist at a distance?'

It is made explicit in the first passage, already quoted, that Berkeley himself adopts an extreme idealistic interpretation. For him mind is the only absolute reality, and the unity of nature is the unity of ideas in the mind of God. Personally, I think that Berkeley's solution of the metaphysical problem raises difficulties not less than those which he points out as arising from a realistic interpretation of the scientific scheme. There is, however, another possible line of thought, which enables us to adopt anyhow an attitude of provisional realism, and to widen the scientific scheme in a way which is useful for science itself.

I recur to the passage from Francis Bacon's *Natural History,* already quoted in the previous lecture:

'It is certain that all bodies whatsoever, though they have no sense, yet they have perception: . . . and whether the body be alterant or altered, evermore a perception precedeth operation; for else all bodies would be alike one to another. . . .'

Also in the previous lecture I construed *perception* (as used by Bacon) as meaning *taking account of* the essential character of the thing perceived, and I construed *sense* as meaning *cognition.* We certainly do take account of things of which at the time we have no explicit cognition. We can even have a cognitive memory of the taking account, without having had a contemporaneous cognition. Also, as Bacon points out by his statement, '. . . for else all bodies would be alike one to another,' it is evidently some element of the essential character which we take account of, namely something on which diversity is founded and not mere bare logical diversity.

The word *perceive* is, in our common usage, shot through and through with the notion of cognitive apprehension. So is the word *apprehension,* even with the adjective *cognitive* omitted. I will use the word *prehension* for *uncognitive apprehension:* by this I mean *apprehension* which may or may not be cognitive. Now take Euphranor's last remark:

'Is it not plain, therefore, that neither the castle, the planet, nor the cloud, *which you see here,* are those real ones which you suppose exist at a distance?' Accordingly, there is a prehension, *here* in this place, of things which have a reference to *other* places.

Now go back to Berkeley's sentences, quoted from his *Principles of Human Knowledge.* He contends that what constitutes the realisation of natural entities is the being perceived within the unity of mind.

We can substitute the concept, that the realisation is a gathering of things into the unity of a prehension; and that what is thereby realised is the prehension, and not the things. This unity of a prehension defines itself as a *here* and a *now,* and the things so gathered into the grasped unity have essential reference to other places and other times. For Berkeley's *mind,* I substitute a process of prehensive unification. In order to make intelligible this concept of the progressive realisation of natural occurrences, considerable expansion is required, and confrontation with its actual implications in terms of concrete experience. This will be the task of the subsequent lectures. In the first place, note that the idea of simple location has gone. The things which are grasped into a realised unity, here and now, are not the castle, the cloud, and the planet simply in themselves; but they are the castle, the cloud, and the planet from the standpoint, in space and time, of the prehensive unification. In other words, it is the perspective of the castle over there from the standpoint of the unification here. It is, therefore, aspects of the castle, the cloud, and the planet which are grasped into unity here. You will remember that the idea of perspectives is quite familiar in philosophy. It was introduced by Leibniz, in the notion of his monads mirroring perspectives of the universe. I am using the same notion, only I am toning down his monads into the unified events in space and time. In some ways, there is greater analogy with Spinoza's modes; that is why I use the terms *mode* and *modal.* In the analogy with Spinoza, his one substance is for me the one underlying activity of realisation individualising itself in an interlocked plurality of modes. Thus, concrete fact is process. Its primary analysis is into underlying activity of prehension, and into realised prehensive events. Each event is an individual matter of fact issuing from an individualisation of the substrate activity. But individualisation does not mean substantial independence.

An entity of which we become aware in sense perception is the terminus of our act of perception. I will call such an entity, a *sense-object.*

For example, green of a definite shade is a sense-object; so is a sound of definite quality and pitch; and so is a definite scent; and a definite quality of touch. The way in which such an entity is related to space during a definite lapse of time is complex. I will say that a sense-object has *ingression* into space-time. The cognitive perception of a sense-object is the awareness of the prehensive unification (into a standpoint A) of various modes of various sense-objects, including the sense-object in question. The standpoint A is, of course, a region of space-time; that is to say, it is a volume of space through a duration of time. But as one entity, this standpoint is a unit of realised experience. A mode of a sense-object at A (as abstracted from the sense-object whose relationship to A the mode is conditioning) is the aspect from A of some other region B. Thus the sense object is present in A with the mode of location in B. Thus if green be the sense-object in question, green is not simply at A where it is being perceived, nor is it simply at B where it is perceived as located; but it is present at A with the mode of location in B. There is no particular mystery about this. You have only got to look into a mirror and to see the image in it of some green leaves behind your back. For you at A there will be green; but not green simply at A where you are. The green at A will be green with the mode of having location at the image of the leaf behind the mirror. Then turn round and look at the leaf. You are now perceiving the green in the same way as you did before, except that now the green has the mode of being located in the actual leaf. I am merely describing what we do perceive: we are aware of green as being one element in a prehensive unification of sense-objects; each sense-object, and among them green, having its particular mode, which is expressible as location elsewhere. There are various types of modal location. For example, sound is voluminous: it fills a hall, and so sometimes does diffused colour. But the modal location of a colour may be that of being the remote boundary of a volume, as for example the colours on the walls of a room. Thus primarily space-time is the locus of the modal ingression of sense-objects. This is the reason why space and time (if for simplicity we disjoin them) are given in their entireties. For each volume of space, or each lapse of time, includes in its essence aspects of all volumes of space, or of all lapses of time. The difficulties of philosophy in respect to space and time are founded on the error of considering them as primarily the loci of simple locations. Perception is simply the cognition of prehensive unification; or more shortly, perception is cognition of prehension. The actual world is a manifold of prehensions; and a 'prehension' is a 'prehensive occasion'; and a prehensive occasion is the most concrete finite entity, conceived as what it is in itself and for itself, and not as from its aspect in the essence of another such occasion. Prehensive unification might be said to have simple location in its volume A. But this would be a mere tautology. For space and time are simply abstractions from the totality of prehensive unifications as mutually patterned in each other. Thus a prehension has simple location at the volume A in the same way as that in which a man's face fits on to the smile which spreads over it. There is, so far as we have gone, more sense in saying that an act of perception has simple location; for it may be conceived as being simply at the cognised prehension.

There are more entities involved in nature than the mere sense objects, so far considered. But, allowing for the necessity of revision consequent on a more complete point of view, we can frame our answer to Berkeley's question as to the character of the reality to be assigned to nature. He states it to be the reality of ideas in mind. A complete metaphysic which has attained to some notion of mind, and to some notion of ideas, may perhaps ultimately adopt that view. It is unnecessary for the purpose of these lectures to ask such a fundamental question. We can be content with a provisional realism in which nature is conceived as a complex of prehensive unifications. Space and time exhibit the general scheme of interlocked relations of these prehensions. You cannot tear any one of them out of its context. Yet each one of them within its context has all the reality that attaches to the whole complex. Conversely, the totality has the same reality as each prehension; for each prehension unifies the modalities to be ascribed, from its standpoint, to every part of the whole. A prehension is a process of unifying. Accordingly, nature is a process of expansive development, necessarily transitional from prehension to prehension. What is achieved is thereby passed beyond, but it is also retained as having aspects of itself present to prehensions which lie beyond it.

Thus nature is a structure of evolving processes. The reality is the process. It is nonsense to ask if the colour red is real. The colour red is ingredient in the process of realisation. The realities of nature are the prehensions in nature, that is to say, the events in nature.

Now that we have cleared space and time from the taint of simple location, we may partially abandon the awkward term prehension. This term was introduced to signify the essential unity of an event, namely, the event as one entity, and not as a mere assemblage of parts or of ingredients. It is necessary to understand that space-time is nothing else than a system of pulling together of assemblages into unities. But the word *event* just means one of these spatio-temporal unities. Accordingly, it may be used instead of the term 'prehension' as meaning the thing prehended.

An event has contemporaries. This means that an event mirrors within itself the modes of its contemporaries as a display of immediate achievement. An event has a past. This means that an event mirrors within itself the modes of its predecessors, as memories which are fused into its own content. An event has a future. This means that an event mirrors within itself such aspects as the future throws back on to the present, or, in other words, as the present has determined concerning the future. Thus an event has anticipation:

> 'The prophetic soul
> Of the wide world dreaming on things to come.'

These conclusions are essential for any form of realism. For there is in the world for our cognisance, memory of the past, immediacy of realisation, and indication of things to come.

In this sketch of an analysis more concrete than that of the scientific scheme of thought, I have started from our own psychological field, as it stands for our cognition. I take it for what it claims to be: the self-knowledge of our bodily event. I mean the total event, and not the inspection of the details of the body. This self-knowledge discloses a prehensive unification of modal presences of entities beyond itself. I generalise by the use of the principle that this total bodily event is on the same level as all other events, except for an unusual complexity and stability of inherent pattern. The strength of the theory of materialistic mechanism has been the demand, that no arbitrary breaks be introduced into nature, to eke out the collapse of an explanation. I accept this principle. But if you start from the immediate facts of our psychological experience, as surely an empiricist should begin, you are at once led to the organic conception of nature of which the description has been commenced in this lecture.

It is the defect of the eighteenth century scientific scheme that it provides none of the elements which compose the immediate psychological experiences of mankind. Nor does it provide any elementary trace of the organic unity of a whole, from which the organic unities of electrons, protons, molecules, and living bodies can emerge. According to that scheme, there is no reason in the nature of things why portions of material should have any physical relations to each other. Let us grant that we cannot hope to be able to discern the laws of nature to be necessary. But we can hope to see that it is necessary that there should be an order of nature. The concept of the order of nature is bound up with the concept of nature as the locus of organisms in process of development.

NOTE. In connection with the latter portion of this chapter a sentence from Descartes' 'Reply to Objections . . . against the Meditations' is interesting:—'Hence the idea of the sun will be the sun itself existing in the mind, not indeed formally, as it exists in the sky, but objectively, i.e., in the way in which objects are wont to exist in the mind; and this mode of being is truly much less perfect than that in which things exist outside the mind, but it is not on that account mere nothing, as I have already said.' [Reply to Objections 1, Translation by Haldane and Ross, vol. ii, p. 10.) I find difficulty in reconciling this theory of ideas (with which I agree) with other parts of the Cartesian philosophy.

Process

That "all things flow" is the first vague generalization which the unsystematized, barely analyzed, intuition of men has produced. It is the theme of some of the best Hebrew poetry in the Psalms; it appears as one of the first generalizations of Greek philosophy in the form of the sayings of Heraclitus; amid the later barbarism of Anglo-Saxon thought it reappears in the story of the sparrow flitting through the banqueting hall of the Northumbrian king; and in all stages of civilization its recollection lends its pathos to poetry. Without doubt, if we are to go back to that ultimate, integral experience, unwarped by the sophistications of theory, that experience whose elucidation is the final aim of philosophy, the flux of things is one ultimate generalization around which we must weave our philosophical system.

At this point we have transformed the phrase, "all things flow," into the alternative phrase, "the flux of things." In so doing, the notion of the "flux" has been held up before our thoughts as one primary notion for further analysis. But in the sentence "all things flow," there are three words—and we have started by isolating the last word of the three. We move backward to the next word "things" and ask, What sort of things flow? Finally we reach the first word "all" and ask, What is the meaning of the "many" things engaged in this common flux, and in what sense, if any, can the word "all" refer to a definitely indicated set of these many things?

The elucidation of meaning involved in the phrase "all things flow," is one chief task of metaphysics.

But there is a rival notion, antithetical to the former. I cannot at the moment recall one immortal phrase which expresses it with the same completeness as the alternative notion has been rendered by Heraclitus. This other notion dwells on permanences of things—the solid earth, the mountains, the stones, the Egyptian Pyramids, the spirit of man, God.

The best rendering of integral experience, expressing its general form divested of irrelevant details, is often to be found in the utterances of religious aspiration. One of the reasons of the thinness of so much modern metaphysics is its neglect of this wealth of expression of ultimate feeling. Accordingly we find in the first two lines of a famous hymn a full expression of the union of the two notions in one integral experience:

> Abide with me;
> Fast falls the eventide.

Here the first line expresses the permanences, "abide," "me" and the "Being" addressed; and the second line sets these permanences amid the inescapable flux. Here at length we find formulated the complete problem of metaphysics. Those philosophers who start with the first line have given us the metaphysics of "substance"; and those who start with the second line have developed the metaphysics of "flux." But, in truth, the two lines cannot be torn apart in this way; and we find that a wavering balance between the two is a characteristic of the greater number of philosophers. Plato found his permanences in a static, spiritual heaven, and his flux in the entanglement of his forms amid the fluent imperfections of the physical world. Here I draw attention to the word "imperfection." In any assertion as to Plato I speak under correction; but I believe that Plato's authority can be claimed for the doctrine that the things that flow are imperfect in the sense of "limited" and of "definitely exclusive of much that they might be and are not." The lines quoted from the hymn are an almost perfect expression of the direct intuition from which the main position of the Platonic philosophy is derived. Aristotle corrected his Platonism into a somewhat different balance. He was the apostle of "substance and attribute," and of the classificatory logic which this notion suggests. But, on the other side, he makes a masterly analysis of the notion of "generation." Aristotle in his own person expressed a useful protest against the Platonic tendency to separate a static spiritual world from a fluent world of superficial experience. The later Platonic schools stressed this tendency, just as the medieval Aristotelian thought allowed the static notions of Aristotle's logic to formulate some of the main metaphysical problems in terms which have lasted tiff today.

On the whole, the history of philosophy supports Bergson's charge that the human intellect "spatializes the universe"; that is to say, that it tends to ignore the fluency, and to analyze the world in terms of static categories. Indeed Bergson went further and conceived this tendency as an inherent necessity of the intellect. I do not believe this accusation; but I do hold that "spatialization" is the shortest route to a clear-cut philosophy expressed in reasonably familiar language. Descartes gave an almost perfect example of such a system of thought. The difficulties of Cartesianism with its three clear-cut substances, and with its "duration" and "measured time" well in the background, illustrate the result of the subordination of fluency. This subordination is to be found in the unanalyzed longing of the hymn, in Plato's vision of heavenly perfection, in Aristotle's logical concepts, and in Descartes' mathematical mentality. Newton, that Napoleon of the world of thought, brusquely ordered fluency back into the world, regimented into his "absolute mathematical time, flowing equably without regard to anything external." He also gave it a mathematical uniform in the shape of his Theory of Fluxions.

At this point the group of seventeenth- and eighteenth-century philosophers practically made a discovery, which, although it lies on the surface of their writings, they only half-realized. The discovery is that there are two kinds of fluency. One kind is the concrescence which, in Locke's language, is "the real internal constitution of a particular existent." The other kind is the *transition* from particular existent to particular existent. This transition, again in Locke's language, is the "perpetually perishing" which is one aspect of the notion of time; and in another aspect the transition is the origination of the present in conformity with the "power" of the past.

The phrase "the real internal constitution of a particular existent," the description of the human understanding as a process of reflection upon data, the phrase "perpetually perishing," and the word "power" together with its elucidation are all to be found in Locke's *Essay.* Yet owing to the limited scope of his investigation Locke did not generalize or put his scattered ideas together. This implicit notion of the two kinds of flux finds further unconscious illustration in Hume. It is all but explicit in Kant, though—as I think—misdescribed. Finally, it is lost in the evolutionary monism of Hegel and of his derivative schools. With all his inconsistencies, Locke is the philosopher to whom it is most useful to recur, when we desire to make explicit the discovery of the two kinds of fluency, required for the description of the fluent world. One kind is the fluency inherent in the constitution of the particular existent. This kind I have called "concrescence." The other kind is the fluency whereby the perishing of the process, on the completion of the particular existent, constitutes that existent as an original element in the constitutions of other particular existents elicited by repetitions of process. This kind I have called "transition." Concrescence moves towards its final cause, which is its subjective aim; transition is the vehicle of the efficient cause, which is the immortal past.

The discussion of how the actual particular occasions become original elements for a new creation is termed the theory of objectification. The objectified particular occasions together have the unity of a datum for the creative concrescence. But in acquiring this measure of connection, their inherent presuppositions of each other eliminate certain elements in their constitutions, and elicit into relevance other elements. Thus objectification is an operation of mutually adjusted abstraction, or elimination, whereby the many occasions of the actual world become one complex datum. This fact of the elimination by means of synthesis is sometimes termed the perspective of the actual world from the standpoint of that concrescence. Each actual occasion defines its own actual world from which it originates. No two occasions can have identical actual worlds.

Section II

"Concrescence" is the name for the process in which the universe of many things acquires an individual unity in a determinate relegation of each item of the "many" to its subordination in the constitution of the novel "one."

The most general term "thing"—or, equivalently, "entity"—means nothing else than to be one of the "many" which find their niches in each instance of concrescence. Each instance of concrescence *is itself* the novel individual "thing" in question. There are not "the concrescence" *and* the "novel thing": when we analyze the novel thing we find nothing but the concrescence. "Actuality" means nothing else than this ultimate entry into the concrete, in abstraction from which there is mere nonentity. In other words, abstraction from the notion of "entry into the concrete" is a self-contradictory notion, since it asks us to conceive a thing as not a thing.

An instance of concrescence is termed an "actual entity"—or, equivalently, an "actual occasion." There is not one completed set of things which are actual occasions. For the fundamental inescapable fact is the creativity in virtue of which there can be no "many things" which are not subordinated in a concrete unity. Thus a set of all actual occasions is by the nature of things a standpoint for another concrescence, which elicits a concrete unity from those many actual occasions. Thus we can never survey the actual world except from the standpoint of an immediate concrescence which is falsifying the presupposed completion. The creativity in virtue of which any relative complete actual world is, by the nature of things, the datum for a new concrescence, is termed "transition." Thus, by reason of transition, "the actual world" is always a relative term, and refers to that basis of presupposed actual occasions which is a datum for the novel concrescence.

An actual occasion is analyzable. The analysis discloses operations transforming entities which are individually alien into components of a complex which is concretely one. The term "feeling" will be used as the generic description of such operations. We thus say that an actual occasion is a concrescence effected by a process of feelings.

A feeling can be considered in respect to (i) the actual occasion felt, (ii) the eternal objects felt, (iii) the feelings felt, and (iv) its own subjective forms of intensity. In the process of concrescence the diverse feelings pass on to wider generalities of integral feeling.

Such a wider generality is a feeling of a complex of feelings, including their specific elements of identity and contrast. This process of the integration of feeling proceeds until the concrete unity of feeling is obtained. In this concrete unity all indetermination as to the realization of possibilities has been eliminated. The many entities of the universe, including those originating in the concrescence itself, find their respective rôles in this final unity. This final unity is termed the "satisfaction." The "satisfaction" is the culmination of the concrescence into a completely determinate matter of fact. In any of its antecedent stages the concrescence exhibits sheer indetermination as to the nexus between its many components.

SECTION III

An actual occasion is nothing but the unity to be ascribed to a particular instance of concrescence. This concrescence is thus nothing else than the "real internal constitution" of the actual occasion in question. The analysis of the formal constitution of an actual entity has given three stages in the process of feeling: (i) the responsive phase, (ii) the supplemental stage, and (iii) the satisfaction.

The satisfaction is merely the culmination marking the evaporation of all indetermination; so that, in respect to all modes of feeling and to all entities in the universe, the satisfied actual entity embodies a determinate attitude of "yes" or "no." Thus the satisfaction is the attainment of the private ideal which is the final cause of the concrescence. But the process itself lies in the two former phases. The first phase is the phase of pure reception of the actual world in its guise of objective datum for aesthetic synthesis. In this phase there is the mere reception of the actual world as a multiplicity of private centers of feeling, implicated in a nexus of mutual presupposition. The feelings are felt as belonging to the external centers, and are not absorbed into the private immediacy. The second stage is governed by the private ideal, gradually shaped in the process itself; whereby the many feelings, derivatively felt as alien, are transformed into a unity of aesthetic appreciation immediately felt as private. This is the incoming of "appetition," which in its higher exemplifications we term "vision." In the language of physical science, the "scalar" form overwhelms the original "vector" form: the origins become subordinate to the individual experience. The vector form is not lost, but is submerged as the foundation of the scalar superstructure.

In this second stage the feelings assume an emotional character by reason of this influx of conceptual feelings. But the reason why the origins are not lost in the private emotions is that there is no element in the universe capable of pure privacy. If we could obtain a complete analysis of meaning, the notion of pure privacy would be seen to be self-contradictory. Emotional feeling is still subject to the third metaphysical principle, that to be "something" is "to have the potentiality for acquiring real unity with other entities." Hence, "to be a real component of an actual entity" is in some way "to realize this potentiality." Thus "emotion" is "emotional feeling"; and "what is felt" is the presupposed vector situation. In physical science this principle takes the form which should never be lost sight of in fundamental speculation, that scalar quantities are constructs derivative from vector quantities. In more familiar language, this principle can be expressed by the statement that the notion of "passing on" is more fundamental than that of a private individual fact. In the abstract language here adopted for metaphysical statement, "passing on" becomes "creativity," in the dictionary sense of the verb *creare,* "to bring forth, beget, produce." Thus, according to the third principle, no entity can be divorced from the notion of creativity. An entity is at least a particular form capable of infusing its own particularity into creativity. An actual entity, or a phase of an actual entity, is more than that; but, at least, it is that.

*   *   *

SECTION V

To sum up: There are two species of process, macroscopic process, and microscopic process. The macroscopic process is the transition from attained actuality to actuality in attainment; while the microscopic process is the conversion of conditions which are merely real into determinate actuality. The former process effects the transition from the "actual" to the "merely real"; and the latter process effects the growth from the real to the actual. The former process is efficient; the latter process is teleological. The future is merely real, without being actual; whereas the past is a nexus of actualities. The actualities are constituted by their real genetic phases. The present is the immediacy of teleological process whereby reality becomes actual. The former process provides the conditions which really govern attainment; whereas the latter process provides the ends actually attained. The notion of "organism" is combined with that of "process" in a twofold manner. The community of actual things is an organism; but it is not a static organism. It is an incompletion in process of production. Thus the expansion of the universe in respect to actual things is the first meaning of "process"; and the universe in any stage of its expansion is the first meaning of "organism." In this sense, an organism is a nexus.

Secondly, each actual entity is itself only describable as an organic process. It repeats in microcosm what the universe is in macrocosm. It is a process proceeding from phase to phase, each phase being the real basis from which its successor proceeds toward the completion of the thing in question. Each actual entity bears in its constitution the "reasons" why its conditions are what they are. These "reasons" are the other actual entities objectified for it.

An "object" is a transcendent element characterizing that *definiteness* to which our "experience" has to conform. In this sense the future has *objective* reality in the present, but no *formal* actuality. For it is inherent in the constitution of the immediate, present actuality that a future will supersede it. Also conditions to which that future must conform, including real relationships to the present, are really objective in the immediate actuality.

Thus each actual entity, although complete so far as concerns its microscopic process, is yet incomplete by reason of its objective inclusion of the macroscopic process. It really experiences a future which must be actual, although the completed actualities of that future are undetermined. In this sense, each actual occasion experiences its own objective immortality.

Fact and Form

All human discourse which bases its claim to consideration on the truth of its statements must appeal to the facts. In none of its branches can philosophy claim immunity to this rule. But in the case of philosophy the difficulty arises that the record of the facts is in part dispersed vaguely through the various linguistic expressions of civilized language and of literature, and is in part expressed more precisely under the influence of schemes of thought prevalent in the traditions of science and philosophy.

In this . . . part of these lectures, the scheme of thought which is the basis of the philosophy of organism is confronted with various interpretations of the facts widely accepted in the European tradition, literary, philosophic, and scientific. So far as concerns philosophy only a selected group can be explicitly mentioned. There is no point in endeavouring to force the interpretations of divergent philosophers into a vague agreement. What is important is that the scheme of interpretation here adopted can claim for each of its main positions the express authority of one, or the other, of some supreme master of thought—Plato, Aristotle, Descartes, Locke, Hume, Kant. But ultimately nothing rests on authority; the final court of appeal is intrinsic reasonableness.

The safest general characterization of the European philosophical tradition is that it consists of a series of footnotes to Plato. I do not mean the systematic scheme of thought which scholars have doubtfully extracted from his writings. I allude to the wealth of general ideas scattered through them. His personal endowments, his wide opportunities for experience at a great period of civilization, his inheritance of an intellectual tradition not yet stiffened by excessive systematization, have made his writings an inexhaustible mine of suggestion. Thus in one sense by stating my belief that the train of thought in these lectures is Platonic, I am doing no more than expressing the hope that it falls within the European tradition. But I do mean more: I mean that if we had to render Plato's general point of view with the least changes made necessary by the intervening two thousand years of human experience in social organization, in aesthetic attainments, in science, and in religion, we should have to set about the construction of a philosophy of organism. In such a philosophy the actualities constituting the process of the world are conceived as exemplifying the ingression (or 'participation') of other things which constitute the potentialities of definiteness for any actual existence. The things which are temporal arise by their participation in the things which are eternal. The two sets are mediated by a thing which combines the actuality of what is temporal with the timelessness of what is potential. This final entity is the divine element in the world, by which the barren inefficient disjunction of abstract potentialities obtains primordially the efficient conjunction of ideal realization. This ideal realization of potentialities in a primordial actual entity constitutes the metaphysical stability whereby the actual process exemplifies general principles of metaphysics, and attains the ends proper to specific types of emergent order. By reason of the actuality of this primordial valuation of pure potentials, each eternal object has a definite, effective relevance to each concrescent process. Apart from such orderings, there would be a complete disjunction of eternal objects unrealized in the temporal world. Novelty would be meaningless, and inconceivable. We are here extending and rigidly applying Hume's principle, that ideas of reflection are derived from actual facts.

By this recognition of the divine element the general Aristotelian principle is maintained that, apart from things that are actual, there is nothing—nothing either in fact or in efficacy. This is the true general principle which also underlies Descartes' dictum: "For this reason, when we perceive any attribute, we therefore conclude that some existing thing or substance to which it may be attributed, is necessarily present."[1] And again: "for every clear and distinct conception (*perceptio*) is without doubt something, and hence cannot derive its origin from what is nought, . . ."[2] This general principle will be termed the 'ontological principle.' It is the principle that everything is positively somewhere in actuality, and in potency everywhere. In one of its applications this principle issues in the doctrine of 'conceptualism.' Thus the search for a reason is always the search for an actual fact which is the vehicle of the reason. The ontological principle, as here defined,

---

[1] *Principles of Philosophy*, Part I, 52; translation by Haldane and Ross. All quotations from Descartes are from this translation.
[2] *Meditation* IV, towards the end.

constitutes the first step in the description of the universe as a solidar-ity[3] of many actual entities. Each actual entity is conceived as an act of experience arising out of data. It is a process of 'feeling' the many data, so as to absorb them into the unity of one individual 'satisfaction.' Here 'feeling' is the term used for the basic generic operation of pass-ing from the objectivity of the data to the subjectivity of the actual entity in question. Feelings are variously specialized operations, effect-ing a transition into subjectivity. They replace the 'neutral stuff' of certain realistic philosophers. An actual entity is a process, and is not describable in terms of the morphology of a 'stuff.' This use of the term 'feeling' has a close analogy to Alexander's[4] use of the term 'en-joyment'; and has also some kinship with Bergson's use of the term 'intuition.' A near analogy is Locke's use of the term 'idea,' including 'ideas of particular things' (cf. his *Essay,* III, III, 2, 6, and 7). But the word 'feeling,' as used in these lectures, is even more reminiscent of Descartes. For example: "Let it be so; still it is at least quite certain that it seems to me that I see light, that I bear noise and that I feel heat. That cannot be false; properly speaking it is what is in me called feel-ing *(sentire);* and used in this precise sense that is no other thing than thinking."[5]

In Cartesian language, the essence of an actual entity consists solely in the fact that it is a prehending thing (i.e., a substance whose whole essence or nature is to prehend).[6] A 'feeling' belongs to the positive species of 'prehensions.' There are two species of prehensions, the 'positive species' and the 'negative species.' An actual entity has a perfectly definite bond with each item in the universe. This determinate bond is its prehension of that item. A negative prehension is the definite exclusion of that item from positive contribution to the subject's own real internal constitution. This doctrine involves the position that a neg-ative prehension expresses a bond. A positive prehension is the definite inclusion of that item into positive contribution to the subject's own real internal constitution. This positive inclusion is called its 'feeling'

---

[3] The word 'solidarity' has been borrowed from Professor Wilson Carr's *Presiden-tial Address* to the Aristotelian Society, Session 1917–1918. The address—"The Inter-action of Body and Mind"—develops the fundamental principle suggested by this word.

[4] Cf. his *Space, Time and Deity, passim.*

[5] *Meditation* II, Haldane and Ross translation.

[6] For the analogue to this sentence cf. *Meditation* VI; substitute *'Ens prehendens'* for *'Ens cogitans.'*

of that item. Other entities are required to express *how* any one item is felt. All actual entities in the actual world, relatively to a given actual entity as 'subject,' are necessarily 'felt' by that subject, though in general vaguely. An actual entity as felt is said to be 'objectified' for that subject. Only a selection of eternal objects are 'felt' by a given subject, and these eternal objects are then said to have 'ingression' in that subject. But those eternal objects which are not felt are not therefore negligible. For each negative prehension has its own subjective form, however trivial and faint. It adds to the emotional complex, though not to the objective data. The emotional complex is the subjective form of the final 'satisfaction.' The importance of negative prehensions arises from the fact, that (i) actual entities form a system, in the sense of entering into each other's constitutions, (ii) that by the ontological principle every entity is felt by some actual entity, (iii) that, as a consequence of (i) and (ii), every entity in the actual world of a concrescent actuality has some gradation of real relevance to that concrescence, (iv) that, in consequence of (iii), the negative prehension of an entity is a positive fact with its emotional subjective form, (v) there is a mutual sensitivity of the subjective forms of prehensions, so that they are not indifferent to each other, (vi) the concrescence issues in one concrete feeling, the satisfaction.

SECTION II

That we fail to find in experience any elements intrinsically incapable of exhibition as examples of general theory is the hope of rationalism. This hope is not a metaphysical premise. It is the faith which forms the motive for the pursuit of all sciences alike, including metaphysics.

In so far as metaphysics enables us to apprehend the rationality of things, the claim is justified. It is always open to us, having regard to the imperfections of all metaphysical systems, to lose hope at the exact point where we find ourselves. The preservation of such faith must depend on an ultimate moral intuition into the nature of intellectual action—that it should embody the adventure of hope. Such an intuition marks the point where metaphysics—and indeed every science—gains assurance from religion and passes over into religion. But in itself the faith does not embody a premise from which the theory starts; it is an ideal which is seeking satisfaction. In so far as we believe that doctrine, we are rationalists.

There must, however, be limits to the claim that all the elements in the universe are explicable by 'theory.' For 'theory' itself requires that there be 'given' elements so as to form the material for theorizing. Plato himself recognizes this limitation: I quote from Professor A. E. Taylor's summary of the *Timaeus*:

> In the real world there is always, over and above "law," a factor of the "simply given" or "brute fact," not accounted for and to be accepted simply as given. It is the business of science never to acquiesce in the merely given, to seek to "explain" it as the consequence, in virtue of rational law, of some simpler initial "given." But, however far science may carry this procedure, it is always forced to retain *some* element of brute fact, the merely given, in its account of things. It is the presence in nature of this element of the given, this surd or irrational as it has sometimes been called, which Timaeus appears to be personifying in his language about Necessity.[7]

So far as the interpretation of Plato is concerned, I rely upon the authority of Professor Taylor. But, apart from this historical question, a clear understanding of the given elements in the world is essential for any form of Platonic realism.

For rationalistic thought, the notion of 'givenness' carries with it a reference beyond the mere data in question. It refers to a 'decision' whereby what is 'given' is separated off from what for that occasion is 'not given.' This element of 'givenness' in things implies some activity procuring limitation. The word 'decision' does not here imply conscious judgment, though in some 'decisions' consciousness will be a factor. The word is used in its root sense of a 'cutting off.' The ontological principle declares that every decision is referable to one or more actual entities, because in separation from actual entities there is nothing, merely nonentity—'The rest is silence.'

The ontological principle asserts the relativity of decision; whereby every decision expresses the relation of the actual thing, *for which* a decision is made, to an actual thing *by which* that decision is made. But 'decision' cannot be construed as a casual adjunct of an actual entity. It constitutes the very meaning of actuality. An actual entity arises from decisions *for* it, and by its very existence provides decisions

---

[7] *Plato, The Man and His Work,* Lincoln MacVeagh, New York, 1927.

for other actual entities which supersede it. Thus the ontological principle is the first stage in constituting a theory embracing the notions of
'actual entity,' 'givenness,' and 'process.' just as 'potentiality for process' is the meaning of the more general term 'entity,' or 'thing'; so
'decision' is the additional meaning imported by the word 'actual' into
the phrase 'actual entity.' 'Actuality' is the decision amid 'potentiality.' It represents stubborn fact which cannot be evaded. The real internal constitution of an actual entity progressively constitutes a decision
conditioning the creativity which transcends that actuality. The Castle
Rock at Edinburgh exists from moment to moment, and from century
to century, by reason of the decision effected by its own historic route
of antecedent occasions. And if, in some vast upheaval of nature, it
were shattered into fragments, that convulsion would still be conditioned by the fact that it was the destruction of *that* rock. The point to
be emphasized is the insistent particularity of things experienced and
of the act of experiencing. Bradley's doctrine[8]—Wolf-eating-Lamb as
a universal qualifying the absolute—is a travesty of the evidence. *That*
wolf eat *that* lamb at *that* spot at *that* time: the wolf knew it; the lamb
knew it; and the carrion birds knew it. Explicitly in the verbal sentence,
or implicitly in the understanding of the subject entertaining it, every
expression of a proposition includes demonstrative elements. In fact
each word, and each symbolic phrase, is such an element, exciting the
conscious prehension of some entity belonging to one of the categories
of existence.

SECTION III

Conversely, where there is no decision involving exclusion, there is no
givenness. For example, the total multiplicity of Platonic forms is not
'given.' But in respect of each actual entity, there is givenness of such
forms. The determinate definiteness of each actuality is an expression
of a selection from these forms. It grades them in a diversity of relevance. This ordering of relevance starts from those forms which are, in
the fullest sense, exemplified, and passes through grades of relevance
down to those forms which in some faint sense are proximately rele-

---

[8] Cf. *Logic*, Bk. I, Ch. II, Sect. 42.

vant by reason of contrast with actual fact. This whole gamut of relevance is 'given,' and must be referred to the decision of actuality.

The term 'Platonic form' has here been used as the briefest way of indicating the entities in question. But these lectures are not an exegesis of Plato's writings; the entities in question are not necessarily restricted to those which he would recognize as 'forms.' Also the term 'idea' has a subjective suggestion in modern philosophy, which is very misleading for my present purposes; and in any case it has been used in many senses and has become ambiguous. The term 'essence,' as used by the Critical Realists, also suggests their use of it, which diverges from what I intend. Accordingly, by way of employing a term devoid of misleading suggestions, I use the phrase 'eternal object' for what in the preceding paragraph of this section I have termed a 'Platonic form.' Any entity whose conceptual recognition does not involve a necessary reference to any definite actual entities of the temporal world is called an 'eternal object.'

In this definition the 'conceptual recognition' must of course be an operation constituting a real feeling belonging to some actual entity. The point is that the actual subject which is merely conceiving the eternal object is not thereby in direct relationship to some other actual entity, apart from any other peculiarity in the composition of that conceiving subject. This doctrine applies also to the primordial nature of God, which is his complete envisagement of eternal objects; he is not thereby directly related to the given course of history. The given course of history presupposes his primordial nature, but his primordial nature does not presuppose it.

An eternal object is always a potentiality for actual entities; but in itself, as conceptually felt, it is neutral as to the fact of its physical ingression in any particular actual entity of the temporal world. 'Potentiality' is the correlative of 'givenness.' The meaning of 'givenness' is that what *is* 'given' might not have been 'given'; and that what *is not* 'given' *might have been* 'given.'

Further, in the complete particular 'givenness' for an actual entity there is an element of exclusiveness. The various primary data and the concrescent feelings do not form a mere multiplicity. Their synthesis in the final unity of one actual entity is another fact of 'givenness.' The actual entity terminates its becoming in one complex feeling involving a completely determinate bond with every item in the universe, the bond being either a positive or a negative prehension. This termination is the 'satisfaction' of the actual entity. Thus the addition of another component alters this *synthetic* 'givenness.' Any additional component is therefore contrary to this internal 'givenness' of the original. This principle may be illustrated by our visual perception of a picture. The pattern of colours is 'given' for us. But an extra patch of red does not constitute a mere addition; it alters the whole balance. Thus in an actual entity the balanced unity of the total 'givenness' excludes anything that is not given.

This is the doctrine of the emergent unity of the superject. An actual entity is to be conceived both as a subject presiding over its own immediacy of becoming, and a superject which is the atomic creature exercising its function of objective immortality. It has become a 'being'; and it belongs to the nature of every 'being' that it is a potential for every 'becoming.'

This doctrine, that the final 'satisfaction' of an actual entity is intolerant of any addition, expresses the fact that every actual entity—since it is what it is—is finally its own reason for what it omits. In the real internal constitution of an actual entity there is always some element which is contrary to an omitted element. Here 'contrary' means the impossibility of joint entry in the same sense. In other words, indetermination has evaporated from 'satisfaction' so that there is a complete determination of 'feeling,' or of 'negation of feeling,' respecting the universe. This evaporation of indetermination is merely another way of considering the process whereby the actual entity arises from its data. Thus, in another sense, each actual entity includes the universe, by reason of its determinate attitude towards every element in the universe.

Thus the process of becoming is dipolar, (i) by reason of its qualification by the determinateness of the actual world, and (ii) by its conceptual prehensions of the indeterminateness of eternal objects. The process is constituted by the influx of eternal objects into a novel determinateness of feeling which absorbs the actual world into a novel actuality.

The 'formal' constitution of an actual entity is a process of transition from indetermination towards terminal determination. But the indetermination is referent to determinate data. The 'objective' constitution of an actual entity is its terminal determination, considered as a complex of component determinates by reason of which the actual entity is a datum for the creative advance. The actual entity on its physical side is composed of its determinate feelings of its actual world, and on its mental side is originated by its conceptual appetitions.

Returning to the correlation of 'givenness' and 'potentiality,' we see that 'givenness' refers to 'potentiality,' and 'potentiality' to 'givenness'; also we see that the completion of 'givenness' in actual fact converts the 'not-given' for that fact into 'impossibility' for *that* fact. The individuality of an actual entity involves an exclusive limitation. This element of 'exclusive limitation' is the definiteness essential for the synthetic unity of an actual entity. This synthetic unity forbids the notion of *mere* addition to the included elements.

It is evident that 'givenness' and 'potentiality' are both meaningless apart from a multiplicity of potential entities. These potentialities are the 'eternal objects.' Apart from 'potentiality' and 'givenness,' there can be no nexus of actual things in process of supersession by novel actual things. The alternative is a static monistic universe, without unrealized potentialities; since 'potentiality' is then a meaningless term.

The scope of the ontological principle is not exhausted by the corollary that 'decision' must be referable to an actual entity. Everything must be somewhere; and here 'somewhere' means 'some actual entity.' Accordingly the general potentiality of the universe must be somewhere; since it retains its proximate relevance to actual entities for which it is unrealized. This 'proximate relevance' reappears in subsequent concrescence as final causation regulative of the emergence of novelty. This 'somewhere' is the non-temporal actual entity. Thus 'proximate relevance' means 'relevance' as in the primordial mind of God.

It is a contradiction in terms to assume that some explanatory fact can float into the actual world out of nonentity. Nonentity is nothingness. Every explanatory fact refers to the decision and to the efficacy of an actual thing. The notion of 'subsistence' is merely the notion of how eternal objects can be components of the primordial nature of God. This is a question for subsequent discussion (cf. Part V). But eternal objects, as in God's primordial nature, constitute the Platonic world of ideas.

There is not, however, one entity which is merely the *class* of all eternal objects. For if we conceive any class of eternal objects, there are additional eternal objects which presuppose that class but do not belong to it. For this reason, at the beginning of this section, the phrase 'the multiplicity of Platonic forms' was used, instead of the more natural phrase 'the class of Platonic forms.' A multiplicity is a type of complex thing which has the unity derivative from some qualification which participates in each of its components severally; but a multiplicity has no unity derivative *merely* from its various components.

SECTION IV

The doctrine just stated—that every explanatory fact refers to the decision and to the efficacy of an actual thing—requires discussion in reference to the ninth Categoreal Obligation. This category states that 'The concrescence of each individual actual entity is internally determined and is externally free.'

The peculiarity of the course of history illustrates the joint relevance of the 'ontological principle' and of this categoreal obligation. The evolution of history can be rationalized by the consideration of the determination of successors by antecedents. But, on the other hand, the evolution of history is incapable of rationalization because it exhibits a selected flux of participating forms. No reason, internal to history, can be assigned why that flux of forms, rather than another flux, should have been illustrated. It is true that any flux must exhibit the character of internal determination. So much follows from the ontological principle. But every instance of internal determination assumes *that* flux up to *that* point. There is no reason why there could be no alternative flux exhibiting that principle of internal determination. The actual flux presents itself with the character of being merely 'given.' It does not disclose any peculiar character of 'perfection.' On the contrary the imperfection of the world is the theme of every religion which offers a way of escape, and of every sceptic who deplores the prevailing superstition. The Leibnizian theory of the 'best of possible worlds' is an audacious fudge produced in order to save the face of a Creator constructed by contemporary, and antecedent, theologians. Further, in the case of those actualities whose immediate experience is most completely open to us, namely, human beings, the final decision of the immediate subject-superject, constituting the ultimate modification of subjective aim, is the foundation of our experience of responsibility, of approbation or of disapprobation, of self-approval or of self-reproach, of freedom, of emphasis. This element in experience is too large to be put aside merely as misconstruction. It governs the whole tone of human life. It can be illustrated by striking instances from fact or from fiction. But these instances are only conspicuous illustrations of human experience during each hour and each minute. The ultimate freedom of things, lying beyond all determinations, was whispered by Galileo—*E pur si muove*—freedom for the inquisitors to think wrongly, for Galileo to think rightly, and for the world to move in despite of Galileo and inquisitors.

The doctrine of the philosophy of organism is that, however far the sphere of efficient causation be pushed in the determination of components of a concrescence—its data, its emotions, its appreciations, its purposes, its phases of subjective aim—beyond the determination of these components there always remains the final reaction of the self-creative unity of the universe. This final reaction completes the self-creative act by putting the decisive stamp of creative emphasis upon the determinations of efficient cause. Each occasion exhibits its measure of creative emphasis in proportion to its measure of subjective intensity. The absolute standard of such intensity is that of the primordial nature of God, which is neither great nor small because it arises out of no actual world. It has within it no components which are standards of comparison. But in the temporal world for occasions of relatively slight experient intensity, their decisions of creative emphasis are individually negligible compared to the determined components which they receive and transmit. But the final accumulation of all such decisions— the decision of God's nature and the decisions of all occasions— constitutes that special element in the flux of forms in history, which is 'given' and incapable of rationalization beyond the fact that within it every component which is determinable is internally determined.

The doctrine is, that each concrescence is to be referred to a definite free initiation and a definite free conclusion. The initial fact is macrocosmic, in the sense of having equal relevance to all occasions; the final fact is microcosmic, in the sense of being peculiar to that occasion. Neither fact is capable of rationalization, in the sense of tracing the antecedents which determine it. The initial fact is the primordial appetition, and the final fact is the decision of emphasis, finally creative of the 'satisfaction.'

SECTION V

The antithetical terms 'universals' and 'particulars' are the usual words employed to denote respectively entities which nearly, though not quite,[9] correspond to the entities here termed 'eternal objects,' and 'actual entities.' These terms, 'universals' and 'particulars,' both in the suggestiveness of the two words and in their current philosophical use, are somewhat misleading. The ontological principle, and the wider doctrine of universal relativity on which the present metaphysical discussion is founded, blur the sharp distinction between what is universal and what is particular. The notion of a universal is of that which can enter into the description of many particulars; whereas the notion of a particular is that it is described by universals, and does not itself enter into the description of any other particular. According to the doctrine of relativity which is the basis of the metaphysical system of the present lectures, both these notions involve a misconception. An actual entity cannot be described, even inadequately, by universals; because other actual entities do enter into the description of any one actual entity. Thus every so-called 'universal' is particular in the sense of being just what it is, diverse from everything else; and every so-called 'particular' is universal in the sense of entering into the constitutions of other actual entities. The contrary opinion led to the collapse of Descartes' many substances into Spinoza's one substance; to Leibniz's windowless monads with their pre-established harmony; to the sceptical reduction of Hume's philosophy—a reduction first effected by Hume himself, and reissued with the most beautiful exposition by Santayana in his *Scepticism and Animal Faith.*

The point is that the current view of universals and particulars inevitably leads to the epistemological position stated by Descartes:

> From this I should conclude that I knew the wax by means of vision and not simply by the intuition of the mind; unless by chance I remember that, when looking from a window and saying 'I see men who pass in the street,' I really do not see them, but infer that what I see is men, just as I say that I see wax. And yet what do I see from the window but hats and coats which may cover automatic machines? Yet I judge these to be men. And similarly solely by the faculty of judgment [*judicandi*] which rests in my mind, I comprehend that which I believed I saw with my eyes.[10]

In this passage it is assumed[11] that Descartes—the Ego in question—is a particular, characterized only by universals. Thus his impres-

---

[9] For example, prehensions and subjective forms are also 'particulars.'

[10] *Meditation* II.

[11] Perhaps inconsistently with what Descartes says elsewhere: in other passages the mental activity involved seems to be *analysis* which discovers *'realitas objectiva'* as

sions—to use Hume's word—are characterizations by universals. Thus there is no perception of a particular actual entity. He arrives at the belief in the actual entity by 'the faculty of judgment.' But on this theory he has absolutely no analogy upon which to found any such inference with the faintest shred of probability. Hume, accepting Descartes' account of perception (in this passage), which also belongs to Locke in some sections of his *Essay,* easily draws the sceptical conclusion. Santayana irrefutably exposes the full extent to which this scepticism must be carried. The philosophy of organism recurs to Descartes' alternative theory of *'realitas objective,'* and endeavours to interpret it in terms of a consistent ontology. Descartes endeavoured to combine the two theories; but his unquestioned acceptance of the subject-predicate dogma forced him into a representative theory of perception, involving a *'judicium'* validated by our assurance of the power and the goodness of God. The philosophy of organism in its account of prehension takes its stand upon the Cartesian terms *'realitas objective,'* *'inspection'* and *'intuitio.'* The two latter terms are transformed into the notion of a 'positive prehension,' and into operations described in the various categories of physical and conceptual origination. A recurrence to the notion of 'God' is still necessary to mediate between physical and conceptual prehensions, but not in the crude form of giving a limited letter of credit to a *'judicium.'*

Hume, in effect, agrees that 'mind' is a process of concrescence arising from primary data. In his account, these data are 'impressions of sensation'; and in such impressions no elements other than universals are discoverable. For the philosophy of organism, the primary data are always actual entities absorbed into feeling in virtue of certain universals shared alike by the objectified actuality and the experient subject (cf. Part III). Descartes takes an intermediate position. He explains perception in Humian terms, but adds an apprehension of particular actual entities in virtue of an *'inspectio'* and a *'judicium'* effected by the mind (*Meditations II* and *III*). Here he is paving the way for Kant, and for the degradation of the world into 'mere appearance.'

All modern philosophy hinges round the difficulty of describing the world in terms of subject and predicate, substance and quality, particular and universal. The result always does violence to that immediate experience which we express in our actions, our hopes, our sympathies,

---

a component element of the idea in question. There is thus *'inspectio'* rather than *'judicium.'*

our purposes, and which we enjoy in spite of our lack of phrases for its verbal analysis. We find ourselves in a buzzing[12] world, amid a democracy of fellow creatures; whereas, under some disguise or other, orthodox philosophy can only introduce us to solitary substances, each enjoying an illusory experience: "O Bottom, thou art changed! what do I see on thee?" The endeavour to interpret experience in accordance with the overpowering deliverance of common sense must bring us back to some restatement of Platonic realism, modified so as to avoid the pitfalls which the philosophical investigations of the seventeenth and eighteenth centuries have disclosed.

The true point of divergence is the false notion suggested by the contrast between the natural meanings of the words 'particular' and 'universal.' The 'particular' is thus conceived as being just its individual self with no necessary relevance to any other particular. It answers to Descartes' definition of substance: "And when we conceive of substance, we merely conceive an existent thing which requires nothing but itself in order to exist."[13] This definition is a true derivative from Aristotle's definition: A primary substance is "neither asserted of a subject nor present in a subject."[14] We must add the title phrase of Descartes' *The Second Meditation*: "Of the Nature of the Human Mind; and that it is more easily known than the Body," together with his two statements: ". . . thought constitutes the nature of thinking substance," and "everything that we find in mind is but so many diverse forms of thinking."[15] This sequence of quotations exemplifies the set of presuppositions which led to Locke's empiricism and to Kant's critical philosophy—the two dominant influences from which modern thought is derived. This is the side of seventeenth-century philosophy which is here discarded.

The principle of universal relativity directly traverses Aristotle's dictum, 'A substances is not present in a subject.' On the contrary, according to this principle an actual entity *is* present in other actual entities. In fact if we allow for degrees of relevance, and for negligible relevance, we must say that every actual entity is present in every other actual entity. The philosophy of organism is mainly devoted to the task of making clear the notion of 'being present in another entity.' This

---

[12] This epithet is, of course, borrowed from William James.
[13] Principles of Philosophy, Part I, 51.
[14] *Aristotle* by W. D. Ross, Ch. II.
[15] *Principles of Philosophy*, Part I, 53.

phrase is here borrowed from Aristotle: it is not a fortunate phrase, and in subsequent discussion it will be replaced by the term 'objectification.' The Aristotelian phrase suggests the crude notion that one actual entity is added to another *simpliciter.* This is not what is meant. One role of the eternal objects is that they are those elements which express how any one actual entity is constituted by its synthesis of other actual entities, and how that actual entity develops from the primary dative phase into its own individual actual existence, involving its individual enjoyments and appetitions. An actual entity is concrete because it is such a particular concrescence of the universe.

SECTION VI

A short examination of Locke's *Essay Concerning Human Understanding* will throw light on the presuppositions from which the philosophy of organism originates. These citations from Locke are valuable as clear statements of the obvious deliverances of common sense, expressed with their natural limitations. They cannot be bettered in their character of presentations of facts which have to be accepted by any satisfactory system of philosophy.

The first point to notice is that in some of his statements Locke comes very near to the explicit formulation of an organic philosophy of the type being developed here. It was only his failure to notice that his problem required a more drastic revision of traditional categories than that which he actually effected, that led to a vagueness of statement, and the intrusion of inconsistent elements. It was this conservative, other side of Locke which led to his sceptical overthrow by Hume. In his turn, Hume (despite his explicit repudiation in his *Treatise,* Part I, Sect.VI) was a thorough conservative, and in his explanation of mentality and its content never moved away from the subject-predicate habits of thought which had been impressed on the European mind by the overemphasis on Aristotle's logic during the long mediaeval period. In reference to this twist of mind, probably Aristotle was not an Aristotelian. But Hume's sceptical reduction of knowledge entirely depends (for its arguments) on the tacit presupposition of the mind as subject and of its contents as predicates—a presupposition which explicitly he repudiates.

The merit of Locke's *Essay Concerning Human Understanding* is its adequacy, and not its consistency. He gives the most dispassionate descriptions of those various elements in experience which common sense never lets slip. Unfortunately he is hampered by inappropriate metaphysical categories which he never criticized. He should have widened the title of his book into 'An Essay Concerning Experience.' His true topic is the analysis of the types of experience enjoyed by an actual entity. But this complete experience is nothing other than what the actual entity is in itself, for itself. I will adopt the pre-Kantian phraseology, and say that the experience enjoyed by an actual entity is that entity *formaliter*. By this I mean that the entity, when considered 'formally,' is being described in respect to those forms of its constitution whereby it is that individual entity with its own measure of absolute self-realization. Its 'ideas of things' are *what* other things are for it. In the phraseology of these lectures, they are its 'feelings.' The actual entity is composite and analysable; and its 'ideas' express how, and in what sense, other things are components in its own constitution. Thus the form of its constitution is to be found by an analysis of the Lockian ideas. Locke talks of 'understanding' and 'perception.' He should have started with a more general neutral term to express the synthetic concrescence whereby the many things of the universe become the one actual entity. Accordingly I have adopted the term 'prehension,' to express the activity whereby an actual entity effects its own concretion of other things.

The 'prehension' of one actual entity by another actual entity is the complete transaction, analysable into the objectification of the former entity as one of the data for the latter, and into the fully clothed feeling whereby the datum is absorbed into the subjective satisfaction— 'clothed' with the the various elements of its 'subjective form.' But this definition can be stated more generally so as to include the case of the prehension of an eternal object by an actual entity; namely, The 'positive prehension' of an entity by an actual entity is the complete transaction analysable into the ingression, or objectification, of that entity as a datum for feeling, and into the feeling whereby this datum is absorbed into the subjective satisfaction. I also discard Locke's term 'idea.' Instead of that term, the other things, in their limited roles as elements for the actual entity in question, are called 'objects' for that thing. There are four main types of objects, namely 'eternal objects,' 'propositions,' 'objectified' actual entities and nexūs. These 'eternal objects' are Locke's ideas as explained in his *Essay* (II, I, 1), where he writes:

> *Idea is the object of thinking*.—Every man being conscious to himself that he thinks, and that which his mind is applied about, whilst thinking, being the ideas that are there, it is past doubt that men have in their mind several ideas, such as are those expressed by the words, "whiteness, hardness, sweetness, thinking, motion, man, elephant, army, drunkenness," and others.

But later (III, III, 2), when discussing general terms (and subconsciously, earlier in his discussion of 'substance' in II, XXIII), he adds parenthetically another type of ideas which are practically what I term 'objectified actual entities' and 'nexūs.' He calls them 'ideas of particular things'; and he explains why, in general, such ideas cannot have their separate names. The reason is simple and undeniable: there are too many actual entities. He writes: "But it is beyond the power of human capacity to frame and retain distinct ideas of all the particular things we meet with: every bird and beast men saw, every tree and plant that affected the senses, could not find a place in the most capacious understanding." The context shows that it is not the impossibility of an 'idea' of any particular thing which is the seat of the difficulty; it is solely their number. This notion of a direct 'idea' (or 'feeling') of an actual entity is a presupposition of all common sense; Santayana ascribes it to 'animal faith.' But it accords very ill with the sensationalist theory of knowledge which can be derived from other parts of Locke's writings. Both Locke and Descartes wrestle with exactly the same difficulty.

The principle that I am adopting is that consciousness presupposes experience, and not experience consciousness. It is a special element in the subjective forms of some feelings. Thus an actual entity may, or may not, be conscious of some part of its experience. Its experience is its complete formal constitution, including its consciousness, if any. Thus, in Locke's phraseology, its 'ideas of particular things' are those other things exercising their function as felt components of its constitution. Locke would only term them 'ideas' when these objectifications belong to that region of experience lit up by consciousness. In Section 4 of the same chapter, he definitely makes all knowledge to be "founded in particular things." He writes: ". . . yet a distinct name for every particular thing would not be of any great use for the improve-

ment of knowledge: which, *though founded in particular things*,[16] en-
larges itself by general views; to which things reduced into sorts under
general names, are properly subservient." Thus for Locke, in this passage, there are not first the qualities and then the conjectural particular
things; but conversely. Also he illustrates his meaning of a 'particular
thing' by a 'leaf,' a 'crow,' a 'sheep,' a 'grain of sand.' So he is not
thinking of a particular patch of colour, or other sense-datum.[17] For
example, in Section 7 of the same chapter, in reference to children he
writes: "The ideas of the nurse and the mother are well framed in their
minds; and, like pictures of them there, represent only those individuals." This doctrine of Locke's must be compared with Descartes' doctrine of *realitas objectiva*. Locke inherited the dualistic separation of
mind from body. If he had started with the one fundamental notion of
an actual entity, the complex of ideas disclosed in consciousness would
have at once turned into the complex constitution of the actual entity
disclosed in its own consciousness, so far as it is conscious—fitfully,
partially, or not at all. Locke definitely states how ideas become general. In Section 6 of the chapter he writes: "and ideas become general
by separating from them the circumstances of time, and place, and any
other ideas that may determine them to this or that particular existence." Thus for Locke the abstract idea is preceded by the 'idea of a
particular existent'; "[children] frame an idea which they find those
many particulars do partake in." This statement of Locke's should be
compared with the Category of Conceptual Valuation, which is the
fourth categoreal obligation.

Locke discusses the constitution of actual things under the term 'real
essences.' He writes (Section 15, same chapter): "And thus the real
internal (but generally in substances unknown) constitution of things,
whereon their discoverable qualities depend, may be called their 'essence.'" The point is that Locke entirely endorses the doctrine that an
actual entity arises out of a complex constitution involving other entities, though by his unfortunate use of such terms as 'cabinet,' he puts
less emphasis on the notion of 'process' than does Hume.

Locke has in fact stated in his work one main problem for the philosophy of organism. He discovers that the mind is a unity arising out of

---

[16] My italics.

[17] As he is in I, II, 15, where he writes, "The senses at first let in particular ideas,
and furnish the yet empty cabinet; . . ." Note the distinction between 'particular ideas'
and 'ideas of particular things.'

the active prehension of ideas into one concrete thing. Unfortunately, he presupposes both the Cartesian dualism whereby minds are one kind of particulars, and natural entities are another kind of particulars, and also the subject-predicate dogma. He is thus, in company with Descartes, driven to a theory of representative perception. For example, in one of the quotations already cited, he writes: "and, like pictures of them there, *represent* only those individuals." This doctrine obviously creates an insoluble problem for epistemology, only to be solved either by some sturdy make-believe of 'animal faith,' with Santayana, or by some doctrine of illusoriness—some doctrine of mere appearance, inconsistent if taken as real—with Bradley. Anyhow 'representative perception' can never, within its own metaphysical doctrines, produce the title deeds to guarantee the validity of the representation of fact by idea.

Locke and the philosophers of his epoch—the seventeenth and eighteenth centuries—are misled by one fundamental misconception. It is the assumption, unconscious and uncriticized, that logical simplicity can be identified with priority in the process constituting an experient occasion. Locke founded the first two books of his *Essay* on this presupposition, with the exception of his early sections on 'substance,' which are quoted immediately below. In the third and fourth books of the *Essay* he abandons this presupposition, again unconsciously as it seems.

This identification of priority in logic with priority in practice has vitiated thought and procedure from the first discovery of mathematics and logic by the Greeks. For example, some of the worst defects in educational procedure have been due to it. Locke's nearest approach to the philosophy of organism, and—from the point of view of that doctrine—his main oversight, are best exemplified by the first section of his chapter, 'Of our Complex Ideas of Substances' (11, XXIII, 1). He writes:

> The mind, being, as I have declared, furnished with a great number of the simple ideas conveyed in by the senses, as they are found in exterior things, or by reflection on its own operations, takes notice, also, that a certain number of these simple ideas go constantly together; which being presumed to belong to one thing, and words being suited to common apprehensions, and made use of for quick dispatch, are called, so united in one subject, by one name; which, by inadvertency, we are apt afterward to talk of and consider as one simple idea, which indeed is a com-

plication of many ideas together: because, as I have said, not imagining how these simple ideas can subsist by themselves, we accustom ourselves to suppose some *substratum* wherein they do subsist, and from which they do result; which therefore we call "substance."

In this section, Locke's first statement, which is the basis of the remainder of the section, is exactly the primary assumption of the philosophy of organism: "The mind, being . . . furnished with a great number of the simple ideas conveyed in by the senses, *as they are found in exterior things, . . .*" Here the last phrase, 'as they are found in exterior things,' asserted what later I shall call the vector character of the primary feelings. The universals involved obtain that status by reason of the fact that '*they are found in exterior things.*' This is Locke's assertion and it is the assertion of the philosophy of organism. It can also be conceived as a development of Descartes' doctrine of '*realitas objective.*' The universals are the only elements in the data describable by concepts, because concepts are merely the analytic functioning of universals. But the 'exterior things,' although they are not expressible by concepts in respect to their individual particularity, are no less data for feeling; so that the concrescent actuality arises from feeling their status of individual particularity; and thus that particularity is included as in element from which feelings originate, and which they concern.

The sentence later proceeds with, "a certain number of these simple ideas go constantly together." This can only mean that in the immediate perception 'a certain number of these simple ideas' are found together in an exterior thing, and that the recollection of antecedent moments of experience discloses that the same fact, of togetherness in an exterior thing, holds for the same set of simple ideas. Again, the philosophy of organism agrees that this description is true for moments of immediate experience. But Locke, owing to the fact that he veils his second premise under the phrase 'go constantly together,' omits to consider the question whether the 'exterior things' of the successive moments are to be identified.

The answer of the philosophy of organism is that, in the sense in which Locke is here speaking, the exterior things of successive moments are not to be identified with each other. Each exterior thing is either one actual entity, or (more frequently) is a nexus of actual entities with immediacies mutually contemporary. For the sake of simplicity we will speak only of the simpler case where the 'exterior thing' means one actual entity at the moment in question. But what Locke is explicitly concerned with is the notion of the self-identity of the one enduring physical body which lasts for years, or for seconds, or for ages. He is considering the current philosophical notion of an individualized particular substance (in the Aristotelian sense) which undergoes adventures of change, retaining its substantial form amid transition of accidents. Throughout his *Essay,* he in effect retains this notion while rightly insisting on its vagueness and obscurity. The philosophy of organism agrees with Locke and Hume, that the non-individualized substantial form is nothing else than the collection of universals—or, more accurately, the one complex universal—common to the succession of 'exterior things' at successive moments respectively. In other words, an 'exterior thing' is either one 'actual entity,' or is a 'society' with a 'defining characteristic.' For the organic philosophy, these 'exterior things' (in the former sense) are the final concrete actualities. The individualized substance (of Locke) must be construed to be the historic route constituted by some society of fundamental 'exterior things,' stretching from the first 'thing' to the last 'thing.'

But Locke, throughout his *Essay,* rightly insists that the chief ingredient in the notion of 'substance' is the notion of 'power.' The philosophy of organism holds that, in order to understand 'power,' we must have a correct notion of how each individual actual entity contributes to the datum *from which* its successors arise and *to which* they must conform. The reason why the doctrine of power is peculiarly relevant to the enduring things, which the philosophy of Locke's day conceived as individualized substances, is that any likeness between the successive occasions of a historic route procures a corresponding identity between their contributions to the datum of any subsequent actual entity; and it therefore secures a corresponding intensification in the imposition of conformity. The principle is the same as that which holds for the more sporadic occasions in empty space; but the uniformity along the historic route increases the degree of conformity which that route exacts from the future. In particular each historic route of like occasions tends to prolong itself, by reason of the weight of uniform inheritance derivable from its members. The philosophy of organism abolishes the detached mind. Mental activity is one of the modes of feeling belonging to all actual entities in some degree, but only amounting to conscious intellectuality in some actual entities. This higher grade of mental activity is the intellectual self-analysis of the entity in an earlier stage of incompletion, effected by intellectual feelings produced in a later stage of concrescence.[18]

The perceptive constitution of the actual entity presents the problem, How can the other actual entities, each with its own formal existence, also enter objectively into the perceptive constitution of the actual entity in question? This is the problem of the solidarity of the universe. The classical doctrines of universals and particulars, of subject and predicate, of individual substances not present in other individual substances, of the externality of relations, alike render this problem incapable of solution. The answer given by the organic philosophy is the doctrine of prehensions, involved in concrescent integrations, and terminating in a definite, complex unity of feeling. To be actual must mean that all actual things are alike objects, enjoying objective immortality in fashioning creative actions; and that all actual things are subjects, each prehending the universe from which it arises. The creative action is the universe always becoming one in a particular unity of self-experience, and thereby adding to the multiplicity which is the universe as many. This insistent concrescence into unity is the outcome of the ultimate self-identity of each entity. No entity—be it 'universal' or 'particular'—can play disjoined roles. Self-identity requires that every entity have one conjoined, self-consistent function, whatever be the complexity of that function.

SECTION VII

There is another side of Locke, which is his doctrine of 'power.' This doctrine is a better illustration of his admirable adequacy than of his consistency; there is no escape from Hume's demonstration that no such doctrine is compatible with a purely sensationalist philosophy. The establishment of such a philosophy, though derivative from Locke, was not his explicit purpose. Every philosophical school in the course of its history requires two presiding philosophers. One of them under the influence of the main doctrines of the school should survey experience with some adequacy, but inconsistently. The other philosopher should reduce the doctrines of the school to a rigid consistency; he

---

[18] Cf. Part III, Ch. V.

will thereby effect a *reductio ad absurdum.* No school of thought has performed its full service to philosophy until these men have appeared. In this way the school of sensationalist empiricism derives its importance from Locke and Hume.

Locke introduces his doctrine of 'power' as follows (II, XXI, 1–3):

This idea how got.—The mind being every day informed, by the senses, of the alteration of those simple ideas it observes in things without, and taking notice how one comes to an end and ceases to be, and another begins to exist which was not before; reflecting also on what passes within itself, and observing a constant change of its ideas, sometimes by the impression of outward objects on the senses, and sometimes by the determination of its own choice; and concluding, from what it has so constantly observed to have been, that the like changes will for the future be made in the same things by like agents, and by the like ways; considers in one thing the possibility of having any of its simple ideas changed, and in another the possibility of making that change; and so comes by that idea which we call "power." Thus we say, fire has a power to melt gold; . . . and gold has a power to be melted: . . . In which and the like cases, the power we consider is in reference to the change of perceivable ideas: for we cannot observe any alteration to be made in, or operation upon, any thing, but by the observable change of its sensible ideas; nor conceive any alteration to be made, but by conceiving a change of some of its ideas . . . . Power thus considered is twofold; viz. as able to make, or able to receive, any change: the one may be called "active," and the other "passive," power . . . . I confess power includes in it some kind of relations—a relation to action or change; as, indeed, which of our ideas, of what kind soever, when attentively considered, does not? For our ideas of extension, duration, and number, do they not all contain in them a secret relation of the parts? Figure and motion have something relative in them much more visibly. And sensible qualities, as colours and smells, etc., what are they but the powers of different bodies in relation to our perception? . . . . Our idea therefore of power, I think, may well have a place amongst other simple ideas, and be considered as one of them, being one of those that make a principal ingredient in our complex ideas of substances, as we shall hereafter have occasion to observe.

In this important passage, Locke enunciates the main doctrines of the philosophy of organism, namely: the principle of relativity; the relational character of eternal objects, whereby they constitute the forms of the objectifications of actual entities for each other; the com-

posite character of an actual entity (i.e., a substance); the notion of
'power' as making a principal ingredient in that of actual entity (substance). In this latter notion, Locke adumbrates both the ontological
principle, and also the principle that the 'power' of one actual entity
on the other is simply how the former is objectified in the constitution
of the other. Thus the problem of perception and the problem of power
are one and the same, at least so far as perception is reduced to mere
prehension of actual entities. Perception, in the sense of consciousness
of such prehension, requires the additional factor of the conceptual
prehension of eternal objects, and a process of integration of the two
factors (cf. Part III).

Locke's doctrine of 'power' is reproduced in the philosophy of organism by the doctrine of the two types of objectification, namely, (α)
'causal objectification,' and (β) 'presentational objectification.'

In 'causal objectification' what is felt *subjectively* by the objectified
actual entity is transmitted *objectively* to the concrescent actualities
which supersede it. In Locke's phraseology the objectified actual entity
is then exerting 'power.' In this type of objectification the eternal objects, relational between object and subject, express the formal constitution of the objectified actual entity.

In 'presentational objectification' the relational eternal objects fall
into two sets, one set contributed by the 'extensive' perspective of the
perceived from the position of the perceiver, and the other set the antecedent concrescent phases of the perceiver. What is ordinarily termed
'perception' is consciousness of presentational objectification. But according to the philosophy of organism there can be consciousness of
both types of objectification. There can be such consciousness of both
types because, according to this philosophy, the knowable is the complete nature of the knower, at least such phases of it as are antecedent
to that operation of knowing.

Locke misses one essential doctrine, namely, that the doctrine of
internal relations makes it impossible to attribute 'change' to any actual
entity. Every actual entity is what it is, and is with its definite status in
the universe, determined by its internal relations to other actual entities.
'Change' is the description of the adventures of eternal objects in the
evolving universe of actual things.

The doctrine of internal relations introduces another consideration
which cannot be overlooked without error. Locke considers the 'real
essence' and the 'nominal essence' of things. But on the theory of

the general relativity of actual things between each other, and of the internality of these relations, there are two distinct notions hidden under the term 'real essence,' both of importance. Locke writes (III, III, 15):

> Essence may be taken for the being of any thing, whereby it is what it is. And thus the real internal (but generally in substances unknown) constitution of things, whereon their discoverable qualities depend, may be called their "essence." . . . It is true, there is ordinarily supposed a real constitution of the sorts of things: and it is past doubt there must be some real constitution, on which any collection of simple ideas co-existing must depend. But it being evident that things are ranked under names into sorts or species only as they agree to certain abstract ideas to which we have annexed those names, the essence of each genus or sort comes to be nothing but that abstract idea, which the general or "sortal" (if I may have leave so to call it from "sort," as I do "general" from *genus*) name stands for. And this we shall find to be that which the word "essence" imparts in its most familiar use. These two sorts of essences, I suppose, may not unfitly be termed, the one the "real," the other the "nominal," essence.

The fundamental notion of the philosophy of organism is expressed in Locke's phrase, "it is past doubt there must be some real constitution, on which any collection of simple ideas co-existing must depend." Locke makes it plain (cf. II, II, 1) that by a 'simple idea' he means the ingression in the actual entity (illustrated by 'a piece of wax,' 'a piece of ice,' 'a rose') of some abstract quality which is not complex (illustrated by 'softness,' 'warmth,' 'whiteness'). For Locke such simple ideas, *coexisting* in an actual entity, require a *real* constitution for that entity. Now in the philosophy of organism, passing beyond Locke's explicit statement, the notion of a real constitution is taken to mean that the eternal objects function by introducing the multiplicity of actual entities as constitutive of the actual entity in question. Thus the constitution is 'real' because it assigns its status in the real world to the actual entity. In other words the actual entity, in virtue of being *what* it is, is also *where* it is. It is somewhere because it is some actual thing with its correlated actual world. This is the direct denial of the Cartesian doctrine, ". . . an existent thing which requires nothing but itself in order to exist." It is also inconsistent with Aristotle's phrase, "neither asserted of a subject nor present in a subject."

I am certainly not maintaining that Locke grasped explicitly the implications of his words as thus developed for the philosophy of organism. But it is a short step from a careless phrase to a flash of insight; nor is it unbelievable that Locke saw further into metaphysical problems than some of his followers. But abandoning the question of what Locke had in his own mind, the 'organic doctrine' demands a 'real essence' in the sense of a complete analysis of the relations, and inter-relations of the actual entities which are formative of the actual entity in question, and an 'abstract essence' in which the specified actual entities are replaced by the notions of unspecified entities in *such* a combination; this is the notion of an unspecified actual entity. Thus the real essence involves real objectifications of specified actual entities; the abstract essence is a complex eternal object. There is nothing self-contradictory in the thought of many actual entities with the same abstract essence; but there can only be one actual entity with the same real essence. For the real essence indicates 'where' the entity is, that is to say, its status in the real world; the abstract essence omits the particularity of the status.

The philosophy of organism in its appeal to the facts can thus support itself by an appeal to the insight of John Locke, who in British philosophy is the analogue to Plato, in the epoch of his life, in personal endowments, in width of experience, and in dispassionate statement of conflicting intuitions.

This doctrine of organism is the attempt to describe the world as a process of generation of individual actual entities, each with its own absolute self-attainment. This concrete finality of the individual is nothing else than a decision referent beyond itself. The 'perpetual perishing' (cf. Locke, IT, XIV, It) of individual absoluteness is thus foredoomed. But the 'perishing' of absoluteness is the attainment of 'objective immortality.' This last conception expresses the further element in the doctrine of organism—that the process of generation is to be described in terms of actual entities.

Objects and Subjects

1. Prefatory.—When Descartes, Locke, and Hume undertake the analysis of experience, they utilize those elements in their own experience which lie clear and distinct, fit for the exactitude of intellectual discourse. It is tacitly assumed, except by Plato, that the more fundamental factors will ever lend themselves for discrimination with peculiar clarity. This assumption is here directly challenged.

2. Structure of Experience.—No topic has suffered more from this tendency of philosophers than their account of the object-subject structure of experience. In the first place, this structure has been identified with the bare relation of knower to known. The subject is the knower, the object is the known. Thus, with this interpretation, the object-subject relation is the known-knower relation. It then follows that the more clearly any instance of this relation stands out for discrimination, the more safely we can utilize it for the interpretation of the status of experience in the universe of things. Hence Descartes' appeal to clarity and distinctness.

This deduction presupposes that the subject-object relation is the fundamental structural pattern of experience. I agree with this presupposition, but not in the sense in which subject-object is identified with knower-known. I contend that the notion of mere knowledge is a high abstraction, and that conscious discrimination itself is a variable factor only present in the more elaborate examples of occasions of experience. The basis of experience is emotional. Stated more generally, the basic fact is the rise of an affective tone originating from things whose relevance is given.

3. Phraseology.—Thus, the Quaker word "concern," divested of any suggestion of knowledge, is more fitted to express this fundamental structure. The occasion as subject has a "concern" for the object. And the "concern" at once places the object as a component in the experience of the subject, with an affective tone drawn from this object and directed toward it. With this interpretation the subject-object relation is the fundamental structure of experience.

Quaker usages of language are not widely spread. Also each phraseology leads to a crop of misunderstandings. The subject-object relation can be conceived as Recipient and Provoker, where the fact provoked is an affective tone about the status of the provoker in the provoked experience. Also the total provoked occasion is a totality involving many such examples of provocation. Again this phraseology is unfortunate; for the word "recipient" suggests a passivity which is erroneous.

4. Prehensions.—A more formal explanation is as follows. An occasion of experience is an activity, analyzable into modes of functioning which jointly constitute its process of becoming. Each mode is analyzable into the total experience as active subject, and into the thing or object with which the special activity is concerned. This thing is a datum, that is to say, is describable without reference to its entertainment in that occasion. An object is anything performing this function of a datum provoking some special activity of the occasion in question. Thus subject and object are relative terms. An occasion is a subject in respect to its special activity concerning an object; and anything is an object in respect to its provocation of some special activity within a subject. Such a mode of activity is termed a "prehension." Thus a prehension involves three factors. There is the occasion of experience within which the prehension is a detail of activity; there is the datum whose relevance provokes the origination of this prehension; this datum is the prehended object; there is the subjective form, which is the affective tone determining the effectiveness of that prehension in that occasion of experience. How the experience constitutes itself depends on its complex of subjective forms.

5. Individuality.—The individual immediacy of an occasion is the final unity of subjective form, which is the occasion as an absolute reality. This immediacy is its moment of sheer individuality, bounded on either side by essential relativity. The occasion arises from relevant objects, and perishes into the status of an object for other occasions. But it enjoys its decisive moment of absolute self-attainment as emotional unity. As used here the words "individual" and "atom" have the same meaning, that they apply to composite things with an absolute reality which their components lack. These words properly apply to an actual entity in its immediacy of self-attainment when it stands out as for itself alone, with its own affective self-enjoyment. The term "monad" also expresses this essential unity at the decisive moment, which stands between its birth and its perishing. The creativity of the world is the throbbing emotion of the past hurling itself into a new transcendent fact. It is the flying dart, of which Lucretius speaks, hurled beyond the bounds of the world.

6. Knowledge.—All knowledge is conscious discrimination of objects experienced. But this conscious discrimination, which is knowledge, is nothing more than an additional factor in the subjective form of the interplay of subject with object. This interplay is the stuff constituting those individual things which make up the sole reality of the Universe. These individual things are the individual occasions of experience, the actual entities.

But we do not so easily get rid of knowledge. After all, it is knowledge that philosophers seek. And all knowledge is derived from, and verified by, direct intuitive observation. I accept this axiom of empiricism as stated in this general form. The question then arises how the structure of experience outlined above is directly observed. In answering this challenge I remind myself of the old advice that the doctrines which best repay critical examination are those which for the longest period have remained unquestioned.

7. Sense-Perception.—The particular agelong group of doctrines which I have in mind is: (1) that all perception is by the mediation of our bodily sense-organs, such as eyes, palates, noses, ears, and the diffused bodily organization furnishing touches, aches, and other bodily sensations; (2) that all percepta are bare sensa, in patterned connections, given in the immediate present; (3) that our experience of a social world is an interpretative reaction wholly derivative from this perception; (4) that our emotional and purposive experience is a reflective reaction derived from the original perception, and inter-twined with the interpretative reaction and partly shaping it. Thus the two reactions are different aspects of one process, involving interpretative, emotional, and purposive factors. Of course, we are all aware that there are powerful schools of philosophy which explicitly reject this doctrine. Yet I cannot persuade myself that this rejection has been taken seriously by writers belonging to the schools in question. When the direct question as to things perceived arises, it seems to me that the answer is always returned in terms of sensa perceived.

8. Perceptive Functions.—In the examination of the sensationalist doctrine, the first question to be asked concerns the general definition of what we mean by those functions of experience which we term "perceptions." If we define them as those experiential functions which arise directly from the stimulation of the various bodily sense-organs, then argument ceases. The traditional doctrine then becomes a mere matter of definition of the use of the word "perception." Indeed, having regard to long-standing usage, I am inclined to agree that it may be advisable for philosophers to confine the word "perception" to this limited meaning. But the point on which I am insisting is that this meaning *is* limited, and that there is a wider meaning with which this limited use of the term "perception" has been tacitly identified.

9. Objects.—The process of experiencing is constituted by the reception of entities, whose being is antecedent to that process, into the complex fact which is that process itself. These antecedent entities, thus received as factors into the process of experiencing, are termed "objects" for that experiential occasion. Thus primarily the term "object" expresses the relation of the entity, thus denoted, to one or more occasions of experiencing. Two conditions must be fulfilled in order that an entity may function as an object in a process of experiencing: (1) the entity must be *antecedent,* and (2) the entity must be experienced in virtue of its antecedence; it must be *given.* Thus an object must be a thing received, and must not be either a *mode* of reception or a thing *generated* in that occasion. Thus the process of experiencing is constituted by the reception of objects into the unity of that complex occasion which is the process itself. The process creates itself, but it does not create the objects which it receives as factors in its own nature.

"Objects" for an occasion can also be termed the "data" for that occasion. The choice of terms entirely depends on the metaphor which you prefer. One word carries the literal meaning of "lying in the way of," and the other word carries the literal meaning of "being given to." But both words suffer from the defect of suggesting that an occasion of experiencing arises out of a passive situation which is a mere welter of many data.

10. Creativity.—The exact contrary is the case. The initial situation includes a factor of activity which is the reason for the origin of that occasion of experience. This factor of activity is what I have called "Creativity." The initial situation with its creativity can be termed the initial phase of the new occasion. It can equally well be termed the "actual world" relative to that occasion. It has a certain unity of its own, expressive of its capacity for providing the objects requisite for a new occasion, and also expressive of its conjoint activity whereby it is essentially the primary phase of a new occasion. It can thus be termed a "real potentiality." The "potentiality" refers to the passive capacity, the term "real" refers to the creative activity, where the Platonic definition of "real" in the *Sophist* is referred to. This basic situation, this actual world, this primary phase, this real potentiality—however you characterize it—as a whole is active with its inherent creativity, but in its details it provides the passive objects which derive their activity from the creativity of the whole. The creativity is the actualization of potentiality, and the process of actualization is an occasion of experiencing. Thus viewed in abstraction objects are passive, but viewed in conjunction they carry the creativity which drives the world. The process of creation is the form of unity of the Universe.

11. Perception.—In the preceding sections, the discovery of objects as factors in experience was explained. The discussion was phrased in terms of an ontology which goes beyond the immediate purpose, although the status of objects cannot be understood in the absence of some such ontology explaining their function in experience, that is to say, explaining why an occasion of experience by reason of its nature requires objects.

The objects are the factors in experience which function so as to express that that occasion originates by including a transcendent universe of other things. Thus it belongs to the essence of each occasion of experience that it is concerned with an otherness transcending itself. The occasion is one among others, and including the others which it is among. Consciousness is an emphasis upon a selection of these objects. Thus perception is consciousness analyzed in respect to those objects selected for this emphasis. Consciousness is the acme of emphasis.

It is evident that this definition of perception is wider than the narrow definition based upon sense-perception, sense, and the bodily sense-organs.

12. Nonsensuous Perception.—This wider definition of perception can be of no importance unless we can detect occasions of experience exhibiting modes of functioning which fall within its wider scope. If we discover such instances of nonsensuous perception, then the tacit identification of perception with sense-perception must be a fatal error barring the advance of systematic metaphysics.

Our first step must involve the clear recognition of the limitations inherent in the scope of sense-perception. This special mode of functioning essentially exhibits percepts as *here, now, immediate,* and *discrete.* Every impression of sensation is a distinct existence, declares Hume; and there can be no reasonable doubt of this doctrine. But even Hume clothes each impression with force and liveliness. It must be distinctly understood that no prehension, even of bare sensa, can be divested of its affective tone, that is to say, of its character of a "concern" in the Quaker sense. Concernedness is of the essence of perception.

Gaze at a patch of red. In itself as an object, and apart from other factors of concern, this patch of red, as the mere object of that present act of perception, is silent as to the past or the future. How it originates, how it will vanish, whether indeed there was a past, and whether there will be a future, are not disclosed by its own nature. No material for the interpretation of sensa is provided by the sensa themselves, as they stand starkly, barely, present and immediate. We *do* interpret them; but no thanks for the feat is due to them. The epistemologies of the last two hundred years are employed in the tacit introduction of alien considerations by the uncritical use of current forms of speech. A copious use of simple literary forms can thus provide a philosophy delightful to read, easy to understand, and entirely fallacious. Yet the usages of language do prove that our habitual interpretations of these barren sensa are in the main satisfying to common sense, though in particular instances liable to error. But the evidence on which these interpretations are based is entirely drawn from the vast background and foreground of nonsensuous perception with which sense-perception is fused, and without which it can never be. We can discern no clean-cut sense-perception wholly concerned with present fact.

In human experience, the most compelling example of nonsensuous perception is our knowledge of our own immediate past. I am not referring to our memories of a day past, or of an hour past, or of a minute past. Such memories are blurred and confused by the intervening occasions of our personal existence. But our immediate past is constituted by that occasion, or by that group of fused occasions, which enters into experience devoid of any perceptible medium intervening between it and the present immediate fact. Roughly speaking, it is that portion of our past lying between a tenth of a second and half a second ago. It is gone, and yet it is here. It is our indubitable self, the foundation of our present existence. Yet the present occasion while claiming self-identity, while sharing the very nature of the bygone occasion in all its living activities, nevertheless is engaged in modifying it, in adjusting it to *other* influences, in completing it with *other* values, in deflecting it to *other* purposes. The present moment is constituted by the influx of the *other* into that self-identity which is the continued life of the immediate past within the immediacy of the present.

13. Illustration.—Consider a reasonably rapid speaker enunciating the proper name "United States." There are four syllables here. When the third syllable is reached, probably the first is in the immediate past; and certainly during the word "States" the first syllable of the phrase lies beyond the immediacy of the present. Consider the speaker's own occasions of existence. Each occasion achieves for him the immediate sense-presentation of sounds, the earlier syllables in the earlier occasions, the word "States" in the final occasion. As mere sensuous perception, Hume is right in saying that the sound "United" as a mere sensum has nothing in its nature referent to the sound "States," yet the speaker is carried from "United" to "States," and the two conjointly live in the present, by the energizing of the past occasion as it claims its self-identical existence as a living issue in the present. The immediate past as surviving to be again lived through in the present is the palmary instance of nonsensuous perception.

The Humean explanation, involving the "association of ideas," has its importance for this topic. But it is not to the point for this example. The speaker, a citizen of the United States and therefore dominated by an immense familiarity with that phrase, may in fact have been enunciating the phrase "United Fruit Company"—a corporation which, for all its importance, he may not have heard of till half a minute earlier. In his experience the relation of the later to the earlier parts of this phrase is entirely the same as that described above for the phrase "United States." In this latter example it is to be noted that while association would have led him to "States," the fact of the energizing of the immediate past compelled him to conjoin "Fruit" in the immediacy of the present. He uttered the word "United" with the nonsensuous anticipation of an immediate future with the sensum "Fruit," and he then uttered the word "Fruit" with the nonsensuous perception of the immediate past with the sensum "United." But, unfamiliar as he was with the United Fruit Company, he had no association connecting the various words in the phrase "United Fruit Company"; while, patriot as he was, the orator had the strongest association connecting the words "United" and "States." Perhaps, indeed, he was the founder of the

Company, and also invented the name. He then uttered the mere sounds "United Fruit Company" for the first time in the history of the English language. There could not have been the vestige of an association to help him along. The final occasion of his experience which drove his body to the utterance of the sound "Company" is only explicable by his concern with the earlier occasions with their subjective forms of intention to procure the utterance of the complete phrase. Also, insofar as there was consciousness, there was direct observation of the past with its intention finding its completion in the present fact. This is an instance of direct intuitive observation which is incapable of reduction to the sensationalist formula. Such observations have not the clear sharp-cut precision of sense-perception. But surely there can be no doubt about them. For instance, if the speaker had been interrupted after the words "United Fruit," he might have resumed his speech with the words "I meant to add the word *Company.*" Thus during the interruption, the past was energizing in his experience as carrying in itself an unfulfilled intention.

14. Conformation of Feeling.—Another point emerges in this explanation, namely, the doctrine of the continuity of nature. This doctrine balances and limits the doctrine of the absolute individuality of each occasion of experience. There is a continuity between the subjective form of the immediate past occasion and the subjective form of its primary prehension in the origination of the new occasion. In the process of synthesis of the many basic prehensions modifications enter. But the subjective forms of the immediate past are continuous with those of the present. I will term this doctrine of continuity, the Doctrine of Conformation of Feeling.

Suppose that for some period of time some circumstance of his life has aroused anger in a man. How does he now know that a quarter of a second ago he was angry? Of course, he remembers it; we all know that. But I am inquiring about this very curious fact of memory, and have chosen an overwhelmingly vivid instance. The mere word "memory" explains nothing. The first phase in the immediacy of the new occasion is that of the conformation of feelings. The feeling as enjoyed by the past occasion is present in the new occasion as datum felt, with a subjective form conformal to that of the datum. Thus if A be the past occasion, D the datum felt by A with subjective form describable as A angry, then this feeling—namely, A feeling D with subjective form of anger—is initially felt by the new occasion B with the same subjective form of anger. The anger is continuous throughout the successive occasions of experience. This continuity of subjective form is the initial sympathy of B for A. It is the primary ground for the continuity of nature. Insofar as that feeling has fallen within the illumination of consciousness, he enjoys a nonsensuous perception of the past emotion. He enjoys this emotion both objectively, as belonging to the past, and also formally as continued in the present. This continuation is the continuity of nature. I have labored this point, because traditional doctrines involve its denial.

Thus nonsensuous perception is one aspect of the continuity of nature.

15. Hume's Doctrine of Custom.—Hume appeals to a doctrine of force and liveliness as an essential factor in an impression of sensation. This doctrine is nothing but a special case of the doctrine of subjective forms. Again, he holds that the force and liveliness of one occasion of experience enter into the character of succeeding occasions. The whole doctrine of "custom" depends on this assumption. If the occasions be entirely separate, as Hume contends, this transition of character is without any basis in the nature of things. What Hume, in his appeal to memory, is really doing is to appeal to an observed immanence of the past in the future, involving a continuity of subjective form.

With this addition, every argument of Part III of Hume's *Treatise* can be accepted. But the conclusion follows that there is an observed relation of causation between such occasions. The general character of this observed relation explains at once memory and personal identity. They are all different aspects of the doctrine of the immanence of occasions of experience. The additional conclusion can also be derived, that insofar as we apply notions of causation to the understanding of events in nature, we must conceive these events under the general notions which apply to occasions of experience. For we can only understand causation in terms of our observations of these occasions. This appeal to Hume has the sole purpose of illustrating the common-sense obviousness of the present thesis.

16. The Flux of Energy.—An occasion of experience which includes a human mentality is an extreme instance, at one end of the scale, of those happenings which constitute nature. As yet this discussion has fixed attention upon this extreme. But any doctrine which refuses to place human experience outside nature must find in description of human experience factors which also enter into the descriptions of less specialized natural occurrences. If there be no such factors, then the doctrine of human experience as a fact within nature is mere bluff, founded upon vague phrases whose sole merit is a comforting familiarity. We should either admit dualism, at least as a provisional doctrine, or we should point out the identical elements connecting human experience with physical science.

The science of physics conceives a natural occasion as a locus of energy. Whatever else that occasion may be, it is an individual fact harboring that energy. The words electron, proton, photon, wave motion, velocity, hard and soft radiation, chemical elements, matter, empty space, temperature, degradation of energy, all point to the fact that physical science recognizes qualitative differences between occasions in respect to the way in which each occasion entertains its energy.

These differences are entirely constituted by the flux of energy, that is to say, by the way in which the occasions in question have inherited their energy from the past of nature, and in which they are about to transmit their energy to the future. The discussion of the Poynting Flux of Energy is one of the most fascinating chapters of Electrodynamics. Forty-seven years ago, when a young graduate student, I first heard of it in a lecture delivered by Sir J. J. Thomson. It was then a new discovery recently published by Poynting. But its father was the great Clerk Maxwell who had expounded all the requisite principles. The sole conclusion with which we are concerned is that energy has recognizable paths through time and space. Energy passes from particular occasion to particular occasion. At each point there is a flux, with a quantitative flow, and a definite direction.

This is a conception of physical nature in terms of continuity. In fact, the concept of continuity was dominant in Clerk Maxwell's thought. But the alternative concept of distinguishable individualism has again emerged into importance in the more recent physics. Electrons and protons and photons are unit charges of electricity; also there are the quanta of the flux of energy. These contrasted aspects of nature, continuity and atomicity, have a long history in European thought, reaching back to the origin of science among the Greeks. The more probable conclusion is that neither can be dispensed with, and that we are only witnessing that modern phase of the contrast which is relevant to the present stage of science.

17. Mind and Nature Compared.—The doctrine of human experience which I have outlined above, also for its own purposes preserves a doctrine of distinguishable individualities which are the separate occasions of experience, and a doctrine of continuity expressed by the identity of subjective form inherited conformally from one occasion to the other. The physical flux corresponds to the conformal inheritance at the base of each occasion of experience. This inheritance, in spite of its continuity of subjective form, is nevertheless an inheritance from definite individual occasions. Thus, if the analogy is to hold, in the account of the general system of relations binding the past to the present, we should expect a doctrine of quanta, where the individualities of the occasions are relevant, and a doctrine of continuity where the conformal transference of subjective form is the dominating fact.

The notion of physical energy, which is at the base of physics, must then be conceived as an abstraction from the complex energy, emotional and purposeful, inherent in the subjective form of the final synthesis in which each occasion completes itself. It is the total vigor of each activity of experience. The mere phrase that "physical science is an abstraction," is a confession of philosophic failure. It is the business of rational thought to describe the more concrete fact from which that abstraction is derivable.

18. Personality.—In our account of human experience we have attenuated human personality into a genetic relation between occasions of human experience. Yet personal unity is an inescapable fact. The Platonic and Christian doctrines of the Soul, the Epicurean doctrine of a Concilium of subtle atoms, the Cartesian doctrine of Thinking Substance, the Humanitarian doctrine of the Rights of Man, the general Common Sense of civilized mankind—these doctrines between them dominate the whole span of Western thought. Evidently there is a fact to be accounted for. Any philosophy must provide some doctrine of personal identity. In some sense there is a unity in the life of each man, from birth to death. The two modem philosophers who most consistently reject the notion of a self-identical Soul-Substance are Hume and William James. But the problem remains for them, as it does for the philosophy of organism, to provide an adequate account of this undoubted personal unity, maintaining itself amid the welter of circumstance.

19. Plato's Receptacle.—In mathematical studies, where there is a problem to be solved, it is a sound method to generalize, so as to divest the problem of details irrelevant to the solution. Let us therefore give a general description of this personal unity, divesting it of minor details

of humanity. For this purpose it is impossible to improve upon a passage from one of Plato's Dialogues. I summarize it with the insertion
of such terms as "personal unity," "events," "experience," and "personal identity," for two or three of its own phrases. "In addition to the
notions of the welter of events and of the forms which they illustrate,
we require a third term, personal unity. It is a perplexed and obscure
concept. We must conceive it the receptacle, the foster-mother as I
might say, of the becoming of our occasions of experience. This personal identity is the thing which receives all occasions of the man's
existence. It is there as a natural matrix for all transitions of life, and is
changed and variously figured by the things that enter it; so that it
differs in its character at different times. Since it receives all manner
of experiences into its own unity, it must itself be bare of all forms. We
shall not be far wrong if we describe it as invisible, formless, and all-
receptive. It is a locus which persists, and provides an emplacement for
all the occasions of experience. That which happens in it is conditioned
by the compulsion of its own past, and by the persuasion of its immanent ideals."

You will have recognized that in this description I have been adapt-
ing from Plato's *Timaeus,*[1] with the slightest of changes. But this is not
Plato's description of the Soul. It is his doctrine of the Receptacle or
Locus whose sole function is the imposition of a unity upon the events
of Nature. These events are together by reason of their community of
locus, and they obtain their actuality by reason of emplacement within
this community.

20. Immanence.—This is at once the doctrine of the unity of nature, and of the unity of each human life. The conclusion follows that
our consciousness of the self-identity pervading our life-thread of occasions is nothing other than knowledge of a special strand of unity
within the general unity of nature. It is a locus within the whole,
marked out by its own peculiarities, but otherwise exhibiting the general principle which guides the constitution of the whole. This general
principle is the object-to-subject structure of experience. It can be otherwise stated as the vector-structure of nature. Or otherwise, it can be
conceived as the doctrine of the immanence of the past energizing in
the present.

This doctrine of immanence is practically that doctrine adumbrated

---

[1] I have used A. E. Taylor's translation, with compression and changes of phrase.

by the Hellenistic Christian theologians of Egypt. But they applied the doctrine only to the relation of God to the World, and not to all actualities.

21. Space and Time.—The notion of Space-Time represents a compromise between Plato's basic Receptacle, imposing no forms, and the Actual World imposing its own variety of forms. This imposition of forms is subject to the perspective elimination required by incompatibilities of affective tone. Geometry is the doctrine of loci of intermediaries imposing perspective in the process of inheritance. In geometry, this doctrine is restricted to its barest generalities of coordination prevailing for this epoch of the Universe. These generalities solely concern the complex of serial relations persistently illustrated in the connection of events.

Our perception of this geometrical order of the Universe brings with it the denial of the restriction of inheritance to mere personal order. For personal order means one-dimensional serial order. And space is many-dimensional. Spatiality involves separation by reason of the diversity of intermediate occasions, and also it involves connection by reason of the immanence involved in the derivation of present from past. There is thus an analogy between the transference of energy from particular occasion to particular occasion in physical nature and the transference of affective tone, with its emotional energy, from one occasion to another in any human personality. The object-to-subject structure of human experience is reproduced in physical nature by this vector relation of particular to particular. It was the defect of the Greek analysis of generation that it conceived it in terms of the bare incoming of novel abstract form. This ancient analysis failed to grasp the real operation of the antecedent particulars imposing themselves on the novel particular in process of creation. Thus the geometry exemplified in fact was disjointed from their account of the generation of fact.

22. The Human Body.—But this analogy of physical nature to human experience is limited by the fact of the linear seriality of human occasions within any one personality, and of the many-dimensioned seriality of the occasions in physical Space-Time.

In order to prove that this discrepancy is only superficial, it now remains for discussion whether the human experience of direct inheritance provides any analogy to this many-dimensional character of space. If human occasions of experience essentially inherit in one-dimensional personal order, there is a gap between human occasions and the physical occasions of nature.

The peculiar status of the human body at once presents itself as negating this notion of strict personal order for human inheritance. Our dominant inheritance from our immediately past occasion is broken into by innumerable inheritances through other avenues. Sensitive nerves, the functionings of our viscera, disturbances in the composition of our blood, break in upon the dominant line of inheritance. In this way, emotions, hopes, fears, inhibitions, sense-perceptions arise, which physiologists confidently ascribe to the bodily functionings. So intimately obvious is this bodily inheritance that common speech does not discriminate the human body from the human person. Soul and body are fused together. Also this common identification has survived the scientific investigation of physiologists who are apt to see more body than soul in human beings.

But the human body is indubitably a complex of occasions which are part of spatial nature. It is a set of occasions miraculously coordinated so as to pour its inheritance into various regions within the brain. There is thus every reason to believe that our sense of unity with the body has the same origin as our sense of unity with our immediate past of personal experience. It is another case of nonsensuous perception, only now devoid of the strict personal order.

But physiologists and physicists are equally agreed that the body inherits physical conditions from the physical environment according to the physical laws. There is thus a general continuity between human experience and physical occasions. The elaboration of such a continuity is one most obvious task for philosophy.

23. Dualism.—This discussion has begged attention to a complex argument. The topic is a large one, and the restrictions of time have made it impossible for the argument to rest upon the way. I will conclude by drawing attention to a general question which is relevant.

Is this discussion to be looked upon as another example of *The Revolt against Dualism?* We have all read with high appreciation Professor Lovejoy's brilliant book in criticism of this revolt. Now, superficially, the position which I have here put forward is certainly an instance of the revolt which he criticizes. But in another sense, I have endeavored to put forward a defense of dualism, differently interpreted. Plato, Descartes, Locke, prepared the way for Hume; and Kant followed upon Hume. The point of this address is to show an alternative line of thought which evades Hume's deduction from philosophical tradition, and at the same time preserves the general trend of thought received from his three great predecessors. The dualism in the later Platonic dialogues between the Platonic "souls" and the Platonic "physical" nature, the dualism between the Cartesian "thinking substances" and the Cartesian "extended substances," the dualism between the Lockian "human understanding" and the Lockian "external things" described for him by Galileo and Newton—all these kindred dualisms are here found within each occasion of actuality. Each occasion has its physical inheritance and its mental reaction which drives it on to its self-completion. The world is not merely physical, nor is it merely mental. Nor is it merely *one* with many subordinate phases. Nor is it merely a complete fact, in its essence static with the illusion of change. Wherever a vicious dualism appears, it is by reason of mistaking an abstraction for a final concrete fact.

The universe is dual because, in the fullest sense, it is both transient and eternal. The universe is dual because each final actuality is both physical and mental. The universe is dual because each actuality requires abstract character. The universe is dual because each occasion unites its formal immediacy with objective otherness. The universe is *many* because it is wholly and completely to be analyzed into many final actualities—or, in Cartesian language, into many *res verae*. The Universe is *one,* because of the universal immanence. There is thus a dualism in this contrast between the unity and multiplicity. Throughout the universe there reigns the union of opposites which is the ground of dualism.

The Grouping of Occasions

Section I.—The Grouping of Occasions is the outcome of some common function performed by those occasions in the percipient experience. The grouped occasions then acquire a unity; they become, for the experience of the percipient, one thing which is complex by reason of its divisibility into many occasions, or into many subordinate groups of occasions. The subordinate groups are then complex unities, each belonging to the same metaphysical category of existence as the total group. This characteristic, namely divisibility into groups of analogous types of being, is the general notion of extensiveness. The peculiar relationships (if any) diffused systematically between the extensive groups of an epoch constitute the system of geometry prevalent in that epoch.

The general common function exhibited by any group of actual occasions is that of mutual immanence. In Platonic language, this is the function of belonging to a common Receptacle. If the group be considered merely in respect to this basic property of mutual immanence, however otherwise lacking in common relevance, then—conceived as exemplifying this general connectedness—the group is termed a Nexus.

Thus the term Nexus does not presuppose any special type of order, nor does it presuppose any order at all pervading its members other than the general metaphysical obligation of mutual immanence. But in fact the teleology of the Universe, with its aim at intensity and variety, produces epochs with various types of order dominating subordinate nexūs interwoven with each other. A nexus can spread itself both spatially and temporally. In other words, it can include sets of occasions which are contemporary with each other, and it can include sets which are relatively past and future. If the nexus be purely spatial, then it will include no pair of occasions such that one of the pair is antecedent to the other. The mutual immanence between the occasions of the nexus will then be of the indirect type proper to contemporary occasions. It is for this reason that the notion of externality dominates our intuition of space. If the nexus be purely temporal, then it will include no pair of contemporary occasions. It is to be a mere thread of temporal transition from occasion to occasion. The idea of temporal transition can never be wholly disengaged from that of "causation." This latter notion is merely a special way of considering direct immanence of the past in its future.

Section II.—The notion of the contiguity of occasions is important. Two occasions, which are not contemporary, are contiguous in time when there is no occasion which is antecedent to one of them and subsequent to the other. A purely temporal nexus of occasions is continuous when, with the exception of the earliest and the latest occasions, each occasion is contiguous with an earlier occasion and a later occasion. The nexus will then form an unbroken thread in temporal or serial order. The first and the last occasions of the thread will, of course, only enjoy a one-sided contiguity with the thread.

Spatial contiguity is more difficult to define. It requires a reference to the temporal dimensions. It can be defined by the aid of the doctrine that no two contemporary occasions are derived from a past wholly in common. Thus if A and B be two contemporary occasions, the past of A includes some occasions not belonging to the past of B, and that of B includes occasions not belonging to the past of A. Then A and B are contiguous when there is no occasion (i) contemporary with both A and B, and (ii) such that its past includes all occasions, each belonging both to the past of A and the past of B. The particular form of this definition is of no great importance. But the principle that the interrelations of the present are derived from a reference to the past is fundamental. It gives the reason why the contemporary world is experienced as a display of lifeless substances passively illustrating imposed characters.

Anyhow contiguity, temporal and spatial, is definable in terms of the doctrine of immanence. By the aid of the notion of contiguity, the notion of a region can be defined as denoting a nexus in which certain conditions of contiguity are preserved. The logical details of such a definition are irrelevant to this discussion.

So far we have been considering various species of nexus, whose sole principle of unity is derived from the bare fact of mutual immanence. We will term this genus of nexus, the genus whose species are discriminated by differences of bare extensive patterns. More briefly, it will be termed the *Genus of Patterned Nexūs*. Every nexus belongs to some species of this genus, if we abstract from the qualitative factors which are interwoven in its patterns.

Section III.—We now pass on to the general notion of a *Society.* This notion introduces the general consideration of types of order, and the genetic propagation of order. The definition depends upon taking into account factors which are omitted in the analysis of the Genus of Patterned Nexūs.

A Society is a nexus which illustrates or "shares in" some type of "Social Order." "Social Order" can be defined[1] as follows:—"A nexus enjoys 'social order' when (i) there is a common element of form illustrated in the definiteness of each of its included actual entities, and (ii) this common element of form arises in each member of the nexus by reason of the conditions imposed upon it by its prehensions of some other members of the nexus, and (iii) these prehensions impose that condition of reproduction by reason of their inclusion of positive feelings involving[2] that common form. Such a nexus is called a 'society,' and the common form is the 'defining characteristic' of that society."

Another rendering[3] of the same definition is as follows:—"The point of a 'society' as the term is here used, is that it is self-sustaining; in other words, that it is its own reason. Thus a society is more than a set of [actual] entities to which the same class-name applies: that is to say, it involves more than a merely mathematical conception of 'order.' To constitute a society, the class-name has got to apply to each member, by reason of genetic derivation from other members of that same society. The members of the society are alike because, by reason of their common character, they impose on other members of the society the conditions which lead to that likeness."

It is evident from this description of the notion of a 'Society,' as here employed, that a set of mutually contemporary occasions cannot form a complete society. For the genetic condition cannot be satisfied by such a set of contemporaries. Of course a set of contemporaries may belong to a society. But the society, as such, must involve antecedents and subsequents. In other words, a society must exhibit the peculiar quality of endurance. The real actual things that endure are all societies. They are not actual occasions. It is the mistake that has thwarted

---

[1] Cf. *Process and Reality,* Part I, Ch. III, Sect. II.

[2] In the original, *Process and Reality,* "of that" in place of "involving."

[3] Cf. *Process and Reality,* Part II, Ch. III, Sect. II.

European metaphysics from the time of the Greeks, namely, to confuse societies with the completely real things which are the actual occasions. A society has an essential character, whereby it is the society that it is, and it has also accidental qualities which vary as circumstances alter. Thus a society, as a complete existence and as retaining the same metaphysical status, enjoys a history of expressing its changing reactions to changing circumstances.[4] But an actual occasion has no such history. It never changes. It only becomes and perishes. Its perishing is its assumption of a new metaphysical function in the creative advance of the universe.

The self-identity of a society is founded upon the self-identity of its defining characteristic, and upon the mutual immanence of its occasions. But there is no definite nexus which is the nexus underlying that society, except when the society belongs wholly to the past. For the realized nexus which underlies the society is always adding to itself, with the creative advance into the future. For example, the man adds another day to his life, and the earth adds another millennium to the period of its existence. But until the death of the man and the destruction of the earth, there is no determinate nexus which in an unqualified sense is either the man or the earth.

Section IV.—Though there is no one nexus which can claim to be the society, so long as that society is in existence, there is a succession of nexūs each of which is the whole realized society up to that stage of its existence. The extensive patterns of the various nexūs of the succession for a given society may be different. In such a case the extensive patterns, so far as they differ, cannot be any element in the defining characteristic of the society. But the extensive patterns of the various nexūs of the succession may be identical, or at least they may have in common some feature of their pattern. In this case the common pattern, or the common feature, can be one element in the defining characteristic of the society in question.

The simplest example of a society in which the successive nexūs of its progressive realization have a common extensive pattern is when each such nexus is purely temporal and continuous. The society, in each stage of realization, then consists of a set of contiguous occasions in serial order. A man, defined as an enduring percipient, is such a

---

[4] This notion of "society" has analogies to Descartes' notion of "substance"; cf. Descartes' *Principles of Philosophy,* Part I, *Principles* LI–LVII.

society. This definition of a man is exactly what Descartes means by a thinking substance. It will be remembered that in his *Principles of Philosophy* [Part 1, *Principle* XXI; also *Meditation* III] Descartes states that endurance is nothing else than successive recreation by God. Thus the Cartesian conception of the human soul and that here put forward differ only in the function assigned to God. Both conceptions involve a succession of occasions, each with its measure of immediate completeness.

Societies of the general type, that their realized nexūs are purely temporal and continuous, will be termed "personal." Any society of this type may be termed a "person." Thus, as defined above, a man is a person.

But a man is more than a serial succession of occasions of experience. Such a definition may satisfy philosophers—Descartes, for example. It is not the ordinary meaning of the term "man." There are animal bodies as well as animal minds; and in our experience such minds always occur incorporated. Now an animal body is a society involving a vast number of occasions, spatially and temporally coordinated. It follows that a "man" in the full sense of ordinary usage, is not a "person" as here defined. He has the unity of a wider society, in which the social coordination is a dominant factor in the behaviors of the various parts.

Also, when we survey the living world, animal and vegetable, there are bodies of all types. Each living body is a society, which is not personal. But most of the animals, including all the vertebrates, seem to have their social system dominated by a subordinate society which is "personal." This subordinate society is of the same type as "man," according to the personal definition given above, though of course the mental poles in the occasions of the dominant personal society do not rise to the height of human mentality. Thus in one sense a dog is a "person," and in another sense he is a non-personal society. But the lower forms of animal life, and all vegetation, seem to lack the dominance of any included personal society. A tree is a democracy. Thus living bodies are not to be identified with living bodies under personal dominance. There is no necessary connection between "life" and "personality." A "personal" society need not be "living," in the general sense of the term; and a "living" society need not be "personal."

Section V.—The Universe achieves its values by reason of its coordination into societies of societies, and into societies of societies of societies. Thus an army is a society of regiments and regiments are societies of men, and men are societies of cells, and of blood, and of bones, together with the dominant society of personal human experience, and cells are societies of smaller physical entities such as protons, and so on and so on. Also all of these societies presuppose the circumambient space of social physical activity.

It is evident that the previous definition of "society" has been phrased so as to suggest an over-simplified concept of the meaning. For the notion of a defining characteristic must be construed to include the notion of the coordination of societies. Thus there are societies at different levels. For instance, the army is a society at a level different from that of a regiment, and similarly for a regiment and a man. Nature is a complex of enduring objects, functioning as subordinate elements in a larger spatial-physical society. This larger society is for us the natural universe. There is however no reason to identify it with the boundless totality of actual things.

Also each of these enduring objects, such as tables, animal bodies, and stars, is itself a subordinate universe including subordinate enduring objects. The only strictly personal society of which we have direct discriminative intuition is the society of our own personal experiences. We also have a direct, though vaguer, intuition of our derivation of experience from the antecedent functioning of our bodies, and a still vaguer intuition of our bodily derivation from external nature.

Nature suggests for our observation gaps, and then as it were withdraws them upon challenge. For example, ordinary physical bodies suggest solidity. But solids turn to liquids, and liquids to gases. And from the gas the solid can again be recovered. Also the most solid of solids is for certain purposes a viscous fluid. Again impenetrability is a difficult notion. Salt dissolves in water, and can be recovered from it. Gases interfuse in liquids. Molecules arise from a patterned interfusion of atoms. Food interfuses with the body, and produces an immediate sense of diffused bodily vigor. This is especially the case with liquid stimulants. Thus the direct immediate experience of impenetrability loses upon challenge its sharp-cut status.

Section VI.—Another gap is that between lifeless bodies and living bodies. Yet the living bodies can be pursued down to the edge of lifelessness. Also the functionings of inorganic matter remain intact amid the functionings of living matter. It seems that, in bodies that are obviously living, a coordination has been achieved that raises into prominence some functions inherent in the ultimate occasions. For lifeless matter these functionings thwart each other, and average out so as to produce a negligible total effect. In the case of living bodies the coordination intervenes, and the average effect of these intimate functionings has to be taken into account.

Those activities in the self-formation of actual occasions which, if coordinated, yield living societies are the intermediate mental functionings transforming the initial phase of reception into the final phase of anticipation. In so far as the mental spontaneities of occasion do not thwart each other, but are directed to a common objective amid varying circumstances, there is life. The essence of life is the teleological introduction of novelty, with some conformation of objectives. Thus novelty of circumstance is met with novelty of functioning adapted to steadiness of purpose.

Life may characterize a set of occasions diffused throughout a society, though not necessarily including all, or even a majority of, the occasions of that society. The common element of purpose which characterizes these various occasions must be reckoned as one element of the determining characteristic of the society. It is evident that according to this definition no single occasion can be called living. Life is the coordination of the mental spontaneities throughout the occasions of a society.

But apart from life a high grade of mentality in individual occasions seems to be impossible. A personal society, itself living and dominantly influencing a living society wider than itself, is the only type of organization which provides occasions of high-grade mentality. Thus in a man, the living body is permeated by living societies of low-grade occasions so far as mentality is concerned. But the whole is coordinated so as to support a personal living society of high-grade occasions. This personal society is the man defined as a person. It is the soul of which Plato spoke.

How far this soul finds a support for its existence beyond the body is:—another question. The everlasting nature of God, which in a sense is non-temporal and in another sense is temporal, may establish with the soul a peculiarly intense relationship of mutual immanence. Thus in some important sense the existence of the soul may be freed from its complete dependence upon the bodily organization.

But it is to be noticed that the personality of an animal organism may be more or less. It is not a mere question of having a soul or of not having a soul. The question is, How much, if any? Any tendency to a high-grade multiple personality would be self-destructive by the antagonism of divergent aims. In other words, such multiple personality is destructive of the very essence of life, which is conformation of purpose.

GEORGE HERBERT MEAD

George Herbert Mead was born on February 27, 1863, in South Hadley, Massachusetts, the son of a Congregational minister. In 1870 the family migrated to Oberlin, Ohio, where young George remained until he graduated from Oberlin College in 1883. Before continuing his formal education Mead spent the following four years teaching and surveying in various parts of the Northwest. Then for a year beginning in 1887 he pursued graduate studies in philosophy at Harvard under James and Royce. In the fall of 1888 he began studies of both philosophy and psychology, first in Leipzig and then in Berlin, which continued until he was appointed an instructor in the Department of Philosophy at the University of Michigan in 1891. There he met John Dewey, who was to become his dearest friend throughout the remainder of his life. In 1893, through the influence of J. H. Tufts, then Chairman of the Department of Philosophy, both Mead and Dewey were enticed to the budding University of Chicago. Though Dewey left there for Columbia University in 1904, Mead remained as chairman of the department, a position he held until his death.

While he published only a few articles of philosophical interest during his lifetime, Mead was extremely influential through his teaching. He delivered brilliant courses on Leibniz, Aristotle, Hume, Kant, and Hegel, and, more significantly, on aspects of his own developing position. His devoted students vowed to see these lectures in print and, after his death, carefully collated student and stenographic notes from two of his most famous courses were published as *Movements of Thought in the Nineteenth Century* and *Mind, Self, and Society*. The appointment of Robert M. Hutchins as President of the University of Chicago in 1930 and the policies he pursued alienated many of the members of the Philosophy Department and clouded the last days of Mead's life. Due to these circumstances, his plan to rewrite his Carus Lectures, delivered in 1930, was never carried out, though they were subsequently published in the rough form in which they were delivered as *The Philosophy of the Present*.

Mead died on April 26, 1931. Since his death respect for his work has grown steadily. He was a highly original thinker and a daring speculator, as the Carus Lectures reveal, but his especial significance in the movement of process philosophy lies no doubt in his careful elaboration of a theory of the self constructed upon the basic categories of the new point of view.

MAJOR PHILOSOPHICAL WORKS BY MEAD

1932 *The Philosophy of the Present.* (Carus Lectures.) Edited by Arthur E. Murphy. LaSalle, Ill.: Open Court. (Contains also two previously published articles, "The Objective Reality of Perspectives" and "The Genesis of the Self and Social Control.")

1934 *Mind, Self, and Society.* Edited by Charles W. Morris. Chicago: University of Chicago Press.

1936 *Movements of Thought in the Nineteenth Century.* Edited by Merritt H. Moore. Chicago: The University of Chicago Press.

1938 *The Philosophy of the Act.* Edited by Charles W. Morris, John M. Brewster, Albert M. Dunham, and David L. Miller. Chicago: The University of Chicago Press. (A collection of Mead's unpublished papers, some of which are very important.)

1964 *Selected Writings of George Herbert Mead.* Edited by Andrew J. Reck Indianapolis: The Liberal Arts Press. (Twenty-five articles published during Mead's lifetime.)

1964 "Two Unpublished Papers," *The Review of Metaphysics,* June, pp. 515–556. Edited and introduced by David L. Miller.

RECOMMENDED WORKS ON MEAD

Natanson, Maurice. *The Social Dynamics of George H. Mead.* Washington: Public Affairs Press, 1956.

Pfuetze, Paul E. *The Social Self.* New York: Bookman Associates, 1954.

Reck, Andrew J. "The Philosophy of George Herbert Mead," *Tulane Studies in Philosophy,* Vol. XII, 1963, pp. 5–51.

The Present as the Locus of Reality

The subject of this lecture is found in the proposition that reality exists in a present. The present of course implies a past and a future, and to these both we deny existence. Whitehead's suggestion that, as specious presents vary in temporal spread, one present can be conceived which could take in the whole of temporal reality, would seemingly leave to us passage but would eliminate the past and the future. Whatever else it would be it would not be a present, for that out of which it had passed would not have ceased to exist, and that which is to exist would already be in that inclusive present. Whether this would still leave the character of passage might be doubted, but in any case the essential nature of the present and of existence would have disappeared. For that which marks a present is its becoming and its disappearing. While the flash of the meteor is passing in our own specious presents it is all there if only for a fraction of a minute. To extend this fraction of a minute into the whole process of which it is a fragment, giving to it the same solidarity of existence which the flash possesses in experience, would be to wipe out its nature as an event. Such a conspectus of existence would not be an eternal present, for it would not be a present at all. Nor would it be an existence. For a Parmenidean reality does not exist. Existence involves non-existence; it does take place. The world is a world of events.

There is little purpose or profit in setting up antinomies and overthrowing the one by the other, or in relegating permanence to a subsistent, timeless world while the event, in which there is nothing but passage, is made the substantial element in existent things. The permanent character that we are interested in is one that abides in existence, and over against which change exists as well. There is, that is, the past which is expressed in irrevocability, though there has never been present in experience a past which has not changed with the passing generations. The pasts that we are involved in are both irrevocable and revocable. It is idle, at least for the purposes of experience, to have recourse to a "real" past within which we are making constant discoveries, for that past must be set over against a present within which the emergent appears, and the past, which must then be looked at from the standpoint of the emergent, becomes a different past. The emergent, when it appears, is always found to follow from the past, but before it appears it does not, by definition, follow from the past. It is idle to insist upon universal or eternal characters by which past events may be identified irrespective of any emergent, for these are either beyond our formulation or they become so empty that they serve no purpose in identification. The import of the infinite in ancient and modern mathematical thought illustrates this impotence.

The possibility remains of pushing the whole of real reality into a world of events in a Minkowski space-time that transcends our frames of reference, and the characters of events into a world of subsistent entities. How far such a conception of reality can be logically thought out I will not undertake to discuss. What seems to me of interest is the import which such a concept as that of irrevocability has in experience.

I will not spend time or rhetoric in presenting the moving picture of the histories that have succeeded each other from the myths of primitive ages up to Eddington's or Jeans' account of "The Universe about Us." It is only of interest to note that the rapidity with which these pasts succeed each other has steadily increased with the increase in critical exactitude in the study of the past. There is an entire absence of finality in such presentations. It is of course the implication of our research method that the historian in any field of science will be able to reconstruct what has been, as an authenticated account of the past. Yet we look forward with vivid interest to the reconstruction, in the world that will be, of the world that has been, for we realize that the world that will be cannot differ from the world that is without rewriting the past to which we now look back.

And yet the character of irrevocability is never lost. That which has happened is gone beyond recall and, whatever it was, its slipping into the past seems to take it beyond the influence of emergent events in our own conduct or in nature. It is the "what it was" that changes, and this seemingly empty title of irrevocability attaches to it whatever it may come to be. The importance of its being irrevocable attaches to the "what it was," and the "what it was" is what is not irrevocable. There is a finality that goes with the passing of every event. To every account of that event this finality is added, but the whole import of this finality belongs to the same world in experience to which this account belongs.

Now over against this evident incidence of finality to a present stands a customary assumption that the past that determines us is *there*. The truth is that the past is there, in its certainty or probability, in the same sense that the setting of our problems is there. I am proceeding upon the assumption that cognition, and thought as a part of the cognitive process, is reconstructive, because reconstruction is essential to the conduct of an intelligent being in the universe. This is but part of the more general proposition that changes are going on in the universe, and that as a consequence of these changes the universe is becoming a different universe. Intelligence is but one aspect of this change. It is a change that is part of an ongoing living process that tends to maintain itself. What is peculiar to intelligence is that it is a change that involves a mutual reorganization, an adjustment in the organism and a reconstitution of the environment; for at its lowest terms any change in the organism carries with it a difference of sensitivity and response and a corresponding difference in the environment. It is within this process that so-called conscious intelligence arises, for consciousness is both the difference which arises in the environment because of its relation to the organism in its organic process of adjustment, and also the difference in the organism because of the change which has taken place in the environment. We refer to the first as meaning, and to the second as ideation. The reflection of the organism in the environment and the reflection of environment in the organism are essential phases in the maintenance of the life process that constitutes conscious intelligence.

I will consider the import of consciousness in a later lecture. At present my interest is only to locate that activity to which cognition belongs and of which thought is an expression. I am distinguishing in particular that existence of the world for the individual and social organism which answers to the more general usage of the term consciousness from that situation which answers to the term "consciousness of." It is the latter which, to my mind, connotes cognition. The distinction between the two falls in with that which I have suggested between the problem and its setting. The setting within which adjustment takes place is essential to the adjustment and falls within what belongs to the "field of consciousness," as that term is generally used—especially when we recognize the implications of that which is more definitely in the field of consciousness. The term "field of awareness" is at times used in the same sense, but it is more apt to carry with it the value of "awareness of" than is the term "consciousness." In other words, in knowledge there is always the presupposition of a world that is there and that provides the basis for the inferential and ideational process of cognition. This of course restricts cognition or "consciousness of" to that which has within it an inferential strain.

Now the world which is there in its relationship to the organism, and which sets the conditions for the adjustment of the organism and the consequent change in and of that world, includes its past. We approach every question of a historical character with a certain apparatus, which may be nicely defined, and this more technically defined material of documents, oral testimony, and historical remains subtends a given past which extends backward from the memories of yesterday and today, and which we do not question. We use the apparatus to answer hypothetically the historical questions which press upon us, and to test our hypotheses when they have been elaborated. It is of course understood that any part of this apparatus and of the past within which it is embedded may itself fall under doubt, but even the most heroic skepticism in its very enunciation cannot get away from the memory of the words and ideas which formulate the skeptical doctrine.

Some such given past is involved in questions bearing upon the past. And this given past extends the specious present. It is true that the ultimate agreement between the meanings of two documents may lie in experience in a specious present, but only upon the supposition of the comparison we have previously made of the documents. This comparison stretches back of us and remains unquestioned until someone points out an error therein and thus brings it into question, but then only upon the basis of his and others' past. Take the ingenious suggestion, of Gosse's father, I believe, that God had created the world with its fossils and other evidences of a distant past to try men's faith; and bring the suggestion up to a half an hour ago. Suppose that the world came into existence, with its exact present structure, including the so-called contents of our minds, thirty minutes ago, and that we had some ulterior evidence analogous to Mr. Gosse's fundamentalist views, that this had taken place. We could examine the hypothesis only in the light of some past that was there, however meager it had become. And this past extends indefinitely, there being nothing to stop it, since any moment of it, being represented, has its past, and so on.

What do we mean, now, by the statement that there has been some real past with all its events, in independence of any present, whose contents we are slowly and imperfectly deciphering? We come back of course to the very corrections which we make in our historical research, and to the higher degree of evidence of that which has been discovered over that which can be offered for the discarded account. Higher degrees of probability and added evidence imply that there is or has been some reality there which we are bringing to light. There is thus a palpable reference to the unquestioned past by means of whose evidence we investigate and solve the problems that arise. And the very fact to which I have referred, that any accepted account of the past, though not now in question, may be conceivably thrown into doubt, seems to imply some unquestionable past which would be the background for the solution of all conceivable problems. Let us admit this for the time being, and ask the further question whether this past independent of any present does enter at all into our investigations—I mean as a presupposition that plays any part in our thinking? If we should take away this presupposition would our apparatus and the operation of it in historical research be in any way affected? Certainly not, if we concern ourselves only with the problems with which historians in social or scientific history are concerned. Here the reference is always and solely to the given past out of which a problem has arisen; and the outlines of the problem and the tests to which presented hypotheses are subjected, are found in the given past. As we have seen, this given past may itself at a later date be affected with doubt and brought under discussion. And yet the possible dubiety of the given past in no way affects the undertaking. This is another way of saying that the dubiety of all possible pasts never enters into the historian's thinking. The only approach to such entrance is the demand that all past pasts should be accounted for and taken up into the latest statement. And every past past, in so far as it is reconstructed, is in so far shown to be incorrect. In the implications of our method we seem to approach a limiting statement, even if at infinity, which would fill out all gaps and correct all errors. But if we are making corrections there must seemingly be some account that is correct, and even if we contemplate an indefinite future of research science which will be engaged in the undertaking we never escape from this implication.

There is another way of saying this, and that is that our research work is that of discovery, and we can only discover what is there whether we discover it or not. I think however that this last statement is in error, if

it is supposed to imply that there is or has been a past which is independent of all presents, for there may be and beyond doubt is in any present with its own past a vast deal which we do not discover, and yet this
which we do or do not discover will take on different meaning and
be different in its structure as an event when viewed from some later
standpoint. Is there a similar error in the conception of correction of
the past error and in the suggestion that it implies the absolutely correct, even if it never reaches it? I am referring to the "in-itself" correctness of an account of events, implied in a correction which a later
historian makes. I think that the absolute correctness which lies back
in the historian's mind would be found to be the complete presentation
of the given past, if all its implications were worked out. If we could
know everything implied in our memories, our documents, and our
monuments, and were able to control all this knowledge, the historian
would assume that he had what was absolutely correct. But a historian
of the time of Aristotle, extending thus his known past, would have
reached a correct past which would be at utter variance with the known
world of modern science, and there are only degrees of variance between such a comparison and those which changes due to research are
bringing out in our pasts from year to year. If we are referring to any
other "in-itself" correctness it must be either to that of a reality which
by definition could never get into our experience, or to that of a goal at
infinity in which the type of experience in which we find ourselves
ceases. It is of course possible to assume that the experience within
which we find ourselves is included in some world or experience that
transcends it. My only point is that such an assumption plays no part
in our judgments of the correctness of the past. We may have other
reasons, theological or metaphysical, for assuming a real past that
could be given in a presentation independent of any present, but that
assumption does not enter into the postulations or technique of any sort
of historical research.

While the conception of an "in-itself" irrevocable past is perhaps
the common background of thinking, it is interesting to recur to the
statement that I made earlier that the research scientist looks forward
not only with equanimity but also with excited interest to the fundamental changes which later research will bring into the most exact
determinations which we can make today. The picture which this offers
is that of presents sliding into each other, each with a past which is
referable to itself, each past taking up into itself those back of it, and

in some degree reconstructing them from its own standpoint. The moment that we take these earlier presents as existences apart from the presentation of them as pasts they cease to have meaning to us and lose any value they may have in interpreting our own present and determining our futures. They may be located in the geometry of Minkowski space-time, but even under that assumption they can reach us only through our own frames of reference or perspectives; and the same would be true under the assumptions of any other metaphysics which located the reality of the past in pasts independent of any present.

It would probably be stated that the irrevocability of the past is located in such a metaphysical order, and that is the point which I wish to discuss. The historian does not doubt that something has happened. He is in doubt as to what has happened. He also proceeds upon the assumption that if he could have all the facts or data, he could determine what it was that happened. That is, his idea of irrevocability attaches, as I have already stated, to the "what" that has happened as well as to the passing of the event. But if there is emergence, the reflection of this into the past at once takes place. There is a new past, for from every new rise the landscape that stretches behind us becomes a different landscape. The analogy is faulty, because the heights are there, and the aspects of the landscape which they reveal are also there and could be reconstructed from the present of the wayfarer if he had all the implications of his present before him; whereas the emergent is not there in advance, and by definition could not be brought within even the fullest presentation of the present. The metaphysical reality suggested by Eddington's phrase that our experience is an adventuring of the mind into the ordered geometry of space-time would, however, correspond to a preëxistent landscape.

There is of course the alternative doctrine of Whitehead that perspectives exist in nature as intersecting time systems, thus yielding not only different presents but also different pasts that correspond to them. I cannot, however, see how Whitehead with the fixed geometry of space-time which he accepts can escape from a fixed order of events, even though the "what" of these events depends upon the integration of eternal objects arising through the action of God, thus giving rise to emergence. The point at issue is whether the necessity with which the scientist deals is one that determines the present out of a past which is independent of that or any present. An ordered space-time involves such a metaphysical necessity. From this standpoint the different pasts of experience are subjective reinterpretations, and the physicist is not interested in making them a part of the whole scheme of events. Whitehead's philosophy is a valiant attempt to harmonize this sort of geometric necessity with emergence and the differences of varying perspectives. I do not believe that this can be accomplished, but I am more interested in the answer to the question, whether the necessity which is involved in the relations of the present and the past derives from such a metaphysical necessity, that is, from one that is independent of any present.

I revert here to my original proposition that a reality that transcends the present must exhibit itself in the present. This alternative is that found in the attitude of the research scientist, whether he confesses it in his doctrine or not. It is that there is and always will be a necessary relation of the past and the present but that the present in which the emergent appears accepts that which is novel as an essential part of the universe, and from that standpoint rewrites its past. The emergent then ceases to be an emergent and follows from the past which has replaced the former past. We speak of life and consciousness as emergents but our rationalistic natures will never be satisfied until we have conceived a universe within which they arise inevitably out of that which preceded them. We cannot make the emergent a part of the thought relation of past and present, and even when we have seemingly accepted it we push biochemistry and behavioristic psychology as far as we can in the effort to reduce emergence to a disappearing point. But granting the research scientist a complete victory—a wholly rationalized universe within which there is determined order—he will still look forward to the appearance of new problems that will emerge in new presents to be rationalized again with another past which will take up the old past harmoniously into itself.

Confessedly, the complete rationality of the universe is based upon an induction, and what the induction is based upon is a moot point in philosophic doctrine. Granted any justifiable reason for believing it, all our correlations greatly strengthen it. But is there such a reason? At this crucial point there is the greatest uncertainty. Evidently the scientist's procedure ignores this. It is not a moot question with him. It is not a question in his procedure at all. He is simply occupied in finding rational order and stretching this back, that he may previse the future. It is here that his given world functions. If he can fit his hypothesis into this world and if it anticipates that which occurs, it then becomes the account of what has happened. If it breaks down, another hypothesis replaces it and another past replaces that which the first hypothesis implied.

The long and short of it is that the past (or the meaningful structure of the past) is as hypothetical as the future. Jeans' account of what has been taking place inside of Aldebaran or Sirius Minor during the past millions of years is vastly more hypothetical than the astronomer's catalogue of what eclipses will take place during the next century and where they will be visible. And the metaphysical assumption that there has been a definite past of events neither adds to nor subtracts from the security of any hypothesis which illuminates our present. It does indeed offer the empty form into which we extend any hypothesis and develop its implications, but it has not even the fixity which Kant found in his forms of intuition. The paradoxes of relativity, what Whitehead terms the different meanings of time in different time systems, reveal the hypothetical nature of the ruled schedules of the past into which we are to fit the events which our physical theories unroll behind us. We may have recourse to the absolute space-time with its coincidences of events and intervals between them, but even here it is open to argument whether this interpretation of the transformations from one frame of reference to another is the final one, whether we have attained the ultimate structure of the physical universe or only a more powerful mathematical apparatus for reaching higher exactitude in measurements and calculations, whose interpretation will vary with the history of mathematical physics. The Minkowski space-time is as much an hypothesis as the de Broglie wave-constitution of matter.

But the irrevocability of the past event remains even if we are uncertain what the past event was. Even the reversible character of physical processes which mathematical equations seem to disclose does not shake this character of space-time experience. It may be thinkable that viewed from some vast distance the order of some of what we call the same events might differ in different perspectives, but within any perspective what has passed cannot recur. In that perspective what has happened has happened, and any theory that is presented must make room for that order in that perspective. There is an unalterable temporal direction in what is taking place and if we can attach other processes to this passage we can give to them as much of certainty as the degree of attachment justifies. Given a certain value for the velocity of a moving body in a certain frame of reference, we can determine where the body will necessarily be. Our problem is to determine just what it is that has preceded what is taking place so that the direction of temporal progress may determine what the world is going to be. There is a certain temporal process going on in experience. What has taken place issues in what is taking place, and in this passage what has occurred determines spatio-temporally what is passing into the future. So far then as we can determine the constants of motion we can follow that determination, and our analysis seeks to resolve the happening in so far as may be into motion. In general, since passage is itself given in experience, the direction of changes that are going on partly conditions what will take place. The event that has taken place and the direction of the process going on form the basis for the rational determination of the future. The irrevocable past and the occurring change are the two factors to which we tie up all our speculations in regard to the future. Probability is found in the character of the process which is going on in experience. Yet however eagerly we seek for such spatio-temporal structures as carry with them deducible results, we nonetheless recognize relations of things in their processes which cannot be resolved into quantitative elements, and although as far as possible we correlate them with measurable characters we in any case recognize them as determining conditions of what is taking place. We look for their antecedents in the past and judge the future by the relation of this past to what is taking place. All of these relationships within the ongoing process are determining relations of what will be, though the specific form of that determination constitutes the scientific problem of any particular situation. The actuality of determination within the passage of direct experience is what Hume by his presuppositions and type of analysis eliminated from experience, and what gives such validity as it has to Kant's deduction of the categories.

It is the task of the philosophy of today to bring into congruence with each other this universality of determination which is the text of modern science and the emergence of the novel which belongs not only to the experience of human social organisms, but is found also in a nature which science and that philosophy that has followed it have separated from human nature. The difficulty that immediately presents itself is that the emergent has no sooner appeared than we set about rationalizing it, that is, we undertake to show that it, or at least the conditions that determine its appearance, can be found in the past that lay behind it. Thus the earlier pasts out of which it emerged as something which did not involve it are taken up into a more comprehensive past that does lead up to it. Now what this amounts to is that whatever does happen, even the emergent, happens under determining conditions—especially, from the standpoint of the exact sciences, under spatio-temporal conditions which lead to deducible conclusions as to what will happen within certain limits, but also under determining conditions of a qualitative sort whose assurances lie within probability only—but that these conditions never determine completely the "what it is" that will happen. Water as distinct from combinations of oxygen and hydrogen may happen. Life and so-called consciousness may happen. And quanta may happen, though it may be argued that such happening stands on a different "level" from that of life and consciousness. When these emergents have appeared they become part of the determining conditions that occur in real presents, and we are particularly interested in presenting the past which in the situation before us conditioned the appearance of the emergent, and especially in so presenting it that we can lead up to new appearances of this object. We orient ourselves not with reference to the past which was a present within which the emergent appeared, but in such a restatement of the past as conditioning the future that we may control its reappearance. When life has appeared we can breed life, and given consciousness, we can control its appearance and its manifestations. Even the statement of the past within which the emergent appeared is inevitably made from the standpoint of a world within which the emergent is itself a conditioning as well as a conditioned factor.

We could not bring back these past presents simply as they occurred—if we are justified in using the expression—except as presents. An exhaustive presentation of them would amount only to reliving them. That is, one present slipping into another does not connote what is meant by a past. But even this statement implies that there were such presents slipping into each other, and whether we regard them from that standpoint or not we seem to imply their reality as such, as the structure within which the sort of past in which we are interested must lie, if it is an aspect of the real past. Passing by the ambiguities which such a statement carries within it, what I want to emphasize is that the irrevocability of the past does not issue from this conception of the past. For in our use of the term irrevocability we are pointing toward what must have been, and it is a structure and process in the present which is the source of this necessity. We certainly cannot go back to such a past and test our conjectures by actually inspecting its events in their happening. We test our conjectures about the past by the conditioning directions of the present and by later happenings in the future which must be of a certain sort if the past we have conceived was there. The force of irrevocability then is found in the extension of the necessity with which what has just happened conditions what is emerging in the future. What is more than this belongs to a metaphysical picture that takes no interest in the pasts which arise behind us.

In the analysis which I have undertaken we come then, *first*, to passage within which what is taking place conditions that which is arising. Everything that is taking place takes place under necessary conditions. *Second,* these conditions while necessary do not determine in its full reality that which emerges. We are getting interesting reflections of this situation from the scientist's criticism of his own methods of reaching exact determination of position and velocity and from the implications of quanta. What appears in this criticism is that while the scientist never abandons the conditioning of that which takes place by that which has gone on, expressed in probability, he finds himself quite able to think as emergent even those events which are subject to the most exact determination. I am not attempting to previse what later interpretation will be put upon the speculations of de Broglie, Schroeder, and Planck. I am simply indicating that even within the field of mathematical physics rigorous thinking does not necessarily imply that conditioning of the present by the past carries with it the complete determination of the present by the past.

Third, in passage the conditioning of that which is taking place by that which has taken place, of the present by the past, is *there.* The past in that sense is in the present; and in what we call conscious experience, its presence is exhibited in memory, and in the historical apparatus which extends memory, as that part of the conditioning nature of passage which reflects itself into the experience of the organic individual. If all objects in a present are conditioned by the same characters in passage, their pasts are implicitly the same, but if, to follow out a suggestion taken from the speculations about quanta, one electron out of two thousand sets energy free, when there are no determining conditions for the selection of this electron over against the other nineteen hundred and ninety-nine, it is evident that the past as exhibited in the conduct of this electron will be of a sort that will not even implicitly be the same as that of the others in that group, though its jump will be conditioned by all that has gone before. If of two thousand individuals under disintegrating social conditions one commits suicide where, so far as can be seen, one was as likely to succumb as another, his past has a peculiarly poignant nature which is absent from that of the others, though his committing of suicide is an expression of the past. The past is there conditioning the present and its passage into the future, but in the organization of tendencies embodied in one individual there may be an emergent which gives to these tendencies a structure which belongs only to the situation of that individual. The tendencies coming from past passage, and from the conditioning that is inherent in passage, become different influences when they have taken on this organized structure of tendencies. This would be as true of the balance of processes of disruption and of agglomeration in a star as in the adjustment to each other of a living form and its environment. The structural relationship in their reciprocal balance or adjustment arranges those passing processes which reflect backward and lead us to an account of the history of the star. As Dewey has maintained, events appear as histories which have a *dénouement,* and when an historical process is taking place the organization of the conditioning phases of the process is the novel element which is not predictable from the separate phases themselves, and which at once sets the scene for a past that leads to this outcome. The organization of any individual thing carries with it the relation of this thing to processes that occurred before this organization set in. In this sense the past of that thing is "given" in the passing present of the thing and our histories of things are elaborations of what is implicit in this situation. This "given" in passage is there and is the starting point for a cognitive structure of a past.

Fourth, this emergent character, being responsible for a relationship of passing processes, sets up a given past that is, so to speak, a perspective of the object within which this character appears. We can conceive of an object such as, say, some atom of hydrogen, which has remained what it is through immeasurable periods in complete adjustment to its surroundings, which has remained real in the slipping of one present into another, or, better, in one unbroken, uneventful passage. For such an object there would have been unbroken existence but no past, unless we should revert to the occasion on which it emerged as an atom of hydrogen. This amounts to saying that where being is existence but not becoming there is no past, and that the determination involved in passage is a condition of a past but not its realization. The relationship of passage involves distinguishable natures in events before past, present, and future can arise, as extension is a relationship which involves distinguishable physical things before structurable space can arise. What renders one event distinguishable from another is a becoming which affects the inner nature of the event. It seems to me that the extreme mathematization of recent science in which the reality of motion is reduced to equations in which change disappears in an identity, and in which space and time disappear in a four-dimensional continuum of indistinguishable events which is neither space nor time is a reflection of the treatment of time as passage without becoming.

What then is a present? Whitehead's definition would come back to the temporal spread of the passage of the events that make up a thing, a spread which is extended enough to make it possible for the thing to be what it is. That of an atom of iron would not need to be longer than the period within which the revolution of each of its electrons around the nucleus is completed. The universe during this period would constitute a duration from the point of view of the atom. The specious present of a human individual would presumably be a period within which he could be himself. From the standpoint which I have suggested it would involve a becoming. There must be at least something that happens to and in the thing which affects the nature of the thing in order that one moment may be distinguishable from another, in order that there may be time. But there is in such a statement a conflict of principles of definition. From one standpoint we are seeking for what is essential to a present; from the other we are seeking for the lower limit in a process of division. I will refer to the latter first, for it involves the question of the relation of time to passage—to that within which time seems to lie and in terms of whose extension we place time and compare times. The thousandth part of a second has a real significance, and we can conceive of the universe as foundering in a sea of entropy within which all becoming has ceased. We are dealing here with an abstraction of the extension of mere passage from the time within which events happen because they become. In Whitehead's treatment this is called "extensive abstraction," and leads up to an event-particle as mathematical analysis leads up to the differential. And an event-particle should have the same relationship to something that becomes that the differential of a change such as an accelerating velocity has to the whole process. In so far, extensive abstraction is a method of analysis and integration and asks for no other justification than its success. But Whitehead uses it as a method of metaphysical abstraction and finds in the mere happening the event, the substance of that which becomes. He transfers the content of what becomes to a world of "eternal objects" having ingression into events under the control of a principle lying outside of their occurrence. While, then, the existence of what occurs is found in the present, the "what it is" that occurs does not arise out of happening, it happens to the event through the metaphysical process of ingression. This seems to me to be an improper use of abstraction, since it leads to a metaphysical separation of what is abstracted from the concrete reality from which the abstraction is made, instead of leaving it as a tool in the intellectual control of that reality. Bergson refers, I think, to the same improper use of abstraction, in another context, as the spatialization of time, contrasting the exclusive nature of such temporal moments with the interpenetration of the contents of "real" duration.

If, on the contrary, we recognize what becomes as the event which in its relation to other events gives structure to time, then the abstraction of passage from what is taking place is purely methodological. We carry our analysis as far as the control of subject matter requires, but always with the recognition that what is analyzed out has its reality in the integration of what is taking place. That this is the result of defining the event as that which becomes, is evident, I think, in the application and testing of our most abstruse hypotheses. To be of value and to be accredited these must present new events springing out of old, such as the expansion or contraction of the universe in Einstein's and Weyl's speculations on the seeming recession at enormous velocities of distant nebulae, or the stripping of electrons from atomic nuclei in the center of stellar bodies in Jeans' speculations upon the transformation of matter into radiation. And these happenings should so fit into our experimental findings that they may find their reality in the concretion of what is taking place in an actual present. The pasts which they spread back of us are as hypothetical as the future which they assist us in prevising. They become valid in interpreting nature in so far as they present a history of becomings in nature leading up to that which is becoming today, in so far as they bring out what fits into the pattern that is emerging from the roaring loom of time, not in so far as they erect metaphysical entities which are the tenuous obverse of mathematical apparatus.

If, in Bergson's phrase, "real duration" becomes time through the appearance of unique events which are distinguishable from each other through their qualitative nature, a something that is emergent in each event, then bare passage is a manner of arranging these events. But what is essential to this arrangement is that in each interval which is isolated it must be possible that something should become, that something unique should arise. We are subject to a psychological illusion if we assume that the rhythm of counting and the order which arises out of counting answer to a structure of passage itself, apart from the processes which fall into orders through the emergence of events. We never reach the interval itself between events, except in correlations between them and other situations within which we find congruence and replacement, something that can never take place in passage as such. We reach what may be called a functional equality of represented intervals within processes involving balance and rhythm, but on this basis to set up time as a quantity having an essential nature that allows of its being divided into equal portions of itself is an unwarranted use of abstraction. We can hypothetically reconstruct the past processes that are involved in what is going on as a basis for the cognitive construction of the future which is arising. What we are assured of by the experimental data is that we comprehend that which is going on sufficiently to predict what will take place, not that we have attained a correct picture of the past independent of any present, for we expect this picture to change as new events emerge. In this attitude we are relating in our anticipation presents that slip into others, and their pasts belong to them. They have to be reconstructed as they are taken up into a new present and as such they belong to that present, and no longer to the present out of which we have passed into the present present.

A present then, as contrasted with the abstraction of mere passage, is not a piece cut out anywhere from the temporal dimension of uniformly passing reality. Its chief reference is to an emergent event, that is, to the occurrence of something which is more than the processes that have led up to it and which by its change, continuance, or disappearance, adds to later passages a content they would not otherwise have possessed. The mark of passage without emergent events is its formulation in equations in which the so-called instances disappear in an identity, as Meyerson has pointed out.

Given an emergent event, its relations to antecedent processes become conditions or causes. Such a situation is a present. It marks out and in a sense selects what has made its peculiarity possible. It creates with its uniqueness a past and a future. As soon as we view it, it becomes a history and a prophecy. Its own temporal diameter varies with the extent of the event. There may be a history of the physical universe as an appearance of a galaxy of galaxies. There is a history of every object that is unique. But there would be no such history of the physical universe until the galaxy appeared, and it would continue only so long as the galaxy maintained itself against disruptive and cohesive forces. If we ask what may be the temporal spread of the uniqueness which is responsible for a present the answer must be, in Whitehead's terms, that it is a period long enough to enable the object to be what it is. But the question is ambiguous for the term "temporal spread" implies a measure of time. The past, as it appears with the present and future, is the relation of the emergent event to the situation out of which it arose, and it is the event that defines that situation. The continuance or disappearance of that which arises is the present passing into the future. Past, present, and future belong to a passage which attains temporal structure through the event, and they may be considered long or short as they are compared with other such passages. But as existing in nature, so far as such a statement has significance, the past and the future are the boundaries of what we term the present, and are determined by the conditioning relationships of the event to its situation.

This relation of the event to its situation, of the organism to its environment, with their mutual dependence, brings us to relativity, and to the perspectives in which this appears in experience. The nature of environment answers to the habits and selective attitudes of organisms, and the qualities that belong to the objects of the environment can only be expressed in terms of sensitivities of these organisms. And the same is true of ideas. The organism, through its habits and anticipatory attitudes, finds itself related to what extends beyond its immediate present. Those characters of things which in the activity of the organism refer to what lies beyond the present take on the value of that to which they refer. The field of mind, then, is the larger environment which the activity of the organism calls for but which transcends the present. What is present in the organism, however, is its own nascent activity, and that in itself and in the environment which sustains it, and there is present also its movement from the past and beyond the present. It belongs to the so-called conscious organism to complete this larger temporal environment by the use of characters found in the present. The mechanism by which the social mind accomplishes this I will discuss later; what I wish to bring out now is that the field of mind is the temporal extension of the environment of the organism, and that an idea resides in the organism because the organism is using that in itself which moves beyond its present to take the place of that toward which its own activity is tending. That in the organism which provides the occasion for mind is the activity which reaches beyond the present within which the organism exists.

But in such an account as this I have been implicitly setting up this larger period within which, say, an organism begins and completes its history as there seemingly in independence of any present, and it is my purpose to insist upon the opposite proposition that these larger periods can have no reality except as they exist in presents and that all their implications and values are there located. Of course this comes back, *first,* to the evident fact that all the apparatus of the past, memory images, historical monuments, fossil remains, and the like are in some present, and, *second, to* that portion of the past which is there in passage in experience as determined by the emergent event. It comes back, *third,* to the necessary test of the formulation of the past in the rising events in experience. The past we are talking about lies with all its characters within that present.

There is, however, the assumed implication that this present refers to entities which have a reality independent of this and any other present, whose full detail, though of course beyond recall, is inevitably presumed. Now there is a confusion between such a metaphysical assumption and the evident fact that we are unable to reveal all that is involved in any present. Here we stand with Newton before a boundless sea and are only gathering the pebbles upon its shore. There is nothing transcendent about this powerlessness of our minds to exhaust any situation. Any advance which makes toward greater knowledge simply extends the horizon of experience, but all remains within conceivable experience. A greater mind than Newton's or Einstein's would reveal in experience, in the world that is there, structures and processes that we cannot find nor even adumbrate. Or take Bergson's conception of all our memories, or all occurrences in the form of images, crowding in upon us, and held back by a central nervous system. All of this is conceivable in a present whose whole richness should be at the disposal of that very present. This does not mean that the aeons revealed in those structures and processes, or the histories which those images connote would unroll themselves in a present as temporally extended as their formulation implies. It means, in so far as such an unbridled conception or imagination can have meaning, that we should have an inconceivable richness offered to our analysis in the approach to any problem arising in experience.

The past in passage is irrecoverable as well as irrevocable. It is producing all the reality that there is. The meaning of that which is, is illuminated and expanded in the face of the emergent in experience, like (a + b) to the 25th power by the binomial theorem, by the expansion of the passage which is going on. To say that the Declaration of Independence was signed on the 4th of July, 1776, means that in the time system which we carry around with us and with the formulation of our political habits, this date comes out in our celebrations. Being what we are in the social and physical world that we inhabit we account for what takes place on this time schedule, but like railway time-tables it is always subject to change without notice. Christ was born four years before A.D.

Our reference is always to the structure of the present, and our test of the formulation we make is always that of successfully carrying out our calculations and observations in a rising future. If we say that something happened at such a date, whether we can ever specify it or not, we must mean that if in imagination we put ourselves back at the supposed date we should have had such an experience, but this is not what we are concerned with when we work out the history of the past. It is the import of what is going on in action or appreciation which requires illumination and direction, because of the constant appearance of the novel from whose standpoint our experience calls for a reconstruction which includes the past.

The best approach to this import is found in the world within which our problems arise. Its things are enduring things that are what they are because of the conditioning character of passage. Their past is in what they are. Such a past is not eventual. When we elaborate the history of a tree whose wood is found in the chairs in which we sit, all the way from the diatom to the oak but lately felled, this history revolves about the constant reinterpretation of facts that are continually arising, nor are these novel facts to be found simply in the impact of changing human experiences upon a world that is there. For, in the first place, human experiences are as much a part of this world as are any of its other characteristics, and the world is a different world because of these experiences. And, in the second place, in any history that we construct we are forced to recognize the shift in relationship between the condi-

tioning passage and emergent event, in that part of the past which belongs to passage, even when this passage is not expanded in ideation.

The outcome of what I have said is that the estimate and import of
all histories lies in the interpretation and control of the present; that as
ideational structures they always arise from change, which is as essential a part of reality as the permanent, and from the problems which
change entails; and that the metaphysical demand for a set of events
which is unalterably there in an irrevocable past, to which these histories seek a constantly approaching agreement, comes back to motivate
other than those at work in the most exact scientific research.

NOTE

Durations are a continual sliding of presents into each other. The present is a passage constituted by processes whose earlier phases determine in certain respects their later phases. Reality then is always in the
present. When the present has passed it no longer is. The question
arises whether the past arising in memory and in the projection of this
still further backwards, refers to events which existed as such continuous presents passing into each other, or to that conditioning phase of
the passing present which enables us to determine conduct with reference to the future which is also arising in the present. It is this latter
thesis which I am maintaining.

The implication of my position is that the past is such a construction
that the reference that is found in it is not to events having a reality
independent of the present which is the seat of reality, but rather to
such an interpretation of the present in its conditioning passage as will
enable intelligent conduct to proceed. It is of course evident that the
materials out of which that past is constructed lie in the present. I refer
to the memory images and the evidences by which we build up the
past, and to the fact that any reinterpretation of the picture we form of
the past will be found in a present, and will be judged by the logical
and evidential characters which such data possess in a present. It is
also evident that there is no appeal from these in their locus of a present
to a real past which lies like a scroll behind us, and to which we may
recur to check up on our constructions. We are not deciphering a manu-
script whose passages can be made intelligible in themselves and left
as secure presentations of that portion of what has gone before, to be

supplemented by later final constructions of other passages. We are not contemplating an ultimate unchangeable past that may be spread behind us in its entirety subject to no further change. Our reconstructions of the past vary in their extensiveness, but they never contemplate the finality of their findings. They are always subject to conceivable reformulations, on the discovery of later evidence, and this reformulation may be complete. Even the most vivid of memory images may be in error. In a word our assurances concerning the past are never attained by a congruence between the constructed past and a real past independent of this construction, though we carry this attitude at the back of our heads, because we do bring our immediate hypothetical reconstructions to the test of the accepted past and adjudge them by their agreement with the accepted record; but this accepted past lies in a present and is subject, itself, to possible reconstruction.

Now it is possible to accept all this, with a full admission that no item in the accepted past is final, and yet to maintain that there remains a reference in our formulation of the past event to a something that happened which we can never expect to resuscitate in the content of reality, something that belonged to the event in the present within which it occurred. This amounts to saying that there is behind us a scroll of elapsed presents, to which our constructions of the past refer, though without the possibility of ever reaching it, and without the anticipation that our continual reconstructions will approach it with increasing exactness. And this brings me to the point at issue. Such a scroll, if attained, is not the account that our pasts desiderate. If we could bring back the present that has elapsed in the reality which belonged to it, it would not serve us. It would be that present and would lack just that character which we demand in the past, that is, that construction of the conditioning nature of now present passage which enables us to interpret what is arising in the future that belongs to this present. When one recalls his boyhood days he cannot get into them as he then was, without their relationship to what he has become; and if he could, that is, if he could reproduce the experience as it then took place, he could not use it, for this would involve his not being in the present within which that use must take place. A string of presents conceivably existing as presents would never constitute a past. If then there is such a reference it is not to an entity which could fit into any past, and I cannot believe that the reference, in the past as experienced, is to a something which would not have the function or value that in our experience belongs to a past. We are not referring to a real past event which would not be the past event we are seeking. Another way of saying this is that our pasts are always mental in the same manner in which the futures that lie in our imagination ahead of us are mental. They differ, apart from their successive positions, in that the determining conditions of interpretation and conduct are embodied in the past as that is found in the present, but they are subject to the same test of validity to which our hypothetical futures are subject. And the novelty of every future demands a novel past.

This, however, overlooks one important character of any past, and that is that no past which we can construct can be as adequate as the situation demands. There is always a reference to a past which cannot be reached, and one that is still consonant with the function and import of a past. It is always conceivable that the implications of the present should be carried further than we do actually carry them, and further than we can possibly carry them. There is always more knowledge which would be desirable for the solution of any problem confronting us but which we cannot attain. With the conceivable attainment of this knowledge we should undoubtedly construct a past truer to the present within which the implications of this past lie. And it is to this past that there is always a reference within every past which imperfectly presents itself to our investigation. If we had every possible document and every possible monument from the period of Julius Caesar we should unquestionably have a truer picture of the man and of what occurred in his lifetime, but it would be a truth which belongs to this present, and a later present would reconstruct it from the standpoint of its own emergent nature. We can then conceive of a past which in any one present would be irrefragable. So far as that present was concerned it would be a final past, and if we consider the matter, I think that it is this past to which the reference lies in that which goes beyond the statement which the historian can give, and which we are apt to assume to be a past independent of the present.

The Genesis of the Self and Social Control

It is evident that a statement of the life of each individual in terms of
the results of an analysis of that which is immediately experienced
would offer a common plane of events, in which the experience of each
would differ from the experiences of others only in their extent, and
the completeness or incompleteness of their connections. These differences disappear in the generalized formulations of the social sciences.
The experiences of the same individuals, in so far as each faces a world
in which objects are plans of action, would implicate in each a different
succession of events. In the simplest illustration, two persons approach
a passing automobile. To one it is a moving object that he will pass
before it reaches the portion of the street that is the meeting-place of
their two paths. The other sees an object that will pass this meeting-
point before he reaches it. Each slices the world from the standpoint of
a different time system. Objects which in a thousand ways are identical
for the two individuals are yet fundamentally different through their
location in one spatio-temporal plane, involving a certain succession
of events, or in another. Eliminate the temporal dimension, and bring
all events back to an instant that is timeless, and the individuality of
these objects which belongs to them in behavior is lost, except in so
far as they can represent the results of past conduct. But taking time
seriously, we realize that the seemingly timeless character of our spatial world and its permanent objects is due to the consentient set which
each one of us selects. We abstract time from this space for the purposes of our conduct. Certain objects cease to be events, cease to pass
as they are in reality passing and in their permanence become the conditions of our action, and events take place with reference to them.
Because a whole community selects the same consentient set does not
make the selection less the attitude of each one of them. The life-
process takes place in individual organisms, so that the Psychology

which studies that process in its creative determining function becomes a science of the objective world.

Looked at from the standpoint of an evolutionary history, not only have new forms with their different spatio-temporal environments and their objects arisen, but new characters have arisen answering to the sensitivities and capacities for response. In the terms of Alexander, they have become differently qualified. It is as impossible to transfer these characters of the habitats to the consciousness of the forms as it is to transfer the spatio-temporal structure of the things to such a so-called consciousness. If we introduce a fictitious instantaneousness into a passing universe, things fall to pieces. Things that are spatio-temporally distant from us can be brought into this instant only in terms of our immediate contact experience. They are what they would be if we were there and had our hands upon them. They take on the character of tangible matter. This is the price of their being located at the moment of our bodies' existence. But this instantaneous view has the great advantage of giving to us a picture of what the contact experience will be when we reach the distant object, and of determining conditions under which the distance characters arise. If the world existed at an instant in experience, we should be forced to find some realm such as consciousness into which to transport the distance or so-called secondary qualities of things. If consciousness in evolutionary history, then, has an unambiguous significance, it refers to that stage in the development of life in which the conduct of the individual marks out and defines the future field and objects which make up its environment, and in which emerge characters in the objects and sensitivities in the individuals that answer to each other. There is a relativity of the living individual and its environment, both as to form and content.

What I wish to trace is the fashion in which self and the mind has arisen within this conduct. It is the implication of this undertaking that only selves have minds, that is, that cognition only belongs to selves, even in the simplest expression of awareness. This, of course, does not imply that below the stage of self-consciousness sense characters and sensitivity do not exist. This obtains in our own immediate experience in so far as we are not self-conscious. It is further implied that this development has taken place only in a social group, for selves exist only in relation to other selves, as the organism as a physical object. exists only in its relation to other physical objects. There have been two fields within which social groups have arisen which have determined their environment together with that of their members, and the individuality of its members. These lie in the realm of invertebrates and in that of the vertebrates. Among the Hymenoptera and termites there are societies whose interests determine for the individuals their stimuli and habitats, and so differentiate the individuals themselves, mainly through the sexual and alimentary processes, that the individual is what he is because of his membership within those societies. In the complex life of the group, the acts of the individuals are completed only through the acts of other individuals, but the mediation of this complex conduct is found in the physiological differentiation of the different members of the society. As Bergson has remarked of the instincts, the implements by which a complex act is carried out are found in the differential structure of the form. There is no convincing evidence that an ant or a bee is obliged to anticipate the act of another ant or bee, by tending to respond in the fashion of the other, in order that it may integrate its activity into the common act. And by the same mark there is no evidence of the existence of any language in their societies. Nor do we need to go to the invertebrates to discover this type of social conduct. If one picks up a little child who has fallen, he adapts his arms and attitude to the attitude of the child, and the child adapts himself to the attitude of the other; or in boxing or fencing one responds to stimulation of the other, by acquired physiological adjustment.

Among the vertebrates, apart from the differentiation of the sexes and the nurture and care of infant forms, there is little or no inherited physiological differentiation to mediate the complexities of social conduct. If we are to cooperate successfully with others, we must in some manner get their ongoing acts into ourselves to make the common act come off. As I have just indicated, there is a small range of social activity in which this is not necessary. The suckling of an infant form, or a dog fight, if this may be called a social activity, does not call for more than inherited physiological adjustment. Perhaps the so-called herding instinct should be added, but it hardly comes to more than the tendency of the herd to stick together in their various activities. The wooing and mating of forms, the care of the infant form, the bunching of animals in migrations, and fighting, about exhaust vertebrate social conduct, and beyond these seasonal processes vertebrate societies hardly exist till we reach man. They exhaust the possibilities in vertebrate structure of the mediation of social conduct, for the vertebrate organism has shown no such astonishing plasticity in physiological differentiation as that which we can trace among the insects, from isolated forms to members of the societies of the termites, the ants, and the bees.

A social act may be defined as one in which the occasion or stimulus which sets free an impulse is found in the character or conduct of a living form that belongs to the proper environment of the living form whose impulse it is. I wish, however, to restrict the social act to the class of acts which involve the cooperation of more than one individual, and whose object as defined by the act, in the sense of Bergson, is a social object. I mean by a social object one that answers to all the parts of the complex act, though these parts are found in the conduct of different individuals. The objective of the act is then found in the life-process of the group, not in those of the separate individuals alone. The full social object would not exist in the environments of the separate individuals of the societies of the Hymanoptera [*sic*] and termites, nor in the restricted societies of the vertebrates whose basis is found alone in physiological adjustment. A cow that licks the skin of a calf stuffed with hay, until the skin is worn away, and then eats the hay, or a woman who expends her parental impulse upon a poodle, cannot be said to have the full social object involved in the entire act in their environments. It would be necessary to piece together the environments of the different individuals or superimpose them upon each other to reach the environment and objects of the societies in question.

Where forms such as those of the Hymenoptera and the termites exhibit great plasticity in development, social acts based on physiological adjustment, and corresponding societies, have reached astonishing complexity. But when the limit of that plasticity is reached, the limit of the social act and the society is reached also. Where, as among the vertebrates, that physiological adjustment which mediates a social act is limited and fixed, the societies of this type are correspondingly insignificant. But another type of social act, and its corresponding society and object, has been at least suggested by the description of the social act based on physiological adjustment. Such an act would be one in which the different parts of the act which belong to different individuals should appear in the act of each individual. This cannot mean, however, that the single individual could carry out the entire act, for then, even if it were possible, it would cease to be a social act, nor could the stimulus which calls out his own part of the complex act be that which

calls out the other parts of the act in so far as they appear in his conduct. If the social object is to appear in his experience, it must be that
the stimuli which set free the responses of the others involved in the
act should be present in his experience, not as stimuli to his response,
but as stimuli for the responses of others; and this implies that the
social situation which arises after the completion of one phase of the
act, which serves as the stimulus for the next participant in the complex
procedure, shall in some sense be in the experience of the first actor,
tending to call out, not his own response, but that of the succeeding
actor. Let us make the impossible assumption that the wasp, in stinging
a spider which it stores with its egg, finds in the spider a social object
in the sense which I have specified. The spider would have to exist in
the experience of the wasp as live but quiescent food for the larva when
it emerges from the egg. In order that the paralyzed spider should so
appear to the wasp, the wasp would need to be subject to the same
stimulus as that which sets free the responses of the larva; in other
words, the wasp would need to be able to respond in some degree as
the larva. And of course the wasp would have to view the spider under
the time dimension, grafting a hypothetical future onto its passing present, but the occasion for this would have to lie in the wasp's tending to
respond in rôle of larva to the appropriate food which it is placing in
storage. This, then, presents another possible principle of social organization, as distinguished from that of physiological differentiation. If
the objects that answer to the complex social act can exist spatio-temporally in the experience of the different members of the society, as
stimuli that set free not only their own responses, but also as stimuli to
the responses of those who share in the composite act, a principle of
coordination might be found which would not depend upon physiological differentiation. And one necessary psychological condition for this
would be that the individual should have in some fashion present in his
organism the tendencies to respond as the other participants in the act
will respond. Much more than this would be involved, but this at least
would be a necessary precondition. A social object answering to the
responses of different individuals in a society could be conceived of as
existing in the experiences of individuals in that society, if the different
responses of these individuals in the complex acts could be found in
sufficient degree in the natures of separate individuals to render them
sensitive to the different values of the object answering to the parts of
the act.

The cortex of the vertebrate central nervous system provides at least a part of the mechanism which might make this possible. The nervous currents from the column and the stem of the brain to the cortex can there bring the acts that go out from these lower centers into relation with each other so that more complex processes and adjustments can arise. The centers and paths of the cortex represent an indefinite number of possible actions; particularly they represent acts which, being in competition with each other, inhibit each other, and present the problem of organization and adjustment so that overt conduct may proceed. In the currents and crosscurrents in the gray matter and its association fibers, there exist the tendencies to an indefinite number of responses. Answering to these adjustments are the objects organized into a field of action, not only spatially but temporally; for the tendency to grasp the distant object, while already excited, is so linked with the processes of approach that it does not get its overt expression till the intervening stretch is passed. In this vertebrate apparatus of conduct, then, the already excited predispositions to thousands of acts, that far transcend the outward accomplishments, furnish the inner attitudes implicating objects that are not immediate objectives of the individual's act.

But the cortex is not simply a mechanism. It is an organ that exists in fulfilling its function. If these tendencies to action which do not get immediate expression appear and persist, it is because they belong to the act that is going on. If, for example, property is a social object in the experience of men, as distinguished from the nut which the squirrel stores, it is because features of the food that one buys innervate the whole complex of responses by which property is not only acquired, but respected and protected, and this complex so innervated is an essential part of the act by which the man buys and stores his food. The point is not that buying food is a more complicated affair than picking it up from the ground, but that exchange is an act in which a man excites himself to give by making an offer. An offer is what it is because the presentation is a stimulus to give. One cannot exchange otherwise than by putting one's self in the attitude of the other party to the bargain. Property becomes a tangible object, because all essential phases of property appear in the actions of all those involved in exchange, and appear as essential features of the individual's action.

The individual in such an act is a self. If the cortex has become an organ of social conduct, and has made possible the appearance of social objects, it is because the individual has become a self, that is, an individual who organizes his own response by the tendencies on the part of others to respond to his act. He can do this because the mechanism of the vertebrate brain enables the individual to take these different attitudes in the formation of the act. But selves have appeared late in vertebrate evolution. The structure of the central nervous system is too minute to enable us to show the corresponding structural changes in the paths of the brain. It is only in the behavior of the human animal that we can trace this evolution. It has been customary to mark this stage in development by endowing man with a mind, or at least with a certain sort of mind. As long as consciousness is regarded as a sort of spiritual stuff out of which are fashioned sensations and affections and images and ideas or significances, a mind as a locus of these entities is an almost necessary assumption, but when these contents have been returned to things, the necessity of quarters for this furniture has disappeared also.

It lies beyond the bounds of this paper to follow out the implications of this shift for logic and epistemology, but there is one phase of all so-called mental processes which is central to this discussion, and that is self-consciousness. If the suggestions which I have made above should prove tenable, the self that is central to all so-called mental experience has appeared only in the social conduct of human vertebrates. It is just because the individual finds himself taking the attitudes of the others who are involved in his conduct that he becomes an object for himself. It is only by taking the rôles of others that we have been able to come back to ourselves. We have seen above that the social object can exist for the individual only if the various parts of the whole social act carried out by other members of the society are in some fashion present in the conduct of the individual. It is further true that the self can exist for the individual only if he assumes the rôles of the others. The presence in the conduct of the individual of the tendencies to act as others act may be, then, responsible for the appearance in the experience of the individual of a social object, i.e., an object answering to complex reactions of a number of individuals, and also for the appearance of the self. Indeed, these two appearances are correlative. Property can appear as an object only in so far as the individual stimulates himself to buy by a prospective offer to sell. Buying and selling are involved in each other. Something that can be exchanged can exist in the experience of the individual only in so far as he has in his own make-up the tendency to sell when he has also the tendency to buy.

And he becomes a self in his experience only in so far as one attitude on his own part calls out the corresponding attitude in the social undertaking.

This is just what we imply in "self-consciousness." We appear as selves in our conduct in so far as we ourselves take the attitude that others take toward us, in these correlative activities. Perhaps as good an illustration of this as can be found is in a "right." Over against the protection of our lives or property, we assume the attitude of assent of all members in the community. We take the rôle of what may be called the "generalized other." And in doing this we appear as social objects, as selves. It is interesting to note that in the development of the individual child, there are two stages which present the two essential steps in attaining self-consciousness. The first stage is that of play, and the second that of the game, where these two are distinguished from each other. In play in this sense, the child is continually acting as a parent, a teacher, a preacher, a grocery man, a policeman, a pirate, or an Indian. It is the period of childish existence which Wordsworth has described as that of "endless imitation." It is the period of Froebel's kindergarten plays. In it, as Froebel recognized, the child is acquiring the rôles of those who belong to his society. This takes place because the child is continually exciting in himself the responses to his own social acts. In his infant dependence upon the responses of others to his own social stimuli, he is peculiarly sensitive to this relation. Having in his own nature the beginning of the parental response, he calls it out by his own appeals. The doll is the universal type of this, but before he plays with a doll, he responds in tone of voice and in attitude as his parents respond to his own cries and chortles. This has been denominated imitation, but the psychologist now recognizes that one imitates only insofar as the so-called imitated act can be called out in the individual by his appropriate stimulation. That is, one calls or tends to call out in himself the same response that he calls out in the other.

The play antedates the game. For in a game there is a regulated procedure, and rules. The child must not only take the rôle of the other, as he does in the play, but he must assume the various rôles of all the participants in the game, and govern his action accordingly. If he plays first base, it is as the one to whom the ball will be thrown from the field or from the catcher. Their organized reactions to him he has imbedded in his own playing of the different positions, and this organized reaction becomes what I have called the "generalized other" that accompanies and controls his conduct. And it is this generalized other in his experience which provides him with a self. I can only refer to the bearing of this childish play attitude upon so-called sympathetic magic. Primitive men call out in their own activity some simulacrum of the response which they are seeking from the world about. They are children crying in the night.

The mechanism of this implies that the individual who is stimulating others to response is at the same time arousing in himself the tendencies to the same reactions. Now, that in a complex social act, which serves as the stimulus to another individual to his response is not as a rule fitted to call out the tendency to the same response in the individual himself. The hostile demeanor of one animal does not frighten the animal himself, presumably. Especially in the complex social reactions of the ants or termites or the bees, the part of the act of one form which does call out the appropriate reaction of another can hardly be conceived of as arousing a like reaction in the form in question, for where the complex social act is dependent upon physiological differentiation, such an unlikeness in structure exists that the same stimulus could not call out like responses. For such a mechanism as has been suggested, it is necessary to find first of all some stimulus in the social conduct of the members of an authentic group that can call out in the individual that is responsible for it, the same response that it calls out in the other; and in the second place, the individuals in the group must be of such like structure that the stimulus will have the same value for one form that it has for the other. Such a type of social stimulus is found in the vocal gesture in a human society. The term gesture I am using to refer to that part of the act or attitude of one individual engaged in a social act which serves as the stimulus to another individual to carry out his part of the whole act. Illustrations of gestures, so defined, may be found in the attitudes and movements of others to which we respond in passing them in a crowd, in the turning of the head toward the glance of another's eye, in the hostile attitude assumed over against a threatening gesture, in the thousand and one different attitudes which we assume toward different modulations of the human voice, or in the attitudes and suggestions of movements in boxers or fencers, to which responses are so nicely adjusted. It is to be noted that the attitudes to which I have referred are but stages in the act as they appear to others, and include expressions of countenance, positions of the body, changes in breathing rhythm, outward evidence of circulatory

changes, and vocal sounds. In general these so-called gestures belong
to the beginning of the overt act, for the adjustments of others to the
social processes are best made early in the act. Gestures are, then, the
early stages in the overt social act to which other forms involved in the
same act respond. Our interest is in finding gestures which can affect
the individual that is responsible for them in the same manner as that
in which they affect other individuals. The vocal gesture is at least one
that assails our ears who make it in the same physiological fashion as
that in which it affects others. We hear our own vocal gestures as others
hear them. We may see or feel movements of our hands as others see
or feel them, and these sights and feels have served in the place of the
vocal gesture in the case of those who are congenitally deaf or deaf
and blind. But it has been the vocal gesture that has preeminently provided the medium of social organization in human society. It belongs
historically to the beginning of the act, for it arises out of the change
in breathing rhythm that accompanies the preparation for sudden action, those actions to which other forms must be nicely adjusted.

If, then, a vocal gesture arouses in the individual who makes it a
tendency to the same response that it arouses in another, and this beginning of an act of the other in himself enters into his experience, he will
find himself tending to act toward himself as the other acts toward him.
In our self-conscious experience we understand what he does or says.
The possibility of this entering into his experience we have found in
the cortex of the human brain. There the coordinations answering to an
indefinite number of acts may be excited, and while holding each other
in check enter into the neural process of adjustment which leads to the
final overt conduct. If one pronounces and hears himself pronounce the
word "table," he has aroused in himself the organized attitudes of his
response to that object, in the same fashion as that in which he has
aroused it in another. We commonly call such an aroused organized
attitude an idea, and the ideas of what we are saying accompany all of
our significant speech. If we may trust to the statement in one of St.
Paul's epistles, some of the saints spoke with tongues which had no
significance to them. They made sounds which called out no response
in those that made them. The sounds were without meaning. Where a
vocal gesture uttered by one individual leads to a certain response in
another, we may call it a symbol of that act; where it arouses in the
man who makes it the tendency to the same response, we may call it a
significant symbol. These organized attitudes which we arouse in our-

selves when we talk to others are, then, the ideas which we say are in our minds, and in so far as they arouse the same attitudes in others, they are in their minds, in so far as they are self-conscious in the sense in which I have used that term. But it is not necessary that we should talk to another to have these ideas. We can talk to ourselves, and this we do in the inner forum of what we call thought. We are in possession of selves just in so far as we can and do take the attitudes of others toward ourselves and respond to those attitudes. We approve of ourselves and condemn ourselves. We pat ourselves upon the back and in blind fury attack ourselves. We assume the generalized attitude of the group, in the censor that stands at the door of our imagery and inner conversations, and in the affirmation of the laws and axioms of the universe of discourse. *Quod semper, quod ubique.* Our thinking is an inner conversation in which we may be taking the rôles of specific acquaintances over against ourselves, but usually it is with that I have termed the "generalized other" that we converse, and so attain to the levels of abstract thinking, and that impersonality, that so-called objectivity that we cherish. In this fashion, I conceive, have selves arisen in human behavior and with the selves their minds. It is an interesting study, that of the manner in which the self and its mind arises in every child, and the indications of the corresponding manner in which it arose in primitive man. I cannot enter into a discussion of this. I do wish, however, to refer to some of the implications of this conception of the self for the theory of social control.

I wish to recur to the position, taken earlier in this paper, that, if we recognize that experience is a process continually passing into the future, objects exist in nature as the patterns of our actions. If we reduce the world to a fictitious instantaneous present, all objects fall to pieces. There is no reason to be found, except in an equally fictitious mind, why any lines should be drawn about any group of physical particles, constituting them objects. However, no such knife-edge present exists. Even in the so-called specious present there is a passage, in which there is succession, and both past and future are there, and the present is only that section in which, from the standpoint of action, both are involved. When we take this passage of nature seriously, we see that the object of perception is the existent future of the act. The food is what the animal will eat, and his refuge is the burrow where he will escape from his pursuer. Of course the future is, as future, contingent. He may not escape, but in nature it exists there as the counterpart of his act. So far as there are fixed relations there, they are of the past, and the object involves both, but the form that it has arises from the ongoing act. Evolutionary biology, in so far as it is not mere physics and chemistry, proceeds perhaps unwittingly upon this assumption, and so does social science in so far as it is not static. Its objects are in terms of the habitat, the environment. They are fashioned by reactions. I am merely affirming the existence of these objects, affirming them as existent in a passing universe answering to acts.

In so far as there are social acts, there are social objects, and I take it that social control is bringing the act of the individual into relation with this social object. With the control of the object over the act, we are abundantly familiar. Just because the object is the form of the act, in this character it controls the expression of the act. The vision of the distant object is not only the stimulus to movement toward it. It is also, in its changing distance values, a continual control of the act of approach. The contours of the object determine the organization of the act in its seizure, but in this case the whole act is in the individual and the object is in his field of experience. Barring a breakdown in the structure or function, the very existence of the object insures its control of the act. In the social act, however, the act is distributed among a number of individuals. While there is or may be an object answering to each part of the act, existing in the experience of each individual, in the case of societies dependent upon physiological differentiation, the whole object does not exist in the experience of any individual. The control may be exercised through the survival of those physiological differentiations that still carry out the life-process involved in the complex act. No complication of the act which did not mediate this could survive. Or we may take refuge in a controlling factor in the act, as does Bergson, but this is not the situation that interests us. The human societies in which we are interested are societies of selves. The human individual is a self only in so far as he takes the attitude of another toward himself. In so far as this attitude is that of a number of others, and in so far as he can assume the organized attitudes of a number that are cooperating in a common activity, he takes the attitudes of the group toward himself, and in taking this or these attitudes he is defining the object of the group, that which defines and controls the response. Social control, then, will depend upon the degree to which the individual does assume the attitudes of those in the group who are involved with him in his social activities. In the illustration already used, the man who buys controls his purchase from the standpoint of a value in the object that exists for him only in so far as he takes the attitude of a seller as well as a buyer. Value exists as an object only for individuals within whose acts in exchange are present those attitudes which belong to the acts of the others who are essential to the exchange.

The act of exchange becomes very complicated; the degree to which all the essential acts involved in it enter into the acts of all those engaged therein varies enormously, and the control which the object, i.e., the value, exercises over the acts varies proportionately. The Marxian theory of state ownership of capital, i.e., of exclusive state production, is a striking illustration of the breakdown of such control. The social object, successful economic production, as presented in this theory, fails to assume the attitudes of individual initiative which successful economic production implies. Democratic government, on the theory of action through universal interest in the issues of a campaign, breaks down as a control, and surrenders the government largely to the political machine, whose object more nearly answers to the attitudes of the voters and the non-voters.

Social control depends, then, upon the degree to which the individuals in society are able to assume the attitudes of the others who are involved with them in common endeavor. For the social object will always answer to the act developing itself in self-consciousness. Besides property, all of the institutions are such objects, and serve to control individuals who find in them the organization of their own social responses.

The individual does not, of course, assume the attitudes of the numberless others who are in one way or another implicated in his social conduct, except in so far as the attitudes of others are uniform under like circumstances. One assumes, as I have said, the attitudes of generalized others. But even with this advantage of the universal over the multiplicity of its numberless instances, the number of different responses that enter into our social conduct seems to defy any capacity of any individual to assume the rôles which would be essential to define our social objects. And yet, though modern life has become indefinitely more complex than it was in earlier periods of human history, it is far easier for the modern man than for his predecessor to put himself in the place of those who contribute to his necessities, who share with him the functions of government, or join with him in determining prices. It is not the number of participants, or even the number of different functions, that is of primary importance. The important question is whether these various forms of activities belong so naturally to the member of a human society that, in taking the rôle of another, his activities are found to belong to one's own nature. As long as the complexities of human society do not exceed those of the central nervous system, the problem of an adequate social object, which is identical with that of an adequate self-consciousness, is not that of becoming acquainted with the indefinite number of acts that are involved in social behavior, but that of so overcoming the distances in space and time, and the barriers of language and convention and social status, that we can converse with ourselves in the rôles of those who are involved with us in the common undertaking of life. A journalism that is insatiably curious about the human attitudes of all of us is the sign of the times. The other curiosities as to the conditions under which other people live, and work, and fight each other, and love each other, follow from the fundamental curiosity which is the passion of self-consciousness. We must be others if we are to be ourselves. The modern realistic novel has done more than technical education in fashioning the social object that spells social control. If we can bring people together so that they can enter into each other's lives, they will inevitably have a common object, which will control their common conduct.

The task, however, is enormous enough, for it involves not simply breaking down passive barriers such as those of distance in space and time and vernacular, but those fixed attitudes of custom and status in which our selves are imbedded. Any self is a social self, but it is restricted to the group whose rôles it assumes, and it will never abandon this self until it finds itself entering into the larger society and maintaining itself there. The whole history of warfare between societies and within societies shows how much more readily and with how much greater emotional thrill we realize our selves in opposition to common enemies than in collaboration with them. All over Europe, and more specifically at Geneva, we see nationals with great distrust and constant rebounds trying to put themselves in each other's places and still preserve the selves that have existed upon enmities, that they may reach the common ground where they may avoid the horror of war, and meliorate unendurable economic conditions. A Dawes Plan is such a social object, coming painfully into existence, that may control the conflicting interests of hostile communities, but only if each can in some degree put himself in the other's place in operating it. The World Court and the League of Nations are other such social objects that sketch out common plans of action if there are national selves that can realize themselves in the collaborating attitudes of others.

CHARLES HARTSHORNE

Charles Hartshorne was born in Kittanning, Pennsylvania on June 5, 1897. Hartshorne's undergraduate career began at Haverford, but it ended after only two years when he volunteered to go to France with the U.S. Army Medical Corps during World War I to serve as an orderly. Shortly after returning to the United States in 1919, Hartshorne resumed his undergraduate career at Harvard University, where, in 1923, he completed his Ph.D. While a student at Harvard, Hartshorne studied with, among others, C. I. Lewis, R. B. Perry, and W. E. Hocking. Upon graduating from Harvard, Hartshorne spent two years in Europe on a Sheldon Fellowship doing postdoctoral work, mostly in Germany, but with some time spent in England and Austria. When he came back from Europe in 1925, Hartshorne returned to Harvard, where he became an instructor and a research fellow. The latter job was truly momentous, as it consisted in his both being a teaching assistant for Alfred North Whitehead and beginning the process of editing the Peirce papers (with Paul Weiss). Indeed, these two thinkers have had a profound influence on Hartshorne throughout his life and career. Hartshorne left Harvard in 1928 for the University of Chicago, where he remained for 27 years. While at Chicago, Hartshorne began in earnest his prolific publishing career, publishing such books as *Man's Vision of God and the Logic of Theism, The Divine Relativity,* and *Reality as Social Process: Studies in Metaphysics and Religion.* Then, in 1955, Hartshorne left Chicago for Emory University. Because Emory had a strict retirement policy at the time, Hartshorne left there for the University of Texas in 1962, at the age of 65. Professor Hartshorne still lives in Austin, Texas, where he has been Ashbel Smith Professor Emeritus since 1978. In Hartshorne's distinguished career, he has published over 20 books and some 500 articles. His distinguished career as a philosopher has been equaled by his international influence as one of the founders (along with Whitehead) of Process Theology, which remains today as the most vibrant theological alternative to classical theism.

In addition to being a well-known and respected philosopher, Hartshorne is also a noted ornithologist, with a specialty in bird songs. In 1973 he published *Born to Sing: An Interpretation and World Survey of Bird Song.* In addition, he has published 16 articles on the subject.

MAJOR PHILOSOPHICAL WORKS BY HARTSHORNE

1934 *The Philosophy and Psychology of Sensation.* Chicago: The University of Chicago Press. Reissued in 1968 by Kennikat Press.

1937 *Beyond Humanism: Essays in the New Philosophy of Nature.* Chicago: Willet, Clark & Company. Bison Book Edition, with new Preface: Lincoln: University of Nebraska Press, 1968.

1941 *Man's Vision of God and the Logic of Theism.* Chicago: Willet, Clark & Company. After 1948 published by Harper and Brothers Publishers, New York. Reprinted, 1964, by Archon Books, Hamden, Conn.

1948 *The Divine Relativity: A Social Conception of God.* The Terry Lectures, 1947. New Haven: Yale University Press.

1950 "Whitehead's Metaphysics," in *Whitehead and the Modern World: Science, Metaphysics, and Civilization, Three Essays on the Thought of Alfred North Whitehead.* By Victor Lowe, Charles Hartshorne, and A. H. Johnson. Boston: The Beacon Press. Reprinted by Books for Libraries Press, 1972.

1953 *Reality as Social Process: Studies in Metaphysics and Religion.* Glencoe, Ill.: The Free Press, and Boston: The Beacon Press. Reprinted by Hafner, 1971.

1953 *Philosophers Speak of God* (with William L. Reese). Chicago: The University of Chicago Press. Reissued in 1976 in Midway Reprints.

1962 *The Logic of Perfection and Other Essays in Neoclassical Metaphysics.* La Salle, Ill.: Open Court.

1965 *Anselm's Discovery.* La Salle, Ill.: Open Court.

1967 *A Natural Theology for Our Time.* La Salle, Ill.: Open Court.

1970 *Creative Synthesis and Philosophic Method.* London: SCM Press Ltd., and La Salle, Ill.: Open Court.

1972 *Whitehead's Philosophy: Selected Essays, 1935–1970.* Lincoln: University of Nebraska Press.

1973 *Born to Sing: An Interpretation and World Survey of Bird Song.* Bloomington: Indiana University Press.

1976   *Aquinas to Whitehead: Seven Centuries of Metaphysics of Religion. The Aquinas Lecture, 1976.* Milwaukee: Marquette University Publications.

1983   *Insights and Oversights of Great Thinkers: an Evaluation of Western Philosophy.* Albany: SUNY Press.

1984   *Omnipotence and Other Theological Mistakes.* Albany: SUNY Press.

1984   *Creativity in American Philosophy.* Albany: SUNY Press.

1987   *Wisdom as Moderation: a Philosophy of the Middle Way.* Albany: SUNY Press.

1990   *The Darkness and the Light: A Philosopher Reflects on his Fortunate Career and Those Who Made it Possible.* Albany: SUNY Press.

1997   *The Zero Fallacy & Other Essays in Neoclassical Metaphysics.* Mohammed Valady, ed. LaSalle, Ill.: Open Court.

RECOMMENDED COMMENTARIES AND DISCUSSIONS ABOUT HARTSHORNE

Cobb, John B. Jr., and Franklin I. Gamwell. *Existence and Actuality: Conversations with Charles Hartshorne.* Chicago: The University of Chicago Press, 1984.

Dombrowski, Daniel A. *Analytic Theism, Hartshorne, and the Concept of God.* Albany: SUNY Press, 1996.

———. *Hartshorne and the Metaphysics of Animal Rights.* Albany: SUNY, 1988.

Gragg, Alan. *Charles Hartshorne.* Series in Makers of the Modern Theological Mind, ed. Bob E. Patterson. Waco, Tex.: Word Books, 1973.

Hahn, Lewis E. (ed.). *The Philosophy of Charles Hartshorne.* La Salle, Ill.: Open Court Publishing Co., 1991.

Kane, Robert and Stephen R. Phillips (eds.). *Hartshorne, Process Philosophy and Theology.* Albany: SUNY, 1989.

Moskop, John C. *Divine Omniscience and Human Freedom: Thomas Aquinas and Charles Hartshorne.* Macon, Ga.: Mercer University Press, 1984.

Peters, Eugene H. *Hartshorne and Neoclassical Metaphysics: An Interpretation.* Lincoln: University of Nebraska Press, 1970.

Reese, William L, and Eugene Freeman (eds.). *Process and Divinity:*

The Hartshorne Festschrift. LaSalle, Ill.: Open Court Publishing Co., 1964.

Sia, Santiago (ed.). *Charles Hartshorne's Concept of God: Philosophical and Theological Responses.* Boston: Martinus Nijhoff Publishers, 1990.

———. *God in Process Thought: A Study in Charles Hartshorne's Concept of God.* Boston: Martinus Nijhoff Publishers, 1985.

Viney, Donald Wayne. *Charles Hartshorne and the Existence of God.* Albany: SUNY Press, 1985.

The Development of Process Philosophy (Introduction to the First Edition)

The term "process philosophy"—first used by I do not know whom, perhaps my friend Bernard Loomer—is one way of pointing to a profound change which has come over speculative philosophy or metaphysics in the modern period in Europe and America. I have myself often used the more noncommittal phrase "neoclassical metaphysics" for much the same purpose, since the emphasis upon process or becoming, though essential, is only one feature of this new way of viewing reality. Also characteristic is the emphasis upon relations and relativity. The Buddhistic phrase, "dependent origination," suggests the connection between the two points. What has an origin is relative to that origin; only what has always been as it is can be "absolute," wholly independent of other things. However, in this essay I shall deal chiefly with process, not relativity. It is not hard to translate talk about being and becoming into talk about absoluteness and relativity. But I shall not always attempt the translation in what follows.

Greek philosophy tended to depreciate becoming and exalt mere being, and—as was consistent—to depreciate relativity and exalt independence or absoluteness. Aristotle summed it up when he held that what was altogether immutable and hence immune to influence from others was superior to that which in any way changed or depended upon other things. Medieval natural theology never explicitly deviated from this attitude, though revealed doctrines of the trinity and the incarnation may have almost explicitly done so. (Did not the Son depend upon the Father without being inferior to Him?)

However, the harmony of some doctrines of the classical natural theology with the Greek attitude is extremely doubtful. Aristotle had denied God's knowledge of contingent and changing things, on the straightforward ground that knowing cannot be independent of what is known. Yet Christian and most Jewish and Mohammedan theists felt obliged, for religious reasons, to affirm God's knowledge of the contingent and changing world. Only a few Mohammedans dared even to hint that this must mean change in God. Christians and Jews would scarcely go so far. The result was a glaring inconsistency which troubled many. For precisely this reason Crescas, and later Spinoza, denied contingency (and by implication change) not only in God but in the world which God knows. For they saw that the known is in the knowing, and if there is contingency and change in the former then there is also in the latter. Thus in Spinoza the Greek bias came to its last great triumph in Western thought. Not only God, but the world, too, was to be made safe from accident or genuine alteration. And indeed, immutable omniscience, implying the immutability of all truth, consorts ill with the view that becoming is real. If there is novel reality, then to that extent the truth also must be novel. To say of future events that they "are going to be" is to imply that their entire character is a present fact, though a fact which, with our human limitations, we have not yet reached. But there the fact is, waiting for us to reach it, or there it is offstage, waiting to come on. In this view, genuine becoming is missing. The truth, the reality, is eternally there, spread out to the divine gaze, though our present experience, being localized in the eternal panorama, cannot behold most of it. As St. Thomas put it, events in time are like travelers on a road who cannot see those far ahead of them though they can all be seen by one sufficiently high above the road looking down upon its entire length, i.e., by God in eternity. Bergson's phrase, "spatializing time," fits this view as a glove a hand. The theory entirely omits the aspect of creation involved in becoming. The entirety of creation cannot be viewed if there is no such totality. How can there be if the actual sum of events receives additions each moment? And what is becoming if not such perpetual adding of new realities? Thomas is assuming the falsity of a certain view of time; process philosophy adopts this view, and not without reason.

Since the eternalistic view reached explicit formulation in theological guise, it was fitting that the process doctrine should also emerge in a theological context. Philosophies of being, which treat becoming as secondary, have acquired powerful religious sanctions; it is therefore well that we should realize from the outset that process philosophy, in its origin at least, is a rival religious doctrine rather than an irreligious one. This is true in two important respects:

(1) The earliest great tradition which espoused a philosophy of becoming was Buddhism. Heracleitos, who said that things are new each moment, was isolated, and in addition obscure, for we have but fragmentary sayings. Only the followers of Buddha produced a great literature expressive of the doctrine that becoming is the universal form of reality. They carried this view through, in some respects, with admirable thoroughness, long before anything like it occurred in the West. Philosophies of being characteristically treat change either as "unreal" or as in principle but the substitution of one set of qualities for another in an abiding "substratum," "substance," or "subject of change." For them, reality consists essentially of beings, not happenings or events. If a being is not of the highest kind, it shows this deficiency by undergoing alterations. If it is of the highest kind, alteration could only be for the worse and hence could have no point. So the highest being is changeless, but the others, poor things, keep changing, apparently in the in principle vain effort to make up for their imperfection. This doctrine is Greek through and through, but, alas, the Church Fathers accepted it. True, the doctrine also arose long ago in the Orient. But there Buddhism came to challenge it, with a subtlety and persistence which had no counterpart in classical and medieval Europe. The Buddhists rejected "substance," including the "soul" as substance. The momentary experiences are the primary realities, and these do not change, they simply become, and what is called change is the successive becoming of events having certain relationships to their predecessors. The "soul" or the self-identical ego is merely the relatedness of experiences to their predecessors through memory and the persistence of various qualities or personality traits. The first great metaphysician in the West to hold this view clearly was Whitehead, in the present century. But we must not get ahead of our story, which is mainly that of the development of process philosophy in the West.

(2) The man who first squarely faced the conflict between the religious doctrine of an all-knowing God and Greek eternalism and decided against the latter was Fausto Socinus, whose sect was destroyed by persecution and whose bold theorizing has been ignored by historians of philosophy (not to their credit, I must add). Socinus rejected the immutability of God in order to be able consistently to affirm the reality of becoming. He did not quite put it in this way. What he said rather was that human freedom is incompatible with immutable divine knowledge of our free acts. However, our freedom is nothing but that

case of becoming which we experience from the inside or by direct intuition, rather than infer from more or less indirect observation. We have to start with events we intimately know! A decision (and we make little ones each moment) is a settling of the otherwise unsettled; it occurs in time, not in eternity; to say that God eternally knows all decisions is to imply that the totality of decisions is a single all-inclusive eternally complete set of realities. But then there is nothing for decisions to decide. We only imagine we are resolving a real indeterminacy when we make up our minds; in truth the resolution is eternal. But if eternal, it has no genuine becoming. We say that we "make" a decision; but religious philosophies of being tell us that God makes everything by a single eternal act. So then I make my decision now and God eternally makes it! But if God makes it, how is it my decision rather than His? Socinus in effect, perhaps without being fully explicit about it, was pointing to the paradox of the double determining of events to which Greek thought in its theological form had led. This brave and honest man had the courage to affirm that we really do make our decisions, and that in so far as we do God does not make them. We have here the idea of self-creation, which later in Lequier, the French philosopher of a century ago, and still later in William James, Dewey, Whitehead, Sartre, and others has been so often stressed. Note that it was a theological idea before it was an atheistic one (in Sartre). But if we, and not God, make our decisions, in what fashion can God know these decisions? He cannot decree them in eternity and, by knowing this decree, know what they are. Rather, He must perceive them as they occur, and then preserve them in memory. Events—at least those events which are free acts—come into being, are created, at a given time; to know them beforehand—even more, to know them eternally—is a logical absurdity, for it is not beforehand, much less eternally, that they exist to be known! Only as and after they occur are there any such entities to be known. Hence that God "fails" to know them eternally or beforehand is not properly a failure, for success here is mere nonsense, and where success is nonsense "failure" is inapplicable. Hence it is quibbling to call God "ignorant" because He does not know things which are not there to be known. This argument was hinted at much earlier (in Cicero, if not before him), but the Socinians were the first to make serious theological use of it. They courageously admitted real change in the divine knowledge, the becoming of new knowledge in God to harmonize with the becoming or creation of new things to be known. There is no total creation for God to know in one finally complete act of knowing. Rather, the totality of the real is enriched each moment by as many acts of freedom as occur in the world. With the growth of reality must come a growth of divine knowledge of reality. All this is somewhat further clarified by Lequier three centuries later—followed by Whitehead, who apparently knew little of his predecessors in this way of thinking.

It is notable that the earliest theist of all, Ikhnaton of Egypt, spoke of God "fashioning himself." Thus self-creation is an old religious idea. One can find it also in ancient India. Medieval anti-process theology may eventually be seen as but an interlude, a detour from which religious thought has happily returned to the main highway. And clearly, if Socinus allows man to determine part of the content of the divine knowledge by man's self-creation, he can hardly wish to deny self-creation to deity. For if God is to change, it surely should be in part voluntarily, and not solely as result of man's initiative. Besides, the self-creativity of man, like all his traits, can only be an imperfect image of what in God must be perfect. So there must be an "Eminent" or divine self-creation, of which ours is but a remote and inferior analogue. If, in making our decisions, we make something of ourselves, then analogously God in making His supreme decisions must in some supreme sense make Himself. Even Lequier seems not to see this implication of the process doctrine. Whitehead is our first great systematic philosopher to see it with any great clarity. But the German psychologist and religious thinker, Fechner, had said something like it in his *Zend-Avesta.*

One can, to be sure, read a sort of process philosophy into Hegel and Schelling. But in these writers there are so many concessions to, or echoes of, Greek thought that dispute concerning their classification is to my mind rather unrewarding. They are process philosophers perhaps—if they are anything clear and unambiguous. But what a big "if" this is! They doubtless helped to do away with the classical metaphysics of being; but that they constructed a viable alternative is much less clear.

Socinus and Lequier attacked the theological center of the philosophy of being and absoluteness and proposed a definite alternative. But they failed to generalize this alternative. Only man's freedom (and God's knowledge of man) was clearly taken out of the old context; the rest of nature could still be looked upon as unfree, and as subject to immutable divine knowledge. This is where Bergson and Whitehead, preceded at least vaguely by Fechner, come in. Bergson treats all life as to some extent free or creative, and definitely hints, in his later works, that all nature is to some extent free. In Whitehead this implication is made sharply explicit. Not only man is a "self-created creature" but every individual is, in some slight degree at least, self-creative, maker of its own decisions, and so of itself. Divinity is the Eminent or supreme form of self-creation, anything else is an inferior form. Whitehead combines this with the Socinian insight that a self-creative creature must also create something in God, for he who makes something in himself makes something in the knowledge of all those who know him, and so makes them to a certain extent. We make our friends and enemies just in so far as we are free and they know us. It could not be otherwise, given the essential meanings of "free" and "know." Since God knows all creatures, and a creature is merely an inferior case of what in God is supreme self-creativity, all creatures whatsoever are in part creators of (something in) God. And so Whitehead refers to God as Creature, or to the divine Consequent Nature—God as consequent upon or partly created by the world. This is how deity must be conceived in a consistent metaphysics of process.

Whitehead is not indulging in eccentricity at this point, he is merely following out the logic of the decision to make creative becoming the universal category. So when he tells us that creativity is the "category of the ultimate," the "universal of universals," he is summing up and crowning a long development. Freedom is now seen as the essence of reality, not a mere special case. To be is to create oneself and thereby to influence the self-creation of those by whom one is known, including God.

Process philosophy, fully thought out, is creationism! Multitudes have talked about God's "creating" of the world, but they usually had no philosophical category adequate to express this idea. All they could do was to say that God was "cause" and the world the effect. They were unable to show in our ordinary experiences of causation any unambiguously creative aspect. The potter shapes the clay, they said, but the supreme Potter, they also said, had shaped the lesser potter completely, and so the only genuine decision was the supreme Potter's. Thus free creation, genuine decision, is banished from the world. But how, from such a world, could we possibly form the conception of divine creation? I believe that three thousand years of speculation have led to this result, foreshadowed by Ikhnaton at the outset: Creativity, if real at all, must be universal, not limited to God alone, and it must be self-creativity as well as creative influencing of others. In the hymns of Ikhnaton there is nothing about mere causality, nothing about inexorable causal relationships, nothing (unless a vague hint or two) about God's determining the details of the creature's actions. The suggestion almost throughout is of free creatures responding to divine freedom, influencing God to delight in the spectacle they afford for Him, while they delight in His beneficent influence upon them. But it took three millennia to change this purely poetic and intuitive vision into a sharply defined philosophical doctrine. Many formidable obstacles had first to be overcome.

Let us look at some of these obstacles. There is the commonsense view, enshrined in European language (not in all languages), that the most concrete realities to which abstractions are to be applied, the real "subjects" which have "predicates" are things, individuals which change from one actual state to another—a person, a tree, a mountain, a star—not happenings. But there is something more concrete than an individual, and that is the actual history of the individual, the succession of "states," for instance, experiences, which constitute the reality of the individual through time. Is it not clear that the entire *actuality* of the individual is in his states, bodily and mental? True, his possibilities are not exhaustively realized by these states; he could have had other experiences; but we are not now asking what he potentially is, only what he actually has been up to now. The sole way to distinguish the individual from the happenings making up his history is in terms of possibility versus actuality, with the states constituting the *entire* actuality. Now I ask: Are not the actual and the concrete the same? Only in abstract terms can one speak of possible happenings; concrete happenings, knowable as such, and actual happenings are one and the same. Hence those who take individuals to be wholly concrete will, if they are clear-headed, be forced, with Leibniz, to identify the individual with the total succession of his states. But then we do not know who a man is until he is dead; we cannot speak of his capability of having done (or experienced) something else; for, as Leibniz said, it would not have been that individual but another who would have done it. The commonsense meaning of individual is destroyed if we simply identify an individual with an actual event-sequence. To save this meaning, and we need it for many purposes, we must admit, with the Buddhists and

Whitehead, that individuality is somewhat abstract, compared to an actual event-sequence. It is the man now, his present actual state, which "has" the man as the same individual from birth to death, not the same individual which "has" the present actual state. We speak of someone's being "in a state" (not of the state as being in him). Whitehead can take this literally; substance philosophers cannot. The point is not that individual identity is an illusion, but that it is abstract. Concretely there is a new man each moment, "born anew" in religious language. But of course, in many important personality traits it may be the same man all the time. And each new state fits onto the one series which started with a certain embryo state in a certain mother. It is always, while the man lives, the same series, but the identity of such a series is somewhat abstract. To see the man as always the very same entity, we must abstract from what is new in him at each moment. Personal identity through experiences is a property of the experiences, they are not properties of the identity, or of the ego. If they were, to know an individual would mean knowing all his future. We should not really know which individual was John until John was dead. This is not how we use the idea of self-identity. It took European philosophy over two thousand years to think through this issue, which Buddhism thought through long ago. Contemporary physics, with its view of reality as consisting in events related in the four dimensions of space-time, helped Whitehead to see the point, but the Buddhists got there without this help.

The argument against the process view has been, "If there is change, something, X, must have changed from state A to state B." Very well, suppose the weather changes from wet to dry, does this mean there is an entity, the weather, as concrete as the wet and dry states? Are these "in" the weather? Surely the weather is in them. Suppose "public opinion" changes, or "the situation" changes—is it not obvious that the "subjects of change" here are relatively abstract entities? Process philosophy generalizes this insight. It treats change as the successive becoming of events related to one another, but also differing from one another in some more or less abstract respects which interest us. Change is the becoming of novelty, and process philosophy is all for that.

Another argument is: Memory shows us that we, the very same persons, were there in the past having certain experiences. But again, no one denies personal self-identity, provided its abstractness or partial nature is recognized. In the past that I recall, "I" was there, just in so far as what is important about "my" personal sequence of experiences was already in the earlier experiences. But why is it that we cannot remember our identical selves as small infants? Surely because in those early states what is now most important about us was not yet actual. To abstract from all that we have become since early infancy is more than we can do and still leave anything worth distinctly recalling as ourselves. But even in fairly early childhood important personality traits were already beginning to emerge, and so we can recall childhood experiences as making us already the "same" person we are now. Still, we certainly cannot ever remember that in the past we were concretely and precisely what we are now, for that we were not! The "selfsame ego" is an abstraction from concrete realities, not itself a fully concrete reality. To see this is the beginning of wisdom in the theory of self-hood. The Buddhists saw it. (Did the Hindus? I am not convinced they did.)

One of the many signs of confusion in substance philosophy is the failure to deal with the obvious logical truth that identity is a symmetrical relation: if X is Y, then Y is X. Very well, if identity explains memory of the past, by the same token it does *not* explain the failure to "remember" the future. If memory is an entity being, or intuiting, that very same entity, then it ought to work equally in both directions. In spite of claims of some students of Psychical research, the lack of real symmetry in this respect is too glaring to be ignored. We anticipate trends, extrapolate them into the future, but we remember not trends but particular incidents. Identity is not the logical structure to express this. And that substance philosophers rarely even mention this point is proof enough of how far they are from clarity as to the real problems. As Whitehead says, identity is "exactly the wrong answer" if the question is: How do we explain the creativity of process, its production of novelty? That it is the same entity does not imply that there are new states of the entity, still less that it is the previous states which are experienced, not the subsequent ones. In general, all attempts to explain becoming as a special case of being, novelty as a special case of permanence, have failed. Becoming is said to be a mixture of being and not-being; this is so incomplete a statement as to be less than a half-truth. Becoming is not simply a mixture of being and not-being, it is a mixture of which a *new* instance is *created* every moment, but in this moment-by-moment creation of *new* cases of being-not-being is the whole mystery of becoming. A *fixed* mixture of what is and what is not would still not be becoming, but at most only a deficient form of being. The *becoming* of new (allegedly) deficient forms of being is simply becoming, and no light is thrown on the *transition* to novelty by the talk about being and its negation. We shall see that, by contrast, being can very well be explicated as an aspect of becoming, permanence as an aspect of novelty. The converse procedure has always failed, though men have often refused to take note of the failure. When they noted it, they excused themselves by declaring becoming "unreal." Its refusal to subordinate itself to being condemned it. But this is sheer question-begging. The necessity of the subordination having been assumed, of course it could also be deduced. But the validity of the assumption is not thereby confirmed; rather the resistance of becoming to the attempted subordination disconfirms the theory!

An important obstacle to the process view is the apparent continuity of becoming—for instance, of experiencing. It seems that experiencing is not a succession of distinct acts or happenings but just one perpetually changing act or happening, at least between waking and sleeping. Here some process philosophers have stopped short and never reached full clarity. This applies to Bergson and Dewey, for instance. And here again Whitehead, preceded by the Buddhists, and to his great credit by William James, carried the analysis through. Continuity is an abstract mathematical concept, not a given actuality. Half a continuum is itself a smaller continuum, but half a man is not a smaller man, nor is half a molecule just a smaller molecule. If happenings are actualities, and even more concrete than individuals, they must be like molecules or men, not like mathematical schema. If experiencing were continuous, then half of a half of a half . . . of an experience would also be an experience. However, though in a tenth of a second we can have an experience, in half of a half of a half of a tenth, it seems we cannot. Were experiencing a continuum, indeed, we should have an infinite number of experiences between waking and having breakfast! This seems quite absurd. But the alternative is that we have a finite number of experiences, and no finite number can make a continuum. James said that each "specious present" was a new unit-happening which comes into actuality as a whole, not bit by bit. Whitehead accepts this, and generalizes it for other types of experiencing than the human, and ultimately for all happenings whatever. Reality consists of the becoming of unit-events, which he calls "actual entities," "actual occasions," "drops of experience." It is only with this doctrine that process philosophy can effectively compete with substance philosophies. For these had the advantage that individuals, at least individual animals, are units such that half a unit is not a unit in the same sense at all. In a room, the number of persons can be definite and finite; but in process philosophies which admit continuity, the number of happenings, even of a given kind, must be infinite in a single second. But then all definiteness is lost, and there are no objective units of reality. Giving up continuity—and here, too, Whitehead was helped by physics, with its quanta, while the Buddhists got there unaided—the difficulty is overcome. True, we cannot perhaps know what corresponds, in other animals and other types of process than human experiencing, to the human specious present of about .1 second. However, in some cases, e.g., birds, we can rather safely posit a greater number of experiences than ten while a clock ticks off one second. In any case this is a question of detail only.

Another difficulty which a process philosopher must deal with is the requirement that his view must *not* mean that literally "everything changes," or as the Buddhists put it, "everything is impermanent," passes away, from which they deduced the unimportance of ordinary human concerns. In meditation, in mysterious Nirvana, the Buddhists felt that they somehow transcended even impermanence, but only in nonrational fashion. It is necessary for a philosopher to have also a more theoretical escape. Buddha hinted once that there was something which does not pass away, but this was about as far as he would go. Here Bergson, along with Peirce, and then most explicitly and clearly Whitehead, has a great addition to make to the tradition of process philosophy. How do we even know that things *have* passed away, if not by preserving in memory at least something of what they have been? In memory, past happenings are still somehow with us. Moreover, in perception also past happenings in a fashion linger on in present experience. We now hear the explosion which in fact took place some seconds ago, we see a stellar explosion which took place years in the past. Memory and perception both somehow embrace the past and preserve something at least of its character. In human memory and perception this "immortality of the past" is faint and fragmentary; but then all human capacities are imperfect, limited. If we are to raise the question of deity at all, why not consider a perfect or divine memory, and a perfect or divine perception of happenings, once they have occurred? In such a perfect memory or perception the past might be literally immortal, adequately preserved in all its quality, all its beauty, forever.

Is this merely introducing God as a trick device to rid us of our difficulties? Yet what can any theory do but explain what otherwise remains inexplicable? And it is no merely emotional need that events should be preserved, that our lives should forever have some place or function in reality after they are over, or after, perhaps, all human life is ended. It is also a logical demand that after events have happened, it should always be true that they have. But if the Buddhists are right, what can make it true that things have happened just as they have? Truth must be true of reality. If the reality keeps fading out, so must truth. But what then would make it true that it had faded? Thus the literal immortality of the past, in principle accounted for by memory and perception, but adequately only in an adequate memory or perception, is required to explain what "truth" means.

One can justify introducing the idea of God into process philosophy in still other ways. I shall deal only with the following. If self-creativity is the universal principle, if all actualities are partly self-determined or free, what prevents indefinitely great confusion and conflict? Confusion and conflict are indeed real, but they are limited: The cosmos does go on in a reasonably foreseeable way, countless sorts of processes fit together into a varied and beautiful whole, and nobody thinks the universe is likely to blow up in universal conflict. The cosmic order can be viewed in one of two ways: (1) The many self-created creatures harmonize together sufficiently to constitute a cosmos, not thanks to any controlling influence or guidance, but purely spontaneously. Either by sheer luck or their own unimaginable wisdom and goodness, they cooperate to constitute and maintain a viable cosmos. (2) The many self-created creatures harmonize together to constitute a viable cosmos thanks to some controlling influence or guidance. This influence or guidance can, in a process philosophy, consist only in a supreme form of self-creative power, a supreme form of process which, because of its superiority, exerts an attraction upon all the others or, as Whitehead likes to put it, "persuades" or "lures" them to follow its directive. I believe a strong case indeed can be made for (2) as against (1). This is the "argument from design" or from order, as process philosophy conceives it.

You can read the great critics of the theistic proofs (say Hume and Kant), but you will not find that they have any clear conception of the argument in this form. For instance, they object that the order of the world, as we know it at least, is far from perfect. But process philosophy does not presume that there is an absolute order but only that, whatever disorder there may be in the cosmos, it *is* a thinkable cosmos, rather than an unthinkable chaos or confusion. And of course the order is not absolute if all creatures are partly self-determined. They respond to the universal lure or directive, but it is they who respond, and just *how* they respond is in some measure their own decision. Yet, though they can cause one another suffering by unfortunate responses, they cannot really disrupt the universe. Were there no universal directive, there seems no way to understand such an invulnerable integrity of the universe. And if it be said that we do not know this integrity to obtain, the reply is, it does not matter whether we know it or merely have faith in it, for to such faith there is no feasible alternative. Life itself is a venture of faith in the orderliness of reality. Only verbally can we renounce this faith. But some of us value, as a precious luxury if nothing more, the possibility of a rational theory of that orderliness. Theism alone can furnish such a theory. The rest is mystery pure and simple.

I wish to deal now with a central doctrine of Whitehead, that in the creative act which is reality itself "the many become one and are increased by one." To see what this means one may take one's own momentary experience as illustration. An experience is a unit-happening, and we have new ones about ten times a second, but they fit together so smoothly that we do not distinctly notice the transitions. In such a unit-experience there are memories of preceding experiences, especially those in the previous second or less, and there are various perceptions. But whatever is remembered and whatever is perceived also consists, from the most concrete point of view, in unit-happenings, analogous to single human experiences. The perceived or remembered happenings are the "many" referred to in the above quotation. That they "become one" is slightly elliptical, for "they are embraced together in a new unit-reality," the experience in question. But the multiplicity of events has thereby been "increased by one," as is obvious. And in the next moment this event, too, will be remembered or perceived, and so "become one" with various other events. Thus the process of experiencing is a perpetual unification of a pluralistic reality which, as fast as it gets unified, becomes pluralistic again, and so can never be finally unified. Process is creative synthesis, the many into a new one producing a new many—and so on forever. The synthesis is creative, for how could a plurality dictate its own increase? Determinism, if carried to the limit, is magic, not rationality. The causal conditions for each free act are previous acts of freedom; creativity feeds upon its own products and upon nothing else! (Whitehead's "eternal objects" may seem to contradict this; if they do, then I should myself reject them.) Because the previous products are retained in the new syntheses, there is (in spite of Buddhism) any amount of permanence in this philosophy. The products of creation are never destroyed by new creation, but always utilized and preserved forever, at least on the divine level.

What Whitehead calls the "principle of relativity" is the principle of creativity looked at in reverse, as it were. Whatever in any sense is, he says, furnishes a "potential" for all subsequent acts of synthesis. "Being" is here defined through becoming: That may be said to be which is available for memory or perception, for integration into ever new acts of synthesis, and in this sense is a potential for all future becoming. *To be is to be available* for all future actualities. This availability is the very meaning of present "reality." There are profound ethical and religious implications of this view which Buddhism (though without giving a clear rationale for them) appreciated, and Whitehead also emphasizes. I call the doctrine "contributionism." Individual existence is nothing more nor less than a contribution to the future world society, the entire life and value of which is destined to be appreciated and enjoyed forever by the Eminent or Divine creativity, this immortality in God being the creatures' only value in the long run. Egocentric motivations essentially consist in metaphysical confusion. And this is why a Buddhist termed the egocentric view "writhing in delusion." For it involves one in an utterly vain and painful attempt to make reality ultimately a contribution to oneself; whereas the final destiny and value of all nondivine life lies beyond the particular self.

It is to be noted that the foregoing doctrine literally defines "being," or permanent reality, in terms of becoming. Thus it is a misconception to suppose that process philosophy, siding with becoming, rejects being. Rather, it is a doctrine of being *in* becoming, permanence in the novel; by contrast, philosophies of being are doctrines of becoming in being, novelty in the permanent. The trouble is that to insinuate anything new into the permanent is to make it a new thing. The old with the least new factor is, as a whole, new. This is inherent in the meaning of "whole," that its parts contribute to it; and with new parts making new contributions there must to that extent be a new whole. Only abstractly, by disregarding the new, can we say that it is the very same whole. But then it becomes a relative and partly subjective matter how far the new is worthy of being disregarded in this fashion. And what is not relative or subjective is the logical necessity that in its concrete entirety the whole reality is always new, however unimportant the novel additions. The only clear alternative to this is Leibniz' denial that in reality anything new is ever added, since the individual contained all his adventures the moment he was born or created. It is a fine example of how little people want to speak precisely that nearly everyone in philosophy has thought he could reject Leibniz' proposal without going on to a philosophy of events and without giving up the meaning of individual needed in ordinary speech (that of an entity identifiable in abstraction from many particular facts about it) and do all this without confusion or inconsistency. Leibniz saw with deadly accuracy the real issue: What does the concretely definite include in this definiteness? If the concretely definite is the individual as identical throughout his career, then at all times the individual's adventures, past and future, are parts of the individual. If the concretely definite is not the individual but the momentary states, then there can be a real distinction between present, past, and future, otherwise not. Leibniz never thought of taking this process view. But he did see once for all the impossibility of having it both ways, that is, taking the enduring individual as the definite or concrete entity and also supposing that the given individual might, as that same individual, take this course or that, make this decision or that, enjoy this experience or that. The common-sense meaning of individual as facing real alternatives is incompatible with the metaphysics which takes the most concrete units of reality to be enduring individuals; it is only consistent with a metaphysics which takes momentary states to be the concrete realities. That this is not a commonplace in philosophy is an illustration of cultural lag. Leibniz gave us our chance to be clear about the point; it is time we took advantage of his contribution.

So far from its being true that Whitehead, for instance, is denying our right to talk of persons as self-identical through change, he is rather protecting this right against the threat of a metaphysics which fails to harmonize with it except thanks to vagueness or ambiguity. There is a somewhat abstract identity of persons and enduring objects. This is just the point, that identity through change is abstractly real. And also, persons and things are *almost* concrete, they are concrete in comparison with obviously abstract entities such as "being human" or "triangle." Aristotelian substantialism was vaguely and roughly correct; Leibniz was precisely and with the clarity of genius wrong; Whitehead is as clear as Leibniz, but faithful to the indispensable elements of the notion of enduring individuality.

The reader may have been worried about the way in which we have taken human experience as the model of reality. Is this not suspiciously anthropomorphic? The answer is, we have taken human experience only as one end of an analogy which may be stretched as wide as one's imagination can stretch it. An amoeba can "learn"and make what look like "choices" or exhibit "strategy" toward a "desired" end. Of course its "experiences" or "feelings" are not much like ours. But to say that they are absolutely different, or (the same) that it has none, is merely to say that we cannot have the faintest idea of what it is like to be an amoeba, or that we can only know about an amoeba what it looks like to a human being observing it. Similarly, we can perhaps only know what a molecule is as a humanly-perceived phenomenon, but cannot know what it is to be a molecule. We can know it as an element in an event of human experience, but not as an event on its own. Whitehead does not deny that one may play safe in this way. But he thinks it is a sheer illusion to suppose that there is some *other* way to try to conceive what an amoeba or atom is in itself than to try to imagine how it feels. He finds no other way. And neither do I. A fair number of philosophers and scientists, from Leibniz down to our time, have agreed with us. The greatest process philosophers (Peirce also) have been universal *psychicalists,* seeing in mind or experience "the sole self-intelligible thing" (Peirce); in this, agreeing with the last great philosopher of being (Leibniz). They find no reasonable explanation of "matter," except as a form or manifestation of "mind." Metaphysics has always tended to reach this result. Northern Buddhism illustrates this, but so does Hinduism. It is only a little below the surface in Plato and Aristotle. The opponents of psychicalistic metaphysics are, whether they know it or not, opponents of all metaphysics. For no clear metaphysical alternative has ever been proposed. Dualism is a problem, not a solution. That experiences do occur cannot be denied; hence, the only open question is, does anything else occur? One may safely defy critics to prove the affirmative. Nonhuman experiences occur, no doubt, but that things constituted by no sort of experience, however different from ours, occur, this no science, no philosophy, can possibly establish. And an intelligible world-picture results from so modulating the idea of experience as such that it coincides with that of reality. At no lesser price can such a picture be had.

Neoclassical metaphysics is the fusion of the idealism or psychicalism which is implicit or explicit in all metaphysics with the full realization of the primacy of becoming as self-creativity or creative synthesis, feeding only upon its own products forever. This creativity may be conceived to have an eminent or divine form as well as lesser forms, and it perpetually immortalizes its products, literally so by virtue of the Eminent creativity. In no other philosophy, I believe, have so many theoretical and spiritual values been united with so much appearance of consistency and clarity. If this is not so, then I am indeed deluded.

A World of Organisms

"... with the magic hand of chance." JOHN KEATS.

"I cannot think that the world ... is the result of chance; and yet I cannot look at each separate thing as the result of design ... I am, and shall ever remain, in a hopeless muddle."

"But I know that I am in the same sort of muddle ... as all the world seems to be in with respect to free will, yet with everything supposed to have been foreseen or pre-ordained."

CHARLES DARWIN, writing to Asa Gray, 1860.

AN "ORGANISM" in this essay is a whole whose parts serve as "organs" or instrument to purposes or end-values inherent in the whole.[1] It is scarcely deniable that organs and organisms exist. A man is aware of realizing purpose, and he is aware of doing so through parts of his body. Hence he is aware that he exists as an organism. It follows that either nature contains two types of wholes, the organic and the inorganic, or all natural wholes are organic. We must choose between a dualism and an organic monism, since an inorganic monism would contradict obvious facts. Is organic monism possible?

It seems not, for just as it is evident that a man is an organism, so it is evident that a mountain is not, although primitive man sometimes thought otherwise. Science exhibits nothing in the behavior of the parts of the mountain to suggest that these parts serve a purpose whose realization is enjoyed by the mountain as a whole. But this fact does not prove that no form of organic monism is possible. There is no evidence that the parts of a finger serve any purpose whose realization is enjoyed by the finger. Not all the parts of an organism are organisms. Yet a

---

[1] For further considerations relevant to the speculations in this chapter, see my contribution to *Philosophical Essays in Memory of Edmund Husserl* (Cambridge: Harvard University Press, 1940). For a defense of the speculative method, see Ch. II of my *Man's Vision of God and the Logic of Theism* (New York: Harper and Brothers, 1940). Also, "Anthropomorphic Tendencies in Positivism," *Philosophy of Science*, VIII, 184–203.

finger may in two senses be viewed as organic: it belongs to an organism; and its own parts, at least on one level, the cells, are or may be organisms. That cells literally enjoy health and suffer from injury is a supposition that conflicts with no facts, while there are facts it helps to explain. The mountain, like the finger, may be part or organ of a larger organic whole, perhaps the entire universe as an organism; and the molecules (or if not these, the atoms) composing the mountain may, like cells, though on a still humbler level, be organic wholes. The submolecular parts may contribute value, in the form of simple feelings, to the molecules, and the molecules may contribute value to the cosmos.

Organic monism, in the sense just indicated, includes within itself a limited or relative dualism. The assertion is not that all wholes are purposive or organic; but that, first, all well-unified wholes are organic, and second, that all wholes whatever both involve and are involved in organic wholes. But what wholes are well-unified? My suggestion is that any whole which has less unity than its most unified parts is not an organism in the pregnant sense here in question;[2] though, according to organic monism, its most unified parts, and some unified whole of which it is itself a part, must in all cases be organisms.

For example, botanists incline to regard the plant cell, rather than the entire plant, as the primary unit of vegetable activity. A plant is a *quasi*-organic colony of true organisms, the cells, and not, like the vertebrate animal, itself an organism. Again, a termite colony exhibits definite analogies to a single animal organism, but to an organism with less unity than termites, say a flat-worm. The colony in relation to its members is not a super-organism but an epi- or quasi-organism. There is little reason to suppose that the colony feels, though good reason to think termites feel. Or again, a mountain has inferior dynamic unity to its own atoms. Remove a part from an atom, and the whole responds with a systematic readjustment of its parts, a response to which the activity of the mountain as a whole offers only a feeble analogy, even if the mountain be a volcano. Thus it is reasonable to deny that mountains, trees or termite colonies enjoy feelings, but not so reasonable to deny that atoms, tree cells, and termites enjoy them.

Similarly, with all the talk about the "group-mind," there are no good indications that human groups are organisms which could think

---

[2] The reasons for this principle are given in my essay on "The Group Mind" in *Social Research*, IX (May, 1942), 248–265.

and feel as individuals. All that one can show is that human beings, like termites and atoms, act differently according to the social environment, the neighbors, which they have. Yet there may be a hidden truth in the group-mind concept. As we shall see, there is reason to think that the cosmic community, the universe, does have a group mind.

The vertebrate organism, as we know it in ourselves, has a group mind, our mind, and this suggests that quantum mechanics is not the whole account of dynamic action. For this mechanics assumes that nothing influences what electrons, protons, atoms, and the like are doing in an organic body except what other electrons and the like are doing. What then of what the man, say, is doing, for instance, thinking? This thinking is not just an arrangement of particles and/or waves; and either the thinking is an effect which produces no effects, a detached miracle in nature, or electrons in the human brain must move as they do partly because the human being thinks as he does.

However, when one is in deep sleep, what goes on in the body may indeed be little more than mere group action—not, to be sure, of particles, but of cells. And if a cell dies, then what happens in its remains will be no longer what it is doing, but what its molecules or atoms are doing. Experiments to show the merely mechanical character of the organism may, in fact, only show that the organism can at times be reduced to an approximately inorganic state.

Let us return to our main thesis, organic monism. Part of the justification of this monism is that the organic principle is sufficiently flexible to explain the relative lack of organic wholeness found in certain parts of nature, whereas the notion of absolutely non-purposive or inorganic wholes throws no light whatever on the existence or nature of purpose. If there are wholes which are directly valuable in and for themselves, there can be groups of these wholes which are valuable not directly, but for the sake of their members, or of some larger whole. Given the concept of purpose as ultimate, we can restrict its application by employing the distinction which purpose involves between end and means, or the distinction between simple and complex purposes, or purposes merely felt and those consciously surveyed. But given mere purposeless stuff or "matter," we have not, in so far, any notion of purpose.

The idea of a means or instrument does not require the notion of mere or dead matter; for an organism can function as a tool for another organism, and this assumes only that organisms influence each other, which in turn follows from the notion, to be considered presently, that all lesser organisms are parts of one inclusive organism, the universe. All that dead matter could add to this is the purely negative and empty notion of something that is absolutely nothing but means. Such an absolute negation seems devoid of philosophical or scientific utility.

There are, however, some apparent difficulties in the organismic doctrine. For example, the definition of organism calls for a whole with parts, and an electron, for instance, is not known to have parts. Even if it has parts, or if one denies the reality of electrons, must there not be something simple, the ultimate unit of being, which being without parts is not an organism? We must here reconsider the meaning of the term "part" as occurring in our definition of the organic. This meaning implies that an organism involves a plurality of entities contributing directly to the value of a single entity, the "whole." But the contributing entities need not be internal to the whole in the sense of spatially smaller and included parts, as electrons are smaller than and within an atom, or atoms within a molecule, and as nothing known is smaller than and within the electron. To render an electron or other particle an organism it is only necessary that neighboring electrons or other particles should contribute directly to each other's values, that is, should directly feel each other. Physics does not assert that particles are in every sense external to each other. On the contrary, a particle, as inseparable from its wave-field, overlaps other particles. This seems to be all the internality that is required by the general idea of organism. With the simplest organisms it is the community of neighboring entities that constitutes the plurality contributing to each entity—in a different perspective, in each case, since no two electrons, say, will have the same nearest neighbors. Where there are no smaller entities as parts, there will be no sharp distinction between internal and external. An ax seems external to a man because the man's immediate intimate relations are with the parts of his own body, so that by contrast the ax is something that contributes to his being and value only indirectly, only by first contributing, through several intermediaries usually, to the parts of his body and thence to his mind. But perhaps a particle, like a disembodied spirit, has no bodily parts. Its intimates, if any, will be its equals, the neighboring particles, or the larger wholes which they and it constitute. It will be an organic democrat and proletarian, but not an organic aristocrat.

One may well ascribe intimates, even though "external" intimates,

to particles; for such entities respond immediately to neighboring particles. If an electron feels anything, it must feel its neighbors, for what
else could it feel? We, on the contrary, feel chiefly our bodies, and
through these, other things. Just this indirectness of feeling, mediated
by entities of lesser power and complexity than oneself, is what is
meant by having a body. To have no body is to have no inferior servants
immediately bound to one's own purposes and feelings. Hence it is the
particle, the lowest, not the highest, organism—in spite of what has
often been said about God—that best fits the idea of an unembodied
spirit. The particle, one might say, is embodied only in its environment,
not in itself.

The mention of God brings us to the question at the opposite extreme
from that about particles. If the simplest of beings can vet have complexity in the sense required for organic wholeness, can the most complex of beings, the universe, have sufficient simplicity in the sense of
unity to be an organism, no doubt the supreme organism? If lack of
internal parts does not prevent organicity, what about lack of an external environment? The same principle, though in opposite application,
solves both problems. All that an organism requires is "an immediately
contributory complexity." An organic whole must deal with or "respond" to some field of entities or environment, but the term, "internal
environment" is not a quibble. An organism can respond to its parts, if
it has them, or its neighbors, if it has them, or to both, if it has both.
An electron has only neighbors, the universe, only parts, to respond to;
but both may be responsive, and in so far, organic, entities.

It may indeed be urged that the only purpose of internal adjustments,
or responses to parts, is to serve as basis for desirable external adjustments, responses to neighbors. But it can, with more truth, be retorted
that external adjustments are desirable only as means for the attainment
of the internal organic state known as happiness. The only error in this
second position is that with organisms other than the cosmos the internal field of response fails to include more than a fraction of the low
and high-grade life in existence. Thus it is not a case of external relations for their own sake, but of such relations for the sake of dealing
with what would otherwise be missed entirely. The cosmos, which
deals with everything through its internal relations, can perfectly well
dispense with external ones (except toward the future, which is never
in its concreteness intrinsic to the present). To view this privilege of

unique inclusiveness of organic unity as a lack of such unity is simply to lose our way among our own abstractions.

But if the universe has organic unity, where, some have asked, is the world-brain? Fechner long ago, following a trail blazed in the *Timaeus,* pointed out how unscientific the question is. On each great level of life the basic functions are performed by organs that have only a remote analogy from one level to another. We smile at the lack of generalizing power shown by those men of earlier times who supposed that microscopic animals must have, in miniature, all the organs of macroscopic ones. Is it any less naive to think that the world, if organic, must have a magnified brain? If any organic level must be a special case, it is the universe, at the opposite end of the scale from that other special case, the particle.

As we have seen, the particle has no special internal organs, because its neighbors serve it as organs. The universe, conversely, has no neighbors as organs, because everything is its internal organ. Everything contributes equally directly to the cosmic value. This means that the world-mind will have no special brain, but that rather every individual is to that mind as a sort of brain-cell. The brain is only that part of the body which most immediately and powerfully affects and is affected by the mind, the value-unity of the whole. The rest of the body is by comparison a house for the nervous system, a quasi-external environment. As the cosmos has no external environment, so it has no gradations of externality, and not even a quasi-external environment, and thus the cosmic analogue of a brain will be simply the entire system of things as wholly internal and immediate to the cosmic mind. A special world-brain, so far from confirming the supposition of a truly cosmic mind, would negate it.

You may object that if the cosmos has no external environment to deal with it does have an internal one, and that the coordination of internal actions requires a brain. But remember that the brain is only a very rough and partial coordinator of internal actions. It has almost no direct control over myriads of actions that go on in the body, even in the brain cavity itself, and this not because of any deficiency of the vertebrate brain in particular, but as a consequence of there being a brain at all as a special organ. What is needed for supreme control is obviously that every organ should be directly, and not via some other organ, such as a nervous system, responsive to the whole. The idea of a perfect yet special brain-organ is a contradiction in terms, but the

idea of a perfect mind, a mind co-extensive with existence and thus
omniscient, is not for all that a contradiction. For such a mind must
have, not a world-part as brain, but the whole world serving as higher
equivalent of a brain; so that just as between a brain cell and the human
mind there is no further mechanism, so between every individual in
existence and the world-mind there is no chain of intermediaries, not
even a nervous system, but each and every one is in the direct grip of
the world-value. The higher the organism, the larger the part directly
responsive to the whole; the highest organism must be the largest organism as all brain, so to speak.

But what, you ask, would the cosmic organism be doing? To what
end is the coordination of internal activities, where no external action
is possible? The answer is that the end is the prosperity of the parts
and of the whole as the integration of the parts. As our enjoyment of
health is our participation in the health of the numerous cells, so the
happiness of the cosmos is the integration of the lesser happinesses of
the parts. The benevolence of God is the only way the psycho-physics
of the cosmic organism can be conceived, as Fechner, one of the first
great experimental psycho-physicists, was at pains to point out. Theologians have generally missed this valuable argument, for reasons
which I believe to be specious.[3]

It has been argued for instance that if the cosmos were one divine
organism there could be no conflict or suffering. All would be perfect
peace, flawless interadjustment. This, I think, is an error.

To show this we must correct the vagueness of our concept of organism, as so far employed. An organism is not a "whole which determines its parts," but something more complex and less dialectical.
Strictly speaking, in so far as an organism is a whole, in the logical
sense, it does not even influence its parts. A collection of agents is not
itself an agent; and if the whole is more than a collection, a genuine
dynamic unity, and yet acts on its parts, then since parts obviously
constitute and by their changes alter the whole in certain of its aspects,
we should have each part in a relation of mutual determination with
the whole, and hence with every other part. How then could we distinguish one part from another or from the whole? Would not every part
be the whole? Only if each part is something in abstraction from the
whole can we analyze the whole as a collection of parts or members.

---

[3] See my *Man's Vision of God*, especially Ch.V.

We can think of a collection distinctly only by adding its members in thought, and this is impossible if the members presuppose the whole.

But surely, you say, an organism is more than a collection, even an organized collection. Yes, but how? Only a creative synthesis of the parts can have its own unity, not identical with the parts and their interrelationships. But the very meaning of such a "synthesis" . . . presupposes the parts as given, prior to the synthesis, and constituting its materials or data, not its products. Thus any actual whole-synthesis has no influence upon the elements entering into it.

Consider a momentary human experience as a synthesis of events which have just occurred in various parts of the organism, especially the cortical parts of it. This experience does not alter the events which it synthesizes. It may, however, influence subsequent events in the brain and hence in the muscles, etc. Only by neglecting the time structure of the situation, as philosophies of being may be expected to do (and they seldom upset our expectations in this regard), have "holistic" philosophies fallen into the confusion of a whole determining its individual parts. The symmetrical idea of "interaction" between whole and parts is due to treating a complex of one-way relations en bloc. What happens in my brain or nerves influences what I feel immediately afterward, and what I thus feel influences what happens in my brain at a slightly later time.

My feeling at a given moment is one, that of my cells is many. The diverse cellular feelings become data for the unitary human feeling, and this feeling is the momentary "whole" summing up the antecedent states of "the parts" and subsequently reacting upon later states of these parts. Thus the many-one action is turned into a one-many action. Not the whole as collection of parts acts upon those very parts, but the one actuality which is my feeling now, and which reflects the actualities previously constituting my body, acts upon the many actualities which subsequently compose that body.

An organism may be viewed as a society—of cells, molecules, or the like. There are two types of such societies. (The distinction goes back to Leibniz.) One type is what might, broadly speaking, be termed a "democracy." It has no supreme, radically dominant member. Certain cell colonies, and probably many-celled plants in general, and some lower forms of many-celled animals, are examples. But a unitary organism in the narrower or more emphatic sense is one with a dominant member, which is the synthetic act, or rather act-sequence, in the vertebrate case corresponding roughly to, or deriving its data from, the nervous system. My "stream of consciousness," an old metaphor which (with reasonable caution) is still usable, is the dominant member in the very complex society of sequences forming my human reality. When I am deeply asleep, there may be no dominant member then actualized. The real agent is always momentary, the stream or sequence of acts being realized only in its members. The abiding ever-identical agent is an abstraction.

In this way we avoid the mysticism of wholes acting on their very own parts, a notion which would imply unrestricted and symmetrical internal relatedness between every part and every other, dissolving all definite structures into ineffable unity, a consequence which has caused clear thinkers to turn away from "holistic" or "organicist" doctrines. To the physiological commonplace which says, the body is a society of cells, we add, not something unknown or speculative, but the given reality of human feelings or experiences, unitary at a given moment (say, during about a tenth of a second), but multiple through time. (They are given not intro- but retrospectively, in long- or short-range memories.) The cellular processes are not the whole of a man, there is also the process of his experiences. This is not a "ghost in the machine," *pace* Gilbert Ryle. In the first place, there is no machine, but a society of living creatures, each a sequence of actual events. To this we add, as an empirical fact, the sequence of human experiences. These too are events, influencing other events.

The Cartesian division of events into extended and material, and inextended and psychic, is based on no clear evidence on either side of the division. Nothing shows that the psychical events, the experiences, are point-like, or that they are nowhere; and nothing shows that the extended events are simply without feeling, or are merely material (spatio-temporal). And both obviously have causal conditions and consequences. Ryle's apparent assumption that anyone who believes in psychical events must regard them as non-causal seems wonderfully arbitrary. Experiences must have data and, as I have argued elsewhere, this is the same as to say that they have causes.[4] And since, at least in memory, experiences are data for other experiences, it follows that experiences can be causes as well as effects.

---

[4] "The Logical Structure of Givenness," *The Philosophical Quarterly*, VIII (1958), 307–316.

The social view of organic unity is that individuals form organs for other individuals. This proposition is convertible: namely, if individuals are organs, organs are individuals, singly or in groups. Now an individual is self-active; if there are many individuals in the ultimate organism there are many self-active agents in that organism. Being is action, what is really many must act as many. The higher is compounded of the lower, not by suppression but by preservation of the dynamic integrity of the lower. The cosmos could not guarantee that the many individuals within it will act always in concord; for to carry out such a guarantee the cosmos must completely coerce the lesser individuals, that is, must deprive them of all individuality. Existence is essentially social,[5] plural, free, and exposed to risk, and this is required by our conception of organism. For if the action of the parts had no freedom with respect to the whole, there would be no dynamic distinction between whole and parts and the very idea of whole would lose its meaning.

It is true that the many individuals, being organs of the cosmic individual, must, according to our definition, contribute to the value of the one, but this contribution is both negative (in a sense) and positive. It includes suffering as well as joy. The all-inclusiveness of the world-mind means, not that it is exalted above all suffering, but that no pain and no joy is beneath its notice. All things make immediate contribution to the one, but they contribute what they are and have, their sorrow as well as their joy, their discord with their neighbors as well as their harmonies.

A century ago in his *Zend Avesta* (Ch. II) Fechner argued that an eminent consciousness must resemble all consciousness in containing a contrast between voluntary and involuntary, active and passive, elements. Even eminent volition cannot act in a vacuum, or merely upon itself. But that upon which it immediately acts must be present within it; for action and its material are inseparable. In Fechner's terms, there must be involuntary impulses even in God, or there can be no divine volition or purposive activity. But these impulses must come from something. Why not from the volitions of the creatures, the lesser individuals? Our deliberate acts set up currents, as it were, in the mind of

---

[5] This essay could have been written as a generalization of "social" instead of "organic." *Cf.* Whitehead, *Adventures of Ideas* (New York: The Macmillan Company, 1933, 1948), Ch. XIII.

God, as the activities of our brain cells set up currents in our human minds. Each of us is a "pulse in the eternal mind" (Rupert Brooke). God then controls, checks, encourages, redirects, these pulses or impulses. But He cannot wholly initiate or absolutely control them, not because of any weakness on His part, but because absolute control of impulses, or indeed of anything, is a contradiction in terms. God is not limited in His power to do what He wishes to do, but He is not so confused as to wish to destroy the very nature of being, which is its organic character as many individuals in one, the many being as real as the one.

The lesser individuals, being more or less ignorant of each other, act somewhat blindly with respect to many of the effects of their acts. The divine love is not contradicted by the discords which result from this blindness; for love includes tolerance for the freedom of others. The divine perfection lies, not in the suppression of freedom wherever it involves risk, for at all points freedom involves risk, but in the wise and efficient limitation of the risks to the optimum point beyond which further limitation would diminish the promise of life more than its tragedy. Perfection is not to be defined independently of freedom, for then it would be meaningless. Rather perfection is to be defined as the supreme way of mitigating the risk and maximizing the promise of freedom, the optimum of control, beyond which or short of which more harm and less good would result. Statesmen know that beyond a certain point interference with the lives of citizens does more harm than good, and this not solely because of the weakness or stupidity of Statesmen but also because of the meaning of good as self-activity. This is part of the reason for the ideal of democracy, that people need first of all to be themselves, and this self-hood no tyrant, human or superhuman, however benevolent, can impose upon them.

But is the cosmos genuinely and organically one? Let us recall that nothing happens anywhere but its effects are communicated with the speed of light in all directions, that the same basic modes of action, expressed in quantum mechanics and relativity, pervade all parts of space. But the unity lies deeper than any such considerations can make clear. All groups short of the universe can break up, fall to pieces in various ways and degrees. But from the cosmic community there is no secession. There is nowhere to go from the universe. It is the only aggregate that is its own foundation. This fits to perfection the idea that it is its own reason or purpose and the integration of all purposes.

We confuse ourselves in this matter by supposing that in the cosmos must be summed up all the loose-jointedness we see in various portions of the cosmos. This would be true if the loose-jointedness were, at each point, the whole story. But it is not. A sand pile is loose-jointed so far as the pile taken as a whole is concerned. Its parts serve no imaginable unitary purpose enjoyed by the pile. But it does not follow that they serve no unitary purpose. There is no unity of action *of* the sand-pile, but there is unity of action *in* the sand-pile, a unity pervading the grains of sand but referring to a larger whole than the pile. Physics tells us that the entire universe acts upon each particle to constitute its inertia. This unity of action is cosmic, and it is unbroken and all-pervasive.[6] All looseness and disintegration presuppose and cannot contradict the cosmic integrity. The one cosmos arranges and rearranges itself from time to time in subordinate centers of activity (which it can properly be said to create, in the sense of eliciting as partly self-determining), but this formation and disintegration of the subordinate centers expresses the cosmic integrity somewhat as a man may rearrange his thoughts around different idea-foci, or make different movements of his body, without ceasing to enjoy the unity of his personality while doing so.

To all the foregoing, it may be objected that explanations in terms of purpose, teleological explanations, have been discredited in science, above all through the work of Darwin. This is a contention with grave implications; for if science, or at least if rational knowledge, cannot deal with purpose, then so much the worse for purpose, for knowledge, and for human life. But perhaps it is only certain forms of teleology that have been discredited. One form of teleology that we are, I think, well rid of is the notion of a single absolute world-plan, complete in every detail from all eternity, and executed with inexorable power. The objection is not solely that God would be made responsible for the imperfect adaptations and discords in nature. There is the further objection that the world process would be the idle duplicate of something in eternity. A God who eternally knew all that the fulfillment of his purpose would bring could have no need of that fulfillment or of purpose. Complete knowledge is complete possession: it is just because a man does not know in detail what "knowing his friends better" would be

---

[6] The action is not, according to physicists, instantaneous. This is a serious complication, though not, I believe, an insuperable difficulty for out thesis.

like that he has the purpose to come to know them better. As Bergson and Peirce[7] were among the first to see, even a world-purpose must be indeterminate as to details. For one thing, an absolute and inexorable purpose, supposing this meant anything, would deny individuality, self-activity, hence reality, to the lesser individuals, the creatures.

It follows that ill-adjustments, evils—apart from moral evil, evil deliberately chosen—are not willed but are chance result of free acts. But if evil results partly by chance, so does good. Nevertheless, the idea that adjustments are the result of natural selection among unpurposed or blind variations is not incompatible with that of cosmic purpose. For the maintenance of the general conditions under which chance and competition will produce evolution may itself be purposive. Darwinism derives generally higher forms of interadjusted species from lower; but interadjustment itself and as such is assumed, not explained. Interadjusted atoms or particles involve the same essential problem. Theism can explain order as a general character of existence; can any other doctrine? And an order capable of evolving such a vast variety of mutually compatible creatures seems all that providence could guarantee, granting that freedom is inherent in individual existence as such.

Why should the dinosaurs be any less satisfying to God or to us because they were not specifically predesigned? What after all did the old teleology accomplish, except to swell the problem of evil to impossible proportions, and to make an enigma of the process of human choice? Chance, the non-intentional character of the details of the world, is the only remedy for these two difficulties. But, as Darwin repeatedly declared, chance cannot explain the world as an ordered whole of mutually-adapted parts.[8] It was because of this dilemma that Darwin gave up the theistic problem: purpose could not explain details, and nothing else could explain order as a general fact.

Here I think Darwin showed admirable care and honesty. There must

---

[7] Peirce seems to hesitate between a classical and a neo-classical idea of God. Compare, in *The Collected Papers of Charles Sanders Peirce*, edited by Charles Hartshorne and Paul Weiss (Cambridge: Harvard University Press, 1934, 1935), pars. 5.119, 588; 6.157, 346, 465 f., 489, 508. As a contrast to Einstein's disbelief in a "dice-throwing God" note 5.588! See also "A Critique of Peirce's idea of God," *Philosophical Review*, L (1941), 516–523.

[8] See F. Darwin, *The Life and Letters of Charles Darwin* (New York: Appleton, 1898), II, 146; I p. 276. I first came upon this quotation in that fine book, *Charles Darwin and the Golden Rule*, by W. E. Ritter (Washington: Science Service, 1954), p. 75.

be cosmically pervasive limitations upon chance, since unlimited chance is chaos; supreme purpose or providence is the sole positive conception we can form of this chance-limiting factor. And Darwin actually suggests that perhaps the solution is "designed laws" of nature, with all details, good or bad, depending upon "what we call chance."[9] But the great naturalist could not think this thought through, declaring that he was quite unsatisfied with it. Why? The answer may at least be guessed at. (1) Darwin, like so many others, tended to think of science as committed to determinism. "What we call chance," he explains elsewhere, is not properly that at all, but causes unknown to us.[10] Moreover, (2) it was probably not apparent to Darwin why cosmic purpose should leave anything to chance, at least apart from human free will. Only a philosophy of universal creativity can untie this knot. The "metaphysics" of his day, about which, with his wonderful modesty, Darwin sometimes spoke with quaint respect, did not present him with a clearly-conceived creationist philosophy. For this he was scarcely to blame.

Since Darwin was on the whole committed to determinism, he could admit no genuine element of chance for providence to limit. God must then do everything or nothing; but to do everything is to do nothing distinctive! It is also to leave nothing for the creatures to do. (The long debate about the efficacy of "second causes" remained on an essentially verbal level, since no party to the dispute would make the one concession which alone would give it content.) The "mud" in which Darwin said he was immersed was the opacity which always characterizes a deterministic world-view.

Darwin also illustrated, though this time less consciously, the absurd consequences of overlooking the truth, so much stressed in this book, that divine perfection cannot exist as a contingent fact only. Thus he worries about the question, what could have been the origin and genesis of the first cause, if we postulate one—as though its existence would be a "fact" among facts, something made whose manner of making we should inquire into.[11] Or, when asked by Gray what would convince him of cosmic Design, he says that this is a "poser," and tries to imagine experiences which would be convincing. Then he gives up the ef-

---

[9] F. Darwin, II, 105.
[10] See the 2nd and last sentences of Ch. V of the *Origin*, 6th Ed.
[11] F. Darwin, I, 276.

fort as "childish."[12] I suggest that it is indeed childish, because it implies that "God" stands for some great special fact, to which lesser special facts might witness, and thus it fails to grasp, as adult thinking about this matter should, the impossibility that the "creator of all things, visible and invisible," the ground of all possibility, should itself be among the things created, or actualized out of some possibility. Or, if not created, actualized out of possibility, in what intelligible sense could it be contingent, or what could its factuality have in common with that of any facts which we know to be such? I labor this point once more, for it seems to me that the learned world, with almost insignificant exceptions, has been missing it "as if by magic," and I know not how to startle, coax, or lead it gently to take a candid look, at last, at the logic of the concepts involved. (This is also my excuse for certain other cases of repetition in this book: I repeat not what nearly everyone in the intellectual world is saying, but what they are ignoring or denying without careful consideration. The same excuse must serve for the polemical tone of much of this book. The theories I attack have so many friends that no one, it seems, need feel badly because of my rather isolated onslaughts.)

The reader may still not quite see why, if teleology, as conceived all along, was a "hopeless muddle," Darwin's contributions made such a difference. Darwin seemed to show that creative potentialities were inherent in the general features of living things. Since teleology had been thought of as unilateral creativity on the part of deity, unshared in any appreciable degree with the creatures, indications that the world had far-reaching potentialities for self-creation were naturally startling. But only because creativity had not been grasped in its proper universality, as the principle of existence itself.

Darwin saw all this, but as through a glass darkly. And he was misled, like many another, by the apparently factual character of the problem. The facts of evil, which he repeatedly mentions as conflicting with the belief in Design,[13] and the at least alleged fact of human freedom (it is not easy to say in what sense Darwin accepted this as a fact) were the obstacles to teleology, plus only the one new difficulty that in fact variations seem not designed but rather random, in all directions, good, bad, or indifferent. However, freedom, chance, and evil in general are

---

[12] *Op. cit.*, II, 169.
[13] II, 105; I, 276, 284.

inherent a priori in the mere idea of existence, construed as a multiplicity of creative processes; and it is arguable that no other construction makes sense (see the previous and the following chapters). As for the randomness effect, neither monolithic design nor rigorous law throws any light upon it. Analysis shows, as Peirce and others have argued, that without chance, its opposing term necessity is unintelligible, and indeed everything is unintelligible. Even in mathematics, one must at some point accept arbitrary decisions, if there is to be any rational necessity. If chance is merely a word for our ignorance, then we are ignorant indeed!

It is true that chance is not something positive, or a cause of anything. It is but the negative aspect inherent in creative spontaneity (to use a phrase whose redundancy is excused by the supposition of many that it is not redundant). Chance is an aspect of the production of additional determinateness, or more simply, of determination as an act: not merely being, but becoming, definite. Determinists want things just to be definite without ever becoming so. This is in effect the denial of becoming itself, or at least its trivialization. Moreover, and this, too, Darwin dimly saw, if the universe is taken as one absolute causal system, while theism is rejected, then it follows that the system as a whole exists only by true and mere chance, that is, neither by intention nor (on pain of an endless regress) thanks to any further cause. So chance is not escaped.

What integrity there was in the honest facing of this impasse, without favoring either of the cheap and easy pretended escapes, by a man who liked to please and console, more than to upset or startle!

Another respect in which Darwin showed wisdom was in his refusal to claim that he had found the solution to the problem of the origin of life on earth. As mere chance cannot explain order, so mere matter cannot explain life and mind. The reason is the same in both cases: chance and matter are essentially negative conceptions which imply but do not explicate something positive. This is overlooked in the case of matter because "extension," spatio-temporality, is positive; but since analysis shows that mind must have this positive character, what distinguishes matter from mind remains merely negative, and therefore the first concept cannot in good logic explain the second. There must be something positive limiting chance, and something more than mere matter in matter, or Darwinism fails to explain life.

Today, some eminent contributors to evolutionary theory—Wright,

Huxley, Teilhard de Chardin, and others—meet the second requirement by denying the self-sufficiency of the concept of matter, which they hold is "mere" only as observed from without, and known only in its bare spatio-temporal relationships, while in its intrinsic qualities it is mind or experience on various levels and scales of magnitude and temporal rhythm, vastly different mostly from our own. Darwin lacked this explanation of matter, hence he could only confess his ignorance by referring to the "creator" (in the famous closing passage of the *Origin of Species*).

By admitting that mind is primordial and only its species emerge, we surmount various difficulties in a more materialistic Darwinism. We then do not have to explain how from a world without any positive principle of organization (would this be a world or anything conceivable?) organic forms are derived. We have only to explain how some forms of integration come from others, or how such forms alter gradually through long, ages. Mind is intrinsically and by its essential core of meaning a principle of integration. Any mind is at least a felt unity, in which various data are responded to in such a way as to attain enjoyment or satisfaction, in some degree, through unity in contrast. The orderliness of the entire world can then be interpreted through this same principle of responsiveness operating on many levels at once, as will be discussed somewhat further in the next chapter. Moreover, if the materialist wants to say that his matter has tendencies toward integration, and so mind is not needed for this, then he can be led to face the other horn of the dilemma of materialism: how to distinguish those forms of integration which show the presence of mind somewhere in a system from those which do not. Any criterion, I affirm, will either be arbitrary or will fail to divide nature into an older portion without mind and a newer with mind. Since Darwin (like most of his critics) knew little about such possibilities for reducing matter to mind (a topic regarding which much progress has been made during the last hundred years), and almost nothing about the microstructure of physical reality which has since been so extensively explored, he was well justified in refusing to deal with the origin of life, save by vaguely attributing it to the power responsible for the world-order generally.

The Vitalists of several decades ago have in a way gained their cause, though in other ways they have been proved mistaken. They have gained their cause in that a living thing is now seen not to be mechanical, if that means anything like, consisting of parts which touch and push or pull each other, and in this manner constitute the actions of the whole. Digestion, metabolism, growth, and nerve action are not essentially mechanical. But then neither are chemical processes generally. The gratuitous denial of organismic characters to the "inanimate" was the first basic error of vitalism. The inanimate is that part of nature in which organic wholeness is confined to the ultra-microscopic level, where it eludes the competence of the human senses. The second mistake was to see in life a third "force," distinct from matter, on the one hand, and mind on the other. But a process either involves sentience (sensation, feeling, memory, and the like) or does not involve it, there is no third possibility; and apart from spatio-temporal structure or behavior, and modes of experience or feeling, there is nothing positive with which we can be acquainted whereby phenomena may be explained. The third mistake was the converse of the first, for just as primitive, minute organisms may be loosely associated to form an apparently quite inorganic assembly or whole, so on a higher level they may also be associated in a somewhat more integrated way which simulates but does not quite constitute an individual organism. Thus a nation may be viewed as an organic individual, but this is generally regarded as a metaphor or illusion. Similarly an embryo in Driesch's experiments seemed to be doing remarkable things, as though inspired with a plan of its growth-aim, when really it was the cells which were doing whatever was done, and any "entelechy" should have been sought on the cellular level.

While there is no third force, there is a third level, or group of levels, of organization, between ordinary atoms or molecules and ordinary perceptible animals and plants: the level of cells, nuclei, and those giant molecules whose chemistry and arrangements constitute the gene-characters by which life is guided. Here things are even more wonderful than anything Driesch observed. Myriads of activities, simultaneous or overlapping in time, effectively coordinated and controlled! It is cells, genes, and things of that order of magnitude which, as it were, "know" (feel) something of what they are up to, not embryos (except when and as they turn into animals with functioning nervous systems). The problem is one of cellular psychology, sociology, or ecology, and then of molecular psychology and ecology. Finally, everything is a matter of individual and social psychology, on we know not how many levels. But this picture cannot be made clear unless it is firmly grasped that the cells of a tree, for instance (or the atoms or molecules of a solid), may be the highest form of dynamic individual in the tree (or solid). Thus the "vegetable soul" (or growth factor) of Aristotle may be like the "soul of the state," a metaphor or illusion. Cellular souls are another matter, for cells really do the growing, while the "growing tree" is merely the overall view of the process. But the cellular souls are almost rather "animal" than vegetable, in Aristotle's sense, for they respond to internal and external stimuli, and control their activities accordingly. They should therefore probably be viewed as sentient, as sequences of feelings, in addition to their molecular constitutions.

The problem of mind and matter is a problem not of two kinds of stuff or force but of the one and the many, and of numerous levels or kinds of oneness and many-ness. Leibniz, with a flash of the highest genius, discovered this, two and one half centuries ago, after all mankind, so far as I can find out, in East and West, had missed it from the beginning. Many, however, are still pre-Leibnizian in their thinking. This is the sad aspect of the story. Here truly is a "cultural lag," and one affecting the scholar almost as much as the plain man.

The great mistake of "teleology" consisted in never seeing clearly the one-many problem in relation to purpose. (At this point Leibniz was not a Leibnizian.) An absolutely controlling purpose would be the sole purpose, and could not have as it aim the creation of other purposes. If there be even two purposes two decisions, then the conjunction of these two into a total reality must in some aspect be undecided, unintended, a matter of chance. Since a "solitary purpose" is meaningless or pointless, chance is inevitable, granted purpose.[14]

Without the recognition of chance, no teleology! Paradoxical as it may sound, only good things which in details come about by chance may concretely fulfill purpose. A man who goes to the theater to be amused can say that he has accomplished his purpose without implying that he knew in advance just what jokes he wished to hear! And so can a parent whose children think and feel in a spontaneous and unforeseen fashion, just as the parent wished they should do. Must God be without analogy to us in this? And if without analogy, could he be God?

---

[14] I find it very odd that [W. G.] Pollard, in [*Chance and Providence* (New York: Scribner's, 1958)], after giving a brilliant exposition of the irreducible role of chance in science, should relapse into precisely the old "muddle" of attributing details (or have I misunderstood him?) to providence. At least he wants to attribute some details. And so it is to be expected that he should ignore the problem of evil and pass off the question of freedom by the old denial that we could hope to understand such things.

The conception of the ultimate or cosmic organism is the remedy for two great errors of political thought, abstract individualism and abstract or mythical collectivism. Neither the human individual nor any human class or race is an absolute end, but only that whole in which men and nations and all existences have their place and value. We are members one of another because we are members of one ultimate body-mind, one inclusive, unborn, and imperishable organism.

But is the cosmos imperishable? What about the "heat death"? The present world-order, as an arbitrary choice out of the infinity of possible orders, is doubtless perishable. For as Goethe put it, in the mouth of Mephistopheles, "Whatever comes to be, deserves to be destroyed". . . . All definite patterns lose their appeal after sufficient reiteration. The history of art and all aesthetic experience show this. It is absurd to suppose that God would be satisfied with less variety than we ourselves require, when we stretch our imaginations sufficiently to see what is involved. So (in spite of astronomers Hoyle and Bondi) I do not doubt that the present quantitative system of the cosmos is doomed. But this is compatible with there being a deeper qualitative identity through change whereby the universe as the "living garment of deity" retains this status forever.

Chance, Love and Incompatibility

Chance, love, and incompatibility are ultimate principles, applicable to all reality. In defending his thesis, I wish also to discuss some of the interrelations of these three concepts themselves. That they are interconnected is evident on a common sense level. By chance-propinquity people come to love each other, and there is often, if not always, some element of incompatibility between them. But of course, if the three ideas named are to be philosophical categories, applicable to all things, their meanings must be refined and extended beyond the ordinary ones. Philosophy (or at any rate, metaphysics) consists in such refinement of meanings to the end of removing their limitations. To object that in this process all identity of meaning must disappear is to declare philosophy an impossible enterprise. The philosopher should then cease to encumber the academic scene. Assuming, however, that continuity of meaning is possible between the special cases drawn from common speech and the universal conceptions arrived at by philosophical refinement, the question is: Are chance, love, and incompatibility favorable starting points for such refinement?

Philosophic attempts to depreciate these ideas are not lacking. Chance has been said to be a word for our ignorance of causes; love, to be but a form assumed by self-interest; and incompatibility has been held to arise solely through arbitrary negation—so that only if we declare that a possible state of affairs excludes another is it impossible, and then but verbally, that both be actualized.[1] Are these contentions justified?

Two of our ideas, chance and incompatibility, seem to be required by logic. Logic rests on the notion of mutually exclusive alternatives, P and not-P. This is a form of incompatibility. But it is also a manifestation of chance. For chance is the alternative to necessity, and if proposition P is true by necessity, then not-P is absurd and, hence, not a

---

[1] See W. H. Sheldon, *America's Progressive Philosophy* (New Haven: Yale University Press, 1942), ch. iv.

genuine proposition. This may indeed be the case with respect to some P's and not-P's, those affirming or denying necessary truths; but logical conceptions cannot be elucidated except on the assumption that not all truths belong to this class. Again, the logical notion of entailment, of "If . . . then," implies chance; for an "if" is correlative to an "if not," and (once more, apart from certain special cases) both must be meaningful, and thus, whichever is true, it is true by chance, not by necessity. The very notion of necessity presupposes that of chance. For the necessary is merely that which is common to a set of chances; or that of whose absence there is no chance! It is the common factor of the chances. Such a common factor is of course abstract. Assume that there are chances, and it is easy to see wherein necessity consists; assume that there is no such thing as chance, and it will, I think, prove impossible (that is, there will be no chance) to give an intelligible account of necessity. This is an example of Morris Cohen's Law of Polarity, the law that categories run in contraries so related that neither of the contrary poles has meaning or application by itself. In every set of chances, there must be abstract common factors, that is, necessities; and there seems no intelligible meaning for necessity except as common factor of a set of chances. Unconditional necessity is, of course, the highly abstract common factor of the universal set of chances, all chances whatsoever; conditional necessity is the more concrete common factor of a limited set of chances. The factor limiting the set is that by which, as we say, the necessary thing is necessitated. The notion that the necessary must in all cases be necessitated by something is, however, a confusion between the restricted and the general case. The unconditionally necessary is not necessitated by anything, for it is merely what all possibilities or chances have in common. (Is there here a problem of logical types?) There is simply no chance of its being absent; not because anything prevents this, but because such "absence" is nonentity, denoting not even a bare possibility. (The sense in which this agrees, and the sense in which it disagrees, with the traditional notion of "necessary being" cannot here be set forth.)

Chance is non-necessity. This negative characterization, however, does not suffice. For, as just pointed out, necessity is merely an abstract aspect of a set of chances; and the concrete is more inclusive and positive than the abstract. Hence, chance must have a positive character. Peirce was one of the first to do justice to this concrete and positive character of chance.

Chance is the particularity of the particular, its Peircian firstness, freshness, spontaneity, originality—or, in Whiteheadian language, its self-creativity. Stated negatively, this is the particular's undeducibility from general concepts, which is all that distinguishes it from the general, and its undeducibility from antecedent particulars (the impossibility of deriving the total truth about it from the truth about them), which is all that distinguishes one particular state of the universe from another. If a particular were necessitated, or if all that is true of it were logically entailed, by the general, the general would be particular. For the general is the partially indefinite. Humanity in general is not the humanity of Lincoln or of Washington, but neutral to the distinction. Now to imply something definite is to be definite; for a meaning includes its implications. Hence, the general cannot imply any determinate particular coming under it. If, again, a particular must occur because another particular, called its cause occurs, then the two are logically inseparable, and indeed the later particular can only be a constituent of the earlier, and so not really later.

However, you may say, cannot a particular be implied by its cause or antecedent particular, plus a causal law? But the complex entity, cause and law, can only be either a particular or a general, and we have already seen that neither can imply the subsequent particular.

If nondeducibility is thus the very particularity of the particular, it follows that all particulars occur by chance, in our sense of the term. Are they then uncaused? Only if caused means deducible from antecedent conditions and laws. But there is another definition of cause that enables us to say that all events are caused, and that all occur by chance. Causality, on any useful definition, is whatever distinguishes from the logically possible, or the thinkable as such, that which is *really* possible in a given actual situation. Many things are thinkable that cannot here and now occur. But whatever here and now can occur is thinkable. The actually possible is thus narrower than the logically possible. There are, however, two ways of conceiving this narrowness. According to the first way, the actually possible is as narrowly limited as the actual itself. Future events that *can* occur are then just as determinate as past events that have occurred. This view is an extreme. It is also a paradox. For if real possibility is as determinate as actuality, what is the difference? Why is not the future actual already? As Whitehead says, "Definiteness is the soul of actuality." The actual particular is the fully unambiguous, that which conforms to the law of excluded middle as applied to predicates. Indeed, this law in this application is best taken as a definition of actuality. But if the future is wholly definite and thus actual, is it not present rather than future? Should we not try a less extreme and less paradoxical assumption? Why not suppose that only *past* actuality down to and including the present is fully definite (that this does not annul the difference between past and present has been shown elsewhere), and that the restricted or real possibilities which are the future so long as it is not yet present are somewhere between this fullness of definiteness and the opposite pole of unrestricted or merely logical possibility? (The more immediate future is, of course, more narrowly restricted than the more remote future, and it is but one step removed from definite actuality.) We can then say: every event is caused, that is to say, it issues out of a restricted or real potentiality; but also, every event occurs by chance, that is to say, it is more determinate than its proximate real potentiality, and just to that extent is unpredictable, undeducible from its causes and causal laws. By its proximate potentiality, an event is put into a class of then and there possible effects. Membership in the class is compulsory for the next event, not open for its decision. But within the class, or in so far as the proximate potentiality is less sharply definite than actuality, there are limits within which the event decides for itself. Insofar it determines or creates itself; or, as Whitehead says, it is *causa sui*. This is really less a paradox than the notion that all determination is by antecedent causes, since the latter notion merely puts the effective determination or decision, by which possibility is restricted, back to some unimaginable beginning of time or act outside of time. Somewhere, some*when*, somehow, the restriction of the logically possible to the determinateness of the actual must be effected. Where better than here and now, in each and every event? If, however, all events thus do the restricting, any one event can do but a certain portion of it. The rest has already been done by antecedent events. This antecedent, not quite complete, restriction of the logically possible is real possibility or causality.

The classic objection to any such doctrine appeals to the Principle of Sufficient Reason, which runs: for everything, there must be a reason why it is as it is, and not otherwise. This means, if anything, a denial of chance as defined above. The Principle has an air of attractiveness. An event for whose exact nature no antecedent reason can be given is insofar, it seems, inexplicable, irrational; to accept it amounts to a defeatist renunciation of the hope of explanation. However, is ex-

planation really thus to be equated with the possibility of deducibility
from causes or reasons? One may use the *word* "explanation" as synonym for such deducibility; but then we shall need another word for a
broader conception of which this is only a special case. To explain, or
deal with rationally, in this broader sense—for which a good word is
"understand"—is to spell out the relations of a thing, its wider context
beyond that apparent to our sense perceptions. This context includes
not only relations of similarity, repetitiveness, and causal deducibility,
but also relations of novelty, nonrepetitive change, and nondeductibility. Relations of nondeductibility are just as legitimate objects of rational grasp as those of deducibility. Indeed, as Bradley, Bosanquet, and
his followers have been making clear for us, somewhat unwittingly, the
very idea of deducibility loses its rational intelligibility the moment we
suppose that everything implies everything else. Reason is not the mere
tracing of necessary relations. It is the correct classification of relations, with respect to necessity and nonnecessity. A mathematician
who could not see that being square does *not* follow from being rectan-
gular would be just as odd as one who could not see that being rectan-
gular *does* follow from being square. A very famous mathematical
discovery consisted in the proof that the parallel axiom of Euclid is
independent of his other axioms, does not follow from them.

If, then, to explain or understand is to classify correctly a thing's
relations, or lack of them, the statement that an event is not wholly
deducible from its antecedent causes may be as much an explanation,
as contributory to understanding, as the statement that in part or in
some features the event is deducible. We must go further. Events would
become un-understandable, just as geometry would become so, were
we to adopt the assumption that all relations are relations of derivability. Temporal derivability is predictability. We say that knowledge is
for the sake of prediction and control. But prediction and control, if
taken without qualification, exclude one another. One predicts an
eclipse, but does not control it. One controls—from moment to moment—one's conversational utterances, but just to this extent one does
not predict them. To predict is to renounce further control; to hold
open for control is to renounce prediction. If I predict what I shall say
tomorrow, I imply that I shall tomorrow make no decisions concerning
my speech; for the decisions must already have been made. If Beethoven had predicted one of his symphonies, he would have created it
already; and if a psychologist had predicted it, he would have been

just such a composer as Beethoven and assuredly no psychologist. The predictor of Newton must be at least a Newton. Such absurdities may help to teach us that—as Dewey has been contending for nearly half a century—the basic function of knowledge is not to focus a mental camera on the future but to discover what *present* limited potentialities, that is to say, partial indeterminacies, are given for resolution in the future. The resolution itself will be the coming of the future, and to talk of predicting its form is to suppose that something can be settled while it is still unsettled. The object of knowledge is not the future as determinate, but present realities as materials from which alone the future can be made.

The ideal of absolute predictability makes sense indeed only if contemplation is in no way relative to action. The defender of chance need not go to the opposite extreme and say that contemplation is merely an adjunct to action. It suffices to say that knowing and doing have mutual relations to each other, so that neither can be solely and absolutely an end in itself. The conception of a knower who sees past, present, and future—or all time from eternity—sees them but reserves no right to make further choices with respect to them, is, I submit, a mythical one which fails to describe even what we wish knowledge to be. The myth once had a theological garb; now one finds it among logicians who have no desire to be theological. The verbal argument for the determinateness of the future, "What will be will be," is a part of this inheritance from medieval theology. It involves, as has been explained elsewhere, a doubtful conception of the relation of truth to time.[2] The future consists of what will be only in so far as its proximate potentiality is determinate; for the rest, it consists of what may-or-may-not-be. To say, "The future when it is present will have determinate character," is not by any valid logical principle equivalent to saying, "There is a determinate character which the future will have."

But can our view do justice to the role of verified predictions in testing scientific theories? In so far as science looks for causal laws, successful prediction is of course a valid criterion. To the extent that such laws obtain, and events are *not* matters of chance but determined by their antecedents in some repetitive way, prediction must be possible. A single success would not, it is true, completely establish the law, for such isolated agreement with prediction might occur by chance.

---

[2] See *Man's Vision of God*, pp. 99–104.

But repeated success without failures renders this unlikely. And in regions of nature where there is good reason to think the element of chance is small, we may proceed for practical purposes as though it were not there at all.

Of course, in addition to the aspects of absolute prediction of the future, there are the conditional predictions. If we were to set off a bomb, such-and-such would be the consequences. This is a statement about the interrelations of certain potentialities in the future, or in some unspecified time. Each potentiality has an infinite comet tail of possible or probable consequences, and whatever properties are spread throughout the tail are necessary consequences. Science enables us, then, first to set aside what definitely will happen, such as eclipses, as not suitable material for preference or decision, and second and above all, it enables us to comprehend as many as possible of the real potentialities (including those of our own character) among which we are to decide, so that we will not overlook possibilities we might wish to favor or oppose and will not imagine that such a potentiality as setting off an explosion is self-enclosed and without ramifications, other than the most obvious ones.

The hold of the Principle of Sufficient Reason upon some philosophers seems to have been due to their not distinguishing with sufficient reasonableness between various meanings of the word reason.

For what do we ask reasons? First of all, for beliefs, for theoretical decisions. The ideal of belief is that it should be determined by evidence. From this relation of belief to evidence, chance is to be excluded. The content of the belief is to represent and be necessitated by the facts. This, however, is for us only an ideal. Human beliefs are not determined solely by evidences, but in part by other factors, such as desires and wishes, whose action, so far a the ideal is concerned, involves an element of chance. In the second place, we ask reasons for practical decisions, for deliberate modes of behavior. What is their ideal? I suggest that, whereas belief has the aim of duplicating facts already in being, practical decisions have the aim of creating new facts. Science is an echo of nature, but technology is not. It is the business of an echo to be faithful. Caprice is to be excluded. But a suspension bridge is no echo, still less is a symphony a poem. It is not even the ideal of these creations to be determined by the world in which they arise. They are to be something new, not wholly modeled on anything antecedent, including antecedent laws or ideals.

Is such creation, underivable from its antecedents, irrational? Not if words are reasonably employed. The function of reason is not, in spite of Leibniz, to dictate to the will the one best action. Reason operates with universals, and these cannot point unambiguously to a particular, hence not to a particular action. The function of reason is to point not to an action better than any other, but to a class of actions better than any other class. Ideally every member of the class is, at least for our knowledge, superior to every possibility outside the class, and equal to any within it. The enactment of any member of such a class is entirely rational, if that means immune to criticism. Suppose I say to a man, "My dear sir, you have acted unwisely; for there is another action you could have performed whose results would probably have been just as good as the one you did perform." Would he not reply, "What of it? Is there unwisdom in an action so well chosen that there is scant probability that it could have been improved upon?" Unwisdom consists in accepting a lesser value where a greater is within reach. If a man were to act like Buridan's ass and refuse, petulantly, to nourish himself because no particular food was best, would not all recognize what an ass that man was? As though a man should refuse to use a nail until he could be assured that one nail in the box was supreme! Any nail of approximately the right size is better than none, any bundle of hay better than none, and one does not starve because no food is known to be the best available. Sufficient reason in conduct is not that a particular act has a ground of preference, but that the class of acts from which a particular act is arbitrarily determined has such a ground. The ass eats hay because he is hungry, and hay is the available food; but he eats just *this* bit of hay perhaps, only because it is as *good as any* he could now have. This reason suffices for the wisest beast or man, or even, I dare affirm, the wisest superhuman being.

To the old, old query, how an act can fail to be determined by its motive, we may reply thus: An element in all motives is the desire that something new, not previously defined, should achieve definition; further, if the motive is antecedent to the act, then it cannot entirely define its subsequent fulfillment for, since definiteness is actuality, a fully defining motive would have actually all that the fulfillment could have; while, if the motive is not antecedent, then its influence upon the act belongs to the latter's self-causation and lends no support to the theory of complete determination by antecedent causes.

In the third place, one may ask for reasons for concrete events. This is the question of causality once more. The causal ideal is that events should be interesting and valuable novelties, connected with antecedent real potentiality but possessing additional determinations. One does not evaluate transactions with a friend in terms of their predictability, but in part in quite contrary terms. Only with low forms of existence, valued chiefly as means, do we tend to distinguish predictable and unpredictable as good and bad. Yet in no case is absolute predictability a valid ideal, and even if it were, events might fall short of it, as of other ideals.

An ideal still to be considered is that of freedom in the ethical sense. Most of us have read dozens of essays striving to show that ethical freedom and responsibility are compatible with causal determinism, or even that they require it. Yet I still think, with William James, that ethical freedom and metaphysical freedom are connected. All kinds of freedom have this in common, that something which, in abstraction from the entity said to be free, is undecided, by virtue of the entity acquires decision. A slave is unfree, because little is decided by him that is left undecided by others. His environment narrows down what he can do to a meager range of alternatives, out of proportion to his human capacities. Unfreedom is, then, an unduly narrow range of alternatives for decision as left open by others. Now some conclude from this that there is no unfreedom in being determined by one's antecedent character or experience, since it is still the self though the antecedent self, which thus determines. One is not enslaved to another person. For legal purposes, perhaps this suffices. But it involves two oversights.

First, if the argument of this essay, and of many other defenses of indeterminism, is sound, to say that men are free provided they can deliberate (and act) unhampered, even though this deliberating is perhaps fully determined by antecedent factors, amounts to saying, "Men are free if they can deliberate, even though perhaps they cannot deliberate." For no real occurrence, least of all one involving the consciousness of wide alternatives and of universals, could be fully determined by its antecedents, or by any law or order which excludes chance and uncertainty. So the famous compatibility of determinism with freedom only means that the fact of ethical deliberation and its unimpeded consequences establishes freedom, regardless of what else be true or false. This is acceptable; but the question, "Could ethical deliberation occur deterministically?" is the question of compatibility over again. And the affirmative answer is assumed, not proved. Admitting that determinism cannot contradict or nullify the *fact* of freedom (nothing can nullify a fact) , it remains to ascertain whether or not this fact nullifies the thesis of determinism.

Second, there is a sense, and we shall see that it is an ethically significant one, in which a human being has a different self every moment. From this point of view, to be limited by one's past self is to be limited by another, in extreme cases a very alien other at that. We return to this topic later, since the same question is involved in the attempted reduction of love to self-interest. Here I will only point out that if today's action is determined by, inferable from, yesterday's self and its environment, then by the same logic it is determined, even though in a sense mediately rather than immediately, still *completely,* by the self and world state of fifty years ago. The self of a squalling infant and its world become the repositories of the freedom that was supposedly mine. And that infant and its world were determined by the natures of the parents and their environments. (According to some forms of scientific determinism one can as well say that we determine our past as that it determines us; but this makes it but the clearer that from no point of view is there anything *otherwise unsettled* for the present self to settle, since neither past nor future leaves us any possibility of action but one.) So, as with excess of determination by neighbors in the case of the slave, so with excess of determination by antecedent character, freedom and responsibility shrink by retreating, in the one case into the environment, in the other into the past. As James said, the question of ethical meaning is not essentially one of the utility of rewards and punishments, or of praise and blame. It is a question of the locus of decision, as a real settling of the objectively unsettled. This locus cannot be in the self-identical person from birth to the present but must be in the act of the given moment. The value of human beings from which derives, for example, our rights over the lower animals, is that in us the particularization of real potentiality which is the generic nature of process occurs on a higher and more conscious level. We are important, as birds and tigers are not, because we, radically more than they, settle now what was yesterday in no sense entirely settled, and because we know that we are doing this, that we are—as Bergson says—artists of actuality, really creating new definiteness.

Quantum physics, by its category of statistical law and its principle of indeterminacy, seems to open a door to such creation. But then it appears to close it again, for practical purposes (though some authorities deny this), by implying the virtually absolute determinacy of organic action, due to the high numbers of particles involved. However, in philosophy it is categories and principles, not quantitative matters, that are at issue. If individuals on the lowest level are unpredictable, perhaps this is because they are individuals, not because they are on a low level. Now we too are individuals, units of reality, indeed we are radically more individual, and our unity is more certain, because more immediately given, than that of electrons. But we are individuals on a high level. Hence a human being need not be so predictable as the consideration of its particles alone would imply. A particle in one's brain is in the neighborhood of human thoughts and feelings, not just of other subhuman particles. Moreover, since absolute order is for all we know through physics inapplicable to units, the theory of real potentiality is at least not excluded. Assuming the theory, must there not be levels of such potentiality as there are of units, rather than merely more or less complex cases of lowest-level potentialities? How my potentiality, or even that of an amoeba, is related to electronic potentiality may not be a matter for simple extrapolation from low-level physics, but for reasoning by analogy, tested if possible empirically. Thus, ethical freedom can, though less simply or conclusively than some perhaps have supposed, derive support from the new physics. For that physics has given up the dream, the pseudo-category, of a causality which in principle excludes chance. Of course, one may prefer to dream on.

To say that the passion for a tidy world has been a source of chaos in philosophy is scarcely a paradox. Absolute tidiness is a contradiction in terms—logical chaos. The attempt to convert men to it produces disagreement—psychological chaos. Absolute order is logical chaos, for order is a channeling of vitalities, of chance-spontaneities; and if the channeling were absolute, exact, complete—there would be no vitality, no channeling, and no order. The closer together the banks of a river, the more precisely the path of individual particles of water can be deduced from the location of the banks. But if, in the effort to restrict the particles to a precise line of flow, one were to bring the banks infinitely close together, there would be no water, no river, and no banks. This is what determinism does. In a deterministic world everything is completely determined—but this everything is precisely nothing. Whatever happens—but hold! Is not, it happens, a synonym for, it chances? The element of chance is not indeed unrestricted. There is real, not merely logical, possibility. But it is still possibility, not inevitability; it involves maybe's, not mere will-be's. Events come with a freshness, firstness, spontaneity, which is their very particularity.

There may seem to be an appearance of contradiction in what we have said so far. We have on the one hand identified chance and possibility. To say there is no chance, and to say there is no possibility, are one and the same. But we have also, it seems, identified chance with the actual particular. (The same wavering seems to be found in Peirce.) Surely possibility and actuality are not the same! Let us see if the paradox can be resolved. That a particular event occurs is never necessary, but always a "matter of chance." This means that the region of possibility with which it is correlated, or which as we say it actualizes, never implies just this determinate mode of actualization. Indeed, this determinate mode is not even one of the antecedent possibilities, but a creation out of them. A particular is not one of the antecedent possibilities or chances, but its occurrence is a matter of chance in that it was antecedently true that the real potentiality could and would be further determined in an as yet undetermined manner. The chance-character or freshness of the particular can, in truth, be viewed from two perspectives: from that of the antecedent phase of process which involves various relatively well-defined alternatives for the next phase; and from that of the particular itself which is the actualization of one of these alternatives. Here to "actualize" means more than a simple change from "merely possible" to "actual," whatever that by itself could mean, but connotes "some additional definiteness" not contained in any of the antecedently obtaining alternatives. Thus, we may agree with Bergson that it is an illusion to project an event backwards into an antecedent possibility of this very event. The antecedent possibility is as innocent of the precise quality as it is of the actuality of the event in question, and indeed the precise or particular quality is the actuality. But it by no means follows, in spite of Bergson (and of his predecessor Lequier, or his follower Jean Wahl) that there were no antecedent possibilities, or that there is any intellectual absurdity in the concept of antecedent possibilities. For by "possibility of particular P" we mean, if we understand ourselves, only that the previous phase of process defined itself as destined to be superseded *somehow,* within certain limits of variation, by a next phase of process. The "somehow" is not, however, a wholly undifferentiated question mark, but involves some modes of contrast, of "alternative possibilities," none of which can coincide in character with the particular which later turns up, but some one of which, or some one region of the continuum of possible quality, will later be recognizable as the *nearest* alternative or region, the one which *with the least further definition* is equivalent to the particular. This relation between particular and its possibility is only a relation of reason for the possibility, but is a real relation for the particular. Process relates itself backwards to its potencies, not forward to particular actualizations of these potencies. It does relate itself forward to the general principle, there will be further actualization, some additional definiteness or other. In this "or other" lies the aspect of chance, or possibility irreducible to any sort of necessity. So much for chance.

Incompatibility, like chance, is inherent in particularity. To be actual, concrete, particular, is to be definite, that is de-finite—limited, this but not that, or that but not this. Only pure potentiality can be unlimited, indefinite, and void of incompatibility. Real potentiality is always limited, exclusive; and actuality is the final portion of limitation or exclusiveness. A poet sitting down with an idea for a poem is in a state of mind in which many decisions as to the detail of the poem are not yet made. As they are made, more and more possibilities are excluded. Only as possibilities are thus shut out, condemned to non-actualization, can anything be actualized. The condemned possibilities are not necessarily inferior or evil. The basic incompatibility is not of good with evil, but of good with good. (Bigots, of course, fail to see this.) Moreover, there may be those who are strongly attached to some of the excluded possibilities. Every legislative act excludes things which for some are genuine values. Always someone loses or suffers. This is an element of tragedy inherent in process itself.

Ah, say some, there must be a supra-mundane, supra-temporal, immaterial realm in which the excluded possibilities may be, or are, fulfilled. This implies, in the first place, that our choices have no significance; that they settle nothing as to what is actual and what is not. If the possibilities we reject are not left unactualized, any more than those we accept, then our choices are cosmically null. In the second place, is there any meaning to the notion of an actuality which excludes no possibility? The total realm of possibility itself excludes nothing, qua possibility. But it excludes everything, *qua* actuality. (To explicate this fully, we should have to discuss the concept of vagueness.) An actuality which excluded nothing would be coextensive with possibility. But then what would make it actuality rather than possibility? What would be the distinction? The mere word, actuality? Is not the more intelligible assumption that the possibilities each of us rejects are cosmically rejected, really excluded from actualization? True, someone else can ride in the plane in my place if I give up my seat. But the more particular possibility I give up is *my* riding in the plane on that trip, and *this* possibility can never be more actualized. Every choice involves just such final and irrevocable exclusions, valid, I suggest, for the most superior being one can conceive. Two men who each wish to share the central thoughts and experiences of the same woman throughout her life are striving to realize values which are incompatible even from the most ultimate perspective. No being whatever will enjoy both the qualities of shared experiences which can ensue if A achieves such a place in the lady's life, and those which can ensue if B achieves it. (To make marriage so loose and flexible that both men can have what they want will mean that neither can have it. Not that all reform is futile in such matters, but that it cannot eliminate incompatibility.)

As the foregoing example suggests, logical incompatibility, P and not-P, is merely the translation into linguistic form of esthetic incompatibility. For, as Peirce, Bradley, and Whitehead have noted, the unity of actuality is given as a felt unity, and its laws are laws of feeling. That one cannot feel blue and red as characterizing the same aspect of experience is because the esthetic values of these qualities are mutually destructive, unless separated and made possibly complementary by some difference of locus. The definiteness of actuality is its value, for in the indefiniteness of mere possibility contrasts are lacking; and value is unity in contrast, beauty in the broadest sense. The supreme example of such unity is the social harmony which is called love. Love, in the form I have chiefly in mind, is the sense of valuable contrast and unity with another. It is distinguished from hate or indifference as positive evaluation from negative or neutral, and from other forms of positive evaluation or liking in that its object is concrete and singular, not abstract, general, or collective, as in love for mathematics or for mankind. It may seem that there is a further ground of distinction, in that the concrete object of love may be itself a subject with its own feelings and intrinsic values, or not such a subject. If panpsychism is correct, this distinction is verbal only. With Leibniz and many others, I hold that mere matter as such is abstract or collective, and that only panpsychism can give content to it as concrete and singular. When we love a house, we really love an abstraction, a shape, a Gestalt, or else we love a vaguely apprehended collection of singulars (molecules, say) whose characters as singulars are for us indeterminate.

However, the classic failure to see the supremacy of love is found perhaps less in the neglect or denial of panpsychism than in the age-old theory of self-interest as the root motivation. This theory has often been criticized; but few are the philosophies in which the criticism goes far enough. It is often said that if the self which is affirmed in self-interest or self-realization is the highest self, all is well. But it is not merely the kind of self which requires examination, but its numerical identity. Am I simply one self throughout my life? And is my body merely this self in its physical or spatial aspect? Then all relations of my present to my past or future are relations of identity, and likewise all relations to my body. From this standpoint, either love of others or self-love is a metaphysical monstrosity, since in the one the object loved simply transcends our identity, whereas in the other it simply remains within it. Thus, the striking empirical parallels between self-love—or self-hatred—and love or hate toward others are explained away. Metaphysically there could be nothing in common, since between sheer identity and sheer non-identity there is no possibility of mediation. Either self-love must not be called love, but just identity, or love of others cannot be love, but only a ruse of self-interest, serving the identical self, and using the other as means to this end. Again, is it much of an account of the remarkable fact that injury to certain bodily cells is felt as injury to me simply to say that I have or am those cells, or that they are my physical or material aspect? Is not the notion of absolute, substantial self-identity, as still often accepted in ethics, a logical and scientific anachronism? Since Bolzano, certainly since Whitehead and Russell, logic has known better. Psychology and physiology also know better. But the situation is confused and requires bold clarification. The first step toward a more intelligible view is to recognize with Scholz and a number of other logicians that absolute identity of the concrete or particular is given in an event or occasion, not in a thing enduring through time, like a person or a body. The merely relative identity of the latter may be called, with Levin and Scholz, genetic identity, *Genidentität.* It is logically much weaker than the absolute identity of an event. This logical weakness is, so to speak, the ethical strength of the situation. My life consists of hundreds of thousands of selves, if by self is meant subjects with strict identity. When I love myself, this is no mere relation of identity, but an interest of a present actuality in other and past actualities, as well as in potentialities for future actualization. And these objects of my love are really loved, in that there is sympathy for them, a delight in the contrast and unity between "my" feelings, those of the present strictly identical experience, and the feelings of past or future experiences in the same sequence. It is not because there is an enduring self that there is self-love; rather, it is the relations of sympathetic memory and anticipation between successive experiences that constitute the enduring genidentical self. Memory is a form of sympathy, feeling by one experience of the feelings of other experiences. Anticipation is a more imaginative and reversed form of the same relation. It is bonds of sympathy, not between an entity and itself, but between an experience with its subject pole or focus or ego, and other experiences with their foci, that *make* self-identity.

But, am I not forgetting the body as the bearer of selfhood? In the first place, the body is many things, not just one. It is, for example, many cells, each of these many molecules. And a cell or molecule is a sequence of states or events. Each of these sequences presents the problem of genetic identity over again. Furthermore, what makes a body one's own? What binds an experience or self to a body? According to Ducasse, one's body is that with which one directly and constantly interacts. This is the minimal explication of the relation. But what is interaction? Ducasse agrees with Hume that we have no a priori insight into causal dependence, whether between physical events or between a physical and a psychical one. True, but we have such insight as between psychical events. This insight is summed up in the idea of immediate sympathy. Accordingly, but one explanation of the mind-body relation is fully intelligible. It says that every human experience immediately sympathizes with certain other experiences of a drastically subhuman type. The spatial spread of these subhuman experiences is the human body, or at least, the most intimate part of it. When I feel toothache, I suffer; am I alone with this suffering, or is it shared with others? The known fact is that I am not the only living thing involved; for nerve cells are living things. We also know that my pain occurs under conditions injurious to some of my cells. All this is as it would be if the sufferings were not mine alone, but shared with the cells.

That the entire field of esthetic experience is illuminated by the foregoing theory is manifest. The emotional expressiveness of visual and auditory data is only to be expected if these sensations are sympathetic echoes of the sufferings and enjoyments of cells. The joyous sunshine *is* joyous, not because visible light is any happier than invisible ultraviolet rays, but because cells stimulated by light are raised to a higher level of self-enjoyed activity. That sense of a world of emotions which constitutes the hearing of music is exactly what is implied if auditory experience is a synthesis of what in actuality is indeed a world of feelings, the miniature, but in its way complex and vast, world of sentient cells. The emergent overall qualities of the synthesis lift this emotional world up to the human level, and the subhuman contributed feelings serve as signs of contrasting emotional qualities which, in generic aspect, are remotely similar between us and cells.

If the concrete sensory aspects of experience are forms of love, what about thought, or the abstract aspects? Has not logic been called the social discipline of thinking? He who will not say what he means and stand by its implications is he who will deceive his neighbors, and very likely himself, that is, he is deficient in sympathy with other experiences. Or again, take the predictive aspect of knowledge. Why predict? There is only one reason, because we sympathize with future experience. Even to know what one means by other experiences is already a social and sympathetic state.

The connection of knowledge with sympathy sets limits to the possible divorce of intelligence and goodness. Did Hitler know his social environment? He saw of it largely what he wanted to see. He saw the weakness of Chamberlain, because that fitted his desires. Did he see the strength concealed in that absurd man, the ultimate love of country and decency? Nothing of the kind. He thought Chamberlain would just go on playing the same game, and the British people with him. One whose mind is filled with the social realities, that is, the joys and sorrows and ideals of those around him, cannot maintain as an island untouched by all this his own egocentric ideal and purposes. The egoist, or if you prefer the fanatic, must manipulate or ration his sympathies (that is, his social relations). Hitler could be kind to a visiting British pacifist. Why not, since the pacifist was his unwitting ally, as well as a cripple? But Hitler could not enter too freely into certain British attitudes because there was that in them which not only was incompatible with the success of his plans but which, worse still, could only be grasped by one whose heart was not quite as Hitler's, a scene of passions that did not dare to own their own names or to see themselves from the standpoint of men of good will.

Some ethical theories seek to furnish sanction for obligation by arguing that since sympathetic emotions are largely pleasant, it is to one's interest to cultivate them. This implies that a man asking for a motive for doing good has for the time being ceased to love his fellows. But if the man has really and utterly put aside all concern for others, then almost all that is human must have left him. And insofar as he does still care about other persons, he *has* a motive for doing good to them—simply that he wants to do so. Must one have a motive for doing what one wants to do? This is to ask a motive for the motive one already has. Yet I am perpetually bedeviled with the suggestion that I must instantly cease to do good if I become convinced that my future welfare will fail to register an increment because I now act on the good will I feel. But what I need in order to act now is not a future motive, but a present one. If I presently feel concern for another and act on this concern, I do now what I now want to do, and it is absurd to ask a reward for doing what one wants to do. That I, the present self, am privileged to act out my wishes is reward enough. The account is closed. Only if I am asked to do good where I do not love or take any interest in the good of others, is it in order to raise the question of reward. For here a motive *is* needed. I may not want to do good to one I do not cherish, unless some other motive can be furnished—for instance, the hope of reward—as lure to my sympathetic interest in future experiences belonging to my sequence. Given this hope, then perhaps I can do what is asked. Frustrate the hope, and I can complain that I have been misled into a bad bargain, but only on the assumption that I did not love. Hope of reward is a substitute for the intrinsic motive of love.

Is there need for this substitute? I answer, there is political, but not ethical or religious, need. The state and society must hold out rewards, including negative ones or punishments, just to the extent that the minimal requirements of social behavior outrun the amount of love that can be presupposed in men generally. But just to the same extent, men will be legally rather than ethically correct in their conduct. They, or we— for to some extent this applies to all of us—are not really good men if, caring little for the good of others, we yet, because of rewards, promote or at least refrain from injuring that good. Bishop Paley actually presented Christian charity as simply self-regard which takes Heaven and Hell into account.[3] Berdyaev well calls such transcendentalized self-

---

[3] *The Principles of Moral and Political Philosophy*, Bk. II, chs. ii, iii.

interest "the most disgusting mortality ever conceived." For it carries
the denial of the primacy of love farther than an irreligious theory
could plausibly carry it, since it is plain enough that in this life concern
for others must often be its own reward. If, then, religion claims as its
merit that it assists love by furnishing all extrinsic motive, we must
reply that this is a merit only on the non-ethical, political level, the
level of police action. It is, I hold, the business of the state and other
social forms to provide whatever rewards or punishments the deficiencies of love make necessary and to do it so thoroughly that nothing of
that sort would be left for any cosmic magistrate.

The function of religion is not to enable us to act as the needs of
others require without love for these others, but to enable us to love
them as we otherwise could not. How can religion do this? There is
only one way. We can only love or cherish people if we become aware
of the beauty, actual or potential, that is in them. The religious idea in
its best ethical form is that of a cosmic setting of men, and of all things,
the consciousness of which exhibits them as more beautiful, more lov-
able than they appear when we ignore this setting. (Even the Kantian
ethics, in some of its aspects, can be interpreted in this fashion.) How
religion effects this enhancement of the sense for the beauty of things
is a topic for another occasion. But I may perhaps mention my conviction that it can be done not by transcendentalizing self-interest, nor yet
by depreciating, even from the most ultimate perspective, the concepts
of chance and incompatibility, but rather by making us aware of a love
which takes upon itself the totality of actualized chances, even the most
painful.

Let us summarize our results and consider one or two practical applications. We have held that all happenings are to some extent by chance,
and that this violates no legitimate ideal of intelligibility or reasonableness. By means of love or sympathy, what happens here and now is
made relevant to what happens there and then. Human self-identity is
merely a particularly important strand of this relevance. Knowledge
and all interest in the past or future are forms of sympathy. Because of
chance and incompatibility between possibilities, the world is partly
wild and ever somewhat dangerous—as William James delighted to
note. His passion here was no more than was needed to correct the bias
of the great tradition in favor of some cosmic, all-detailed, infallibly
executed design, some chain of syllogisms or dialectical progressions
from some blessed first premise out of which, as a necessary conclu-

sion, my hat and your toothache would eventually emerge. A chance world, that is, any world, has a tinge of tragedy in its constitution. A multiplicity of decisions irreducible to any single decision means a multiplicity of relationships that literally no one has decided, if that means chosen. Now in some of these relationships there is social harmony, in some social discord. Just which occur when is a matter of mere chance, not of choice or necessity. It follows that we must give up the dream of an existence beyond the reach of chance and tragedy. Absolute protection against conflict or suffering is a mirage.

This does not exclude every conception of providential guidance of events. Rather it means that Providence can reasonably be conceived, not as a simple alternative to chance, its mere negation or prevention, but only as a channeling of chances between banks less than infinitely close together. The function of Providence is not to enforce a maximal of good to evil, but a maximal ratio of chances of good to chances of evil. That chances of evil remain is not because evil is good or useful after all, but because chances of evil overlap with chances of good. A dead man has no chance of suffering, also none of enjoyment. The principle is universal and a priori. Tone down sensitiveness and spontaneity, and one reduces the risk of suffering but also the opportunities for depth of enjoyment. All the utopias are tame, just because vitality has been sacrificed to reduce risk. Opportunity, willy-nilly, drops too. Tragedy is thus inherent in value.

For thousands of years men have sought some way to avoid recognizing this. Buddhism, Stoicism, the Christian and Mohammedan theory of Providence and of heaven as commonly interpreted, the Marxian dream of a practically conflict-free society, all are tinged with this escapism. And the result is not that tragedy is genuinely averted; just the contrary, the effect of these evasions is itself tragic in high degree. We shall be able better to minimize tragedy when we face it resolutely as in principle inevitable, though in detail always open to amelioration. The Christian idea of the redeemed as wholly happy in the knowledge that others are damned is a tragic renunciation of sympathy which Berdyaev has gone so far as to term sadistic. The notion of an all-arranging, chance-excluding Providence is doubly tragic; it is cruel, for it compels us to try to imagine that our worst tortures are deliberately contrived for our own or someone's good by an allegedly all-loving being, and it is dangerous, for it suggests that we need not use our own resources to avert evil where possible and to help others in danger and privation.

Over and over we find practical programs vitiated by their failure to reckon sufficiently with the principles we have been discussing. Classical economics, although not so worthless or irrelevant as Marxists allege, is nevertheless weakened by two almost metaphysical deficiencies. On the one hand, it toys with the idea of an invisible hand which always and infallibly brings beneficent results out of individual motivations; and on the other, it toys with the idea that human beings should resign themselves to being, outside of family relations, simply selfish and calculating, rather than beings whose very core is love or social solidarity. Thus, it is uncomfortably close to the metaphysical blunders of trying to separate chance from tragedy and of denying the primacy of love. The market may be, and I take it it is, a marvelous mechanism for usefully coordinating actions in ways not intended by the actors; but it is not an absolute or all-sufficient mechanism. Its more or less inevitable tragedies must be carefully compared with those of available alternatives for this and that portion of our economic life. On the other hand, Marxian planning and dictatorship seem excessive limitations upon the chance-spontaneity of the many, and Marxian solidarity seems to ask both too much and too little of human love. Blanket socialistic or antisocialistic dogmas are pseudo-absolutes, not justified by the genuine absolutes, which are the ultimate factors of chance and love in correct mutual adjustment. This adjustment requires that destructive conflict arising from incompatibility of values should be mitigated without paying too high a price in loss of individuality, from which spontaneity, chance, and danger cannot be eliminated. It is through love that tragedy is, not indeed wholly prevented, but made bearable and given whatever beauty it is capable of. The love that can do this is that which expects to share with others the sufferings from which no actuality, human or superhuman—subject as all must be to chance and incompatibility—can entirely escape. Such love is not, as Plato thought, the search for the supreme beauty. In its highest human and superhuman forms it simply is that beauty.

The branch of secular science that is bringing us back to this principle, long ago, though seldom consistently, professed by religious teachers, is psychiatry. Some look to this science to finish the job of discrediting religious ideas. But, as Karl Menninger has pointed out, the basic religious idea (at least in our Judeo-Christian tradition) is identical with that of psychiatry—the idea that love is the key to life's riddles. If it be objected that religious love is *agape,* and that the love with which psychiatrists are chiefly or wholly concerned is *eros,* I reply that in this famous distinction Nygren (with whom I have discussed this matter) none too well expresses his own meaning and has often been misunderstood—as no doubt have the psychiatrists. Theologians and philosophers might well join with Menninger in longing for the day when, as he says, "We shall have accorded to love that preeminence which it deserves in our scale of values; we shall seek it and proclaim it as the highest virtue and the greatest boon. . . . Love is the medicine for the sickness of the world, a prescription often given, too rarely taken."[4] Menninger also quotes from Burton's *Anatomy of Melancholy* some words which suggest a reason why men have so often turned to lesser ideas than that of love, the reason that otherwise the greatness of their theme might have made only too plain the littleness of all that they could say about it. Burton's words are these: "To enlarge [upon] or illustrate the power and effect of love is to set a candle in the sun."[5] Behold then my candle; or rather, behold the sun!

---

[4] Karl Menninger, *Love Against Hate* (Harcourt Brace and Company, 1942), pp. 293–4.

[5] *Ibid.,* p. 260.